PONTIFICAL INSTITUTE OF MEDIAEVAL STUDIES

MEDIAEVAL SOURCES IN TRANSLATION

17

ACKNOWLEDGEMENT

This book has been published with the help of a grant from the Humanities Research Council of Canada, using funds provided by the Canada Council.

ISBN 0-88844-266-1
ISSN 0316-0814

PRINTED BY UNIVERSA — WETTEREN — BELGIUM

KARLAMAGNÚS SAGA
THE SAGA OF CHARLEMAGNE AND HIS HEROES

translated by

CONSTANCE B. HIEATT

VOLUME TWO
[Part IV]
King Agulandus

THE PONTIFICAL INSTITUTE OF MEDIAEVAL STUDIES
59 Queen's Park Crescent East
Toronto, Ontario, M5S 2C4
Canada

1975

TABLE OF CONTENTS

INTRODUCTION

King Agulandus, the fourth, and by far the longest, section of the thirteenth century Old Norse *Karlamagnús saga*, is found in all four manuscripts of the saga;[1] but the versions found in the A-group and the B-group are significantly different, since a later Icelandic redactor has completely revised the A-version. He had good reason to do so, for the A-version is a fairly mechanical (if sometimes inaccurate) translation of its sources, with glaring inconsistencies resulting from the incompatibility of those sources. By the same token, however, the A-version is of special interest to scholars concerned with the sources and analogues.

One of these sources was the early 12th century Latin *Historia Karoli Magni et Rotholandi*, known as the Pseudo-Turpin Chronicle (hereafter abbreviated PT) after, as Smyser put it,[2] "that graceless Unknown who ... had the temerity to pass his chronicle off as the *mémoires* of Archbishop Tylpin, or Turpin, of Rheims, a contemporary of Charlemagne."[3] The other principal source-in fact the

[1] The mss. are designated *A*, *a*, *B*, and *b*; see my introduction to *Karlamagnús Saga*, Vol. I (Toronto, 1975). The only edition of the saga (hereafter designated *Kms.*) giving both the A and B versions of Part IV is that ed. C. R. Unger (Christiana, 1860). In that edition, the *B,b* version is the first printed, and is followed by the *A,a* version, somewhat confusingly labelled "Karlamagnus saga IV b."—The placement of Part IV in the saga is no doubt determined by the way in which it presents Oddgeir the Dane as a mature hero and Rollant as a neophyte; it would, thus, have to come after III, "Oddgeir the Dane," and before those parts of the saga in which Rollant's reputation is clearly established.

[2] H. M. Smyser, ed., *The Pseudo-Turpin* (Cambridge, Mass., 1937), p. 1.

[3] Some recent writers on the subject would not entirely agree with this statement. Ronald N. Walpole, "Sur la Chronique du Pseudo-Turpin," *Travaux de Linguistique et de Littérature* (Strasbourg), III (1965), 7-18, favors an origin at St. Denis and suggests that the historical Turpin/Tilpin was a monk at St. Denis before he became an archbishop: he would thus see some

source of at least three-quarters of the story—was the later 12th century *Chanson d'Aspremont* (hereinafter abbreviated *Asp.*).[4] What these two works had in common was the name of one of Charlemagne's (mythical) heathen antagonists: Aigolandus in PT, Agolant in *Asp.*[5] In other respects the two tales are quite different; the former deals with a campaign in Spain, for example, while the latter concerns one in Italy.[6] The first Norse translator (or compiler: the two translations may have been made separately) simply translated the first part of PT, dealing with the war with Agolandus—but skipping the death of Agolandus—[7]

logic in the association of his name with the work. André de Mandach, *Naissance et développement de la Chanson de Geste en Europe*, I: *La Geste de Charlemagne et de Roland* (Paris and Geneva, 1961), argues for the authorship of one Pierre d'Andouque, advancing arguments for the legitimacy of this Pierre's assuming the cognomen of Turpin. Reviewers generally have shown strong reservations about this and other aspects of Mandach's theory: see, e.g., those of Meredith-Jones in *Speculum*, 37 (1962), 634-637; Walpole in *MLR*, 60 (1965), 613-618; Payen in *RP*, 18 (1964-65), 354-356; Adler in *Archiv*, 199 (1962-63), 425-26. Earlier statements on the origin of PT include that of Joseph Bédier, *Légendes épiques*, III (Paris, 1912), pp. 41-114.—On the dating of PT, see Peter G. Foote, *The Pseudo-Turpin Chronicle in Iceland* (London, 1959), p. 2; but cf. Smyser, pp. 35-36; Ian Short, "*The Pseudo-Turpin Chronicle*: Some Unnoticed Versions and their Sources," *Med. Æv.*, 38 (1969), p. 2; Adalbert Hämel, "Los Manuscritos Latinos del Falso Turpino," in *Estudios dedicados a Menéndez Pidal* (Madrid, 1953), IV, 67-85; Mandach, *passim*.

[4] On the dating of *Asp.*, see Foote, p. 4 and n. 11.

[5] It is possible that *Asp.* was, in a way, based on PT: cf. Phillip August Becker, "Aspremont," *Romanische Forschungen*, 60 (1947), p. 38: "... die christlichen Helden sind vielmehr aus dem Rolandslied übernommen, und ihr heidnischen Gegner stammt aus dem Pseudoturpin."

[6] The saga is not the only work to put the stories together, one way or another: Mouskés included both in his chronicle, setting the action of *Asp.* in Spain, probably for the same reasons as in the case of the saga, but, with less logic, placing the PT portion after the events of *Asp.* See the *Chronique rimée de Philippe Mouskés*, ed. le Baron de Reiffenberg (Brussels, 1836), e.g. ll. 4429-30, and PT section beginning ca. l. 4718. Cf. also René Louis, *Girart, Comte de Vienne, dans les Chansons de geste: Girart de Vienne, Girart de Fraite, Girart de Rousillon* (Auxerre, 1947), I, pp. 134-135.

[7] Mandach (p. 137) is under the impression that Agulandus dies twice in the saga. The source of his confusion would seem to be R. van Waard, *Études sur l'origine et la formation de la Chanson d'Aspremont* (Groningen, 1937),

then picked up *Asp.*, starting at a point roughly one third of the way from the beginning of the poem's action. Thus, in the A-version, the first twenty-three chapters translate, with few omissions (such as the death of Agolandus), the Prologue and first eighteen chapters of PT;[8] in his twenty-fourth chapter, the translator (or compiler) turned to the 199th laisse of *Asp.*,[9] and continued with this source for another hundred chapters, covering its material up to ls. 504, which relates the death of Agolandus. He has been congratulated for improving on the original PT "by omitting religious digressions"[10] (though he did not omit all of these), but his efforts to harmonize the two sources can only be described as minimal. It does not help matters that his source for *Asp.* apparently had several leaves misplaced, which results in a fine confusion in chapters 25-27.[11]

The B-redactor, who, it is generally agreed,[12] was an Icelander, clearly felt that the only thing to do with the A-version was to re-write it so that it would make a more coherent story. He succeeded well enough in this. The B-version is far more readable, as its recent Icelandic editor remarks,[13] and must be taken as the final saga version; it is,

p. 192: "... au chapitre 13 ..., le roi sarrasin s'enfuit avec le roi de Sibil et avec Astumaior... Plus tard (ch. 23...), le premier est tué, tandis que l'autre, Altumant, ... se rend à Charlemagne en se faisant baptiser." Van Waard meant that the "roi de Sibil" was killed, not "le roi sarrasin" (Agolandus).

[8] Chapter numbers in the longer texts, such as the Codex Calixtinus (hereafter designated CC); Smyser gives the corresponding chapter numbers of the longer versions in the margins of the "Synopsis" of his edition, which is of a shorter text and has different numbering.

[9] Laisse numbers are those of the edition by Louis Brandin (Paris: 2nd ed., 1924; 2 vols.). The only other edition of more than a small fragment is that of the Berlin ms. ed. Immanuel Bekker (Berlin, 1847); as I could not locate this in a number of libraries, including the B.L. and the Bodleian, it is obviously not readily accessible.

[10] Henry Goddard Leach, *Angevin Britain and Scandinavia* (Cambridge, Mass., 1921), p. 247.

[11] Ls. 242 is in the middle of 235, while 238-241 are inserted before 230; cf. E. F. Halvorsen, *The Norse Version of the Chanson de Roland* (Copenhagen, 1959), p. 55, and van Waard, 211-212.

[12] See, e.g., Halvorsen, p. 55.

[13] Bjarni Vilhjálmsson, ed., *Karlamagnús saga og kappa hans* (Reykjavík, 1950), I, p. xxvii; for this reason, as well as because of the lacunae in the A-

in addition, interesting as probably representing the work of the compiler of the B-version of the entire saga.[14] But since it is a complete revision,[15] it cannot be used to fill the lacunae in the A-version, although it may occasionally provide hints as to the nature of missing passages.[16]

The relationship of the two versions is further complicated by the fact that the B-redactor knew and used another redaction of the PT portion of the A-text: that used by the author of the *Tveggja postola saga Jóns ok Jacobs* (hereinafter designated as TPS),[17] the 83rd through the 88th chapters of which clearly derive from an A version of the saga,[18] with almost no indication that any other PT text has been consulted.[19] "B," on the other hand, has certainly used the PT version

texts, he prints only the B-version, with the addition of the Ferakut chapters in A, missing in B. These are printed as a separate unit at the end of the "Saga af Agulando," which constitutes the second volume of this three volume edition.

[14] See Foote, p. 22. On the other hand, Peter Hallberg argues in *Stilsignalement och författarskap i norrön sagalitteratur* (Nordistica Gothoburgensia 3, Göteborg, 1968) that *Agulandus B* shows a special kinship *only* with the tenth part of the saga, "Um kraptaverk og jartegnir" ('Miracles and Signs'). If he is correct, it would be unlikely that the author of these two parts could be the original B-redactor. Hallberg identifies the author of these two parts of the saga as Berge Sokkason, known to be author of *Nikolás saga erkibyskups II* and *Michaels saga*, whose hand he also detects in *Tveggja postola saga Jóns ok Jacobs, Jóns saga postola B, Maríu saga, Thomas saga erkibyskups II, Guðmundar saga Arasonar, Clárus saga*, and *Drauma-Jóns saga*. Hallberg's methods are, however, open to criticism. See, e.g., the review by H. A. Roe in *Scandinavian Studies* 42 (1970), 76-80. For Hallberg's discussion of *Agulandus B*, and the *Karlamagnús saga* in general, see Chapter 15 of his book: "Författarskap inom Karlamagnús saga," p. 104 ff.

[15] As Halvorsen puts it (p. 37), "an entirely new tale."

[16] See, e.g., ch. 59, n. 19.

[17] Ed. C. R. Unger, in *Postola sögur* (Christiana, 1874), pp. 666-675.

[18] Cf. Halvorsen, pp. 38-42; Foote, pp. 9-15. Foote's most convincing parallel is that of PT 103/7-8, *altissimus scilicet quantum solet volare in sublime corvus* with TPS 670/33-34, *svá hátt í lopt upp, sem fugli et venjuligt at hefja sik*, as against *Kms.* A (267/11-12) *þar sem hrafn er vanr at fljúga* (p. 12).

[19] For its exception, see Foote, pp. 52-54.

of Vincent of Beauvais[20] as well as the A-version—and the A-text used was not, of course, necessarily the same as those in the surviving manuscripts. Thus when the B-version has a reading which does not agree with either of the extant A texts, or the version of A found in TPS, or that of Vincent, but which does seem to correspond with one manuscript or another of PT, the source student may be faced with a complex problem: does the reading come from the original A-text, as against the versions preserved, or has the redactor used still another source? In most cases, however, such variants are of a sort likely to arise by pure chance in the course of translation.

One of the intractable difficulties faced by anyone who wishes to determine exactly what the B-redactor did or did not get from the A-version, as against some other source of PT material, is the confusing state of scholarship on the PT itself. While modern readers are unlikely to share the sentiment of some of our ancestors that this chronicle is preferable to the versions of the poets,[21] it was an enormous success in its time, as is attested by the extraordinary number of surviving manuscripts: over 150 have been identified in Latin alone, as well as a similar number of early translations into various vernaculars.[22] Its influence was also vast, turning up in "historical" accounts (such as the *Speculum historiale*);[23] in literature, including innumerable later *chansons de geste*; and in art, as in the Charlemagne window at Chartres. Only a few of the extant manuscripts have been published, and, inevitably, none of these is exactly the text used by the original Norse translator.

In general, the PT texts fall into two classes, the "longer" and "shorter" versions. But within these groupings—which cannot themselves be considered homogenous—there are several distinct sub-

[20] In the *Speculum historiale*, Book 24.

[21] Cf. Walpole, p. 16.

[22] Cf. Mandach, e.g., p. 16, and Short, *passim*.

[23] But not all: for example, the Chronicle of Matthew Paris (in *Chronica majora*, ed. Henry R. Luard, London, 1874; Rolls Series 57) may revive confidence in the historical judgment of the thirteenth century, since Paris seems to have adhered to non-legendary sources as strictly as he could.

divisions.[24] The version on which our translation was based appears to have been a "longer" text similar to that of the Codex Calixtinus, as published by Meredith-Jones,[25] and, it is generally thought, of the group he designates as "C."[26] The characteristic variant readings of this group are represented in the notes to the M-J text by those of one manuscript in this group, "C_3."[27] It is, however, highly questionable that the source was really very close to any C-text currently available.

The most distinctive characteristic of the C-group as noted by M-J is that these manuscripts omit an allusion to Ogier the Dane and the "songs" in his honor: but this statement is in the A-version of the saga.[28] Among the saga readings Foote cites as similar to the C-group,[29] most are, if taken individually, rather dubious, as Foote himself admits; the only really striking example is the reference to Roland's "courtesy" in placing a stone under the head of the sleeping giant: "Rollant var ungr at aldri ok kvikr á ser *ok kurteiss í öllum sinum hætti*" (italics added) clearly has something to do with M-J's C_3 reading "Rotholandus ut erat iuvenis alacer *et nobilis animi*," as against the CC "Rotolandus vero, ut erat iuvenis alacer." Only the C-group, by all reports, has an addition like that found here in the saga.

Mandach, commenting on Foote's article, says "si M. Foote avait eu à sa disposition un tableau systématique des caractéristiques de la ver-

[24] The stemma is still controversial; for accounts, see Short, pp. 3-5; Mandach, *passim*, and the reviews of his book (cf. n. 3 above).

[25] *Historia Karoli Magni et Rotholandi ou Chronique du Pseudo-Turpin* (Paris, 1936); hereafter designated M-J.

[26] Foote, p. 3; Mandach, p. 136, e.g.

[27] M-J's group C is called "W" by Adalbert Hämel, "Aus der Geschichte der Pseudo-Turpin Forschung," *Romanische Forschungen*, 57 (1943), 229-245; see esp. p. 244. Mandach follows M-J in designating the group as C, and the ms. in question C_3. — No other ms. of the C group has been printed. I have checked certain readings in two other C mss. in the B.L. but neither seems to be any closer to the peculiarities of our source.

[28] M-J, p. 12; cf. Walpole, "Note to the Meredith-Jones Edition of the *Historia Karoli Magni et Rotholandi ou Chronique du Pseudo-Turpin*," *Speculum* 22 (1947), p. 261.

[29] "A Note on the Source of the Icelandic Translation of the Pseudo-Turpin Chronicle," *Neophil.* 43 (1959), 137-142, esp. p. 140.

sion C-Cœur de Lion et de son auteur, le Religieux Prorichard, il nous aurait donné une démonstration parfaite," and, citing the text quoted above, adds, "il est évident que le texte norrois suit celui de C-Cœur-de-Lion et non les autres" (p. 136). But is the case really strong enough to be considered proved? It does not appear so, when we look at the "tableau systématique" which Mandach gives us on the preceding pages (131-132). Of his fourteen characteristics of the C-group (which do not include any mention of the generally omitted Ogier reference), only six can be used to prove anything about the saga, since the rest occur in sections of PT omitted in the Norse translation. Of these remaining six, only one occurs in the saga: the one cited by Foote and quoted above. Not one of the other five is to be found in the saga.[30] In fact, Mandach's checklist appears to undermine, rather than strengthen, Foote's case. If these changes are in fact characteristic of all—or even most—of the C-group, then it is very doubtful that the source of the saga belonged to the group.

That there may be other factors confusing the issue is, unfortunately, clear. For one thing, Mandach sometimes has the facts wrong, especially in regard to the saga, which, quite clearly, he has not actually read himself. He remarks, for example, "Ni la version norroise, ni la traduction galloise n'offrent l'Epître de Turpin à Leoprandus" (p. 138), which is simply not so: *both* the Norse and Welsh versions include the letter.[31] For another, the variants apparently distinguishing one group, or manuscript, from another can be

[30] The other five applicable passages are, using Mandach's numbers: (5), in PT 18 (*Kms.* a 23), Charlemagne's sword is identified by name (Gaudiosa, Joyeuse); (7) in PT 10 (*Kms.* A,a 8), Charlemagne calls on the help of the Almighty in the midst of the battle; (8) in PT 12 (A,a 11), Charlemagne adds to his theological arguments the statement that since the heathens do not know their creator, they shall have no inheritance on earth or in heaven; (9) in PT 17 (A,a 15), Charlemagne is reluctant to give Roland permission to fight the giant because Roland is young, etc.; (10) in PT 18 (*a* 23), Charlemagne is amazed to see his men fleeing because he does not know the reason; (11) in PT 17 (A,a 18), the giant tells Roland he has never met anyone more tiring.

[31] For the Welsh version, see Robert Williams, ed. and trans. "Campeu Charlemaen," in *Selections from the Hengwrt Mss.*, Part IV (London, 1880).

elusive or difficult to interpret.[32] When we compare any chapter of the saga translation with M-J's notes on C_3 variants, in most cases we simply cannot be sure which readings the translator had before him. If we look at the beginning of the Prologue, we can see that where CC reads "Salutem in Christo" and C_3 "Salutem in Domino," the saga's greeting is "in Jesus Christ," which could certainly have been suggested by either variant. And such seems to be the usual case.

On the other hand, a phrase in chapter 3 of PT, "sine contrario," which M-J says is *only* in CC, appears to be reflected in the saga's statement that Karlamagnus went to Compostella from Pamplona by the "direct road," and, in the first chapter a reference to Spain which is missing in the C variant is found in the A,a text of the saga. Of course, these are points which could easily be explained by the vagaries of translation, or may be represented in other PT texts which M-J had not examined. There are a number of cases in which the saga seems to be drawing on another identifiable manuscript tradition: an unabridged text similar to those represented in Smyser's edition by the manuscripts which he designates A and M.[33] At least two of the correspondences here seem striking: A,a 2's "En lærisveinar hans fœrðu hans in helga líkama aptr í Galiciam ok styrktu þá enn heilaga kristni með sínum kenningum" as translating "Deinde eius discipuli ipso ab Herode rege perempto ac corpore illius a Iherosolimis usque in Galiciam per mare translato in eadem terra Galicie fidem Christi et

[32] To see a "courtly" personality emerging from the C-revisions, for instance, may seem a bit dubious if the only strong example is Roland's "courtesy," when most of the other examples adduced do not seem very good proof of any such character. One such is the reference to Charlemagne's sword by name in PT 18, on which Mandach comments (p. 131): "Il n'est donc pas étonnant que le Religieux Prorichard [putative author of C] sache que l'épée de Charlemagne s'appelle *Joyeuse*..." But there is no reason why any reader of PT should be ignorant here: the sword is mentioned by name earlier, in Ch. 8, in a great many versions, including B.L. Cotton Nero a xi, which Mandach groups with the very oldest texts.

[33] In Mandach's listing, these are mss. M3-A1-Paris (B.N. lat. 17.656) and M2S-Smyser (Madrid, B.N. 1617). The correspondences are listed in Foote, "Note," esp. p. 141.

predicationem apostoli confirmaverunt," and later in the same chapter (but from the next chapter of PT), "svá kýs hann þik til þess af öllum konungum" corresponding to "ex omnibus te principibus elegit."

Foote concludes that the resemblances to the abridged texts occur in the first seven chapters of the saga, while those corresponding to the C-group begin in ch. 8. But, there are a great many passages in the first seven chapters which, while based on PT, are not found in the abridged version, and a great many C characteristics which are not in the later chapters, as has already been noted. At least one reading in the saga's source is not found in the abridged version or in the C-group or in CC: in A,a 3, translating PT 4 (6 in the abridged version), the Norse translator is quite clearly translating Lat. *clava* 'club' rather than *clavis* 'key,' the reading of the vast majority of PT mss. As far as can be ascertained from the currently available information on PT mss., the 'clava' reading occurs only in two manuscripts of the A-group, the closely related A_{10} and A_{11},[34] and in the early printed editions, all of which, according to Hämel, stem from the same manuscript, a "D" version.[35] There is no other good reason to think the source of the saga had a close relationship to an A or D ms.[36]

There is, further, at least one mysterious reference in the saga for which no source, parallel, or other explanation seems to be available. In A,a 15, the beginning of the "Ferakut episode" (from PT 17), the saga tells us that the giant came from "Kuerna" (or "Kverna") as well as from Syria. It is possible that this is a locale transferred from elsewhere in PT by the translator, by pure chance: a list of Spanish towns in PT 3, omitted in the saga, includes *Crunia* (la Coruna), which is at least within shouting distance of "Kuerna." But it is equally possible that the saga is following another, unknown, source. For

[34] B.N. n.a.l. 369 and B.L. Harley 3500; Mandach, p. 369, considers A_{10} a copy of the ms. originally copied from a St. Denis original for Baudouin V of Hainaut, and A_{11} a copy of A_{10}.

[35] Pp. 230-231; the ms. is Mandach's D_{85}: see p. 375. On the 'clava' variant, see M-J, pp. 102 and 291-292; Foote, "Note," p. 142.

[36] It does not, for example, show the characteristic spellings of either group; see, e.g., Mandach, pp. 98-99.

example the word might have been derived from a form of spelling for Chaldea, a more likely place of origin for a Syrian giant.[37]

In any case, then, if the basic text for the PT section of the saga was of the C type, it was strongly contaminated with at least one other type, and probably more than one. Foote suggests that this contamination is likely to have been "of a kind similar to that detected by Hämel in other manuscripts of PT, where the best explanation of the state of the text is that a copy of a version belonging to one class has been corrected by reference to a manuscript of another class."[38] It is perhaps not so strange that it shows a generally strong resemblance to CC, itself just such a thoroughly hybrid manuscript, which Mandach sees as a B text, derived from a blending of "HA" and C traditions, which were in turn derived from A and D traditions—[39] a state of affairs which seems to cover pretty well all the possibilities. Thus, while it may be that there is an unpublished PT ms. somewhere which would clear up some of these questions once and for all, it seems, in the end, necessary to use the M-J edition of CC as the best "source" for the purpose, and I have consistently so done except in cases where there was specific reason to prefer another text.[40]

When, however, we look at the different manuscript traditions of the saga itself, we find the matter further complicated. It sometimes ap-

[37] Chaldea is referred to once in at least two French derivatives of PT, the *Chronique rimée* of Philippe Mouskés, I, p. 257, l. 6463, in a passage concerning PT's "Salamcadis" (called 'Salant' by Mouskés), and in what appears to be its source, B.N. ms. fr. 2137, ed. Fredrik Wulff (Lund, 1879), p. 46, 17-21; cf. Walpole, *Philip Mouskés and the Pseudo-Turpin Chronicle*, Univ. of Calif. Publ. in Mod. Philology, vol. 26, no. 4, Univ. of Calif. Press, 1947, pp. 331-343.

[38] "Note," p. 141, referring to Hämel's *Überlieferung und Bedeutung des Liber Sancti Jacobi und des Pseudo-Turpin* (Munich, 1950), p. 356.

[39] See his App. C, esp. table on p. 301.

[40] Some readings have been checked against the transcriptions of the text of Walter Muir Whitehill (*Liber Sancti Jacobi, Codex Calixtinus*, I; Santiago de Compostella, 1944) and Hämel (*Der Pseudo-Turpin von Compostela*, ed. Mandach, *Sitzungsberichte der bay. Akad. der Wissenschaften*, Phil.-Hist. Klasse, 1965, I, 1-105), but the corrections to be found there are, while no doubt of considerable importance to students of PT itself, not very helpful for present purposes.

pears that the two manuscripts of the older version, mss. *A* and *a*, are not themselves following the same source. In A,a 7, for example, we come upon a list of names including one given in *A* as "Texphin," which corresponds to the *Texephinus* of CC. In *a*, however, the name is "Terhpin," which appears to represent the *Teremphinus* (variously spelled : Terenphinus, Therophinus) of the abridged versions.[41] There are occasions when a number given in one manuscript corresponds to the abridged version while the number in the other is that of CC. It is possible that the scribe of one of these manuscripts had recourse to another PT manuscript and was correcting as he went along, thus introducing further contamination.

In the case of the B-redactor, it is quite clear that reference was made to a version of PT other than that which has been preserved in *A* and *a*, since a number of details are preserved in the B-version which are not to be found in *A* or *a*. They may, of course, have been in the Aa prototype. Some of them can be found in the TPS version, since, as noted above, it seems to have been based on an older A-version, and was, in turn, a source for the B-version. In the B Prologue, for example, we find "í þeim stað er landsmenn kölluðu á þeim tíma Librarum Domini," which corresponds to TPS's "í þeim stað er Liberum donum heitir," but to nothing in the extant manuscripts of the A-version—or to anything in any printed text of PT, for that matter. But there are other details in B,b which are not in TPS either, such as the account of the grave of St. Torquatus at "Acennoa," and the name of the "sea of Petronus." Many such details seem to have come from Vincent of Beauvais, as does the account of the honor to, and vision of, St. Denis in chapters 3 and 4 of the B-version.

It does not appear that B corrected TPS by checking with Vincent. For example, Vincent does not seem to have the name of *Liberum donum* or *Librarum Domini*.[42] But it remains that we cannot be sure whether the TPS writer knew Vincent at first hand, or at what point in the process each individual influence may have slipped in. For one

[41] See Smyser, p. 64.

[42] Unless the omission is a peculiarity of the edition I consulted, in *Speculi maioris IV* (Venice, 1591).

thing, we must not lose sight of the fact that we do not have the original A-version, or, probably, the original B-version: and maybe not even the original TPS.

There is also some question as to whether the "original A-version" was one original or two; that is, were the saga versions of PT and *Asp.* written and seamed together by the same man in one continuous process, or were they two separate translations, independently composed, then combined by an A-compiler? Foote concludes, largely on stylistic grounds, that the translation is actually two translations by two different hands.[43] He believes that the PT chapters were translated in Iceland, early in the thirteenth century, while *Asp.* was translated in Norway rather later. If so, both texts may have been in circulation in complete forms (it must be remembered that the extant saga versions do not represent all of either PT or *Asp.*), which would add still another missing link to the chain of sources: and yet another stage at which contamination of various sorts may have entered.

If it can be held that the principal source of this part of the saga belonged to the C-group of PT manuscripts, it may be worth noting that this group appears to have had a special connection with Britain.[44] In this case, here, as elsewhere in the saga, the source material would have been likely to have come to Scandinavia via Britain. However, later versions of PT material in Anglo-Norman and Middle English, although reasonably plentiful, do not seem to show any special kinship with the saga. Most, perhaps all, of these later English versions stem from a particular Old French translation which would seem to have been based on a "C" manuscript tradition of PT; none of the earmarks of this later tradition, however, appear in the saga.[45]

[43] *Pseudo-Turpin*, pp. 35-40 and 44-47.

[44] See Foote, *Pseudo-Turpin*, p. 3, and "Note"; Walpole, "Note," 260-262; M-J, p. 22 (remarks that all the mss. of his group C, with two exceptions, are in the B.L.). Walpole corrects M-J in noting that the characteristic "Ogier" omission is found *only* in C mss., not in ms. A, as M-J says.

[45] Cf. Short, pp. 16-17; Walpole, *Charlemagne and Roland, a Study of the Source of Two Middle English Metrical Romances*, Univ. of Calif. Publ. in Mod. Philology, vol. 21, Univ. of Calif. Press, 1944, e.g., p. 434. — On pp. 403-407, Walpole lists characteristics of this group, few of which occur in passages included in the saga, but two can be checked: (1) the addition that

Complex as the matter of the saga's source of PT material may seem to be, the relation of the latter—and by far the greater— portion of the tale to *Asp.* is all too similar a problem. It is possible that the saga version represents a somewhat earlier form of the *Asp.* material,[46] but, as van Waard concluded (p. 264), any theory of the antiquity of the saga version must be viewed with caution, since, while it is shorter than the Wollaton Hall text of *Asp.* (hereinafter abbreviated W) published by Brandin, it corresponds to this text remarkably closely. But here, as in the PT section, the saga version agrees now with one extant manuscript and now with another, and, just as it is difficult to determine which PT manuscript is closest because of the state of PT scholarship, the state of *Asp.* scholarship impedes any firm conclusions on the saga's relationship with the *Asp.* manuscripts.

In the case of PT, the student has a good many published versions more or less available, even if this represents only a fraction of the total. Only one complete text of *Asp.* has been printed, and that edition gives few variants. Brandin lists nine other manuscripts which, to one extent or another, he consulted, but there are at least ten more which were not used at all.[47] Several selections from other manuscripts have been published, but most of them are passages from parts of *Asp.* which are not included in the saga version and thus do not help in the present instance.[48] As Curtius remarked, "Eine kritische Ausgabe wäre

Christ dies on the cross, in translating PT 17 *quia omnis qui nascitur, moritur.* [interpolation] *Si credendum nativitate...* (2) alteration of PT 3 *quasdam scilicet sine pugna, quasdam cum magno bello et maxima arte* to a statement that some were taken by miracles alone and others by battle. In neither case does the saga version have the characteristic change. Similarly, the points of resemblance between the *Chronique Bordelaise* and Willem de Briane's A-N text, cited by Mandach, *Chronique de Turpin: texte anglo-normand* (1963), II, 25-26, have no parallels in the saga text.

[46] Cf. S. Szogs, *Aspremont: Entwicklungsgeschichte und Stellung innerhalb der Karlsgeste* (Halle, 1931), 125-131; van Waard, p. 202.

[47] Cf. J. Monfrin, "Fragments de la Chanson d'Aspremont conservés en Italie," *Romania* 79 (1958), 237-41.

[48] Three such are those published by Ernest Langlois, in "Deux fragments épiques: Otinel, Aspremont," *Romania* 12 (1883), 433-58 (*Asp.*, 446-458), containing 395 verses from the beginning of ms. P_4; P. Meyer, "Fragment d'Aspremont conservé aux Archives du Puy-de-Dome," *Romania* 19 (1890),

sehr erwünscht. Aber werden wir sie erleben?"[49] As no such critical edition has appeared, remarks on the saga's relationship to *Asp.* here must be described as tentative at best, based as they are on a few printed fragments and consultation of a handful of the manuscripts: an exhaustive study of the *Asp.* manuscripts was clearly beyond the scope of the present work.[50]

The manuscripts which are thought to be closest to the saga's source are the two designated L_2 (B.L. Lansdowne 782)[51] and P_2 (B.N. ms. fr. 25529).[52] Claudine I. Wilson's study of lss. 437-439[53] concludes that

201-236, giving the end of *Asp.* according to the fragment and comparing a selection from near the beginning of the poem in eight mss; and W. Meyer, "Franko-italienische Studien, II, 2: Aspremont," *Zeitschrift für romanische Philologie* 10 (1886), 22-42, containing 537 verses of P_2 and P_3, but only the opening of the poem.

One interesting but unhelpful related fragment is that from ms. Camb. addit. 3303 published by Paul Meyer in *Romania* 35 (1906), 22-31, as "Fragment d'une chanson de geste relative à la guerre d'Espagne." This is an episode in which Ogier duels with Agolant in Spain, but it corresponds to nothing in either PT or *Asp.* Roland, Oliver (who is absent from *Asp.* and only marginally present in the part of PT relating to Aigolandus), and Ganelon all figure; Ogier wins Broiefort from Agolant.

[49] Ernst Robert Curtius, "Über die altfranzösische Epik II," *Romanische Forschungen* 61 (1948), p. 447.

[50] In discussing the mss. of *Asp.*, both in this introduction and in the notes to the text, I have made use of Roepke's ms. designations, as those most frequently encountered in discussions of *Asp.*: see Fritz Roepke, *Studien zur Chanson d'Aspremont* (Greifswald, 1909). Unfortunately they differ from those used by Brandin and some others; van Waard, who follows Roepke, gives a table of these symbols on p. 189, noting, e.g., that Brandin's "C" (Benary's "D"; see Walter Benary, "Mitteilungen aus Handschriften der *Chanson d'Aspremont*," *Zeitschrift für romanische Philologie* 34 [1910], p. 2) is Roepke's P_2.

[51] The Peterborough ms.; Mandach claims—citing no specific evidence—that this is the closest representative of the "archaic" source (assumed to be an A-N version) in "À la découverte d'un nouvel 'Aspremont' de la Bibliothèque des Gonzague de Mantoue," *Cultura neolatina* 21 (1961), 116-122. No selections from this ms. have been printed; I have consulted it—and some others—in the B.L.

[52] Some relevant parts of this ms. have been printed by Brandin (Appendix, pp. 181-188), Benary (the selections in the article cited above are based on P_5—B.N. nouv. acq. fr. 10.039—but he gives variants from P_2, among others,

these two manuscripts correspond generally to each other, rather than to W; however, her chart shows that the order of L_2 is not as close to the saga's as is that of P_2. Another section of the poem in which there are significant differences among the manuscripts is the debate scene, lss. 316-334 in W, A,a chapters 40-45 and 59-65, B,b 59. Two of the *tirades* translated in the saga, the speeches of Pliades and Gorhant of Florence, are found in P_2[54] but not in W or L_2.[55] L_2 has, in fact, exactly the same order and participants here as W, except that there is apparently a part missing where a page ends, cutting off the end of Manuel's speech; the next page picks up that of Pantalis in such a way that Sinagon is cut out completely, while Pantalis vanishes into Manuel; and, similarly, Gorant's speech is combined with that of Acesalon in a way which seems to eliminate both Acesalon and Meadas. Missing or skipped pages in the original from which this copy was made no doubt explain these variants. W's "li rois de Balfainie" (l. 6305), the only debater whose omission in the saga cannot be explained by lacunae or simple error, is represented in L_2 in the same order as in W.[56]

Checking the wording of the saga against various manuscript versions of *Asp.* has not produced any conclusive evidence for the special closeness of any one manuscript. Perhaps the clearest example may be seen in the section of P_2 printed by Haase, which corresponds with W, in Brandin's edition, beginning with l. 8542. The differences between the two versions of *Asp.* in question are often very small ones, but

in his notes), and Carl Haase (*Weitere Studien zur 'Chanson d'Aspremont,'* Greifswald, 1917).

[53] "La Chanson d'Aspremont: le problème de Laisses 437-439," *Revue de phil. franç.* 37 (1925), 21-28.

[54] Cf. van Waard, p. 205.

[55] Nor, for that matter, in L_1 (B.M. Old Roy. 15 E VI) or L_3 (B.L. Add. 35.289).

[56] He is also represented in L_3, which has exactly the same order as Wollaton Hall (although its spelling of names is even more peculiar than that of the saga: e.g., W's 'Hogiers,' L_2's 'Hohier,' turns into 'Hoel' in L_3). L_1 also follows the same basic order, but differs from W, L_2, and L_3 in that it condenses the debate drastically, cutting down the participants to six—possibly out of impatience: we are told that "Roy Agolant Ulien ne penst plus endurer."

there are places where the saga version is clearly closer to P_2. On the other hand, there are also places where the saga is just as clearly closer to W.[57] A,a chapters 94 to 97 are notable here: they generally correspond to P_2, and this section is missing, or very generally summarized, in W. Nevertheless, such details as numbers are often at variance with those of P_2, and some points, such as the sparrow-hawk motif near the beginning of A,a 97, are not there at all.

Comparison with the section of P_2 printed by Brandin is equally inconclusive. There are striking points of resemblance and equally striking differences. The latter part of A,a 112 together with 113 will be found in this volume at the end of chapter 72; this section corresponds to the P_2 text which appears under the heading 'II' in Brandin's edition, pp. 183-188, with the numbering of the similar W laisses. At first glance, the greater affinity of the saga to P_2 seems obvious: the order of the saga is, here, that of P_2, which is quite different from W. However, the wording and details of the saga are still not necessarily based on P_2. For example, Ogier and Naimes report disaster to Charlemagne, in the words of W, "Drois emperere mals vos est avenu./Des dose pers avons les nœf perdu." In P_2 they report at greater length:

> Riche rois, sires, com somes confondu!
> Ne somes mie bien doi mile escu.
> Des doze pers q'aviez esleü,
> Que vostre niés Rolanz ot retenu,
> En icest champ an sont li nœf perdu.

The Oddgeir and Nemes of the saga are almost as brief as their prototypes in W, but they put the matter rather differently, adding a statistic which appears in neither French manuscript and apparently reporting that nine of the twelve peers survive, rather than that nine are lost: "Lord, much of our troop is fallen; we have no greater a host than fifteen thousand men now, and nine of the twelve peers."

There is at least one point in A,a 113 where the saga text appears to be closer to W than to P_2. When Berengier comes to the aid of the em-

[57] Some of these differences are remarked in the notes to the translation; see below, esp. notes to chs. 67 and 68.

peror, l. 170 of the P_2 selection reports "C'est Berengiers, cui il tient a son dru," while W 8926 reads "C'est *li marcis* Berengiers qui pres fu" (italics added). The latter seems to be the explanation of the saga's "Baeringur *of Markun.*" But another curious fact is that in the last sentence of the chapter *a* is clearly closer to W while *A* approximates the P_2 version. W 8940, "Ainc en cest siecle si grans joie ne fu," is almost exactly *a*'s "they had never been more joyful since they came into the world," while *A*'s "they rejoiced greatly over his coming" may be a translation of P_2's "Grant joie an ont tuit an l'estor eü."

In general, then, the saga's source may often have been closer to P_2[58] than to W, but it was not invariably so by any means. Thus, since W is about as close as we can now get to the original, in the current state of textual work on the poem, and since it is the only version which is easily available in its entirety, it seems proper to use it as a basis for comparison in evaluating saga variants. Hereafter in this volume it should be understood that "*Asp.*" refers to Brandin's edition, unless another version is specifically indicated. Inevitably, this means that when a note says that a passage is "not in *Asp.*" it means that it is not in that edition: the possibility remains that it may be found elsewhere in manuscripts which the present writer has been unable to consult at length.

A glance at the textual notes to almost any of the later chapters of the saga will demonstrate to the reader how helpful *Asp.* is in deciding between manuscript variants, though it is not, of course, the only criterion which can be used. It is generally assumed that ms. *a* is closer to the French original than ms. *A*; van Waard goes so far as to say "Chaque fois qu'il y a désaccord entre A et a, le dernier donne une traduction plus proche du poème français que le ms. A, comme j'ai pu le constater." The situation does not, however, appear to be really this clear-cut. About half of the fragment of *Kms.* in the Oslo Riksarkiv which is known as Fragment 2[59] consists of passages from the saga of

[58] And, sometimes, other mss., but results of checking points against the available selections of such mss. as P_3 and P_5 are even more doubtful. E.g., P_5's version of the baptism of Balam, printed by Benary, p. 19, omits a passage that is in W and in the saga: *Asp.* 7058-64, found in A,a 73.

[59] Hereafter abbreviated Fr2; it is printed by Unger in an appendix, pp. 558-562.

Agulandus. Since this fragment is undoubtedly older than the extant more nearly complete manuscripts, we would expect it to agree with *a* against *A*, and this is indeed often the case. But it is not invariably so. For example, *A* 49 and Fr2 agree in reading "in all this great multitude," where *a* gives "in his troop."[60] Similarly, the phrase "The heathen answered" in *A* 48, found in Fr2, is omitted in *a*.[61] Fr2 itself is, moreover, not free of errors; in the immediately following sentence, the fragment says "they took the chief standard into *our* power" (italics added), while both *A* and *a* give a more reasonable "*their* power."

It would, then, be dangerous to give *a* automatic preference in choosing variant readings. Comparison with *Asp.* and, in the considerably fewer places where such comparison is available, Fr2, indicates that while the odds may be in favor of *a*, yet *A* is the most justifiable choice in a very large number of instances. When no comparison is available at all, the choice for this translation has often been made on a basis of "sense," or even more arbitrary and subjective grounds: the reader is warned to consider the variants given in the footnotes if he is concerned at all with the minutiae of the text.

Those who may look for textual clues to *Asp.* in the saga version are likely to find their confidence in the Norse translation somewhat undermined by such obvious details as names. It is evident that the translator, the scribes, and/or the redactor did not recognize a great many place names and thus often misread them drastically. Roën appears as 'Kuin' or 'Kum' in A,a 91;[62] the B-redactor gives us 'Kun.' Personal names are at least as often transformed: 'Acesalon' turns up as 'Talamon,' 'Manuel' becomes 'Samnel,' and a few ghostly characters emerge from various sorts of misunderstandings: for example, *Asp.* "le roi d'Angalion" (4501) becomes 'Giulion,' and one 'King Malgerian' appears to owe his existence to a misreading of *Asp.* 6385, "Molt nos ont ore rendu *mal geredon*" (italics added).

The translator's errors are, sadly, not limited to difficulties in recognizing names. His grammar often failed him, as when, frequently enough to be noticeable, he confused singular or dual with plural

[60] Cf. ch. 51, n. 17.
[61] Cf. ch. 51, n. 8.
[62] Cf. ch. 66, n. 7.

pronouns. It certainly seems that the translator of *Asp.*, whether or not he was the same as the translator of PT, did not know French as well as he (or his colleague) knew Latin. It would not be surprising, of course, if the French original had been less legible than the Latin. And, in all fairness, it should be noted that French-speaking scribes themselves had a good deal of trouble with proper names in the *chansons de geste*: a comparison of the spellings for names used in various manuscripts for the participants in *Asp.*'s debate scene shows quite a variety of names, where at least one presumably French-speaking scribe (that of L_3) makes the saga look relatively accurate.

In any case the A,a version of the saga cannot, by itself, be accepted as a reliable guide to an earlier state of the *Chanson d'Aspremont*, if only because it is obviously incomplete. Not only does it lack the beginning and ending, which there are clear signs the original translator knew,[63] but extensive lacunae occur in both manuscripts in A,a chapters 25, 41, and 42. As has been noted above, it would also appear that the saga's original had some leaves misplaced, and thus the jolts which the reader experiences at the beginning of *a* 26 and the middle of *a* 27[64] make it clear that in this case the order of W must be preferred.[65] Another mix-up seems to have occurred in the sequence of A,a 31-36; since A,a 35-36 is transposed from a sequence which ends in the first half of 31, the transitions between 31 and 32 and between 34 and 35 seem quite illogical, although there is no such difficulty

[63] For example, he remarks that the heathen ladies were married to Christians after conversion (*A* 124). The division of the A,a version into "books," which is obviously following his source since the first such notation occurs well into the *Asp.* portion of the saga and suddenly announces "Here ends the fourth book," may well indicate that the saga version is derived from a complete translation which had been divided into "books," since no known ms. of the poem itself has such divisions. If such a division had been made into ten books, each of which comprised ca. 1000 lines of the poem, this would accord well with the book divisions noted in A,a. Cf. Gustav Storm, *Sagnkredsene om Karl den Store og Didrik af Bern hos de nordiske Folk* (Christiana, 1874), p. 56, and Knud Togeby, *Ogier le Danois dans les littératures européennes* (Munksgaard, 1969), p. 89.

[64] The lacuna in *A* here is an insufficient explanation for the lapse.

[65] Cf. van Waard, pp. 210-212.

about that between 35 and 36.[66] As in the previous case, the W order is far more satisfactory.

The way in which the saga divides the crucial debate scene is probably deliberate, since the subject is introduced, in rather different ways, each time. Nonetheless, the effect is deplorable, and one can well sympathize with the B-redactor, who re-amalgamated the two parts. The transition from the end of *a* 45 to the beginning of *a* 46 is notable, and A,a's attempt to revive the subject from the beginning in 58 is bound to strike the reader as repetitious, despite the presumed fresh start.[67]

All this confusion is justification enough for the B-revision, as a result of which we now have two quite different texts, of value to different readers for different reasons. The A,a versions may be of particular help to students of *Asp.* in the clues they present to the structure of the original, as van Waard concluded (p. 202), but it is of course the B-texts we must turn to if we wish to read the saga as a work in its own right. This is not just because it is the only complete and coherent version, but because it is here that we can see the literary hand of the saga-writer at work, ordering and transforming his matter into an independent saga of some interest. Admirers of the "family sagas" may not be impressed with the degree to which the redactor achieved the "fuldkommen sagamæssigt Præg" with which Unger (p. x) credits him, but there can be no doubt that his achievement is impressive when we compare the finished work with the rather bare bones piled up for him by the original translator(s).

Naturally enough, the literary qualities of the work are quite different from those of *Asp.* The French poem has been interesting to different readers for a variety of reasons,[68] but its most intriguing aspect as a work of literature must surely be the ambiguous and shifting relationship between Charlemagne—no background figure here, but an active, heroic leader of men—and Girart d'Eufrate, more properly, no

[66] *Ibid.*, 212-213.
[67] *Ibid.*, 214.
[68] E.g., Szogs, who appears to have been the first scholar to comment on the literary value of the work (ch. II, "Der literarische Wert der Dichtung," pp. 33-59) and also to demonstrate its popularity and influence (88-117).

doubt, de Fraite or Frate.[69] The ambiguity has completely disappeared in the B-version of the saga, where we find Girard presented as an unquestionably loyal ally. But this was obviously inevitable since the compiler of the A,a version left out both the beginning and the end of *Asp.*, so that the B-redactor, who clearly did not have a complete text of *Asp.* before him,[70] could have had no notion of Girard's recalcitrance or of the ominous parting between the two men. The only real clue he would have found in the A,a version would be the passage concerning Turpin in *a* 26.[71] Understandably enough, he omitted this passage in his revision: removed from its context as it is, it must have seemed inexplicable.

The shape and character of the saga of Agulandus has, of course, been in part determined by the way in which *Asp.* was combined with PT. Among other results, Rollant must appear here as a mature hero, not the inexperienced youth who is *Asp.*'s Roland; thus he tends to emerge as the principal hero, although Girard remains prominent, as do, to a lesser extent, others, including Oddgeir. A central plot-conflict is firmly held to throughout: that between Agulandus and Karlamagnus, and all that they stand for. Lesser heathens (among whom Jamund is much the most prominent) show aspects of the general inferiority of the heathen culture, while the various French heroes exemplify, in their different ways, the virtues of theirs.

The unity of the effect is such that although the action is often episodic no sub-plots can be identified which do not turn out to be essentially part of the overall theme. Thus, the conversion of the pagan Balam is one more demonstration of the attractive virtue of the Christian cause, while the defection of Amustene is both an example of heathen treachery and the natural outcome of the heathen society's internal dissensions, mutual distrust, and inhumanity: it is important

[69] Cf. Louis, pp. 159-176. — There are a number of resemblances between this character and Girart de Vienne (*Kms.* Geirard of Viana), who probably represent the same original character; Louis deals with this question at considerable length, and gives a putative stemma showing the relationships between "Girart de Fraite," *Girart de Vienne*, and *Asp.* on p. 145.

[70] As, for example, his version of the relations between Balam and Nemes proves.

[71] See at end of ch. 39.

because it demonstrates that society's self-defeating quality. The tale has the archetypal strength of a semi-mythic struggle between powers of light and darkness, strengthened in its universality by the appeal of defending home and country against the ruthless greed of predatory invaders, for in the B revision it is made clear as early as chapter 6 that the Saracen's intentions are not simply to regain Spain but to establish their control over Rome, the heart of European Christendom. Yet the saga writer takes care not to allow the conflict to slip to the elementary, and fundamentally dull, level of Good-Guys-Versus-Bad-Guys; his Saracens are human and sometimes admirable, while his Christians are aware of their human frailty. Ultimately the heathens are the victims of their own mistakes and false assumptions, as well as of their stubbornness in the face of the disaster they have brought on themselves. Even so, there is real heroism in the hopeless last stand of Agulandus, which makes a fitting ending for this version of the tale.

In translating other parts of the saga, I have made a practice of collating all four manuscripts (or as many of the four as are available for a given passage); but this is obviously not practicable in the case of Part IV, since the two versions are so widely separated. The B-version deserves to stand on its own, for all the reasons noted above. Yet for some purposes A,a is obviously more useful. To date, the only summary (there has been no modern translation otherwise) of this part of the saga is one based on the B-version,[72] and it has misled some students of the subject to whom the A-version was inaccessible.[73] The A-version is also interesting in that it alone preserves the "Ferakut" episode, which is the source[74] of a number of later *chansons de geste* and romances. Since fragments of an earlier manuscript of Part IV (Fr2) are available for comparison with mss. *A* and *a*, the A-version

[72] Gaston Paris, "La Karlamagnus-saga," *Bibliothèque de l'École des Chartes*, 6th ser. (1865), 1-18, based on Unger's Danish summary, pp. lxiv-lxxv of his ed.

[73] See, e.g., Foote's note on Szogs's difficulties, *Pseudo-Turpin*, p. 4, n. 13.

[74] Or analogue? Cf., e.g., Martin de Riquer, *Les Chansons de Geste françaises*, 2nd ed., trans. Irénée Cluzel (Paris, 1957), p. 211 ff.; Paris, *Histoire poétique de Charlemagne* (2nd ed., Paris, 1905), p. 266; Smyser, p. 32, n. 3. — The popularity of the episode in Scandinavia is witnessed by other works on the subject: see, e.g., Vilhjálmsson, p. xxvii.

has particular importance for textual studies and, of course, as the prime source of the B-version, it is helpful to the student of that version.

For these reasons it seemed necessary to translate both versions. However, in the belief that anyone who wished to read a connected narrative should certainly read the B-version, I have appended the relevant sections of A,a to the end of the derived chapters in B, rather than giving A,a as a separate continuous narrative. The resultant proximity of corresponding sections made it possible to avoid a cumbersome duplication of footnotes—which have, as much as is feasible, been added to the A-version rather than the B-version, especially when they deal with relationships with PT or *Asp.* A chart is provided for the convenience of those who may wish to read the A,a account consecutively.

In choosing ms. variants from *B* and *b*, I have followed principles similar to those which guided the choices between *A* and *a*, giving, as there, all significant variants in footnotes. As in the A,a version, it appeared that *b* was frequently, but not invariably, to be preferred over *B*. Again, there is a ms. fragment which gives a little of the text in a version against which it is interesting to check the other manuscripts: the Þjóðminjasafn fragments. It usually conforms to the *b* readings, but its independent variants are so minor as to be worthless for present purposes.[75]

The question of how to render proper names is a perpetual difficulty for all translators of Scandinavian literature; doubly so for those of us who are dealing with material which is not originally Scandinavian. While the policy adopted for the purposes of this translation has already been stated in my introduction to Vol. I, the saga of Agulandus presented further degrees of difficulty, since it abounds in both French and Latin names, some terribly garbled, in Scandinavian versions: no simple, consistent solution seemed to present itself. I have, however,

[75] For example, where *B* gives no conjunction and *b* has *ok* 'and,' the fragment gives *en* 'but' or 'and.' — See Jakob Benediktsson, "Skinnblað úr Karlamagnús sögu," *Skírnir* 126 (1952), 209-213. Foote (*Pseudo-Turpin*, p. 6) accepts Benediktsson's conclusion that this fragment is probably a leaf from the Bb original from which both *B* and *b* are derived, but the evidence seems to be on the scanty side.

generally observed the principles recently stated by Einar Haugen:[76] "Names which are only names should be kept intact (aside from appropriate transliteration, which I should prefer to see without the accents of length) since they convey no other information than the identity of the person or place, and to translate them would be overtranslation. But much speaks for the translation, wherever possible, of names that convey (to native speakers) further information about the place or person ..." To be sure, Haugen was speaking of literature which is Scandinavian in origin, while the present saga is a Scandinavian version of literature of far different origins; still, rather than go back to Latin or Old French forms—often quite different—or to modernize to French, which is not the language of the translation, or English, where many of these names are generally unknown, it seems generally best to continue to use the Scandinavian forms. Any other procedure would have involved enormous problems and, indeed, a degree of misrepresentation.

In so doing, I have, of course, "transliterated," and dropped the masculine nominative strong case ending, according to normal procedures for English translation. Deciding which forms conveyed "further information about the place or person" was sometimes rather difficult: it is hard to be sure whether the original translator really knew much about the geography of the work when he (or they) used so many different names for the same place. But, equally, he used widely varying forms of names for the same person, whether through following different sources, or through noting the variants in an individual source, or through scribal errors. I have, thus, retained a great many of the oddly varying spellings. When the reader finds a man's name spelled one way in one place and another later on, he may sometimes have good cause to suspect that the translator has failed to identify the two forms as belonging to the same person. If the reader is confused, I hope that the notes and glossary of names will be of assistance to him.

The few names I have put into Modern English forms are those which, there is no question, were recognized by the original translator and audience: Rome, Jerusalem, St. James, and Herod Agrippa, for example.

[76] "On Translating from the Scandinavian," in *Old Norse Literature and Mythology, a Symposium*, ed. Edgar C. Polomé (Austin, Texas, 1969), 17-18.

BIBLIOGRAPHICAL REFERENCES

The following works are referred to in the notes to this volume with sufficient frequency to make it appropriate to use abbreviations or short titles hereafter:

Brandin, Louis, ed. *La Chanson d'Aspremont.* 2 vols. Paris, 2nd ed. 1924. (Brandin; the poem is also designated *Asp.*)

Cleasby, Richard, and Gudbrand Vigfusson. *An Icelandic-English Dictionary*; 2nd ed., with supplement by Sir William A. Craigie. Oxford, 1957. (C-V.)

Foote, Peter G. "A Note on the Source of the Icelandic Translation of the Pseudo-Turpin Chronicle," *Neophil.* 43 (1959), 137-142. (Foote, "Note.")

——. *The Pseudo-Turpin Chronicle in Iceland: a Contribution to the Study of the Karlamagnús saga.* London, 1959. (Foote, *Pseudo-Turpin.*)

Louis, René. *Girart, Comte de Vienne, dans les Chansons de Geste: Girart de Vienne, Girart de Fraite, Girart de Roussillon.* 2 vols. Auxerre, 1947. (Louis; all noted p. numbers herein refer to vol. I.)

Mandach, André de. *Naissance et développement de la Chanson de Geste en Europe*, I: *La Geste de Charlemagne et de Roland.* Paris and Geneva, 1961. (Mandach.)

Meredith-Jones, C., ed. *Historia Karoli Magni et Rotholandi ou Chronique du Pseudo-Turpin.* Paris, 1936. (M-J; the work itself is also designated PT.)

Roepke, Fritz. *Studien zur Chanson d'Aspremont.* Greifswald, 1909. (Roepke.)

Smyser, H. M., ed. *The Pseudo-Turpin.* Cambridge, Mass., 1937. (Smyser.)

Unger, C. R., ed. *Karlamagnus Saga ok Kappa Hans.* Christiana, 1860. (Unger; the work itself is also designated *Kms.*)

van Waard, R. *Études sur l'origine et la formation de la Chanson d'Aspremont.* Groningen, 1937. (van Waard).

Vilhjálmsson, Bjarni, ed. *Karlamagnús saga og kappa hans.* 3 vols. Reykjavík, 1950.

KARLAMAGNÚS SAGA

Part IV

King Agulandus

SYNOPSIS, I: the A-version

N.B. : Paragraph numbers below correspond to chapter numbers of mss. A and a. Lower-case letters within paragraphs are intended to facilitate correlation with the synopsis of the B-version. These letters indicate the blocks into which A-version material was cut up by the *B* redactor to be used (or omitted) in *B*. The superscript number at the end of each summarized chapter or chapter section indicates the number of the *B* chapter at the end of which the indicated part of the *A* text will be found. Italicization of the *B* chapter number indicates omission of the material concerned in *B* itself.

1. Archbishop Turpin, in a prefatory letter written at Vienne, where he is recovering from wounds, greets Leoprand, dean of Aachen, at whose urging he now sets forth the true facts of the campaigns on which he accompanied Karlamagnus in Iberia.[prol]

2. (a) St. James, after converting Galicia, was martyred in Jerusalem; his disciples then brought his body back to Spain. But Christianity there was almost completely wiped out by the time of Karlamagnus.[prol] (b) When that emperor had subdued many lands, and intended to cease his campaigns, he saw a vision of a starry way leading to Galicia. Soon after, St. James appeared to him in a dream, telling him to win back Iberia from the Saracens and to see that the saint's burial place was properly honored. After this vision appeared three times, Karlamagnus prepared to undertake the expedition.[1]

3. (a) There, his first conquest was Pamplona, where the city walls fell miraculously in answer to the emperor's prayer. He spared the lives of such Saracens as were willing to be baptized, executing the rest. Many Saracens were much impressed by the French and made peace eagerly. Karlamagnus then journeyed to the grave of St. James; thrusting his spear into the sea, he rejoiced at having won to the farthest boundary of the land. Soon all the area was subdued, the inhabitants converted or killed. Among the cities, one was particularly difficult to conquer; but the emperor finally prayed to St. James, and

the walls of that city fell, too. Karlamagnus cursed it, and it has been uninhabitable ever since, along with four others. He also destroyed all heathen shrines and images,[2] (b) except one in Cadiz called "Salem-cadis", so powerfully possessed by demons that no Christian can approach it.[2] (c) With the gold won as tribute in Iberia, Karlamagnus built churches to St. James there,[2] (d) and in Germany and France.[4]

4. (a) On his return to France, Karlamagnus heard that a heathen king of Africa named Agulandus had invaded Spain, destroying Christendom there. Therefore, Karlamagnus organized another expedition,[10] (b) with Duke Milon leading the army. At this time, an edifying event occurred, as follows:[11]

5. While the French army was camped in Bayonne, a certain knight died, having bequeathed the value of his horse as alms for the poor. But the kinsman entrusted with the bequest spent the money on himself instead. Thirty days later, the dead man appeared to him in a dream, reproaching him, and telling him he would be carried off to hell the next day. That morning, terrible sounds, as of howling beasts, were heard, and the delinquent executor vanished into the air; his body was later found dashed to pieces.[12]

6. (a) Karlamagnus caught up with Agulandus near the River Céa.[13] (b) Near this place, the emperor had a church built in honor of Sts. Facundus and Primitivus.[16] (c) Agulandus challenged Karlamagnus to battle, with even numbers matched; battle was then waged between groups of various sizes on each side, and all the heathens fell.[17] (d) On the night before the third day, when the entire armies were to meet, the French warriors drove their spears into the ground: in the morning many were found to have rooted and grown leaves and flowers; though the spears were cut down, groves sprang up from the roots and may be seen there to this day. These spears belonged to the men who were destined for martyrdom that day,[18] (e) including Duke Milon. In that battle, Karlamagnus lost his horse and was hard pressed, but he drew his sword Gaudiola and led the fight against the heathens.[19] (f) The next day, four Roman counts arrived with reinforcements for Karlamagnus,[19] (g) and Agulandus fled;[20] (h) Karlamagnus then returned home.[*20*]

7. (a) Agulandus now raised a great host of heathens,[5] (b) including several kings;[8] (c) with their help he conquered the city of Agen. He

then sent a message to Karlamagnus offering rich rewards if he would submit to him, but his real purpose was to see the emperor so he might recognize him to kill him in battle. Karlamagnus, however, rode from camp with a small troop of knights; leaving all but one on a nearby hill, he disguised himself as a messenger and rode to Agulandus, whom he told that the emperor awaited him nearby with a token escort. Then having had a good look at the defences of the city, he rode quickly back to camp with his knights, so that Agulandus found no one there when he rode out with a huge force to capture him.[20] (d) After raising an army in his own realm,[21] (e) the emperor besieged Agen, until finally Agulandus had to flee ignominiously.[21]

8. (a) Agulandus now held the city of Saintes, and when Karlamagnus came with his army demanding surrender, offered to do battle the next day.[21] (b) That night, the French drove their spears into the ground on the plain where they were camped, near the river Charente. Again, the spears of those doomed to suffer martyrdom in the day's battle were found in the morning to have taken root and sprouted. The 4000 men who owned these spears rode first into battle, and killed many Saracens before they fell. Karlamagnus lost his horse in the battle, but led his men to victory:[21] (c) finally the Saracens had to flee into the city, where they were besieged, until Agulandus was driven to flee out along the river. In pursuit, the French killed two Saracen kings and almost 4000 others. Agulandus now went over the pass of Cize to Pamplona, sending Karlamagnus a challenge to fight him there.[21]

9. (a) Karlamagnus went home to raise a great army, proclaiming a general amnesty, freeing serfs, providing money for the poor and arms for those who could use them, and offering similar inducements to all who would join the expedition; thus he gathered a great host.[22] (b) This army included all the greatest leaders: Turpin, Rollant, Oliver, and many others.[11]

10. (a) This huge army gathered and went through the pass of Cize to Pamplona, where Karlamagnus sent word to Agulandus to give up the city or fight.[22] (b) Agulandus asked for a truce while he gathered his troops, though his real motive was to meet Karlamagnus face-to-face so he would be able to recognize him. Karlamagnus agreed to his request.[16]

11. (a) When the two kings met, Karlamagnus reproached Agulandus for harrying his lands. Agulandus, delighted to find that Karlamagnus spoke Arabic, replied by asking what right he had to these lands, which were not part of his patrimony. Karlamagnus replied that Christ had ordained that all lands should bow to Christian rule. Agulandus argued that the heathen law, that of the prophet Maumet, was better, but Karlamagnus replied that this is a false faith: those who adhere to it will go to hell while Christians are to be saved. Thus, he said, Agulandus must choose between baptism or death. Agulandus answered that rather than betray his faith, he would fight, on the condition that the faith of the winning side should be considered vindicated—promising that he and his men would be baptized if defeated alive. When the Christians won the ensuing battle, he agreed to be baptized the next morning,[17] (b) although some of his men demurred.[18]

12. When Agulandus came to be baptized the next day he found Karlamagnus at table with his knights and clergy. Surprised by the variety of clerical attire, Agulandus inquired as to its significance, and was informed. Then he asked about the ill-clothed and ill-fed wretches on the floor nearby; told that they represented messengers of Christ, he said that it was a poor faith that led his host to treat his own men well but God's men wretchedly. Refusing baptism, he offered to do battle again.[18]

13. (a) In the next day's encounter, about a hundred thousand men fought on each side.[22] (b) After a hard battle, the Saracens were put to flight; Karlamagnus then camped for the night at the bridge of the Arga. But during the night, without his knowledge, some thousand of his army went out to plunder the dead on the battlefield; on their way back, they were ambushed and slaughtered by heathens.[23]

14. The next day Karlamagnus heard that the prince of Navarre had come to Montjardin to challenge him. On the way to battle, the emperor prayed for a sign from God to show which of his men would fall in the day's fighting. The next morning, the doomed men were found to have red crosses on their shoulders. Thinking to change God's decree, Karlamagnus left these marked men locked in his chapel. In the ensuing battle the Saracens were routed, but when Karlamagnus returned all the men locked in the chapel were found to be dead.[24]

15. Soon after, word came of the challenge of a giant from Syria, who had come to Nájera, sent by the Emir of Babylon, with an army of

Turks and Armenians. This giant, Ferakut, was invulnerable and had the strength of forty men. He demanded single combat with one of the French; but when Oddgeir the Dane went out to duel, Ferakut swept him up under his arm and carried him off. He did the same to all others sent out subsequently, until Rollant demanded to be allowed to challenge him.[24]

16. The giant grasped Rollant, but when he tried to carry him off Rollant pulled him back and they both fell off the horse. They then fought until both had lost their horses and were reduced to using fists and stones as weapons; Rollant could not wound Ferakut, but the giant could not catch him either. Finally Ferakut asked for a truce until morning.[24]

17. The next day they met without weapons, by agreement, except for a sword for Ferakut and a staff for Rollant, who also used all the stones at hand. The giant, though still unwounded, was fatigued at midday and asked for time to rest. Rollant helpfully pillowed his head with a stone to ease his sleep; the truce was scrupulously observed, as was the custom.[24]

18. When Ferakut awoke, Rollant asked why he could not be wounded; the giant replied—in Arabic, which Rollant understood—that he was vulnerable only in the navel. He then asked Rollant his name, kindred, and religion. On hearing that the French fight for Christ, he asked what the nature of Christ is. Rollant's credal reply led him to protest that there is only one god, not three; Rollant answered that there are three persons in the one godhead.[24]

19. Ferakut then demanded how three could be one; Rollant replied with such examples as that one almond consists of three elements, shell, skin, and kernel. The giant then questioned how God, begotten by no one, could beget a son; Rollant answered with the analogy of Adam, who was likewise begotten by no one but begot children himself. The giant's questions on how God could become man, and without human seed, Rollant answered similarly.[24]

20. The giant next asked how a virgin could conceive; Rollant cited such analogies as maggots. The giant asked how God could die, and Rollant replied that all flesh must die.[24]

21. Ferakut asked how he could live again. Rollant replied that all men will, and that some already have, citing various examples of

resurrection, such as lions reviving dead cubs and the dead revived by prophets. The giant asked how he could ascend back to heaven, and Rollant replied that what comes down may go up, as birds do, among others.[24]

22. Ferakut now challenged Rollant to vindicate his faith by fighting again. Almost trapped under the giant's bulk, Rollant was eventually able to get at his sword and pierce him in the navel. The mortally wounded giant was then carried into the town by his men; but the Christians soon took it and freed the prisoners.[24]

23. Karlamagnus now heard that the kings of Seville and Cordova, who had escaped from his last battle with Agulandus, were challenging him. But when the emperor rode into battle, the Saracens put forward a group of men dressed like devils, shaking tambourines; this sight and sound so frightened the horses of the French that they panicked uncontrollably and the French had to flee up a mountain. The next day they blindfolded their horses and stopped their ears, so that such antics had no effect on them. The battle turned against the Saracens, who now gathered around their standard, which was on an ox-cart. When Karlamagnus cut this down, the Saracens were put to flight; the king of Seville was killed and the king of Cordova, after fleeing into the city, surrendered and agreed to be baptized.[25]

24. (a) Jamund, son of Agulandus, now decided to mount a campaign of his own against the Christians, and gathered a host.[26] (b) Word of this reached Karlamagnus,[27] (c) and the two armies met. The Christians put the heathens to flight,[28] (d) capturing much booty, including the idols of the heathens.[29] (e) When Jamund had upbraided his men for cowardice, he sent a messenger to his father's camp to summon Balam, Triamodes, and others.[33]

25. (a) Balam, hearing what had happened, secretly prayed to God that he might live to be baptized.[33] (b) Without the knowledge of Agulandus, seven divisions of the heathens were mustered. Jamund spoke to the leaders and told them of his ignominious defeat, the loss of the gods, and his narrow escape when his horse was killed under him, adding that he regretted his former disregard of his father's advice.[34] [(c) In the French camp, Duke Girard and his men, coming to help the emperor, were soon to be drawing near; but neither group recognized the other; each mistook the other for heathens. (Fragment 2a.)[37]] (d) The French army was mustered into some five divisions.[39]

26. (a) Karlamagnus, who was impressively dressed,[40] (b) met Girard, who embraced him, though Turpin, witnessing it, recalled that Girard had tried to attack him.[39] (c) Girard pledged the aid of his men.[39]

27. (a) After thanking Girard,[39] (b) Karlamagnus armed.[40] (c) Girard, seeing a heathen host approach, went to muster his men.[41] (d) The sixth and seventh divisions completed the host of Karlamagnus,[39] (e) who spoke to his men, encouraging them before battle ; so did the pope.[41]

28. Balam's division led the first attack.[42]

29. (a) The battle raged;[42] (b) Girard then led his men to join in.[43]

30. After two full days of battle, many men had been killed.[45]

31. (a) During the night, everyone had uncomfortable quarters: the men stayed on horseback, swords drawn, with no chance to eat or drink.[46] (b) Girard had killed a knight.[46]

32. (a) Triamodes killed a French knight.[49] (b) Jamund and Bolant encountered Oddgeir and Anketill; the latter killed Bolant.[44]

33. (a) The French eventually killed or put to flight many heathens.[45] (b) But they lost many men, and Jamund's sword, Dyrumdali, was so good he was a great danger to Karlamagnus.[44]

34. That morning, Girard had rallied his men.[48]

35. (a) He rode into a ravine.[48] (b) Karlamagnus spent the night grieving for lost men,[45] (c) while his army watched, unfed. Jamund was angry to see his men fleeing. Balam reminded him that he had told the truth about the French.[46]

36. At daybreak, the small French host rode against twenty thousand heathens. Jamund killed an important French knight, and many others on the French side were in trouble. Oddgeir, much battered, reported that a prisoner had informed him that Jamund did not wish to summon his father; thus Karlamagnus should summon reinforcements to take advantage of the situation.[47]

37. (a) Messengers were sent to summon every man left in camp. Battle resumed; Salomon killed Bordant and took the horn Olifant, but Jamund regained it.[47] (b) The messengers, meanwhile, summoned every man and boy in the camp,[53] (c) including the boy Rollant,[53] (d) and they adapted impromptu gear such as banners made of tablecloths.[53]

38. Girard led a great charge against Jamund's host.[48]

39. The Christians, sweeping the field, approached Jamund's chief standard; Girard and his men dispersed or killed most of the heathens guarding it, and the leaders there, Magon and Asperant, thought it prudent to escape. Jamund did not know of this. Girard captured the standard.[48]

40. (a) When Magon and Asperant reached the camp of Agulandus, many there thought they had betrayed Jamund.[58] (b) Melkiant defended their action.[59] (c) Kalades criticized Agulandus, and especially Jamund, for starting the expedition at all.[59]

41. Galinger said it would be best to wait until they knew the whole truth. Another man accused the two fugitives of treachery.[59]

42. (a) Talamon advised delay.[59] (b) Ulien disagreed, calling for a stiff sentence.[59]

43. Pliades called for an even more severe sentence.[59]

44. Gorhant of Florence, a kinsman of the accused, defended them.[59]

45. Malavent offered to defend them in combat himself.[59]

46. (a) Triamodes killed Milon, and was killed by Baeringur.[49] (b) Riker and a comrade slew two kinsmen of Jamund.[50]

47. Balam rebuked Jamund for complaining, reminding him that he, Balam, had warned him. Jamund blew Olifant to encourage his men and went on fighting.[50]

48. (a) Jamund fought bitterly.[49] (b) Girard, now resting, sent most of his men back to the battle.[48] (c) A heathen messenger brought Jamund word of the fall of his standard; but he and his friends Salatiel and Rodan thought they could still win against the now depleted French troop.[51]

49. (a) Oddgeir killed Salatiel; Nemes killed his companion.[51] (b) Christian leaders told Karlamagnus they would fight on, despite heavy odds.[52]

50. (a) Valteri brought Karlamagnus word of Girard's capture of the chief standard.[52] (b) Now word came of the arrival of the young reinforcements.[53]

51. Droim met the troop of boys. The heathens were appalled to see so many reinforcements join the French. Jamund tried to encourage his men, but now Girard arrived, and Jamund found himself in great danger.[53]

52. Jamund fled, mourning his own foolishness. Balam reproved him for complaining of what his own folly had caused.[54]

53. In flight, the horse of one of Jamund's comrades broke down, and Jamund decided to turn and fight. Oddgeir killed Goram; Jamund killed Oddgeir's horse and fled, but Balam turned back and challenged Karlamagnus, who knocked him from his horse. After a skirmish with Nemes, Balam surrendered, saying he wished to be baptized, and identified himself. Nemes rejoiced. But, meanwhile, Rollant saw Nemes's horse, and, thinking Nemes had fallen, took it and rode off.[54]

54. Jamund, in flight, stopped to drink from a spring. Karlamagnus found him there and told him to put his helmet back on, arm, and fight. Jamund, not recognizing the emperor, offered to enrich him if he would surrender; when he identified himself, Jamund demanded various territories. They fought; Jamund particularly noticed the emperor's helmet, which had special protective qualities.[55]

55. (a) Finally Jamund tried to wrest away the helmet. Just as he was about to succeed, Rollant rode up and struck him down with an improvised club. Gaining Jamund's sword in the fight, Rollant killed him,[55] (b) and took his horse and arms. Just then Oddgeir and Nemes arrived.[56]

56. Oddgeir and Nemes reproved the emperor for risking his life and agreed that Rollant should have the spoils. They left Jamund's body under an olive tree, commenting on his valor.[56]

57. (a) Karlamagnus returned to his men and lodged in Jamund's tent.[57] (b) Girard and his men went back to the tower to rest.[57]

58. Meanwhile, Agulandus was playing chess.[58]

59. (a) Magon and Asperant arrived while Agulandus was sitting at chess and told him of the battle and the fall of Jamund's standard, saying they did not know where Jamund now was. Agulandus, furious, accused them of treachery and called a council to decide their fate.[58] (b) Their kinsman Amustade (later called Amustene) warned the others of the dangers of a harsh verdict.[59]

60. Akvin replied that they were obviously traitors.[59]

61. Akarz of Amflors criticized Agulandus and Jamund and counseled delay.[59]

62. Abilant advocated a rigorous execution.[59]

63. Amustene (not to be confused with Amustade/Amustene) agreed that they were traitors and offered to fight anyone who disagreed.[59]

(64) Samnel said this was simple jealousy of the fugitives' powerful family and opposed such a sentence.[59]

65. Sinapis advocated an extreme penalty, challenging any who might disagree.[59]

66. Ulien and Madequin announced an adverse verdict to Agulandus, who sentenced the fugitives to be drawn to death, their remains cast in a pit and defiled by whores before being burned. Before sentence was carried out, the accused told what they could of Girard's attack, to no avail.[59]

67. After the execution, messengers arrived and confirmed Jamund's loss of the four idols.[60]

68. The spokesman, Valdibrun, continued his tale of disaster, saying he no longer thought the gods had any power. He urged Agulandus to attack quickly while the French troops were depleted, saying he was not sure what had become of Jamund.[60]

69. (a) Agulandus mustered his army, though warned that the French were keen enemies,[60] leaving behind a troop to guard the queen.[60]

70. (a) Madequin was confident of victory.[60] (b) The four divisions of the heathen army were led by formidable leaders, but Amustene/Amustade went reluctantly, grieving for his cruelly executed nephews.[60]

71. (a) While Agulandus prepared to attack, (b) Karlamagnus and his men enjoyed the notable amenities of Jamund's tent.[57]

72. The French feasted in this wonderful tent, illuminated by carbuncle stones with magic powers.[57]

73. (a) Balam was baptized by the pope and christened Vitaclin by Karlamagnus.[57] (b) He then said he would not conceal anything from the emperor.[61]

74. Vitaclin showed Karlamagnus and the pope the embarking army of Agulandus reflected in the tent's remarkable mirror; Karlamagnus then sent for Girard. When he arrived, Karlamagnus asked Girard why he had not had himself crowned a king; Girard answered with a homily on the rights and wrongs of kingship. He was then

shown the ominous reflections. The leaders asked Vitaclin for further information.[61]

75. Vitaclin pointed out and described the various heathen groups and their leaders.[61]

76. Girard urged Karlamagnus to muster his troops, and went to gather his own. Karlamagnus promised rich rewards to his men, who armed themselves with spoils from the battlefields.[62]

77. Rollant and three other youths, however, were aggrieved to be left out. They enlisted the support of Nemes and Oddgeir.[62]

78. Nemes and Oddgeir interceded for the boys; when Karlamagnus said he was too young, Rollant threatened to leave him. Remembering that Rollant had saved his life, the king finally consented.[62]

79. Girard reported back to his men, and sent his sons Milon and Girard to be knighted by Karlamagnus.[62]

80. (a) Karlamagnus knighted all the young men,[62] (b) girding Rollant with Dyrumdali (after declining Oddgeir's suggestion that he try it out on a pile of rocks).[62] (c) He put the other young men under Rollant's command.[62]

81. (a) Karlamagnus then gathered eleven of the bravest knights, naming them, with Rollant, as twelve peers.[62] He then knighted Milon, Girard's son, honoring him with the promise of marriage to an heiress as well as a fine sword.[62]

82. (a) He also knighted young Girard and gave him a fine sword and a horse and royal saddle.[62] (b) The pope sang Mass, and the newly dubbed knights made offerings. The pope preached a sermon, then produced a relic of the holy cross and blessed the host.[63]

83. Agulandus confessed uneasiness about Jamund to his nobles. Madequin told of a forboding dream; Maladient proposed sending an embassy demanding tribute and submission from Karlamagnus. Agulandus appointed Galinger to join Ulien in such a mission.[64]

84. (a) Karlamagnus arranged his host in five divisions,[63] (b) one of which was raised by the pope;[63] (c) the emperor himself put them in order.[63]

85. (a) When the messengers from Agulandus arrived,[64] (b) Karlamagnus had just asked Oddgeir to watch specially over Rollant.[63]

86. Galinger demanded that Karlamagnus return the idols, render lavish tribute, and come himself as a penitent in homage, saying that if

he did so, renouncing his faith, Agulandus would let him keep his crown. The king said this would be difficult, and told them the gods had been broken up and distributed among the harlots. Ulien and Galinger threatened that Agulandus would wipe out the French. Karlamagnus sent the pope to tell Girard of their demands.[64]

87. Girard counseled that Agulandus be sent the head and arm of Jamund as tribute. These were duly laid before the messengers, who were shocked and grieved. Ulien tried to challenge someone to single combat, but had to go back with the sorry tribute.[64]

88. (a) The French saw a great host of heathens drawn up. (b) The messengers met various leaders, all inquiring eagerly about the success of their mission ; all were horrified to learn the truth.[65]

86. Agulandus was similarly disillusioned, and grieved greatly over the remnants of his son. Galinger told him Karlamagnus was a formidable man and summarized the beliefs of the Christians.[65]

90. (a) Agulandus recalled his preparations, and bewailed Jamund's bad companions.[65] (b) Then he kissed the dead head of his son.[65]

91. (a) The army of Karlamagnus was drawn up. Three unknown knights (actually, saints) appeared before the first division.[67] (b) The pope asked two men to take the relic of the cross into battle, but both declined; Turpin then offered to do so and was accepted.[66]

92. As the heathen drew near, Turpin took the cross and Oddgeir and all his men venerated it. Oddgeir then noticed the three mysterious knights and asked who they were. One replied that he was George, and Oddgeir realized that it was the saint. St. George said Rollant was to be granted the right of first attack.[66]

93. The Africans attacked. St. George encouraged Rollant to kill Madequin. Then Oddgeir and the other saints (Demetrius and Mercurius) joined the battle.[67]

94. The Christians, with the help of the saints, dispelled or killed many heathens.[67]

95. (a) Turpin bore the holy cross before the heathens, who were terrified at its bright beams.[67] (b) Rollant now approached the second heathen division.[69]

96. Duke Girard organized his men to attack. Meanwhile, a heathen spy reported their approach to Agulandus. Girard approached fearlessly, though, of course, much outnumbered.[68]

97. As Girard approached, Ulien told Agulandus he would dispatch the small band of Christians. Agulandus rewarded him by promising to make him his heir, which displeased Galinger; Ulien and Galinger would have fought if Agulandus had not been there.[68]

98. Ulien, with his comrade Jafert, led a host against Girard; Clares immediately killed Jafert. The Africans, not well armed, were worsted and began to flee. Ulien, almost despairing, killed Valteri and did as much harm to the Christians as he could.[68]

99. (a) Basin (Boz) challenged him to stay; after some fighting, Ulien saw others coming up and fled.[68] (b) Messengers now brought bad news of how the battle was going to the furious Agulandus.[68]

100. The heathens attacked strongly and the battle looked bad for the Christians; Earl Hugi rode out to help.[69]

101. Akarz now found his men falling back, attacked by Salomon. He complained about the effect of the cross and fled. But the division of Kalades now raised strong battle against the Christians.[69]

102. Salomon arrived to help the French drive back the heathens, but the savage heathen bowmen shot down many of the horses.[69]

103. Among the young men who now distinguished themselves was Grelent, who killed Kalades. Rollant then killed Akarz.[69]

104. (a) Oddgeir and Hugi looked for Rollant and were relieved to find him alive. The Christians triumphed greatly, with the help of the cross and the three saints. Most of the heathens fled,[69] (b) except Eliadas and Pantalas, who were now attacked by the Christians.[70]

105. Though outnumbered, the young men of the French vowed to repay the emperor's generosity and attacked bravely.[70]

106. Salomon and his Bretons arrived in time to succor the hard-pressed French. Droim also came; soon many Africans fell.[70]

107. (a) Turpin, bearing the cross, and the three saints caused much consternation among the heathens, and Eliadas fled.[70] (b) But the French leaders, and especially the horses, were tiring, and a messenger was sent to Karlamagnus asking for help.[70]

108. After his encounter with Boz, Ulien returned to Agulandus, saying that now he would never govern Europe.[71]

109. Agulandus berated Ulien for having given bad advice and then proven a coward. Ulien told how he came to be defeated. Eliadas then arrived so battered Agulandus could not recognize him, and reported

the death of Madequin. Now Karlamagnus was seen to be approaching; Agulandus was still confident that he would conquer the French.[71]

110. Amustene now called together his sons and told them he planned to desert, return to Africa, and take over the realm. They agreed to this plan enthusiastically.[71]

111. As the French attacked, Amustene told Agulandus he would rally his men, and left the chief standard with his followers; then he went to the ships, taking all the booty he could, and breaking up or burning the ships left behind.[71]

112. (a) Girard's troop now approached the chief standard. Ulien recognized them and disillusioned Agulandus, who thought them to be Amustene returning with help. Ulien was sent by Agulandus to attack Girard's men, with some initial success.[73] (b) Meanwhile, Oddgeir, Rollant, and their comrades, having won four battles, encircled a group of heathens, but were too tired to proceed.[70] (c) Karlamagnus joined the fray[72] (d) and killed Gundrun. Battle raged, but there were numerous French losses.[72]

113. (a) The pope told the French God was testing them.[72] (b) Turpin gave the cross to the pope and went to fight himself.[72] (c) In the midst of crucial battle, Karlamagnus prayed to God for help and rallied his men. His own horse was killed under him, and Baeringur helped rescue him, getting him another horse by striking down its heathen rider.[72]

114. (a) Girard rallied his men to attack Ulien and advanced toward the chief standard of Agulandus. Girard arranged his men in close formation, with those in the midst on foot.[72] (b) Agulandus wondered where Amustene was. Karlamagnus was lucky to have the saints on his side.[73]

115. The heathens, driven from the standard, joined battle with the French. Eventually, the troops of Eliadas and Pantalas were routed.[74]

116. The French pursued and completely drove off their opponents.[74]

117. Moadas and Abilant drove the French back under their standard, but Fagon rallied them. In the hard fighting which followed, many leaders were knocked from their horses; Karlamagnus prayed for divine aid and killed Abilant. Fagon heard the emperor's war-cry.[74]

118. Fagon took his troops to the aid of the emperor, exhorting them to prove their worth.[74]

119. Fagon gave the standard to Remund and attacked, killing Moadas and Matusalem.[74]

120. The Africans fled, pursued by the French.[74]

121. (a) Ulien, infuriated to see his men killed and put to flight, killed Edvard and berated those who were deserting him. He then attacked Riker; Riker killed him. The rest of the Africans now panicked.[74] (b) Girard pushed the attack under the chief standard, and at last it fell. Agulandus tried to escape.[75]

122. While Karlamagnus remained on the field with the remnant of his army, Girard pursued Agulandus.[75]

123. Agulandus made a stand on the battlefield; soon his horse was killed. Karlamagnus sent help to Girard; the Africans fled when they saw them coming.[75]

124. (a) Agulandus lamented his fate, but put up a strong fight with a great axe. Since he killed all who approached, Karlamagnus called off the attack and sent a message offering him amnesty if he would become a Christian; Agulandus refused. Clares then drove his spear into Agulandus; Rollant was now able to cut off his head.[75] (b) There were almost no heathen survivors, but the women were given a truce and later converted and married to Christians.[75]

125. (a) Karlamagnus then travelled around Hispania restoring Christianity, building churches, and putting the land in order. Those who had fallen were given Christian burial,[76] (b) and the emperor returned to France, where his presence was sorely needed.[76]

SYNOPSIS, II : the B-version

N.B.: Paragraph numbers below correspond to chapter numbers of mss. B and b. Numbers and lower case letters after the chapter numbers indicate the corresponding sections of the A-version; see the synopsis of that version for the content. Material separately summarized below is new to (or in different form in) the *B* text.

Prologue. 1, 2a.

1. 2b.
2. 3a, 3c.
3. Karlamagnus returned to St. Denis, in Paris, and told the people of his victories and his intention to build churches in Paris to St. James and St. Denis.
4. He then prayed to St. Denis that those who fell in Spain might be granted remission of sins. St. Denis appeared to him in a dream, saying that his prayer had been granted through the intercession of St. James. 3d.
5. At this time there was a very powerful king in Africa, ruling over many nations; his name was Agulandus, and he had a son named Jamund. (Cf. 7a.)
6. Jamund drew about himself many bad companions. Now Agulandus heard of the campaigns in Iberia of Karlamagnus, and called a council. One of his kinsmen, King Ulien, urged him to lead an expedition against the Christians in Iberia; Agulandus agreed, proclaiming his intention to put Iberia and Italy under the rule of Jamund. To gain maximum help in this project from four of the principal heathen gods (Makon, Maumet, Terrogant, and Jupiter), he announced that he would send his four idols to Arabia to be splendidly adorned with gold and jewels.
7. While his messengers took the gods to Arabia, Agulandus prepared for war. Jamund was urged by his friends to go on ahead, but refused, since he thought the campaign was an excuse to deprive him of his patrimony.

8. The gods came back so splendidly decorated that Agulandus was overwhelmed with joy. Then with his son Jamund and many great kings in his train, he set sail from Africa most splendidly. (cf. 7b).

9. When he arrived in Iberia, Agulandus proceeded to destroy Christendom there. Why did St. James allow this? Probably because it seemed Karlamagnus had won his promised reward in heaven too easily; too few men had achieved martyrdom; and perhaps because there were still too many heathens in the southern part of the land. In any case, St. James now arranged it that Karlamagnus heard what was happening in Iberia.

10. Karlamagnus, much grieved at the tidings, called his men together and announced his intention to lead another expedition to Iberia. (Cf. 4a.)

11. 9b, 4b.

12. 5.

13. In the course of harrying Iberia, Agulandus took a strong tower, which he gave to his son to hold; Jamund, however, continued to accompany him. They now reached the valley of the river Céa. (Cf. 6a.) Hearing that Karlamagnus had advanced to Bayonne, he called a council; a king named Balam advised sending a messenger to offer Karlamagnus rewards if he should surrender to Agulandus. Agulandus agreed, and sent Balam himself.

14. Balam delivered the message to Karlamagnus, who treated him so courteously that the Saracen was much impressed. Karlamagnus gave him a number of horses, but sent back the message that he intended to take what rewards he wished without submitting to Agulandus.

15. Balam reported, back at the Saracen camp, that the Christians were so valiant and so determined that it would be foolish to attack them. Infuriated, the Saracens denounced him for having been bribed by the Christians. Since, however, Balam reported there were far fewer Christians than the number of their own host, Agulandus, confident that he could vanquish them with a fraction of his army, sent Jamund back to hold the tower.

16. Karlamagnus now rode out with his army until they came within view of the heathen host. 6b. He then called a council; Turpin advised meeting with the heathen king to offer him a choice of bap-

tism, retreat, or battle. Karlamagnus agreed, and Agulandus accepted an invitation to meet, thinking that Karlamagnus would submit to him. (Cf. 10b.)

17. 1a. (Cf. 6c.)

18. 11b, 12, 6d.

19. 6e. Duke Nemes was taken prisoner, and would have been executed had it not been for the intercession of Balam, who, remembering the courteous treatment he had experienced in the camp of Karlamagnus, paid a huge ransom for Nemes, and sent him back to Karlamagnus with a horse to take the place of the one the emperor had lost in battle. 6f. Balam then reported events to Jamund, with whom he remained.

20. 6g, 7c.

21. 7e, 8a, 8c.

22. Karlamagnus then sent to the pope for help. 9a. The pope joined the emperor's army, with a great host. 10a, 13a.

23. 13b.

24. 14.

25. 23.

26. 24a; they ravaged the land.

27. 24b; he sent a troop commanded by Salomon and Droim to scout the situation.

28. The Christian scouts met with Jamund's band, defeated them and put the survivors to flight. (cf. 24c.)

29. 24d.

30. Lord Girard of Burgundia, hearing of the troubles in Hispania, decided to join Karlamagnus, and went with a large troop, including his sons and nephews; first they headed for Jamund's tower.

31. Jamund, seeing Girard's men camped outside the tower, thought them the same band as before and determined to attack.

32. Girard's men routed the heathens and captured the tower.

33. 24e, 25a.

34. 25b.

35. The scouts of Karlamagnus saw Girard's troop, but, not recognizing it, mistook it for heathens; Salomon had some difficulty getting anyone to ride to Karlamagnus for help.

36. When the emperor came, in response to Salomon's message, he first disposed of the heathen idols, then rode with a small troop to scout the situation.

37. Girard rallied his men to fight the heathen host.

38. When Girard's men met those of Karlamagnus they started to fight, but in the nick of time, they identified themselves to each other; a joyful meeting eventuated. (Cf. Fr.2a.)

39. 26c, 27a, 25d, 27d.

40. 27b, 26a, 27b.

41. 27e, 27c.

42. 28, 29a.

43. 29b.

44. 33b, 32b.

45. 33a, 30, 35b.

46. 31a, 35c.

47. 36, 37a.

48. 34, 35a, 38, 39, 48b.

49. 48a, 32a, 46a.

50. 46b, 47.

51. 48c, 49a.

52. 49b, 50a.

53. 37b, d, 50b, 51.

54. 52, 53.

55. 54, 55a.

56. 55b, 56.

57. 57a, 71b, 72, 73a, 57b.

58. 58, 59a, 40a.

59. 59b, 60 (Aquin), 41; Gordant advised delay (cf. 42a); 42b; Pantalas stated that it was dangerous to rush to an unfounded verdict; Gundrun felt such words amounted to treason against Agulandus (cf. end of 42b); 61, 62, 40b, 65, 66.

60. 67, 68, 69a, 70a, 71a.

61. 73b, 74, 75.

62. 76, 80a, c, 79, 81b, 82a.

63. 84b; Karlamagnus then explained the situation to the army; 82b, 84a, c; 85b.

64. 83, 85a, 86, 87.

65. 88b, 89, 90b.

66. Girard, after giving Karlamagnus some counsel on strategy, went to rally his men. 91b, 92.

67. 88a, 91a, 93, 94, 95a.

68. 96, 97, 98, 99a.

69. 96b, 100, 101, 102, 103, 104a.

70. 104b; 107b, 105, 106, 107a, 112b.

71. 108, 109, 110, 111 (Amustene told Agulandus he would guard the ships ...).

72. 112c, 113b, 112d, 113c, a.

73. 112a, 114a.

74. The heathens, under Moadas and Abilant, attacked. Karlamagnus killed Abilant. At a crucial moment, the emperor blew his horn, and Fagon heard (cf. 115, 116, 117). 118, 119, 120, 121a.

75. 121b, 122, 123, 124a.

76. 125a.

The Order of the A-text

This translation includes the entire A,a version of the saga. As noted above, this version is here printed not as a consecutive whole but in the order which most clearly shows how it was used as source material for the B,b version. Because of the drastic re-arrangement of the material in the B-version (the extent of which may be judged by comparing the A and B synopses), a reader who wishes to read the A-version consecutively will need to turn to the sections of A at the ends of the B chapters in the order given in the following table. Superscript numbers here refer to subdivisions of a section, such subdividing having been frequently necessitated by the complexity of the revision:

Prologue
1
2
3
4
11^{1}
12
13
16
17^{1}
18^{2}
19
5
8
20
21
22^{1}
11^{2}
22^{2}
17^{2}
18^{1}
22^{3}
23
24
25
26
27
28
29
33
34
39^{3}
40^{2}
39^{1}
$40^{1,3}$
41^{2}
39^{4}
41^{1}
42
43
45^{2}
46^{1}
49^{2}
44^{2}
45^{1}
44^{1}
48^{1}
45^{3}
46^{2}
47
53^{1}
48^{2}
58^{2}
59^{4}
59^{2}
49^{3}
50
49^{1}
48^{3}
51
52
53
54
55
56
57^{1}
58^{1}
$59^{1,3,5}$
60
57^{2}
61
$62^{1,3,2,4}$
63^{2}
64^{1}
$63^{3,1,4}$
64^{2}
63^{5}
64^{3}
67^{1}
65
67^{2}
66
67^{3}
69^{1}
68
69^{2}
70^{1}
71
73^{1}
70^{2}
72
73^{2}
74
75
76

PROLOGUE

In the name of Our Lord, Jesus Christ:[1] here begins a part of the saga of the famous lord Karlamagnus, the emperor, son of King Pippin[2] of France; wherein it is fully set forth how the said emperor Karlamagnus freed—with divine assistance and the intercession of St. James[3]—Hispania[4] and Galicia from the power of Saracens and Africans. With mighty arm, God freed Hispania because he intended especially and everlastingly to honor that realm, for the sake of his blessed friend the apostle James, brother of John.[5] And therefore, in order that these renowned deeds which God granted in his times to gain God's grace and the triumphant advancement of Christian men should be held in the memory of all later men in the world, to the praise and glory of God and true knowledge and entertainment, the lord Karlamagnus expressly ordered the emperor's most intimate friend, the excellent lord Turpin, archbishop of Rens,[6] to write of the liberation of Hispania.

The bishop bears witness in the letter which he writes to Leofrandus,[7] deacon of Achis,[8] that he himself was present when God openly worked these great wonders for his people, by reason of the prayer and merit of St. James; this the bishop sets forth as follows:[9]

"Turpin, by the grace of God father and leader of the Christians of Rens, and comrade of the famous lord Karolus Magnus, sends Leo-

[1] *b*: "In nomine domine."

[2] Pepin.

[3] *Jacobus*, passim.

[4] Since the term usually refers to the entire Iberian peninsula, including modern Portugal and part of France, it has been retained throughout in preference to 'Spain'.

[5] *Jon*.

[6] Rheims.

[7] PT Leoprandus.

[8] Aquisgranum; Aachen, Aix-la-Chapelle.

[9] Up to this point, the Prologue, which is not in A,a, corresponds roughly to the Latin *Prefatio*.

frandus, deacon of Achis, loving greetings in Jesus Christ, the Son of God. When you sent me a message asking me to write exactly how the most mighty lord Karlamagnus won Hispania from the power of the Saracens, I was suffering from wounds in the city of Vehenna,[10] and I thought I could not fully do as you entreated, since I was somewhat handicapped at that time; then I remembered how this work was undertaken in duty to God in heaven, to the honor and glory of the holy James—whom the matter especially concerns—and to the eternal fame of Emperor Karlamagnus.

Because I know of your goodness, and for God's grace and love of the apostle James, as well as for affection for the emperor, I began my statement with the perilous circumstances which started these events, and next told the exact nature of everything which happened at that time in Hispania, together with all the famous wonders the Lord God then manifested to strengthen his Christians and the glorious victory which was granted to the emperor there against God's enemies and his, although at the cost of great weariness and bloodshed among his men; and the holy work done by the emperor, to the honor of God and the blessed apostle St. James, in the building of churches and holy monasteries in the fourteen years during which he dwelled in Hispania; and all the events which I myself saw with my own eyes—all this I send to you, written down in friendship.

And since you have written that those dealings between Christian men and heathens in Galicia are not found fully written down in the annals which are kept in the city of Sendene,[11] it may well be that the man who wrote the said annals was not a close witness to the deeds which were performed there, and that the men who told him the version which he later wrote down were not as trustworthy as he thought. But I hope that God will so guide me that this account of mine shall not clash with the said annals. — May the true God guard you, and strengthen your might and will."

So says Archbishop Turpin, beginning, then, his report as it is recorded:

[10] Vienne.
[11] St. Denis.

The excellent apostle of the Lord, the glorious James, son of Zebedeus, first preached God's message in the west of Hispania, illumining dark souls with the clear light of the true faith; but the great hard-heartedness and ingrained evil ways of the people of that land were little changed or softened, despite the apostle's warning, especially when the highest men of the realm sharply spurned the salvation he offered them, completely despising his teaching. And since the sublime James, dear friend of God, gained little fruit from his trouble and labor at that point, he returned, with his disciples, to his native country, the land of Jerusalem,[12] there to fulfill, according to God's will, his mission of the splendid, glorious victory of martyrdom, caused by the hard savagery of the rancorous Jews—suffering, for the love of God, a painful death in torment inflicted with a sharp-edged sword under the wicked king Herod Agrippa.

But after the apostle's victory, the lord God saw to it that his holy body was conveyed by seven disciples, most miraculously, away from Jerusalem[13] to Hispania, thus establishing his sovereignty so that those same people who had had the sweet teaching of the living apostle before should now receive the true help from the proximity of his dead body, and that this land and realm, which the apostle had marked out as his own with his bodily presence, should be his as long as the world is inhabited. And, truly, the design was beautifully carried out, for God's mercy, working through the sublime miracles of James and the valuable preaching of his disciples, converted all parts of Hispania to the Christian faith, so that the body of God's friend was revered with all honor and buried splendidly in the city the people of that country then called Librarum Domini, which is now named Compostella.[14]

The holy faith then flourished well and beautifully in Hispania for a long time, until ungodly Saracens and Moabites[15] raged in warlike fashion with plunder and manslaughter against the aforesaid realm, burning towns and castles alike, tearing down churches and other holy places, slaying every man who would not deny his God; and so com-

[12] *Jorsalaland.*

[13] *B: Afsolum*; *b*, *Jorsolum.*

[14] Modern Santiago de Compostella.

[15] Morabites, Almoravides; cf. M-J p. 296, Smyser p. 25.

pletely did those enemies dismember holy Christianity that almost no one could be found left in the district who granted due honor to the true God and to his blessed friend James.

The Saracens held Hispania under their despicable rule right up to the days of Karolus Magnus, and because of the foul cloud which, in those times, enveloped all the aforesaid lands—rising from their godless services, which were everywhere performed daily, in wretched worship of cursed graven images—the bright beams of the shining gems, famous for their preciousness, fruit of the miracles of St. James and each one more valuable than any worldly treasure, were hidden, and rested deep and secret in the earth for as long as divine Providence ordained.

Now the shameful news became widely known: cursed Saracens held sway over Hispania and Galicia. The next part thus begins there, telling how the almighty God uprooted the thorn from the field of his most beloved friend, the glorious James.

A,a: (1)

Turpin, by God's grace archbishop of the city of Reins,[6] comrade of the great king Karlamagnus[16] in Hispania,[17] sends Leofrandus, deacon of Akis,[8] greetings in Jesus Christ. Because when I was staying in the city of Venna,[10] suffering somewhat from wounds, you sent word to me asking that I write how our so great and so famous emperor Karlamagnus liberated the land of Hispania and Galicia from the sway of Saracens, I, then, wish to write truly, and send you, set down in writing, those wonderful great miracles and that glorious victory which he won from the Saracens in Hispania, which we saw with our own eyes, following him for the fourteen years during which he travelled through Hispania and Galicia with his army. Now since you have written to me that you did not find the famous great tidings of what the emperor did in Hispania fully written down in the annals which are kept in the city of Sendine, you may well discern that he who wrote the annals was not close to these events; yet, this work shall not be discordant with those annals. May God give you long life with good health.

[16] *a: Karl*, here and in many other places.

[17] *a*: *Spania*.

(2) God's glorious apostle James first preached Christianity in Galicia. After that he journeyed to Jerusalem and was there beheaded by King Herod Agrippa. But his disciples bore his sacred body back into Galicia, and further strengthened holy Christianity there with their teaching. Now, in the course of time, Christianity was much destroyed in Galicia, so that there was almost no Christendom there in the days of King Karlamagnus ...[18]

[18] The A,a version is a fairly close translation of PT and generally follows the same chapter divisions, while B,b is obviously at some distance. But the actual wording, even when it means much the same thing, is often further removed than may be evident in the translation; cf., e.g., B's *sá sem sagðan annál hefir samsett, væri eigi nálægr þeim hlutem er þar gerðust* ("the man who wrote the said annals was not a close witness to the deeds which were performed there") as against A's *sà sem þann annál ritaði var eigi nær þessum tiðendum* ("he who wrote the annals was not close to these events"). But B,b may sometimes be closer to the Latin; A,a renders *propriis oculis intuitus sum* as *vér sám várum augum* 'we saw with our own eyes,' while B,b gives *ek sjálfr sá mínum augum* 'I myself saw with my own eyes.' (It is possible that Aa's ms. of PT gave *sumus* rather than *sum.*)

KARLAMAGNUS SAGA

PART FOUR

King Agulandus
Translation

CHAPTER I

How St. James Appeared to Karlamagnus

When the most famous lord who had ever lived in the north lands, Karolus Magnus, first of all the kings of the Franks[1] to hold the Roman empire, had conquered a great realm in Italy[2] and made many lands subject to him under the rule of the Roman empire—Anglia,[3] France,[4] Germany,[5] Burgundia,[6] Lotaringia,[7] and many others which lie between the two seas, together with untold cities taken from the Saracens,—he intended to put aside warfare, to rest after great labor and no longer to risk himself and his men in battle and war.

Now, when the emperor had steadfastly made this resolution in his heart, it was granted to him one night to see over his bed a wonderfully great starry road, which rose up from the Frisian sea and ran between Germany[8] and Gaul,[9] Italy, and Aquitania,[10] and then over Gaskunia,[11] Balda,[12] and Nafaria[13] all the way west to Hispania and Galicia. Since Lord Karlamagnus saw the course of the stars, as described, again and again during the night, being a wise man he thought that so rare a sight must signify something momentous. And as he pondered con-

[1] *Frakka.*
[2] *Italia.*
[3] Understood as England by the A,a translator.
[4] *Francia.*
[5] *Þyverskan.*
[6] Burgundy.
[7] Lorraine.
[8] *Theothonia.*
[9] *Gallia*; France.
[10] *Akvitania.*
[11] Gascony.
[12] The Basque territory.
[13] Navarre.

tinually over the matter, one night there appeared to him in a dream a glorious man, beautifully attired, of radiant appearance and gracious countenance, who spoke to the emperor in loving words, so saying: "My sweet son," says he, "what are you doing?"

When the emperor heard himself so courteously greeted in such gracious speech, he had no intention of being silent in return; he therefore answered, "Who are you, good sir, who greet me so affectionately?"[14]

The handsome man answered, "I am the apostle James, foster-son of the Lord Jesus Christ, and son of Zebedeus and brother of John the evangelist. Jesus, son of the holy Virgin Maria, called me to him from the sea of Galilee in his inexpressible mercy; but Herod, most merciless of kings, had me beheaded with a sword. My body, although most men do not know it, lies in Hispania in the region of Galicia, which realm is now subject to the heinous[15] power of Saracens and Moabites. I am amazed that you do not deliver my land from their power when you have won so many realms, cities, and holdings for Roman Christendom. Therefore, know that as God has made you more powerful than any other king in the world, so he has also appointed you to free my realm from subjection to heathen peoples: and for that cause you will gain a bright crown of eternal glory.

"And that was also the meaning of the starry way which appeared to you. You are to go to these lands with your great army, forward into Hispania, to lay waste that evil nation and free the land from its shameful thralldom to the heathens; further, you shall gladly find my grave, and build and erect my chapel. After you have done this, all the people of Italy shall come there on pilgrimage. For this they shall receive God's absolution for all sins, and, praising God, they shall proclaim great wonders and unheard-of miracles which, in his infinite might, he vouchsafes to perform: people shall continue to make this journey until the end of the world. Now go, as quickly as possible," says James the apostle to Karlamagnus the emperor, "for I shall be your mighty helper,granting you help in this expedition and in your af-

[14] *b*: courteously.

[15] *b* adds "evil."

fairs; and I shall cause your labors to grow great in the sight of God. The honor you shall receive from this will be eternal glory in heaven, and your name shall always be praised as long as the world endures."

After these words, the apostle departed from the emperor's sight, and he awoke, thinking about this vision with great joy. Yet he delayed the journey to Hispania for a little while, waiting for further confirmation of the apostle's promise of what he was to gain, so that the apostle James appeared to him a second and a third time, in the same way as the first occasion.

But when the emperor had been strengthened by the apostle's third appearance, he had no desire to delay his journey any longer, and had a proclamation sent throughout the neighboring districts, summoning to him many leading men; among them was the excellent lord Turpin, archbishop of Rens, who first set down this account. The emperor also summoned no less a multitude of common people, and when they all came together in one place he clearly expounded to them his vision of the apostle James, making it known that he intended to take his army to the land of Hispania to destroy the accursed evildoers who had too long occupied the possessions of the Lord and his blessed friend James.[16] Cheering, all the men agreed to this eagerly, and praised God for his grace.

A,a (2)

... This same emperor, the great Karlamagnus, having, with much labor and strife, subjugated many great kingdoms—England[17] and France,[18] Germany,[19] Bæjaraland,[20] and Burgun[6] and Latorigia[7] and Italy, and many other realms between the two seas which are not recorded here, and having subjected to his rule as part of the Roman empire many outlying cities which had been under the power of the Saracens, now intended to allow himself peace and rest after much labor[21] and long toil, no longer risking himself or his men in warfare

[16] *Jacobus*.
[17] *Sic*.
[18] *Frakkarik:*, 'realm of the Franks.'
[19] *Þyðverskt land*.
[20] Bavaria.
[21] Literally 'sweat,' translating Latin *sudor*.

and battle. At this moment he saw in the heavens a starry road rising up from the Frisian[22] sea, which went between Germany and Galicia,[23] Italy and Aquitaine; then the way reached over Gaskunia and Basda,[12] Nafara[13] and Hispania, all the way to Galicia, where the holy remains of the hallowed apostle James were, although most men who were in the land at that time did not know this.

Now when King Karlamagnus saw that starry way again and again during the night, he pondered over what it might betoken. And when he had earnestly turned this over in his mind, there appeared to him in a dream the sublime vision of a man of beautiful form, who spoke to him in this manner: "My son, what are you doing?" He asked, in return, "Who are you, lord?" The other responded, "I am James the apostle, foster-son of Jesus Christ, and son of Zebedeus and brother of John[24] the evangelist. God called me to him at the sea of Galilee, and King Herod Agrippa had me beheaded by the sword. My body now lies, although most men do not know it, in the land of Galicia,[25] over which the Saracens have shameful rule. I am amazed that you do not deliver my land from the power of these enemies, when you have brought so many great lands and cities under your rule; therefore I wish to make it known to you that as God has made you more powerful than any other worldly king, so he chooses[26] you among all kings, in accordance with the vision which appeared before, to free the land from the oppression of the Moabites; for this you shall receive from him a crown of eternal glory.[27]

"The starry way that you saw under the heavens also meant this: that you shall go from these lands into Galicia, with your great army, destroying the heathen hosts and thus delivering the land, and seek out my chapel and grave. After your time, all the nations between the two seas shall make pilgrimages, receiving God's remission of their sins, and proclaim praises of God and the miracles and wonders he per-

[22] *A*, French.
[23] *Sic*, but no doubt in error for *Gallia*.
[24] *Johannes*.
[25] *a*: Galilee.
[26] *A*: "I choose," but cf. PT *elegit*.
[27] *A*: reward.

forms: they shall make this journey from your days until the end of the world. Now go as quickly as possible, for I shall help you in all things, making your works mighty; because of them I shall obtain for you a crown in heaven from God, and your name shall be praised until the Last Days."

With such words, the blessed apostle James appeared to King Karlamagnus three times. And the king drew strength from the apostle's promise, and drew together a great army, and travelled into Hispania to destroy the heathen hosts with his might.

CHAPTER II

Karlamagnus Converts the Heathens to Christianity

In due time, when the glorious lord Emperor Karlamagnus had prepared his army well and nobly, he began his journey out from France, proceeding from there until he came into the territory of Hispania, to the city which is called Pamphilonia:[1] a great city, with the strongest of walls. Karlamagnus besieged it for three months, but because of the enormous strength of the city it was not taken by skill or any kind of warlike device. And when the emperor saw that this city was not to be won by any human stratagem, he turned to almighty God in heaven for aid, saying, "Lord Jesus, hear my prayer, and give this city into my power, to the glory of thy blessed name, since I came into this land for the sake of thy faith—to deliver it from the shameful rule of the heathen hosts. I also call upon you,[2] glorious James, praying to you to help now, and stand by me: if you truly appeared to me, then break down the strong walls of Pamphilonia."

And after the emperor had spoken these words, all the men present saw the extremely strong[3] walls of the city fall down in the twinkling of an eye, so that now the emperor and his men gained ready entry. The wicked Saracens were now compelled to give up the city, against their will, and the Emperor Karlamagnus gave them two choices: either accept the true faith or suffer immediate death. Those who agreed to the faith won honor and freedom, and he had all the others, young and old, beheaded.

And when the Saracens who dwelled in the cities nearby heard how the walls of Pamphilonia had miraculously fallen down, and all of its

[1] Pamplona.
[2] *B*: my.
[3] *B*: hard.

former strength had quickly dissolved, they were very much troubled in their minds: so much so, that because of the great fear which God now allowed to overcome their hearts, they ran right out of their dwellings and made their way before the emperor, bearing with them tribute, and put themselves and all that they had in his power and at his disposal. The heathen people wondered greatly at the men of Karolus because of their beauty and fine apparel and all their courtesy; this caused them to meet courteously with him and his men, and they gave up their weapons most peacefully.

Now he proceeded quickly along the straightest way to the place where St. James lay in Compostella, which was at that time very small,[4] the old and ruined remains of a fort. Compostella stands in the west of the land of Galicia, very near the sea which is called Perocium mare.[5] Thus the emperor went to the shore, and thrust his sharp spear into the sea, giving thanks to almighty God and the blessed apostle James that he had led his great army as far in the regions of the earth as it was suitable for him to do.

After that, Karlamagnus turned on his journey back, liberating on the way all the land of Hispania and Galicia from the heathens. At this time there were in Galicia thirteen cities, including Compostella, and in Hispania twenty-six,[6] among which was a city called Acennoa[7] which was the resting place of God's excellent martyr Torkvatus,[8] who had in former times been a servant of the holy apostle James; in honor of him, it is truly written, the olive tree which stands by the martyr's grave blooms every year on his feast day, with beautiful full-grown bloom, as a divine gift.

These cities, together with all the neighboring districts, lands and realms, villages and castles, the emperor made subject to him: some

[4] Not in A,a, but this preserves PT *quamvis tunc temporis parva*.

[5] *B*: the sea of Perxotium.

[6] Note that these figures are very different from the grandly vague "five hundred" of A,a. The cities listed in PT III vary somewhat from one ms. to another, and can be variously understood; generally, though, thirteen are listed as in Galicia, and more than a hundred in Spain.

[7] *B*: *Atennoa*; PT Aceintina, Acentina; Gaudix. This is another detail from PT omitted in A,a.

[8] Torquatus; *b, Torqilatus*.

easily, with a sound truce; some through skill and knowledge; and some with great danger and heavy toil—as especially four cities called Venoza, Kaparia, Sonora, and Oda, and a fifth called Lucrina,[9] which is in Valle Veride. This he besieged, in the end, for three months, but could not conquer by any skill or any kind of force until he called on St. James for help, praying that he might break down the strength of Lucrina as he had Pamphilonia before; and this then truly came to pass, for no strong city walls could withstand the coming of God's apostle.

Because of the great labor which Karlamagnus endured before these cities, he cursed their very foundations, and God so supported this deed of his that a most foul spring, with hideous black fish dwelling in it, welled up in this Lucrina: no man dared inhabit these five cities after because of the emperor's words.

All the graven images, temples, and heathen shrines which the emperor found in Hispania, he caused to be burnt, laid waste, or broken down. The excellent lord Archbishop Turpin baptized, by the king's counsel, all the heathen people who wanted to turn away from their false faith, after converting all those who had forsaken the faith they had formerly received through the disciples of James. And all those so wretched that they would rather endure sudden death than accept the true faith were killed or carried away in slavery.

When these things had all been carried out, Karlamagnus turned west again to Compostella, collecting all the most skillful artisans from his land, and had a great minster painstakingly raised in thanksgiving to St. James. And when the church was completed, he honored it with many ornaments, fine bells, beautiful books, and becoming vestments, along with other sorts of the very best apparel suitable for the daily use there of chaste monks gathered together under the rule of St. Ysidore,[10] laying down so many goods there, both for fasts and feast

[9] The corresponding list here in PT is, simply, *Lucerna Ventosa, Capparra,* and *Adania*. The translator has apparently taken *Ventosa* as a separate city; *Sonora* appears to be an expansion of the *Sona* found in A,a and J. *Oda* looks like a corruption of *Adania*; it is possible that the translator was as puzzled by the name as modern scholars have been (see, e.g. M-J p. 280) and thought it might be two names rather than one, thus sorting out 'Ada' (*Oda*) and '... nia,' which somehow became *Sona*. Cf. also M-J p. 275, Smyser p. 19, n. 2.

[10] Isidore of Seville.

periods, that those who served had all they needed in abundance. Nor did he stop there, but proceeded to raise up holy churches far and wide in the land about, giving in abundance such equipment as the gold and silver which the kings and other leaders of Hispania had offered to him.

When Karlamagnus had stayed in these lands for three years, and had busied himself about these matters, as you have heard, he let his men know that he intended to go home to France, leaving Hispania in the keeping of all-ruling God, under the faithful supervision of the holy James.

A,a (3)

The city named Pampilonia was the first which Karlamagnus besieged; for three months he could not conquer it because its walls were so strong. Then Karlamagnus prayed to God, saying, "Lord Jesus Christ, give this city into my power, for the honor of thy name, since for the sake of thy faith I came to the unbelieving[11] people of this land. Hear me, blessed apostle James: let me conquer this town, if it is true that you appeared to me!"

Then all the walls of the town were thrown down to the ground, through the gift of God and the prayer of the blessed apostle James; by this means King Karlamagnus conquered the city. The king spared the lives of all the Saracens who wanted to be baptized, and all those who did not so wish he had killed.[12]

And when the Saracens heard these wonderful[13] tidings, they submitted to him wherever he went, and sent tribute before him, and gave cities and districts into his hands. The Saracens marveled at the emperor's people because of their good looks and fine clothes, and they therefore treated him and his army in a seemly and peaceful fashion when they gave up their weapons.

From there, Karlamagnus took the direct road to the grave of the holy apostle James. And when he had come to the ocean, he thrust his

[11] *a* omits adj.; cf. PT *gentem perfidam*.
[12] *a*: beheaded; PT *trucidavit/ feriendos tradidit*.
[13] *a* only; PT *mirabilibus* (M-J only).

spear into the sea and thanked God and the blessed apostle James that he had led his great army into the part of the earth where he had advanced as far as he could. Archbishop Turpin, advised by King Karlamagnus, baptized all those people in Galicia who had put aside the Christianity taught to them by the apostle James and his disciples, or those who had not received the faith in baptism[14] before. But then he had all those who did not wish to be baptized beheaded, or given into the power of Christians in slavery and oppression.

After that King Karlamagnus conquered all of Hispania from sea to sea; in that expedition he conquered five hundred cities and strongholds in Galicia and all over the land of Hispania. Now all of that land, west from Africa[15] to the sea, submitted to the empire of King Karlamagnus. All these lands, cities, and districts were now under his rule and made peace with him—although some only after strife and great exercise of skill—except for one city, which was among the strongest fortresses in the land, called Luctena[9] in Norse: this he did not manage to conquer by siege. It was in a place called "green valley" in Norse. But finally, when he had besieged this city for four months, he prayed to God and the blessed apostle James: and at once the walls of this town fell down. They have never been built up again to this day. A spring with black waters welled up in this place, and black fish appeared in it.

These cities overcome with laborious difficulty—Luctuosa, Venzoza, Caparia,[16] Oda, Sona[9]—no man dared to inhabit or to build up again unto this day, because of the curses which the king laid on the cities.

King Karlamagnus tore down all the graven images and idols of the Saracens and heathens which he found in Hispania,[17] except for one idol in the land of Alandaluf.[18] This idol was called Salemcadis:[19] the

[14] *A* omits "in baptism," which is needed to clarify the meaning; cf. PT *qui nondum babtizati erant.*

[15] *Afrika.*

[16] *a*: *Luktena, Venoza, Capara; Luctuosa* appears to be a form derived from the full name of 'Lucerna ventosa.' (Cf. n. 9 above.)

[17] The content of this paragraph, which follows the first two-thirds of PT VI, is not found in B,b.

[18] Andalusia; this form provides a clue to the PT text used by the original translator. Cf. Hämel, *Uberlieferung*, pp. 40-41.

[19] *a, Salamkades*; PT Salam Cadis, the colossus of Cadiz.

idol was in the city called Cadis, and "Salam" is the word for god in the language spoken by people of Arabia.[20] The Saracens say that the Maumet they worship made this idol in his own name, and that by magic arts he sealed into this idol a sort of king of devils who possesses, in his strength, this city and the idol;[21] because of this, no one can destroy it. If any Christian comes near it, he becomes ill, but if an ailing Saracen comes to it and honors it and prays for its mercy, he goes away healed. If a bird sits on this idol, it dies at once. The idol itself is made in this way: a four-sided stone stands on the shore of the sea, where the raven is accustomed to fly; made by Saracen art, it becomes thinner higher up. On this pillar stands the image, cast of the finest brass in the form of a man. He faces south, and has in his right[22] hand a huge club.[23] The Saracens say that this club shall fall from the hand of the idol in the year when a French king is born who shall make all Hispania Christian, at the end of the world; and as soon as the Saracens shall see this club fall down, they will all flee away from Hispania.

Karlamagnus used the gold which had been given to him by the kings and leaders of the Saracens in Hispania, during the three years he had stayed there,[24] to add to the minster of the holy apostle James, and he adorned that minster with handsome and precious ecclesiastical ornaments[25] and appointed for it a bishop and canons under the Rule of Bishop Ysodore.[10] ...

[20] Smyser, p. 123, "actually corruption of word for 'idol'"—cf. M-J, p. 291.

[21] *a* omits "in his own name ... idol," which translates PT *in nomine suo ... fabricavit/ optineret.*

[22] *a* only, translates *dextera.*

[23] Cf. Introduction on the significance of this word.

[24] *A* omits from "of the Saracens ..." The *a* version represents an expansion of PT's *reges et principes Yspanie*, and—although the action modified appears to be misunderstood—*per tres annos in illis horis.*

[25] Vestments may be the meaning, but it is not entirely clear; *kirkjuskrúði* may translate either *palliis* or the entire phrase *palliisque, libris ceterisque .../ libris et palliis atque campanis vel ceteris ornatibus*, more fully rendered in the B,b text.

CHAPTER III

Karlamagnus Visits St. Dionisius

When Hispania had been delivered and put in good order, the excellent lord Emperor Karlamagnus departed from Hispania with his host, bearing much gold and silver back to France[1] with him, and visited the home of God's holy friend Dionisius[2] who rested[3] in that most renowned city of Paris. He called together all the people of that city, and those of the places nearby, and made known to them the famous victory which almighty God, with the intercession of St. James, had granted, and the deliverance of Hispania; he said that, mercifully, they had suffered little loss of life in opposing so great a crowd of Saracens as were to be found in that land. The emperor was so inspired that all who heard these things gave praise to immortal God and his most beloved friend the apostle James, patron of Hispania. Karlamagnus said, further, that as a sign of thanksgiving and token of love for James he intended to raise a church to his glory in the city of Paris before he left; he also revealed without further delay that he intended to augment the honor of St. Dionisius and his church in that same Paris at that time, to repay him for the help which he believed Dionisius himself had granted in this expedition. Thus he brought it about that the entire host gave its approval to everything the emperor wished.[4]

[1] "Galicia"—apparently an error for *Gallia*.
[2] St. Denis.
[3] I.e., lay buried.
[4] For A,a basis, see passage at end of Chapter 4.

CHAPTER IV

St. Dionisius Appears to Karlamagnus

The next night, after the event which has just been related, Emperor Karlamagnus went into the church of Dionisius and kept watch there during the night, praying for help from God.[1] With devout heart, the emperor prayed especially for this: that St. Dionisius would obtain God's remission of sins for the souls of the men who had fallen in Hispania before the weapons of the heathen. As soon as the emperor had made his prayer and gone to sleep, St. Dionisius appeared to him, speaking to him thus, in gracious words: "Karolus," said he, "your prayer has been heard, for because of the intercession of your patron James, God has granted to me that all of those you have called to mind who fell in these times in Hispania, and those who shall so fall in the future, shall win forgiveness of all their misdoings, both greater and lesser."

After that Dionisius departed; and the emperor awoke, giving thanks to almighty God. And as soon as the next morning came, he revealed the vision. All his listeners praised almighty God for this grace. The emperor then had a church raised in Paris in honor of James.

After that the emperor left Paris and went to Aquisgranum, the city in which he most often stayed when he was at home in France. There he had a most mighty church erected, equipped as handsomely as possible, to the honor and glory of God's sublime mother, the eternally virgin St. Maria. In this city the emperor had another church built in honor of the apostle James, and a third church of James was built in the city of Tholosa.[2] Karlamagnus also raised up a fourth church to honor St. James between the city of Aza[3] and the city of St. John which is called Sordue;[4] near this church there is a street which is

[1] *B* adds, "and others."

[2] Toulouse.

[3] Ais-en-Gascogne, Dax; PT Axa.

[4] St.-Jean de Sorde; PT sanctum Iohannem Sordue.

called Via Jacobita.[5] He also had built here a great monastery in honor of God and St. James.

Now, as Emperor Karlamagnus had so labored, under the inspiration of the Holy Spirit, for his own salvation and that of others, you shall hear next after this of another chieftain who won renown for himself, incited by a very different spirit.

A,a (3)

... And with the rest of the great quantity of gold and silver which he had gained in Hispania, he had many churches and monasteries built in Germany[6] and France[7] and Gaskunia, almost all of which he consecrated to the glory and honor of the apostle James.[8]

[5] The Way of St. James.

[6] *A*: *Þyðversky*; *a*: *Þyversku*.

[7] *Franz*.

[8] This is a summary of the last third of PT VI, which lists the five churches mentioned in B,b chs. 2 and 4, plus a sixth not mentioned there (*ecclesiam que est apud Biterrensium urbem*, an Augustinian monastery of St. James at Béziers), none of which has anything to do with St. Denis, who plays so important a role in B,b chs. 3 and 4; in fact, St. Denis is not mentioned anywhere in the corresponding chapters of PT after the introductory letter to Leoprand. However, the B,b version is drawing on a much later chapter of PT, XXX, some of which, including the vision of St. Denis, is fairly literally translated here. In this case, it seems clear that B,b is drawing on Vincent of Beauvais's *Speculum historiale*; cf., e.g., Foote, p. 19.

CHAPTER V

King Agulandus

At this time, a great and mighty heathen king called Agulandus[1] ruled over Africa.[2] He had married a lady of a great family, as behoved such a king; she was a wise woman, courteous, and very handsome—no one more beautiful could have been found in all of Africa. She and Agulandus had one son, who was named Jamund:[3] he was a young man, full of arrogance and pride, strong, and formidable, hardy and daring with weapons, as shall be made clear later.

King Agulandus was extremely mighty—no heathen king was ever more powerful, for more than twenty crowned kings were obliged to pay tribute to him, although some of them ruled over many realms. Among the leaders who ruled in Africa at that time were many close kinsmen of Agulandus and some of his most intimate friends. A countless number of people were ruled by him, only a few of whom can be named: Saracens, Mauri,[4] Moabites, Ethiopians,[5] Nardi,[6] Africans, Persians.[7] The heathen sages said that if the fleetest mule, one brought from Jerusalem for the purpose, were to set out on a full summer's day[8] journey, it still could not go all the way around his kingdom.

Jamund, son of Agulandus, was the tallest of men, handsome in appearance, most accomplished; and, for the sake of the love he bore him, Agulandus gave his son a crown, and granted him many great men to serve him. But he was not to take over the government of the realm until after his father's death.

[1] PT Aigolandus, *Asp.* Agolant.
[2] *Affrica.*
[3] *Asp.* Eaumon, Almes.
[4] Moors.
[5] *Ethiopes.*
[6] Possibly PT Pardos?
[7] *Perse.*
[8] *b*: "all the way to the sea."

A,a (7)

After that, Agulandus drew together countless people: Saracens and Misturios,[9] Moabites and Ethiopians, Pardos[10] and Africans,[11] Persians.[12]

[9] *a*: *Misterios*; presumably corresponds to PT Mauros (Moors).

[10] Cf. n. 6.

[11] *Affricanos*.

[12] *Persas*.—Most of the details in the B,b version here (and in the next three chapters) are drawn from *Asp.* rather than PT, and summarize information gleaned in various places there.

CHAPTER VI

Agulandus Consults with his Men

Now when Jamund had received this honor, his pride grew boundless, and he gathered around him young, unsettled men, whose fellowship he sought. He listened eagerly to their counsels, although they could give no good counsel to either themselves or him. And although Agulandus was much displeased, Jamund pursued this course to such an extent that he took under his protection men who had been driven away from his father's service for various crimes. But, because of the love Agulandus bore for his son, and because of the great fear he inspired, no one dared speak against his conduct.

His state continued thus, until Agulandus heard the truth about how Karlamagnus, with his mighty hand, had freed Hispania from the Saracens. Agulandus was much angered by this; calling together his counselors and all the chief men of his land, he said to them, "Good lords," says he, "I believe you have all heard the tidings that our tributary land of Hispania, which our people have held a long time, has now fallen from our power before a great triumph of Christian men; it is now truly reported that their leader, who is called Karlamagnus, has dared to attack Hispania, in enmity to us and to our god, and has killed the men, destroyed the cities, torn down the temples, broken apart the images and completely forbidden their worship—and has subjected all the land to that religion which is most disagreeable to my heart. Now, when I heard such things, my mind was somewhat troubled, for I do not know what will seem best to you to do: and this is what I now wish to determine."

Next, a king stood up whose name was Ulien. He was a heavy man, given to vehement speech, and quick to become angry if anything displeased him. He derived his eminence from a mighty realm and a great family, for he was a nephew of Agulandus. He therefore spoke boldly, saying thus: "Agulandus, it is not fitting for so powerful a king as you to be much disturbed that so poor a land as Hispania has been lost to your glory, for as soon as you wish you may win that and more back from the holdings of the Christians: just as you choose. It may seem to you that many of your champions are better knights than I; yet I vow to Makon[1] that there is none so great in the Frenchman's host that I shall not boldly oppose two or three. Do not hesitate, lord, to lead your army to Hispania. I assure you faithfully that all their strength shall not endure any more than this little wisp of straw which I squeeze together in my big hand."

So spoke the haughty Ulien, who did not know what he was talking about.

Agulandus answered, "You say well, kinsman Ulien, and it must be precisely so. I can fully trust your knightly prowess, and that of my other champions. And since my son Jamund is a man well suited for leadership, while I have no wish to divide up my own power, I not only intend to conquer Hispania itself but to put Italy into his hands as well, and to set his throne in Rome,[2] which is said to be the foremost city in these lands. In order to accomplish this, we shall pray to our gods to stand firm with us, and to revenge all harms from our enemies and theirs.

"And, while many of our gods are great, four among them are the greatest help of all; that is, the mighty Makon, powerful Maumet,[3] great Terrogant[4] and Jupiter the strong: these four we shall have with us on the journey. And in return for the full favor that they grant to help us, we shall give them, as we should, the greatest of dignities to honor them: we shall adorn them all with brightest gold, set with the most precious gems, engraved with surpassing skill. Since in all of Africa are found neither such skilled masters nor such precious materials as are due these gods, I shall send to Arabia, where all the most precious riches, gold and gems, are abundantly produced, for the most skillful craftsmen in that land, so that they may adorn our gods

[1] Mahomet, Mohammed, from O.F. Mahon; understood as a heathen god.

[2] *Roma*.

[3] Another spelling for Mahomet; but here the two are taken to be separate deities.

[4] Another Saracen "deity": O.F. Tervagant, Eng. Termagant.

with the most beautiful materials that can be obtained there. It is truly fitting that just as we have a greater kingdom than that of any other king in the world, so also should the gods we worship be more splendidly embellished, and with more precious materials, than other gods."

When the king had finished his speech, they all rose to their feet crying out at once, and said, "May all the gods help you, good king,[5] and call you to their dwellings, for the great splendor you grant to honor them!"

The king then ended the council, and each man returned to his own place.

[5] *b*: lord.

CHAPTER VII

How Agulandus and Jamund Received Advice

Agulandus now sent messengers to Arabia with his gods. They took about as much time on this journey as was to be expected. While they were away, many friends came to Agulandus, urging him to take his army to Spain as soon as possible; he received their advice with favor and said that as soon as the gods returned home he would prepare his army.

Now Jamund was urged by his friends not to delay but to go on before his father and gain power for himself. But he took little interest, letting Agulandus bear all the responsibility for the expedition, for he thought it of little import even if his father failed disgracefully.[1] If this should come about, he intended, in his pride, to go forward boldly and conquer all the realm for himself, with the backing of his men; for he thought it clear that Agulandus intended to fight the Christians for the realm in order to get him away from Africa. Thus he thought his father wanted to rob him of his patrimony.

[1] *b*; *B*'s "even if he won disgrace" may refer to Jamund himself rather than Agulandus; it is possible that it means "Jamund did not care what people thought of him," but the context seems to demand that Jamund be considering the possibility of his father's failure.

CHAPTER VIII

Agulandus Prepares His Expedition to Hispania

As the messengers neared home, Agulandus rode in great state well out on the way to meet them in order to honor the gods, for he was very curious to see how their beauty[1] and ornament had been changed. And when he saw them so splendid that you could never have found their like, he went almost out of his mind for the boundless gladness he felt in his heart: the wise men of the heathens said that these accursed heathen images were adorned with a quantity of most precious gems, gold, and silver easily sufficient to buy seven of the mightiest cities.

As Agulandus came back to himself—bad as that was—he spoke in this way to those who stood nearby: "Who has seen any god as mighty as these? No one, no, certainly no one at all! If these face their enemies[2] and ours with wrathful eyes and frowning brows, all their strength shall melt into ashes, for now, in reward for our deeds, they have already granted that Karlamagnus has gone away from Hispania to his own lands. That realm was left behind without a protector, and thus nothing more is necessary than that we show Karlamagnus, and Hispania, a small part of our power. If it should be necessary to call for more strength—though the gods will not allow this to come about—there will be quite enough to call upon."

Now Agulandus had shrilling trumpets sounded, and gathered together a great multitude from the nearby cities, choosing from among them as many as he wished to follow him. When the army[3] was ready, Agulandus rode out of his city with great pomp, forward to the sea. Ships were soon ready there, many and great, laden with the finest

[1] *B*, fame.
[2] *b*; *B*'s "friends" is obviously wrong.
[3] *b*; *B*: the lord.

provisions which could be had: food and drink, gold and silver, horses, clothes, and all the very best goods. Then each and every man came aboard to his appointed place. King Agulandus took great pride in his strength, for it now seemed to him beyond any doubt that nothing could harm him, for in his train he had the four gods named above, in whom he trusted for every help: but the more he trusted in them, the worse he would receive.

Jamund, his son, was there, and many other chiefs, kings, earls, dukes, and barons. And these especially were the leaders of the army, as are here named: Texbin,[4] king of Arabia; Bacales, king of Alexandria; Avit, king of Bugie; Aspin, king of Agapia; King Fantim[5] of Marab;[6] Alfing, king of Mariork;[7] Manio, king of Mecque;[8] Ebravit of Sibil.[9] With these, King Agulandus sailed away from Africa.

His journey was most splendid: the sea flashed far and wide when the bright sun shone on the rich ships with their gilt dragon-prows, glowing weather vanes, marvellously beautiful sails of various colors—red as blood or white as snow. If Agulandus could return home to Africa with such a show of might, it would be well for him: and better than was actually to be.

A,a (7)

... In this army were these leaders: Texphin,[10] king of Abia;[11] Bakales,[12] king of Alexandria; Avit,[13] king of Bugia;[14] Ospin, king of

[4] *b*; *B*: *Gezbin*.
[5] *B*, *Famni*.
[6] Morocco.
[7] Majorca.
[8] Mecca.
[9] Seville.—for further information on these names, cf. A,a text and notes 10-24.
[10] *a*, *Terhpin*; PT Texephinus, but some mss. give forms closer to *a*'s, such as Teremphonus/Terenphinus/Therophinis.
[11] PT Araba, 'Arabia.'
[12] PT Burrabellus/Burrahellus.
[13] *A*, *Avid*; PT Avitus.
[14] Bugie, a city near Tunis (Smyser, p. 113).

Agapia;[15] Partin, king of Marak;[16] Alfing,[17] king of Maiork;[18] Mamonon,[19] king of Mekua;[20] Ebrauid,[21] king of Sibil;[22] Altumaior,[23] king of Korduba.[24]

[15] PT Ospinus, Agabia.

[16] The two latter are listed only in *a*; 'Partin' seems to bc a conflation of PT's Fatimus/Faturius/Fatinus, of Barbaria, and Ailis of Maroc, but cf. variant *cum aliis multis, regem Marroc* (M-J, p. 115). In this instance, *b* is closer to the PT name of the king, though its version of the name of the realm is more corrupt than A,a's.

[17] *a, Alfuskor*, PT Aphinorgius.

[18] PT Maiorice.

[19] PT Maimonen/Mamonen.

[20] *A, Meana*.

[21] *a, Ebiauin*, PT Ebraum/Ebrahim.

[22] *A, Sibilus*, PT Sibilia.

[23] *A, Estimator*, PT Altumaior; note that he is omitted in B,b.

[24] Corduba.

CHAPTER IX

Agulandus Arrives in Hispania

As soon as this enemy of God arrived in Hispania with his attendants, a change quickly took place there, for the emperor Karlamagnus was no nearer than his home in France, and the land was leaderless. Thus these limbs of the devil made war on the flock of God and his most holy apostle James with great warfare, breaking down Christianity, killing Christian men or driving them off into exile, and appointing in its place disgraceful heathen practices with devilish services to cursed graven images.

Now, what good reason moved God's blessed apostle James, who was guarding Hispania, as he undertook at the time when Karlamagnus went home to France, that he let his land be subjected to the power and rule of accursed heathens again, and allowed churches to be broken down and temples with heathen altars raised, when James certainly knew that no honor was given to his dear master Jesus while the sons of Hell ruled? Why would he agree to such long suffering—unless it seemed to him that the emperor Karlamagnus had been awarded the crown he had asked for from Heaven with less toil than it was worth, and, too, that far fewer had given their lives to win the entry of James to the house of Christ with Karlamagnus than the apostle had intended; thus he wished to stir up greater battle, so that he could draw them all with him to heaven, as he wished, in defending his land. He may well have had yet a third intention: the southern region was still very much thronged with multitudes of insolent, cursed heathens, and it was thus necessary that they be made to give way and go back home to the abode of their patron Makon and those others in whom they put their trust.

Because of divine considerations such as these, the apostle James arranged it that King Karlamagnus became aware of the truth—that

King Agulandus of Africa had come forth against God; and, faced with these tidings, he prepared himself in the manner that shall now be related.[1]

[1] This sounds very much in the style of Pseudo-Turpin, but I have not found any source for it.

CHAPTER X

Karlamagnus Summons his Men

At this time, when these events had been proceeding in Hispania as has just been told, the excellent lord Karlamagnus sat at Aquisgranum[1] in France. And when he heard the tidings of woe, he was much grieved in his heart and was greatly kindled with godly zeal; he sent an urgent message and letter everywhere about the realm, summoning all the leaders to come in strength to Aquisgranum as quickly as possible. And because of the great love and true obedience which the emperor's subjects cherished towards their lord, each and every one hastened to make the journey to which he was summoned, the greater along with the lesser men, into the appointed place; those who were nearest came most quickly.

Now when many great leaders of the Franks had come together in the place named, and when each of them who had been called was there, the emperor himself rose up and spoke in this way: "May God repay you, good lords, for the devoted homage which, for God's sake, you grant to me; because of this, I tell you that many of you shall earn, even better than I, the same honor that is mine. For you shall consent night and day to my will and command, gladly laying down your lives, which the true God gave you, as all other things you have held, for God's grace and mine: thus you shall repay him for all good things.

"Now I shall reveal the cause for which I have now called you together. Great occasions of sorrow have come to my ears, for it is truly reported that the Christianity which the land of Hispania—which belongs to my holy patron James—received from God, with our help, is now altogether destroyed: trodden down by a heathen dog, king of Africa, Agulandus by name. Therefore I see that St. James must intend me and my men to stand up again to free his land, for his honor and

[1] *Aguisgranum*: Aachen.

our souls' health. Then hear this, my good friends: I shall take this army to Hispania, and shall gain whichever God's providence ordains, a fair victory or speedy death. I expect that it seems to St. James we have taken our rest quite long enough.

"Now, although not all the army which God shall send to our aid has come here as yet, we shall nonetheless prepare our host with the best horses, weapons, and clothing, and hasten with our army into wherever in the land of Hispania it seems most suitable for us to await the reinforcements which will come later. I also hope this: that if the leaders there hear that we are close to them, they may pass timidly from the land."

All who heard these words from the emperor answered with one voice: "Good lord," they said, "gladly do we wish to follow your counsel in this matter and in every other, so long as God lends us life, for your foresight has long availed us well, both as to spirit and as to body. We will thus trust again in God's will and the help of St. James the apostle."

A,a (4)

Now when King Karlamagnus returned home to France, a heathen king of Africa who was called Agulandus came into Hispania, and conquered all that kingdom with a great army. He brought down all the Christianity that King Karlamagnus had established there, killing all the Christian men or driving them from the land. And when King Karlamagnus heard this news, he went to Hispania again, with his host ...

CHAPTER XI

The Leaders of the Host of Karlamagnus

When Emperor Karlamagnus had readied his army in such good and noble fashion that no one could possibly find fault, he hastened on his journey from France with so magnificent a company that there was not such another in all Italy.[1] In this army were such fine leaders that there were no better. One of them, first and foremost, was the excellent lord Turpin, archbishop of Rens, who has been spoken of before: he was specially appointed by God and the emperor to baptize men, consecrate churches, and give pastoral guidance to the people. A second leader was Milon,[2] duke of Angler, brother-in-law of the emperor, and at this time chief in command of his army. A third leader was Rollant,[3] nephew of Karlamagnus. He was earl of Ornonianens[4] and had 4,000 of the boldest knights with him. A fourth was Oliver, earl of Gebenens; he was the son of earl Ramerus, and had three thousand valiant knights. A fifth was Arastagnus, king of Britannia, with seven[5] thousand knights. Sixth was Engiler, duke of Aquitania. The city of Aquitania was first erected by the emperor Augustus, according to the accounts of men of the past; around it lay a great district with mighty strongholds, which takes its name from the city and is called Aquitania. Four thousand warriors followed Engiler, men who bore all weapons boldly but were especially excellent at shooting with bows. A seventh was Oddgeir[6] the Dane, with ten thousand good knights.

[1] Latter clause in *B* only.
[2] Here, *Milun*.
[3] Roland.
[4] For derivation of this name and others here, see the A,a version and notes 13-57.
[5] *b*, four.
[6] Ogier.

Eighth, Nemes,[7] the most noble duke of Bealfer,[8] with five thousand. Ninth, Gundabol,[9] king of Frisia, with four thousand. Tenth, Lanbert of Biturica, a powerful leader, with twelve thousand. Eleventh, Samson,[10] duke of Burgundia, with two thousand. Twelfth, Eystult[11] earl of Lingunia, with three thousand fighting men.

With all these, and many others, lord Karlamagnus went on until he had come to the town, or city, which is called Benona.[12] There he stayed with his army, waiting a while for the leaders who were coming later; therefore next shall be related a circumstance that came about in this place, told in the manner in which archbishop Turpin wrote it down. In his own words, it begins so:

A,a (9)

... And these were the names of the leaders who were most valiant warriors in the army of King Karlamagnus:

Turpin, Archbishop of Rens; Rollant, commander of the army, earl of Cenoman and lord of Clave,[13] nephew of King Karlamagnus, the son of Duke Milon of Angler[14] and the lady Berta,[15] sister of King Karlamagnus, and with him, four thousand good[16] warriors; Olifer was also a commander of the army: the most valiant and skilled of knights and the strongest in wielding a sword, he was earl of Gibbon[17] and son

[7] Naime.

[8] Bavaria.

[9] *b, Gundebol.*

[10] Sanson.

[11] *b, Gistubert.*

[12] Bayonne.

[13] *a, Slave*; PT *comes cenomannicus et Blavii dominus*: count of le Mans and lord of Blaye; this last is, Smyser remarks, "peculiar to" PT; see p. 27, n. 2.

[14] Here *Anglier*; Milon d'Aiglent.

[15] *a, Gilim*, no doubt correcting the PT account to agree with the first part of the saga; *A* follows PT.

[16] Adj. in *a* only, corresponding to the *virorum fortium* of the abridged version of PT; CC has *virorum bellatorum*.

[17] *a, Gilin*; PT *comes gebennensis*, count of Geneva. Note that the B,b version is nearer PT here.

of earl Reiner[18] and had three[19] thousand good warriors; Eystult, earl of Lingun,[20] son of earl Otun,[21] had three thousand warriors; Arastang,[22] king of Brittania,[23] who had seven thousand warriors (there was also then another king of Brittania, of whom we shall not speak now);[24] Engeler, duke of Aquitania,[25] had four thousand warriors, all of whom were well skilled with all sorts of weapons and best at shooting a bow. This city of Aquitania, after which all the land that belongs to it is called, was founded by the emperor Augustus, but after the death of duke Engeler[26] this city became deserted and it has never been re-established since.[27]

Also there were Jofrey, king of Bordel,[28] with three thousand warriors; Gerin and[29] Golias;[30] Saloman,[31] comrade of Eystult, and Baldvini,[32] brother of Rollant; Gandebeld, king of Frisia,[33] with four thousand knights; Del, earl of the city of Narras[34] with two[35] thousand knights; Arnald of Bernald,[36] with two thousand good warriors; Nauman, duke of Beiare,[37] with five thousand good warriors; Oddgeir,

[18] PT Rainerus, Reinerus; Renier de Genvres.

[19] *A*, 4, but cf. PT *tribus*.

[20] Estultus comes lingonensis, Estoult de Lengres.

[21] PT Odo, Odon de Lengres.

[22] Here *Arakstan*.

[23] Arastagnus rex Britannorum.

[24] PT *alius tamen rex tempore istius in Brittania erat* ... cf. Smyser, p. 67.

[25] Engelerus dux Aquitaniae, Engelier le Gascon.

[26] *a, Engiler*.

[27] "Small wonder, since the city never existed."—Smyser, p. 27, n. 3.

[28] Bordeaux; Gaiferus rex burdegalensis, Gaifier de Bordele, Gaufroi de Bordiaus.

[29] *a, Gescir* of; PT Gerinus, Gelinus; Gerin, one of the Twelve Peers.

[30] PT Gelerus/Galerus; Gerier (sometimes sp. Geler, Gelier, etc.), one of the Twelve Peers and almost invariably paired with Gerin.

[31] Salemon de Bretaigne.

[32] Balduinus, Bauduïn.

[33] Gandelbodus/Gandeboldus rex Frisiae, Gondebuef le Frison.

[34] Oellus/Hoellus, of Nantas; e.e., Hoël de Nantes.

[35] *a*, 4, but PT *duobus milibus*.

[36] *a, Berit*; Arnaldus de Berlanda/Bellanda, Hernaut de Beaulande.

[37] *a, Naunal* of *Berare*, i.e., Naimes, duke of Bavaria; PT's Naaman dux Baioriae, correctly identified by the B-redactor as "Nemes of Bealfer": but it is dubious that the A,a translator here recognized the same character he later

King of the Danes,[38] with ten thousand good warriors—of him songs are chanted to this day of how he performed untold wonderful deeds; Lambert, prince of Biturika,[39] with two thousand warriors; Samson, duke of Burgunia,[40] with two thousand warriors; Constantin, prefect of Rome,[41] with twenty thousand warriors; Romald[42] of Albaspania;[43] Gauter of Termis[44] and his brother Vilhjalm;[45] Gara, duke of Lotoringia,[46] with four thousand warriors; Begon,[47] and Afrig of Burgunia;[48] Bernard of Nobilis;[49] Guinard;[50] Esturmid,[51] Thidrek;[52] Juor;[53] Bæring;[54] Haro;[55] Guinelun,[56] who later became a traitor.

calls "Nemes" (e.g., ch. 39) in the part of the saga translated from Aspremont.

[38] Ogerius/Otgerius rex Dacie, here the saga translator certainly recognized the name.

[39] Lambert de Berri (Bourges).

[40] Sanson de Borgoigne.

[41] If this is the king of Rome of this name mentioned in *Ogier*, the tradition is certainly confused, since there he is a relative of the heathen king Corsuble (cf. *Kms.* III, ch. 34, "Constant the Courteous"). Mouskés mentions a "Coustentins Romme" in his list of the heroes; see l. 7060 (p. 281).

[42] *a, Rombald.*

[43] Rainaldus de Albo Spino/Reinaldus de Albaspina; Renaut d'Aubespin.

[44] Gaulterus de Turmis/Galterius de Termis, Gautier de Termes.

[45] William; PT Guielinus/Guielmus. Willelmus; I have found no indication of which of the many Guielins and/or Guillaumes occurring in the *chansons de geste* he may be.

[46] *A, Loringa*; Garinus Lotharingiae dux; Garin le Loherant.

[47] PT Bego; Begon de Belin, brother of Garin le Loherant.

[48] Albericus burgundionus; Auberi le Bourgoing.

[49] Berardus de Nublis; the city appears to be the mysterious town of Nobles, or Noples, but I have been unable to find any Berart or Bernard associated therewith.

[50] Guinardus, elsewhere apparently called Girardus—but there seem no grounds to identify him with Girard d'Eufrate of *Asp.* who figures prominently in the latter part of the saga account.

[51] *a, Estorant*; Esturmitus; Estormi?

[52] Tedricus; Thierri l'Angevin.

[53] Yvorius; Ivorie, one of the Twelve Peers.

[54] Berengarius; Berengier, one of the Twelve Peers.

[55] PT Ato/Hato; Oton, one of the Twelve Peers, generally paired with Berengier.

[56] *a, Guilulun*; Ganalonus, Ganelon.

In the army of King Karlamagnus were the various mounted men who have been enumerated, but of men on foot no count was kept. The leaders who have been named were the most valiant champions in the world, and God's knights among Christian men in their day.

(4)

... Duke Milon of Angler[57] was chief commander of the army.

Now I shall write of an event that will show men what responsibility it is to take charge of the lawful gifts which men give on their deathbeds for the sake of their souls.

[57] *Angleriz*; Milon's name is here given as *A, Nisto, a, Justo.*

CHAPTER XII

About Almsgiving

When Emperor Karlamagnus stopped in the city of Benona, a certain knight of the army, Romaticus by name, became ill; and when he neared death he was shriven and received the Body of God together with the last sacrament. After this, Romaticus summoned a knight who was distantly related to him and spoke thus: "Good friend," says he, "take the beautiful horse which I own and sell it for money enough, and give all the price to the poor, for my salvation, as soon as I am dead."

Romaticus then passed away, and the knight sold the horse for one hundred shillings of silver—which he took for himself, and did not give to the poor; rather, he wasted all the horse's price in a few days, on drink, food, and clothes, and did not intend to give the least bit to even one poor man.

When thirty days had passed after the death of Romaticus, he appeared in a dream to this knight, speaking to him with a curt glance: "There you lie; having, in your greed, done ill to me. Know that when I departed from this life, my Redeemer had, in his mercy, forgiven me all my sins because I gave my horse to be a comfort to those who are his limbs. But because you, with unjust greed, took the alms for yourself and denied to God's poor the comfort which I gave them for my soul's help, I have suffered many torments in all this time which has passed since my death. But now heavenly mercy so ordains that you shall come and take my place tomorrow, and I shall be led to rest in Paradise."

Then the knight awoke, frightened, and at once revealed what had appeared to him during the night. It seemed a wonderful and terrible thing to all his hearers; and as they spoke of this matter among themselves, those who stood nearby heard, up in the air, a great commotion, with terrible sounds like the roaring of lions or the howls of wolves or the bellowing of bulls, and right then this knight was carried away from the sight of men. He was never seen alive again.

As news of this unheard-of event spread around the army. many went searching for him, both on foot and on horseback, for four days together, and they could not find him. But twelve days later his body was found smashed to pieces on a mountain three days' journey away from the place where he was first seized. All now understood that the disturbance in the air which they had heard was made by unclean spirits, who had fiercely cast down this wretched man's body in that place and carried off his soul with them into the place prepared for eternal torment.

By these things it was clearly revealed what a grave fault it is, in the eyes of God, greedily to take for oneself the alms good men give for their souls' salvation, whoever does it, whether he is a relation or not; for if a man does not in such deeds do what is proper, he incurs great guilt, when Holy Church and poor men need the property. He will certainly pay with his soul when he dies, for that which he kept back for his own comfort turns into his great affliction. In this it may also be seen that whatever a Christian man gives while he is still living, or another gives afterwards for him, for his soul, it is very necessary that it be delivered up as quickly as possible; for as long as the good deed is delayed, the soul's need has not been completed, and it must suffer in pain until that which was promised is fulfilled.[1]

This tale ends here, and next we shall turn back to Agulandus.

A,a (5)

When Karlamagnus was staying in the city of Baion[2] with his army, a knight whose name was Romarik[3] gave his horse for the sake of his soul when he was shriven and given extreme unction. After his death, his kinsman, whom he had charged to give the horse's value to the poor, sold his horse for one hundred shillings of silver, but spent this money on himself in a few days for food and drink and clothing. After thirty days, however, the dead man appeared to him and spoke these

[1] This expansion of a single sentence "moral" in PT does not come from any ms. version I have seen.

[2] Bayonne.

[3] PT Romaricus.

words: "I gave my money into your hands to give to poor men for my soul's sake; know that God then forgave all my sins. But because you wrongly took my alms, I have been in terrible torment for thirty days. Tomorrow, however, you shall come and take my place, while I shall go to Paradise."

Now when people heard this dream of his in the morning, they thought it a most wonderful vision. Immediately they heard a noise in the air above him, like the roaring of lions or the howls of wolves or the bellowing of bulls; and in that instant this wretched man was taken up into the air, so that no man ever saw him alive again. For four days a search for him went on, afoot and on horseback, but he was not found. Then, twelve days after that event, his body was found all broken into pieces on a mountain four days' journey away from the place where he had been carried off: devils had cast him down fiercely.

CHAPTER XIII

Agulandus Holds a Council

Now we shall speak of how King Agulandus went all over the land of Hispania, harrying it; he took city after city, castle after castle, breaking down Christianity[1] and establishing heathendom in its place, as has been said before. He conquered a strong tower from Christian men with such hard fighting that no matter what valiant men were to guard it they could not muster nearly enough strength to withstand him. Jamund, son of Agulandus, took this tower, to defend it with his men, but went on further with Agulandus until, at the time when Emperor Karlamagnus was in Baion,[2] they came to a flat, broad plain, in the midst of which lies the river which is called Segia;[3] there they set up their army tents.

And when Agulandus had learned that Karlamagnus was in Baion, he called all his counsellors to him, and spoke thus: "Good leaders," says he, "we do not need to conceal from ourselves that the Christian king Karlamagnus is piling conceit on pride in coming to meet with us. I am amazed at his notions, if he thinks he can govern this land and drive us away in shame! One can only suppose that he does not realize our strength and the almighty power of our gods. But now let us consult as to how we should proceed."

As Agulandus calls for the advice of his counsellors, they propose various courses; some say that the only thing to do is to send all the army against Karlamagnus as quickly as possible and force him to retreat into his own realm, or to kill him, thinking, in their imprudence, to take great tribute from him. Two of the chief men led these two schools of thought: Ulien, who was mentioned before, and

[1] *b*, churches.

[2] Note that in chs. 11 and 12 B,b used the spelling 'Benona' for Bayonne; now A,a's 'Baion' is used; confusion in switching sources may have led to this inconsistency.

[3] *b, Seggja.*

Madequin the Strong, who was so huge that you might say he was more like a giant than like an ordinary man.

But in their midst the king who was called Balam[4] now stood up. He was a high-minded man, wise and trustworthy, bold in his speech and eloquent in delivery. He spoke thus to Agulandus: "Most mighty leader," says he, "everyone knows that it would be beneath the dignity of your majesty to kill that little group of Christian men which follows Karlamagnus, but that it would increase your honor and glory to entice him to accept your rule by fair promises and gracious words, making it evident that in this case you will not attack him; and if he is a wise man, as I indeed believe him to be, then he will know how to perceive your great good will and accept your terms with thanks, giving himself and his realm up into your keeping. If he does not wish this, it will be perfectly proper that he take a bad fall. Therefore my counsel is that you send a bold and subtle messenger to the emperor: one who will carry out your errand firmly, whatever happens for better or worse, and can clearly understand the words of the emperor and his men."

Agulandus answers, "That is the best advice, and it shall be so. But I do not see anyone so well suited for this journey as you, Balam; and therefore you shall go, taking as many men with you as seems best to you. Observe, as you do so, how great or strong a host they have, and tell us whatever else you find."

Balam then says, "Lord. I am your liegeman, and shall obey your order: I shall gladly perform this journey according to your wish."

A,a (6)

Now when King Karlamagnus and Duke Milon[5] came into Hispania with their host, they looked there for King Agulandus, and, as they carefully tracked him down, they met with him at the river which is called Segia,[6] a very lovely river, narrow, and smooth ...

[4] *Asp.* Balan.

[5] *A, Milo*; *a, Justo*.

[6] *a, Seggia*; PT Ceia; the river Céa, in Spain.

CHAPTER XIV

Balam Goes to the Court of Karlamagnus

Balam then equipped himself and his men with the most handsomely ornamented weapons and clothes and went on his way until he arrived in Baion, where he dismounted from his horse and went before the emperor as soon as he had leave to do so. Although Balam had never before seen Emperor Karlamagnus, he readily saw where he was sitting among the others; he greeted the emperor and spoke thus: "May you rest in peace and tranquillity, most valiant leader of the Christian peoples!"

The emperor received him well, inquiring who he was. He answers, "I am called Balam, retainer of the most mighty king Agulandus, sent to your army by him to bring your host a message. Since his lordship has learned of your presence nearby, it seemed to him that there could be no other explanation for your errand than that you seek to come to his court humbly, as it behoves you to do. And since he thought it might be, when you know you have committed offences against him, that you hardly expect to win his mercy, he therefore bade me tell you that he will gladly grant it to you, though you have seized Hispania, thereby taking his possession from him. Not only will he overlook the trouble you have caused him: he even offers to let you take out of his realm as much gold and silver treasure as seems best to you, if you will now gladly and easily submit to his rule and make amends for your previous trespass. But if, in your pride, you will not thankfully accept this offer of peace—such as no one has ever gained before from such a leader—and impudently proceed against his lordship, then you may believe my words: no place in all of Hispania is secure enough to protect you against his power. Even if you were much mightier and had half again as great a host as you now do, you still would not have half the power of Agulandus."

When Balam has said such things, the emperor answers gently, as he was accustomed to, even if something sharp had been said to him, and speaks thus: "You convey the message of your lord well and faithfully. Stay with us for a while, therefore, and rest yourself. But tell me, good friend, where is Agulandus, your master?"

Balam answers: "Right in that flat plain which lies by the river which is called Segia. He awaits your arrival there."

The emperor then says, "Praise be to almighty God and the blessed James, for I intend to go there as soon as God permits me. However, Agulandus is not right in thinking that I would not dare to ask for forgiveness of the one against whom I trespass: but that is not Agulandus. It is, rather, my Lord Jesus Christ, whom I am bound to serve as best I can; indeed, I have committed many and great trespasses against him, but not against Agulandus."

Their conversation then ended. Balam stayed for a little while with Karlamagnus, reflecting on the customs and behaviour of the Christian men, all of which he found most pleasing to his mind: in fact, he thought their faith seemed mightier and more remarkable than that of the heathen peoples. And when he had inquired into all these matters as he wished, he prepared to leave. When the emperor learned of this he had a number of fine, well-equipped horses led to him, saying to Balam, "Good friend," says he, "take as many of these as you wish, but bear my message to King Agulandus: I intend to take so much gold and silver from his treasury as he himself shall think sufficient, without granting any honor to him in exchange."[1]

[1] Based on later *Asp.* material; cf., e.g., ch. 54.

CHAPTER XV

Balam Tells Agulandus About Karlamagnus

Now Balam went on until he came to the encampment of Agulandus, where he dismounted from his horse before the tent of Agulandus, greeted him, and spoke thus: "Karlamagnus, king of the Christians, sends you this greeting: that you should await him in this place, if your heart does not fail you."

Wrathfully, Agulandus then answers, "Did you then see this puffed-up Karlamagnus?"

"Certainly," says Balam; "in good health and spirits in every way, except that it seems to him your meeting is too long postponed. I have never seen a man more remarkable than he, and, to tell you the truth, while his host is much smaller than yours, I have never seen anyone more valiant than they, nor better armed. I only heard one thing feared there, and that was that you might not dare await them. Indeed, then, my advice would be that you not risk battle with them, for what I tell you is no foolishness: never in the world would you conquer their realm or put them to flight."

When King Agulandus and his men hear such a speech from the messenger they are furiously enraged against him, and speak thus: "Truly, you deserve great punishment for your treachery. You have betrayed your leader Agulandus, accepted bribes from the Christians and become their friend: therefore no attention shall be given to your report. But tell, now, how great a host has Karlamagnus?"

Balam answers, "What use is it for me to tell you anything when you will only believe what appears to you? Now know this to be true: he has a troop less than half the size of that of Agulandus, yet he shall completely overcome you."

Agulandus, hearing this, calls his son Jamund to him, and speaks thus to him: "Now I am certain that the Christians have no such troops here as we do; therefore you shall go off with your troops to the strong building you took, to guard and defend it as best you can.

Balam the messenger shall go with you, along with our four gods, for I see that my own troop alone will be enough to conquer Karlamagnus."

So it came about in this way that Jamund went away from his father, never to see him again except at home in the dark region of hell itself. Agulandus stayed behind, in the valley mentioned before, with his men.[1]

[1] *Asp.* ; cf., e.g., ch. 46.

CHAPTER XVI

Karlamagnus and Agulandus Agree to Meet

When the messenger Balam had left Baion, Emperor Karlamagnus called together his leaders and spoke to them in this way, saying, "We have stayed for a while in this place awaiting our troops, but they still have not come. While I am sure that King Agulandus has become aware of our expedition, it is quite unlikely that he is bringing his great army here against us, and in order not to hide ourselves here like foxes in a lair, we should go forward thither, with the guidance of God and St. James."

It was so done: they went, with all the host, from the city, and searched very carefully for Agulandus until they came to a flat, fair valley. In this valley the Frenchmen saw the camp of the heathens, very splendid, with all sorts of different colors. And when Karlamagnus saw that, he gave thanks to almighty God and to St. James, saying, "Praise and glory to you, most sublime God, who have guided us here on the right way to meet with your enemies, with the help of your blessed apostle! I therefore vow to you, Lord, that I shall have a church built to your glory on this plain, if I succeed in purging this land of heathens."

This promise of the emperor was indeed well kept, for later a handsome minster was built there, thanks to the emperor, and consecrated to God's two martyrs Facundus and Primitivus.[1]

Here Karlamagnus had tents pitched, and when this was done he asked his wisest men, Archbishop Turpin and his kinsman Rollant and Duke Milon, how they should now proceed. Archbishop Turpin answers, "Lord," says he, "no one needs to give you advice, but I will tell you mine. It seems to me that it would become you best, and gain the most, to have a conference with the heathen king and find whether he will accept the true faith or give up the land and go home, with

[1] Third-century martyrs; see M-J, 295-296, and Smyser, p. 24, n. 1.

nothing accomplished, to his realm. If he does not wish to accept either of these, our alternative then is to test their valor in battle."

The emperor said it should be so. Men now went to Agulandus with this message.

As soon as Agulandus knew that Karlamagnus had come, he rejoiced and thought that now he would soon gain what he wanted; he ordered all his army to arm itself and prepare for battle as well as possible, saying that now his men would win themselves silver and gold, land and property. And when Agulandus received the message that the emperor asked to meet with him in peace, it seemed likely to him that Karlamagnus was doing this because he wished to submit to his power; he therefore agreed to it.

The men who had taken the message came back to the emperor, and told him what had happened with Agulandus—that he was preparing his army for battle, but had agreed to the meeting. The emperor had his men arm, nor was there any lack of the most splendid armor that anyone might wish to have. The emperor says that they shall ride peacefully to the conference, but be prepared for whatever may arise.

A,a (6)

... There Karlamagnus had established the greatest[2] of churches and consecrated it to God's martyrs Fakunus and Primitibus,[1] and also established there a rich town, where he put a fine monastery ...

(10) ... Now when King Agulandus saw that he would not be able to keep control of the city, he chose to fight against King Karlamagnus, stipulating that King Karlamagnus allow him a truce to prepare his army and to summon those who were nearby to this battle in complete peace.

—But what King Agulandus really wanted was this: he wanted to recognize King Karlamagnus if he should meet him in battle, and therefore wanted a meeting with him. King Karlamagnus agreed to it.

[2] *a*; *A*'s "fairest" is, however, close to the PT's *grandis et decora*; cf. CC *ingens et optima*.

CHAPTER XVII

The Meeting Between Karlamagnus and Agulandus

Now when both were ready, they rode forward towards the plain which lay between the camps. Emperor Karlamagnus rode in front of his host, while Agulandus, on the other side, came straight towards him, for each of them could be easily distinguished from the army by his stature and armor. And as they drew near enough so that each could clearly understand the other's words, Emperor Karlamagnus spoke to Agulandus, saying, "You have given me much to complain of, Agulandus, since, with greedy, wrongful tricks, you have taken from me my lands of Hispania and Gaskunia, killing all the Christians you could, those who wished to flee into my dominion; you have broken down my towns and castles and laid waste with fire and iron to all this land which I had won by the strength of God and St. James, and converted to Christian law."

When Agulandus heard Karlamagnus speak in the language of Arabians,[1] which he himself knew best, he rejoiced greatly, and spoke thus to the emperor: "I ask you, Christian, to tell me why you took that land away from our people, when it never belonged to you or your father, or any of your forefathers."

Karlamagnus answered, "Because almighty God redeemed this land from the power of you heathens, establishing under Christian rule this patrimony of his, of which you robbed him; therefore I was obligated to convert it back into a Christian nation, as well as any other land I could: for all heathen nations ought rightly to bow to our law."

Agulandus then said, "It is most improper for our land to lie under rule of your people, for we have a much more worthy law than you. We honor Maumet, the mighty messenger of God, and obey his com-

[1] *Arabiamenn.*

mandments; thus we celebrate almighty God, who has revealed the future to us in the precepts of Maumet. These we keep and honor, and from them we gain life and power; if you observed them you might be happily surprised."

Karlamagnus then answered, "Truly, Agulandus, you are in error in this faith of yours, for we hold God's commandments, but you hold a false belief. We believe in one God—Father, Son, and Holy Spirit—while you believe in a devil which inhabits your graven images. Our souls come, after bodily death, to everlasting joy, if we hold to the right faith with good works; but the souls of you who trust in graven images go to eternal pain, burning without end in hell itself. It may thus be seen that our law is better than yours. Choose, then, from two alternatives: be baptized, with all your host, and save your life, or come to battle with me, and you shall then find a wretched death."

Agulandus answers, "I shall never allow myself to be baptized and so deny that Maumet is almighty; rather, I shall fight with my people against you and your men, with this stipulation: that that faith which wins the victory shall be judged to be the better, and to that which is victorious be eternal honor, while to that which loses, eternal shame. And if I am conquered alive, I and all my men shall be baptized."

Karlamagnus then answers, "It pleases me very well to have it stand so; but in order that you shall not attribute our victory to human strength rather than to the power of the true faith, this battle shall be conducted in the manner of a duel, so that one goes against one, twenty against twenty, and so on in this way until it is fully proven to you."

Agulandus agreed so to do. Then Karlamagnus sent twenty knights forward against twenty heathens, and the match finished in such a way that all the heathens fell. Next, forty from each side went forth, and again all the heathens fell. Then a hundred rode against a hundred, and things went as before: the heathens fell. At last a thousand rode against a thousand, and most of the heathens fell, but some fled. At this point, all the Christians praised their Lord, as was fitting. But Agulandus came to Karlamagnus to make a truce; he affirmed that it was clearly revealed in this event that Christian law was more valuable than the religion of heathen people, and therefore he agreed to come the next morning and receive the true faith. Thus they part, and each goes to his camp.

A,a (11)

When King Agulandus was ready, he rode out of the city with all his host, and when he had come a little way out of the town, he left his host behind him and rode forward with sixty of the most valiant knights to meet King Karlamagnus. And so soon as they met, King Karlamagnus said, "You have given me much to complain of, if you are Agulandus, who has, by trickery, taken from me my lands of Hispania[2] and Gaskunia, which I had conquered, by God's strength, and converted to Christian law. And you have killed all the Christians who wished to flee into my realm that you could seize. You have broken down my cities and castles and laid waste my land with fire and iron."

And when King Agulandus heard King Karlamagnus speak in the language of the Arabians, which he himself knew best, he rejoiced greatly and said to King Karlamagnus, "I ask you to tell me why you took that land from our people when it never belonged to you, or to your father, or to his father."

King Karlamagnus answers, "Because our Lord, Jesus Christ, maker of heaven and earth, appointed the Christian nations to be over all the nations of the world. It was, therefore, my greatest desire to convert your people to our law."

Agulandus then said, "It is most improper for our nation to be subject to yours, for we have a much more worthy law than you. We honor Maumet, God's messenger, and obey his commandments; and thus we celebrate almighty God, who has revealed the future to us in the precepts of Maumet. These we keep and honor, and from them we gain life and power."

King Karlamagnus answers: "You are in error in this faith, Agulandus, for we hold God's commandments, while you hold the law of a liar. We worship and trust in one God—Father and Son and Holy Spirit—while you believe in a devil which inhabits graven images. After death our souls will go to[3] everlasting joy because of our faith, but your souls shall go to eternal pain in hell. Therefore it may be seen

[2] "and Galicia," *A* only; apparently not in PT.

[3] "mercy and," *a* only, and not in PT.

that our law is better than yours. Now take whichever choice you wish: that you be baptized, with all your host, and save your life,[4] or come to battle with me, where you shall find a wretched death."

King Agulandus answers, "I shall never allow myself to be baptized and so deny that my god[5] Maumet is almighty; rather, I shall fight with my people against you and your nation, with this stipulation: that the faith which wins is best, and to that whichever is victorious be eternal honor, while to that which loses, eternal shame. And if I am conquered alive, I and all my men shall be baptized."

Next, King Karlamagnus sent twenty knights against twenty Saracen knights on the field where the battle was held, and all the heathens fell. Then King Karlamagnus sent forty knights against forty men of Agulandus, and things went as before. Next he sent a hundred knights against a hundred of Agulandus, and when, for the first time, the Christians turned in flight, they all fell because they put more trust in their own military skill than in God's mercy. But next a thousand went against a thousand, and all the Saracens[6] fell.

Then a truce was made, and King Agulandus came to speak with King Karlamagnus; he affirmed that the law of the Christian men was better than that of the Saracens, and therefore he promised that he would be baptized in the morning...

(6)

... And when each of them had come nearer to the other, King Agulandus offered battle to King Karlamagnus, asking him to choose whether he wished to send twenty against twenty, or forty against forty of each troop—or a hundred against a hundred or a thousand against a thousand or two against two or one against one. Karlamagnus then sent a hundred against a hundred knights of King Agulandus, and all the Saracens fell. After that, they each sent two hundred knights, and all the heathens, who were Mauri, fell.

[4] *A* only, but cf. PT *tu et gens tua*.
[5] *A* only, but cf. PT *deum meum*.
[6] *A*, heathens; PT *Sarraceni*.

Then King Agulandus sent two thousand knights against two thousand knights of King Karlamagnus,[7] and some of the knights of Agulandus fell and some fled.[8] On the third day, after King Agulandus secretly sent out his champions,[9] he became quite certain that Karlamagnus had a smaller army than he, and he demanded a battle of the total armies the next day; Karlamagnus agreed to this ...

[7] *a*: "three hundred against three hundred;" PT gives 2000 here.

[8] *a*: "some of them [presumably the knights of Agulandus] fell, and some of the knights of Karlamagnus." *A* follows PT.

[9] I.e., on a spying mission; cf. PT *secrete*.

CHAPTER XVIII

The Second Meeting of Karlamagnus and Agulandus

When Agulandus came to his encampment, he related to those who were there everything that had happened between him and Karlamagnus, and how it had come about that he intended to be baptized; and he told his men to do the same. Many of them agreed, but some refused.

Immediately on the next day, Agulandus went forth to the camp of Karlamagnus and arrived just at the time when he was sitting at table with his troops.[1] And when Agulandus came into the emperor's tent, he looked around the table. All of those of high rank sat with the emperor—bishops, monks, canons, priests, knights,—and he wondered that these people were so variously dressed; he therefore asked the emperor precisely what each one of them was. Karlamagnus explained everything to him, speaking so: "These men whom you see have handsome clothing of one color are bishops and priests, and are called masters of our laws; they absolve us of our sins, through God's mercy, and grant divine blessing. Those whom you see in black clothing are abbots and monks, who pray for us night and day; those who are dressed in white clothing are called canons. Their customs are like those of the former, but they are famous as scholars."

"I did not know of any such," says Agulandus, "nor would I have thought help any the nearer if the like had trailed after me. But tell me now what men those are who sit outermost, on the bare earth, and have before them neither table nor cloth and little food and drink, attired wretchedly in comparison to the others."

Karlamagnus answers, "Those are messengers of our Lord Jesus Christ, and are called special limbs of God. We have as many as thir-

[1] *b*, servants.

teen all told every day at our feast, in remembrance of our Redeemer and the twelve apostles who were with him at the time he was[2] here on earth."

Agulandus then says, "All those who sit up with you, whom you call your men, have enough food and drink and good clothes, but those whom you call God's special men and his messengers, you have sit on the earth far away from you, in shameful condition both as to food and drink and as to clothing. A deed to be wondered at: ill served is their lord, when his messengers are so shamefully received! Therefore I call your law, which you praise and call good, bad; and I would be sorry if I left my former creed to place myself under such a law."

Karlamagnus answers: "Agulandus," says he, "do not let this matter turn aside your good intention, for it is in accordance with godly arrangement, and not contempt for his commands, that poor men should have such food and clothing as they need to live but not be sated with expensive and abundant delicacies nor go in fine clothes: for if that were done, they could not be called poor, and then they would not bear like him the humility the Master himself, and his disciples, deigned to bear in this world. He so arranged things in order that they might keep true humility among the poor, and not pride themselves in great riches and an easy life."

Agulandus would not pay attention to anything like this, asking him, rather, to give him permission to leave, offering to do battle with the whole army against Karlamagnus: then he rides away again to his camp.

But Emperor Karlamagnus made better arrangements for poor men who followed the army thereafter.

Now he ordered his host to prepare their weapons and horses as well as possible. They did so. And when all were well prepared, they thrust their spears down into the plain out before the camp the night right before the battle; but when the Christian men went the next morning, each to take out his spear, many of them had grown bark[3] and the fairest of blooms. All of those who saw this occurrence were much struck with wonder, and attributed it to divine mercy; then they chop-

[2] *B*, fared.

[3] Literally, "bark and birch bark."

ped down the spear-shafts as close to the earth as they could. But it is truly told that from the roots of the chopped-off spear-shafts which stayed behind in the earth, fair groves sprang up, as straight as a shaft, with many[4] branches and lovely leaves that may still be seen. These groves which sprang up from the shafts were mostly of ash, and as many spears bloomed as might suffice for four thousand men.

A,a (11)

... And thus when he came to his army he told the kings and leaders that he wished to be baptized, and told them to do the same; some agreed to that, but some refused.

(12) The next day King Agulandus went to the court of King Karlamagnus, intending to receive baptism there. And when he came before the table of King Karlamagnus, he saw tables prepared, standing there, and men who sat at the tables variously attired. Some were dressed as bishops, according to Christian custom, some dressed as knights; some were in black monk's attire, and some white; some were dressed as secular clergy, and many were clothed in another way, in accord with various habits. Then King Agulandus asked King Karlamagnus closely which man each one was, in his attire. King Karlamagnus says, "Those men who have clothing of one color are priests, and masters of our law; they absolve us of our sins and give us God's blessing. Those whom you see in black cloaks are abbots and monks, more holy than those named before: they pray for us night and day. But those in white clothes are canons, who hold the best rule and sing all the time."

Then King Agulandus saw twelve poor men wearing beggar's clothing, sitting together in one place, on the earth, having neither table nor cloth and little food and drink. And now King Agulandus asked who these wretched creatures[5] might be. Emperor Karlamagnus then answers, "Those are God's people, messengers of our Lord Jesus Christ; we have at our feast every day as many as there were of his twelve[6] apostles with him."

[4] *b*, fair.
[5] *a*, they; not in PT.
[6] *a* only; PT *duodem*.

King Agulandus then said, "All of those who sit up at the table with you are your men, and have good drink , food, and clothing; but those whom you indeed call God's men and his messengers, you have sit on the earth far away from you, shamefully furnished with meat and drink and clothing. Ill served is their lord when his messengers are so shamefully received! I see that the law which you praise is a bad one."

Now he would by no means receive baptism, but, rather, asked to be allowed to take his leave at once, and offered to do battle with King Karlamagnus.[7]

King Karlamagnus now perceived, when King Agulandus would not receive baptism, that poor men, who should be God's messengers, were too poorly provided for.[8] He now took care that they were clothed and fed as well as any in the army.

From this it may be seen that it is a great sin to mistreat poor men.

(6)

... The Christians now readied their weapons for battle. And that evening, before the battle, they stuck their spear-shafts down into the plain out in front of the camp.[9] But early the next day, when the men came so that each could take his spear, all of those who were to fall as martyrs in battle that day found their spear-shafts had grown bark and blossoms. They were filled with wonder by this strange occurrence, and attributed it to God. They then cut off their spears as close to the earth as they could, but from the roots which remained in the earth from the spear-shafts which had been cut, lovely groves sprang up, straight, like shafts, with many branches and fair leaves, which can still be seen there. And these groves which sprang up from these shafts were full of ash trees.

[7] *A*: "'Now I will by no means receive baptism.' And he asked for leave to depart at once, offering to fight him first; and they agreed to a battle." The *a* version is somewhat closer to PT.

[8] *a*: "that Christian men were providing shamefully for poor men, whom they should feed and clothe for God's sake."

[9] *A*: "the doors of the hall:" cf. PT *castra*.

CHAPTER XIX

Balam Comes to the Aid of Nemes

When both the Christians and the heathens had formed their battle ranks, they charged each other with much din and clashing of weapons while horns and trumpets blasted on both sides. Many sharp exchanges of blows could be seen here. Foremost in the host of Karlamagnus rode those who bore the blooming spears which have been described; the Lord God had ordained that all of them should earn the fair crowns of martyrdom on that day. The most important man among them was Duke Milon of Angler,[1] who passed into God's keeping in that battle.

Karlamagnus rode boldly forward into the ranks of the heathens and killed many men with his sword called Gaudiola; but the Saracens so pressed at the emperor that they killed his horse under him. He then defended himself courageously, with two thousand of his men among many Saracens. With the care of God and St. James, however, he returned unscathed to his people.

Many heathens fell on that day, as well as the number of Christians already mentioned. As the day passed by, the battle stopped and everyone went back to his camp. The heathens had then captured the most valiant leader in the host of Karlamagnus, Duke Nemes of Bealfer.[2]

Just then the messenger Balam, who has been spoken of before, was sent by Jamund, who was then staying in the tower, to enquire what was going on between the Christians and the heathens. And when he knew the truth of what had just happened—how Karlamagnus had lost his best horse in the battle and that Nemes, one of the emperor's

[1] *Angeler.*
[2] *Bealfuer.*

greatest champions, was now held prisoner by the heathens—he remembered how well the French had received him and how nobly the emperor had treated him in his court when he was sent there by father and son: thus it seemed to him proper that they be treated with equal courtesy, if he could bring it about; and so he did.

When Agulandus had come into his tent, and Duke Nemes was led before him and doomed by him to suffer death forthwith, Balam comes with his men before Agulandus and speaks so: "Lord," says he, "consider the way in which Karlamagnus dealt with me when I was sent by you. He had the opportunity to have me killed, if he had so wished. Now do as well, to show your own virtue. Let this brave man have his life and send him unharmed back to his people, and let your magnanimity be shown in this."

Agulandus answers, "No, Balam," says he, "it shall not be that this man should be released at your word alone."

Balam then says, "Although you do not wish to give him up for words alone, money shall not be lacking to redeem him. Take as much gold and silver, horses, weapons, and valuable clothing for this man as you yourself wish. If that does not help, know that the blood of many of your men will be shed before this man is slain."

And when Agulandus hears this fine speech, including a firm threat from Balam, he speaks thus: "Take him with you, Balam, and pay us such treasure as you have agreed."

He does so, taking Duke Nemes into his custody, and arranging for goods to be sent to the city, as much as pleased Agulandus: for, though he was now bound to do this, he had brought sufficient wealth with him to ransom a man, however much was demanded—and indeed, he was so well blessed with friends that whatever he wanted was ready to hand. Balam then said to Duke Nemes, "Go to Karlamagnus now and take him my greetings. Since I have heard that he has lost his horse, take with you this white horse which I wish to give him: I do not believe that there is a better one in the heathen host, nor a better one to go into battle with him."[3]

[3] This white horse appears to have been a detail which struck many readers of *Asp*, cf. ch. 54 (where it is derived from a line found in L^2: "a Charlemaine donat le cheval blanc", between the lines which are 5744-45 in *Asp.*), and

Nemes thanks him fittingly for what he has done, and then proceeds to the court of Karlamagnus, to whom he takes Balam's greeting, with the horse, telling of the noble way in which he has behaved to free him. The emperor, delighted to see Nemes, for he had been much distressed by his disappearance, says, "Praise be to God and St. James that you, good friend, are freed from the power of the Saracens—and, if it be their will, I pray that you may never get into such a terrible position again. But it is much to be lamented that so valiant a warrior as Balam should not be acquainted with his Creator."

As they were talking about such matters, word came to the emperor that four counts had come from Rome to their aid, with four thousand of the best knights; they awaited Karlamagnus in Baion. The emperor is now overjoyed at all this—both the release of Nemes and their arrival.

It is to be said of Balam, however, that he departed hastily from the army of Agulandus when Nemes had gone, going to meet Jamund, whom he told what he had learned of the dealings between Christians and heathens.

A,a (6)

... Duke Milon, father of Rollant, won the martyr's palm in this battle, with all those of God's martyrs who had had the blooming spear-shafts, as has just been told. In this battle Karlamagnus lost his horse, and when the emperor was in a dire position, with two thousand Christian foot-soldiers against many thousand Saracens, he drew his sword, which was called Gaudiola,[4] and cut down many of the Saracens in the midst of them. And when both Christians and heathens saw that the day was passing away, they both went home to their tents.

On the next day after this a host came from Rome, four counts[5] with four thousand excellent knights, to the aid of King Karlamagnus ...

references elsewhere, such as that in *La Chevalerie Ogier de Danemarche* (ed. Mario Eusebi; Milan, 1963), 4447-49.

[4] *A*, *Gandiola*; Joyeuse.

[5] *marchisar*, in *a* only.

CHAPTER XX

Karlamagnus Visits Agulandus in Disguise

When Agulandus learned that four leaders with a great host had come to the aid of the emperor, he did not think his situation was as promising as it had been before. He therefore turned his army around and went off to the town which is called Agenna, because he thought he could do better fighting there, against less strength. Although this city of Agenna had strong walls, there was not enough of a force there to withstand attack, so that Agulandus conquered it and established himself and his army there. He then thought he had seized so secure a stronghold that no one was powerful enough to attack its great might and do the least bit of harm; thus he now is so far gone in pride and arrogance that he thinks that everything will go exactly as he wants it to.

He thus sends men to Karlamagnus, offering to give him a great deal of gold and silver if he would give up his kingdom and pay homage to him. When the emperor hears this message from Agulandus, he does not refuse: he says that he will probably come in answer to the message. At that, the messengers return and tell Agulandus that Karlamagnus received their message well; and he rejoices exceedingly at that news, so that now he thinks he will have everything his own way if they meet.

But when the messengers had left, the excellent lord Karlamagnus devised new plans, since, because of the high arrogance which he clearly perceived in this conduct, he saw that this message from Agulandus had been concocted in bad faith. He therefore adopted the counsel God gave him and rode off from the army in secret, with seventy knights, until he came to the top of the mountain which stood near the city of Agenna, from which the city might be clearly seen. Here he dismounted from his horse and removed all his regal clothing, dressing himself in other garments; he took his spear by the handle and laid his shield on his back, preparing himself in every way after the manner of a messenger; with only one knight to accompany him, he then went down from the mountain, where he left his men, telling them to wait there.

Indeed, this expedition[1] of Karlamagnus was based on fearless faith and great trust in God's grace, going with only one other man voluntarily into the hands of his enemies; but he knew that the honor and freedom of holy Christianity depended upon his doing his part readily—and certainly St. James was not far from the emperor at that time when he went boldly forth to the city.

Watchmen ran out of the city towards them at once to ask who they might be. They were told that these were men sent by Emperor Karlamagnus to Agulandus. When the guards had heard this, they led them at once into the hall where Agulandus and his chief men sat, and when they came before the king they greeted him and spoke in this way: "We are sent to you by Karlamagnus. Our errand is to tell you that he has come here, according to his promise, with sixty knights. He wishes to give up his kingdom and become subject to you: therefore he asks you to come to talk with him, bringing sixty knights of your own."

And when Agulandus hears that, he says, "Well have you performed your errand. Tell this to Karlamagnus: he should stay where he is, and I shall certainly come."

The emperor then went out of the city, carefully observing how the city might best be conquered—for that was his primary business in Agenna. Then, leaving the city behind, he returned to his men on the mountain, mounted his horse, and rode as quickly as possible back to his camp. But what could this have been if not the work of God: Karlamagnus spoke to Agulandus and was not recognized by him, although he had seen him shortly before, as has been told. May God be praised for this, and for all the works he daily performs against all probability!

As soon as Karlamagnus had left the city, King Agulandus called together his great army and went with seven[2] thousand knights to the

[1] *b*, plan.
[2] *b*, four.

place where he thought he would find Karlamagnus with only a few men, for he intended to slay the emperor. But when he came to that place his journey was fittingly rewarded; he missed Karlamagnus but revealed his own treachery and bad faith. Thus he returned to the city with shame and disgrace, considerably lower in spirits than before, as was proper; nothing was changed except for the worse, and he must suffer what speedily resulted from his own villainy.

A,a (6)

And when Agulandus knew that, he turned and fled with all his army. King Karlamagnus, however, went home to France with his great host.

(7)

... Now when King Agulandus had conquered the city of Agenna[3] with his great army, he sent a message to Karlamagnus with a few knights[4] and promised to give him sixty[5] horses laden with gold and silver and other riches, too, if he would submit to his rule. He said this because he wanted to learn to recognize King Karl's appearance, so that he could the more easily strike and kill him if it should happen that they met in battle. And, as Karlamagnus understood his false message, he rode from his realm with two thousand of the boldest knights, and set up his camp near the town of Agenna, not more than four miles from the city where Agulandus stayed with his army.

King Karlamagnus then came out secretly from his host up onto a nearby mountain, with sixty knights, so that he could see the city; and there he left these knights behind, together with his royal garments, putting on worse clothes. Laying his shield on his back and without a spear, as it was the custom for the messenger of a leader to go in the

[3] Agen, in Germany.

[4] This phrase is deliberately placed in an ambiguous position because it seems to mean that Agulandus sent a few knights with the message; yet it must be based on PT's statement that Agulandus told Karlamagnus to come with only a few knights.

[5] *A*, forty; PT, sixty.

midst of hostility, he proceeded to the city, taking one knight with him. Now when men came out to meet them from the city and asked them who they were, they said they were messengers to King Agulandus from the great emperor King Karlamagnus.

These men were led into the city and[6] came before King Agulandus; King Karlamagnus and his comrade said:[7] "King Karlamagnus sends us to tell you that he will gladly serve you and that he has come here with sixty knights; he waits for you to come with sixty knights to talk with him peacefully."[8]

And when the king heard this message, he armed himself at once and told them to tell King Karlamagnus to await him. King Agulandus did not know the emperor, though he had spoken with him,[9] while King Karlamagnus could well recognize Agulandus and had considered how best to win the city. He had seen all the kings who were in the town.

He then went up on the mountain to his knights, and returned with them to his host. King Agulandus rode out of the city as quickly as he could, with seven thousand knights, intending to kill King Karlamagnus if he could find an opportunity ...

[6] *A*, "Now when these men, " is more distant from PT.

[7] *A*, "King Karlamagnus said to King Agulandus," but cf. PT *dixerunt*.

[8] *a*'s version is shorter and leaves out the offer to submit to Agulandus, but this is in PT.

[9] *A*, "seen him clearly;" *a* is closer to PT.

CHAPTER XXI

The Battle Between the Kings

As soon as Karlamagnus returned to his tent, he ordered his army to prepare for action at once, and he then made for the city of Agenna. But because it was strongly fortified and was strongly guarded within, he besieged the city for six months without gaining anything; and in the seventh month, when all the machines and devices with which commanders were accustomed to conquer cities and castles had been well and skillfully prepared, the emperor called on St. James the apostle to grant his blessed aid to Christians so that this city might be won to his honor, and to scatter the band of predators who were wrongfully holding it.

Indeed the apostle heard the emperor's prayer, for the Frenchmen waged so vigorous an attack, with the support of the apostle, that to Agulandus there appeared to be no other hope, if he wished to save his life, than to flee from the city with his chief men and all of the host that could escape. And thus he arranged it, fleeing the city at night with all his host, going out through the low, small openings of the city[1] to the town which is called Santun, which he fortified strongly within: he thought all would be well with him now, since he had escaped the attack of the French.

But when Karlamagnus heard that Agulandus had fled from the city he entered victoriously in great state and had all the Saracens who would not receive baptism or become his subjects killed. Karlamagnus stayed in the city a short time before he learned where Agulandus was with his Saracens. He then attacked him with his army and besieged the city. This city of Santun[2] stands very near the river which is called Karant, which ran along one side of the city.

[1] PT *latrinas.*

[2] *b, Samtun.*

The emperor gave Agulandus two choices: either give up the city or fight. Agulandus would rather fight with Karlamagnus than give up the city without a struggle; therefore they both prepare for battle. Agulandus rides out of the city and the emperor rides against him: a violent struggle ensues, with many men falling on both sides. But since the blessed apostle James stood with his own troops, the greatest slaughter befell the Saracens; many of them fell dead, for wherever Rollant and his companions touched with their weapons, bandages were quite unnecessary. The heathens were soon so battered and worn out that they fled back into the city, shutting it after them strongly.

The Christians now set up their camps all around the city, except where the river flowed. And when Agulandus realized he could not hold the city, he fled out at night over the river, since there did not seem to him to be any more acceptable way to escape. But as soon as the French knew of this, they set after him with great force and killed the king of Agabia and the king of Bugie[3] and almost four thousand heathens. Agulandus, however, fled with his host all the way to the city of Pamphilonia, which has been mentioned before. Karlamagnus had had it built up again, and strongly fortified, after the great downfall it had suffered before the attack of St. James, as has been told.

Since Agulandus thought this city much stronger, he decided to stay here. He now sent messengers to the places where he thought he was most likely to get help, for in the third engagement between the French and the Saracens he had lost a great host and many of his champions; he thus summoned a huge army to join him, wherever he might get them. Yet, in his pride, he would not allow anyone to let Jamund know how his affairs had gone, for it seemed to him no little shame if he, so old and mature, should have to accept help from this youth: it seemed preferable to him to try a fourth time and see how dealings went between him and the Christians.

He therefore sent word to Karlamagnus saying that he awaited him in the city of Pamphilonia.

A,a (7)

... but he rode away into his own realm, collected a huge host, and then returned to Hispania, where he went to the city of Agenna and

[3] Literally "King Bugie," but cf. above, A,a 7, at end of Ch. 8.

besieged the town for six months. In the seventh month, King Karlamagnus prepared all the machines and devices with which it was customary for a leader to conquer a city or castle and made a fierce onslaught.

Then King Agulandus, and the kings and leaders who were there with him, fled secretly through the low small openings of the city at night, and thus they escaped the power of Karlamagnus at that time. But the next day King Karlamagnus rode victoriously into the city in great state, and many Saracens were killed then.

(8) King Agulandus now stayed in the city which is called Santunes.[4] When King Karlamagnus heard that, he sought him out and ordered him to give up the town. But he would not give up the city, and offered, rather, to come out of the city and fight against him in such a way that whoever won the battle would hold the city.

On the night immediately before the agreed-on battle, war tents and battle gear were set up on the meadow between the river Karant[5] and the castle which is called Talaburg;[6] there the Christians drove their spears into the plain before their camps, and in the morning those Christians who fell as martyrs in the next day's battle found that their spear-shafts had bark and leaves. These men rode out first the next day, killing many Saracens, and all of them fell, a total of four thousand men.[7]

King Karlamagnus lost his horse there, and when he was on foot in the midst of many heathens, he was helped by his men and killed many people of the Saracens, until, exhausted and defeated, they fled into the city. Now King Karlamagnus set up his camp all around the city, except where the river ran. At last King Agulandus fled out on the river with his army one night.

And as soon as King Karlamagnus became aware of that, he set after him and killed the king of Agabia[8] and the king of Bugia, and almost

[4] PT Sanctonas; "Saintes, city of France, on the route to Compostella," Smyser, p. 123.

[5] PT Charanta; the Charente.

[6] PT Talaburgus; Taillebourg.

[7] Note that while B,b omits the repeated miracle, this number is picked up in B,b chapter 18.

[8] *A, Agapia*; PT Agabia.

four thousand heathens. King Agulandus now fled from Portus Cepheros[9] all the way to the city of Pampilon[10] and sent word to King Karlamagnus to come there to fight with him. As soon as King Karlamagnus heard that, he went back home to his own realm, and now summoned as large a host as could be found in his realm to join him.[11]

[9] *A, Portos Sephereos*; PT portus Cisereos; Port de Cize, a pass through the Pyrenees.

[10] Another spelling for Pamplona.

[11] The Norse translator is not to be blamed for the repetitiousness of this chapter: he is simply following PT.

CHAPTER XXII

The Pope Joins Karlamagnus

Emperor Karlamagnus is now in the city of Santun, where he hears where Agulandus had fled and that he is collecting a great host; and since the holy apostle James has gathered to himself many of the French from the army which followed the emperor to Hispania, he sends messengers to Rome asking that the apostolic lord pope himself raise an expedition from Rome to save holy Christianity in Hispania, with the greatest muster of troops he could get in France. He offered to free all the serfs and bondsmen in France, with their families, from all thralldom; those who were in bonds or prisons were released and given their freedom, while those who had before earned the emperor's displeasure and fallen out with him, he offered to take back into his favor. Similarly, all evil-doers and robbers were offered truce and grace, if they would give up their former ways and follow God's knights; he offered to give back the patrimonies of those who had forfeited them, and made the poor wealthy, and with urgent messages to come forward, he summoned to this expedition both friend and foe, natives and aliens,[1] learned and ignorant, young men and old, promising that they would receive appropriate[2] rewards from him as well as an eternal reward from God himself, since it should indeed be that with divine strength and their help, he might easily overcome God's enemies in Hispania.

And as soon as this proclamation of the emperor reached the lord pope, he gladly agreed to the emperor's request, and, quickly making it known all over Italy, gathered into his train many citizens of Rome itself, of whom the leader was the prefect[3] Constantinus. The lord pope

[1] *B* only, but cf. A,a.

[2] *b*, great.

[3] *B, prospectus.*

took with him the relic of the Lord's cross which was most honored and worshipped in Rome itself, intending to have it at hand to help the Christians. He then left Rome with a splendid following, as was suitable for such a lord.

Many leaders joined the pope's train every day, for as soon as they heard the emperor's message each one prepared himself and his host as quickly as he could. Thus the lord pope travelled on, until he and his retinue approached the emperor, who, when he became aware of the approach of the apostolic lord, praised almighty God and rode out of the city where he and his host were staying to meet the pope and welcome him, with great affection and gladness; he led him to his tent with great pomp and rejoicing, telling him all that had passed between himself and Agulandus up to that time.

When all of the emperor's army came together in one place, it was such a great multitude that, as is truly written, this army covered the earth for two days' journey in length and breadth[4] and for a distance of twelve miles one could hear the noise of men and neighing[5] of horses. With all of this army, the emperor made for Pamphilonia. First went the leader who was called Arnald of Berid[6] with his host, and next earl Eystult[7] with his army. After that was Arastagnus,[8] king of Brittania; then Reinald[9] de Albaspina with his train; next, Gundebol,[10] king of the Frisians, with his troop; then Oddgeir the Dane; and then all the other leaders, one after another with the Emperor Karlamagnus and the lord pope, with the main army, last.[11]

When Karlamagnus came to Pamphilonia, he wished first to find out whether Agulandus would give up the city, and if not, he offers to do battle with him. Agulandus chooses battle, asking however, that

[4] Latter in *B* only, but cf. A,a.
[5] *B*, pacing.
[6] Cf. *a*, *Berit*.
[7] *b*, *Eistul*.
[8] *B*, *Aragstanus*.
[9] *B*, *Arinald*.
[10] *B*, *Gundilber*.
[11] Note that this list differs from that in *A* in including Reinald, but not Constantin[us] and Engeler.

Karlamagnus wait a short time while he made his army ready to fight, and he was granted this.

The emperor arranged his army in five battle ranks, and made Arnald of Berid leader of the first rank. The emperor had a greater, and better prepared, host than the heathens; therefore Agulandus divided his army into four ranks. It is said that he had a hundred thousand men, while the Christians had a hundred thousand thirty-three.

A,a (9)

King Karlamagnus now offered to free all the serfs in France, with all their families, if they would go on this expedition to Hispania with him. And for this expedition he released men who were confined in dungeons and gave money to those who had been destitute; he pardoned evil-doers and restored the inherited property of those who had forfeited it. And of those who were well-armed and skilled in fighting he made knights, and those whom he had justly cast out of his service and friendship he restored to their former offices. And, with urgent word to go forth, he called for this expedition with him both friends and enemies, natives and aliens, in order that he might the sooner destroy God's enemies in Hispania.

When this army was now gathered together, Archbishop Turpin absolved the troops from all their sins and gave them his blessing. King Karlamagnus now began his journey to Hispania against King Agulandus ...

(10)

This army came together in the place called Borddal.[12] The ground the army covered was two days' journey in both length and breadth, and for a distance of twelve miles one could hear the neighing of horses and the noise of their harnesses. Arnald of Bernald[13] was the first to travel out through Portos Cisereos[14] to Pampilon, and earl Eystult

[12] Bordeaux.

[13] *a, Bernind.*

[14] *a, Portus cisterios.*

went after him with his host; next went Oddgeir, king of the Danes, with his host, and Constantin, duke of Rome, with his host; next, King Arastang, and Duke Engeler, with his host; and next, King Gandebol, with his host. King Karlamagnus himself went last, with all the main army. And when King Karlamagnus arrived at the city of Pampilonia, he ordered King Agulandus to give up the city (for he had built up the city again after its destruction, and fortified the castle), or come out of the city and hold battle with him ...

(13)

The next morning both armies came to the appointed field to battle, on the same terms that have been specified. King Karlamagnus had one hundred thousand, and thirty thousand, and four thousand, while King Agulandus had one hundred thousand. The Christians divided themselves into four ranks, but the Saracens[15] into five[16] ...

[15] *A,* heathens; PT *Sarraceni.*

[16] PT: *erat exercitus [Karoli] .c. triginta quatuor milia et exercitus Aigolandi .c. milibus,* Smyser; M-J, C.XXX.IIII *milibus.*

CHAPTER XXIII

The Victory of Karlamagnus

Now when Karlamagnus had arranged his divisions as he wished, he encouraged the army with many words, urging each and every one of them to strive like a good warrior and win for himself at once both wealth in this world, with honor and fame, and an eternal reward without end from the King of Kings. Next, the lord pope stepped forward and blessed all the host, promising that all of those who went bravely forward under the emperor's banner would receive forgiveness of their sins if they gave up their lives and bodies into the power of almighty God and his blessed apostle James,[1] for whose sake this army had come together in this place; all of them agreed to do so as they were urged.

As soon as Agulandus had prepared his army, he at once rode out from the city onto a flat plain. Now might be heard tumult and great din of weapons, for neither side forbears to blast the trumpets and shrilling horns, shouting loud war-cries, so that the earth all around shook, far and wide, as they met. Arnald of Berid made the first charge in this battle; with his troop, he rode courageously forward against the foremost division of Saracens. He was the most gallant of men, and all of his troop was especially well equipped, both as to weapons and as to clothing.[2] Thus he struck on both sides as soon as the armies met, riding right through the midst of the crowd of heathens, dealing death to many men; and so sharply did he press forward with his troop that soon they broke through the first rank of Africans. Another division of the host of Agulandus then rode against them and withstood them for a short time before they went the same way as the first rank.

[1] At this point a lacuna in *b* begins and *B* is thus the only basis for the B,b version of the next fourteen chapters.

[2] I.e., armor.

When Agulandus saw his men undergo such a great defeat, he became extremely angry and sent all his host into the battle at once. But the Frenchmen, seeing this, had no desire to hold back from the attack and held the field of battle courageously, so that they surrounded the heathens with their army and killed many of them, hewing with swords, laying about with spears, cutting down one after another as if they were saplings, until a great fear came over Agulandus: he saw the Christians make a great advance in the battle, and all the field covered with the bodies of his men, while those that still lived quivered and quaked with fear, each one preparing to flee away as far as he can go. Thus he sees there is nothing else to do but to try to escape. And so he does, fleeing with the small troop that was able to follow him to his ships, sailing to Africa with little honor and great dread. He is well content to let his son Jamund try his prowess against the Frenchmen now, and so he settles in the city called Visa[3] with his queen and other followers.

But as soon as the French know of the flight of the heathens, they follow them boldly and kill so many that few are able to escape: so much blood was shed that day that it was ankle-deep. King Altomant and Ebraus of Sibil fled away with a small troop and hid in the nearby mountains; some looked for help to the city of Pamphilonia, taking shelter there, but that did not help them much: when the battle came to an end, Karlamagnus went into the city and had every son of the Saracens he could find killed.

After this battle and the splendid victory which God and St. James granted to Karlamagnus, he went with his army to the bridge of Argus, where he camped for the night. But during that night certain men, without the emperor's knowledge, went stealthily back, out of greed, to the place where the dead lay and took for themselves great loads of gold and silver, which lay in plenty on the fields, and other treasures; and when they were on their way back, they were taken by surprise by the two kings named before, Ebraus and Altomant, with

[3] *Asp.* Rise, Reggio. — Auberi de Trois-Fontaines, writing in 1227-81, says that Charles advanced to ***Regium*** in Calabria, where Roland, after being armed as a knight, killed the Saracen *Eadmundus* and Charles his father *Aigolandus*, with "Gerardus de Frado" in his army. Quoted in Louis, p. 134.

the Saracens who had escaped, who attacked them and killed them all, so that nearly a thousand Christians fell there. The heathens were well pleased with their work and rode off in the night, and did not stop until they came to Corduba.

But when the emperor learned what had happened, he was displeased over this expedition, for, because of the foolishness and greed of his men, the Saracens had hewn a great gap in their flock.

A,a (13)

... Now when the first divisions met, the Christians quickly triumphed over the Saracens. The second divisions then went forward, and the same thing happened. And when the Saracens saw such a great defeat of their men, they came out of the city to the battle with all their men, but Karlamagnus encircled them completely with his army. Arnald of Bernald was the first to attack, with his army, and hacked his way into the middle of the heathen host; he struck on either side with great might and did harm to many men. There was great howling and uproar on both sides then and the Christians went at the heathens with all their might, killing so many that few escaped. King Agulandus fled, and so did the king of Sibil [and] King Astumaior of Korduba, with a small troop. So much blood was shed on that day that it was ankle-deep, and the power of our Lord Jesus Christ and the holy faith[4] was so revealed in this battle, for it won honor in the triumph of the Christians while the Saracens were destroyed in this victory.

After this battle[5] King Karlamagnus went with his army to the bridge of Argua,[6] where he camped for the night. But during that night certain Christian men, without the knowledge of King Karlamagnus, went to the place where the dead lay, and took there gold and silver and all sorts of treasures, as much as they could carry, and then turned back towards their camp. Astumaior of Korduba was hiding in the mountains with his fleeing host, on the way taken by these Christians; he saw their expedition now and came upon them unawares with the Saracens, and killed them all; not one escaped. A thousand men fell there.

[4] *a*; "the power of our faith."
[5] *a*, and victory.
[6] PT Arga; Puente la Reina.

CHAPTER XXIV

About Divine Providence

The day after that battle which the excellent lord Emperor Karlamagnus waged against Agulandus, who had now fled away to his own lands from Hispania, the emperor heard that a leader from Nafaria who was called Furra had come to the bottom of the mountain which the people of that land call Garzdin. This leader wanted one thing: to attack Karlamagnus and do battle with him, for when Furra heard that the emperor had come into Galicia, he was afraid that he might attack his kingdom of Nafaria. He had, therefore, assembled a host and intended to seek out Karlamagnus and vanquish him in battle, if things went as he wished.

When the emperor heard that, he set out with his army for the mountain, bidding Furra to surrender to his rule. He, however, offered to fight against him. Thus both sides prepared for battle. But on the night before the battle the emperor kept watch in his tent, and he devoutly prayed to God and the holy apostle James that he might win victory in this battle; and also he prayed that God show, with a sign of his grace, how many of the Christians would suffer death from the heathens in this strife. And almighty God miraculously revealed himself in answer to this prayer of the emperor, for in the morning, when the army was prepared, the mark of a red cross was visible over the armor on the shoulders of those men whom Divine Providence destined to die.

And when Emperor Karlamagnus saw the holy mark, so that it might not be concealed how many must fall before the enemy's weapons if they came into battle, he wished to try to see whether the situation might be changed if another plan was adopted, and he had all who were marked with this sign gathered together in his chapel and locked them inside it; then he went to battle against the men of

Nafaria. And, to tell of their dealings quickly, Furra fell, and four thousand heathens with him, but none of the Christians.[1]

But when evening fell, the emperor turned back to his camp and unlocked the dwelling in which the knights were shut: there he saw Divine Providence splendidly fulfilled, for those who had been placed there hale and strong in the morning were all now found dead when he returned. In this event it was revealed that none may pass by the hour of death appointed for him by God.

Karlamagnus then conquered Nafaria, with the districts which lie around it.

A,a (14)

On the next day King Karlamagnus heard that a leader from Nafar was at the mountain of Garzin[2] who above all wanted to fight with him. Thus, when King Karlamagnus came to the mountain of Garzin, they agreed to hold battle the next day.[3] The night before battle King Karlamagnus prayed God to show him by a sign which men were to fall in the battle. And when all the army of King Karlamagnus was prepared for battle, a red cross-mark was seen over the armor on the shoulders of those men who were fated to die. When King Karlamagnus saw that, he had all these men shut in his chapel,[4] thinking to save their lives thus, in that they would not fall in the battle. What happened showed that the ways of God are hidden. Karlamagnus won the victory, and four thousand men of Nafar and Saracens fell there;[5] but when King Karlamagnus came back to the camp, they found the hundred and fifty of their men whom King Karlamagnus had left shut up in his chapel, and they were all dead.

Karlamagnus conquered the town at the mountain of Garzin[6] and all Nafar with it.

[1] The latter phrase indicates that the source here is the abridged PT; cf. Smyser, p. 32.

[2] Here, *Garthin*; PT Garzin; Montjardin. From this point until after the next mention of the mountain's name, *A* only.

[3] *a* now makes up for its gap by adding "when King Karlamagnus had come to the mountain." A's sequence parallels that of PT.

[4] Here, A,a translates as *kapella*, while *B* uses the Lat. *oratorium*.

[5] Again, *B* seems to be following PT more closely.

[6] *a, garthin.*

The Battle with Ferakut: an episode omitted in B

A,a 15-22

(15) Soon after that Emperor[1] Karlamagnus was told that a giant from Kuerna[2] of the clan of Goliath had come from Siria[3] to the city of Nager,[4] with twenty thousand Turks[5] and Armenians.[6] He was called Ferakut[7] and was sent by Ammiral[8] of Babilonia[9] against King Karlamagnus; he feared neither missile nor spear and had the strength of forty strong men. Because of this, King Karlamagnus went at once to the city of Nager. And when Ferakut learned of his coming, he came out of the town to meet King Karlamagnus and demanded that a knight be sent against him in single combat. As this procedure seemed fitting to them, King Karlamagnus sent out Oddgeir the Dane to do single combat against the giant. But when the giant saw him, he went up to him blithely, embraced him and all of his weapons with his right arm, and, taking him up lightly under his arm,[10] carried him into the city as if he were a gentle sheep.

Next, King Karlamagnus sent Reinald[11] of Albaspania into single combat. And as soon as the giant came up to him, he took lord Reinald under his other arm, carried him into the town, and cast him into prison. Two lords were sent next, Constantin of Rome and earl Eleon;[12] but Ferakut took them both under his arms and thus carried

[1] *a*, King.

[2] This locality does not appear to be in any ms. of PT, at least in the corresponding chapter. Elsewhere, in a list omitted in *Kms.*, *Crunia*, La Coruna, is mentioned, and it is conceivable that this is intended; but this is only a desperate conjecture.

[3] Syria.

[4] PT Nagaras; Nájera, in Spain.

[5] *Tyrkir*.

[6] *Armeniar*; not in PT.

[7] Here, *Ferakuth; a, Ferakurtt*, passim; PT Ferracutus.

[8] *a*, the king; PT *Admirandus*, i.e., Emir.

[9] Babylon.

[10] *A*: "he received him in a fine embrace, took him up lightly under his right arm;" *a* is closer to PT here.

[11] *A, Reinbald*.

[12] *a, Elon*; PT Oellus, Hoël.

them into the town and cast them in prison. After that the emperor sent twelve[13] men to fight with the giant, two at a time, but he[14] cast them all into prison.

And when King Karlamagnus had seen these dealings, he did not want to risk any more of his men against the giant's strength. Rollant now asked for leave to fight with the giant, and with much difficulty received permission from King Karlamagnus.

(16) Now when lord Rollant and the giant met, the giant picked him up in his right hand and put him on his horse in front of him, intending to take him thus back into the town. But when Rollant regained his strength and trust in almighty God, he grasped the giant by the chin[15] and managed to pull the giant over the back of the horse; they both fell off the horse onto the earth. But when they got to their feet they leapt onto their horses. Rollant drew his sword, intending to kill the giant, but instead chopped his horse right down the middle. Now the giant stood on his feet, with sword in hand,[16] and threatened Rollant with terrible blows. Rollant then cut at the giant's sword arm so hard that the sword fell out of the giant's hand, but he still was not wounded. Now when the giant had lost his sword, he struck Rollant's horse on the brow with his fist so that the horse died at once. And when they were both standing on their feet, they fought with fists and stones until the hour of nones,[17] when Ferakut asked for a truce until the morning.

(17) In the morning they both came to the battlefield unarmed, as they had previously agreed.[18] Ferakut had his sword with him, but that did not help him much when Rollant had the giant's permission to hit him with the crooked stick he had brought to the battlefield with him, and to pelt him with balls of stones, of which there was supply enough lying there. But his blows did not harm the giant, who stood there un-

[13] PT twenty.

[14] *a*: "the giant did as before and ..."

[15] *A*, neck; PT *per mentum*.

[16] *A* only, but corresponds to PT *spatamque ... manu tenens*.

[17] Presumably three p.m.

[18] PT is clearer here: the agreement was that they would come without horses and spears.

protected until midday; then he began to get sleepy, and asked Rollant to give him a truce to sleep for a while. And, since Rollant was young in years, and lively, and courteous in all his manners,[19] he picked up a stone and laid it under the head of the giant, so that he might sleep more calmly than before.—Indeed, King Karlamagnus had ordered that the rules which Christian men and heathens set down between them should be firmly kept, so that no one took a life when a truce was in effect; therefore no one dared to do any harm to the giant while he slept.

(18) But when Ferakut woke up, Rollant sat by him and asked him how it was that he was so strong and hardy that he was not harmed by weapons,[20] stones, or cudgel. The giant answered in the language of Hispania,[21] which Rolland understood: "I cannot be wounded except in the navel." And, as he looked at Rollant, the giant then said, "Of what race do you come, that you fight with such strength?"

"I am," said Rollant, "of the French nation."

Ferakut asked, "What is the faith of the French?"[22]

Rollant answered, "By God's grace, we hold the Christian faith, and the precepts of Jesus Christ; it is for his faith that we fight against heathen people."

And when the giant heard the name of Christ, he then asked, "Who is this Christ in whom you believe, or what is he?"

Rollant answered, "Son of God the Father, born of a virgin, he suffered on the cross, and, having harrowed Hell, he rose up from the dead on the third day after his passion; and on the fortieth day he ascended into Heaven, and now he sits at the right hand of God the Father."

Ferakut then said, "We believe that the maker of heaven and earth is one god,[23] having neither father nor son; and as he was begotten by no

[19] This phrase may be of significance in determining the ms. tradition behind the translation; cf. Foote, "Note ...," p. 140.

[20] *A*, iron, is not quite as close to PT *gladium*.

[21] This would seem to be Arabic.

[22] *A*, that nation; PT *Franci*.

[23] Most of this sentence is missing in *a*; *A*'s version is very close to PT.

one, so he begot no one, and he is thus one god, not three."

Rollant answers, "You say truly that he is one god, but your faith is unsound in that you do not believe that he is one god but also threefold. If you believe in God the Father, then believe in the Son and the Holy Spirit, three persons."

Ferakut said, "If you call the father god, and the son god, and the holy spirit god, then you are saying there are three gods—which cannot be—rather than one god."

Rollant said, "I do not say that: rather, I believe in one God in Trinity. There are three persons in the godhead, co-eternal and equal,[24] separate persons in unity, and eternal in power. The angels in heaven worship God the Three in One, as Abraham saw three angels and bowed to one of them."

(19) The giant said, "Show me how three things can be one thing!"

Rollant answered, "I can show you that in earthly things: as there is in one harp, when it is struck, three elements—skill, strings and hand—so there is in the godhead Father, Son, and Holy Spirit, one God; and as one almond consists of shell, skin, and kernel, so there are three persons in the godhead, one God. In you yourself there are three parts—body, limbs, and soul, yet you are one man: so you may see in the godhead unity and trinity."

Ferakut said, "I now understand how God can be one and three, but I do not see how he could beget a son."

"Do you believe," said Rollant, "that God created Adam?"

"Certainly I believe that," said the giant.

Rollant then said,[25] "As Adam was begotten by no one, yet had children, so was God the Father begotten by no one, yet he begot his Son divinely himself, according to his will, surpassing that which any earthly tongue could tell."

The giant said, "What you say pleases me well,[26] but that God became man I can by no means believe."

[24] These adjectives missing in *a*, but they translate PT *coaeterne, coaequales*.

[25] *a* only.

[26] *a* only; PT *Placet mihi quae dicis.*

Rollant answered, "That same God who created heaven and earth out of nothing, could, through his Holy Spirit, arrange that his Son take on humanity, in human flesh, without human seed."[27]

The giant said, "I am now trying to understand how God's Son might be born of the womb of a maiden, without the presence of a man."

Rollant answers, "God himself made Adam without the seed of another man, and he, the same God, let his Son be born of a maiden without the presence of a man; and as God's Son was begotten of a Father without a mother, so he was born of a mother without a human father, and such a conception was fitting and suitable for God."

(20) The Giant said, "I very much wonder how a maiden might beget a child."

Rollant answered, "Maggots and[28] fishes, birds and bees, and many other creeping things come to be and take life from flesh or wood, or from some other secret matter, by divine power, without any seed of their own kind; so might a pure maiden by God's will, without man's seed, give birth to both God and man."

"It may well be," says the giant, "that he was born of a maiden; but by no means could he die on the cross, if he is, as you say, God's Son."

Rollant answers, "Since God's Son was born as man, he died as man, for all that exists and is born in this world must needs die; and if you believe in the Nativity, then you must believe in the Passion, Death, and Resurrection."

a (21) "How can I believe in his resurrection?" said Ferakut.

"Because," said Rollant, "God's Son was born to die and on the third day after, to rise again."

Now when the giant heard these words, he wondered greatly, and said to Rollant, "Why do you want to tell me so many things that come to nothing? It is impossible for a dead man to live again."

[27] *a*, presence; PT *semine*.

[28] Here several pages are missing in *A* ; *a* is thus the only source for the rest of this episode.

"Not only," says Rollant, "did the Son of God himself rise from the dead, but, indeed, all men shall rise from the dead, all who have lived from the very beginning until the end of the world; and they shall then receive the reward for their deeds, whether good or ill, before the judgment seat of God. That same God who causes a great tree to grow from a little root, and makes a tiny grain of wheat rotting in the earth to come back to life and produce fruit, shall also cause a man's skin and bone, rotten and turned to dust, to be revived and live again, joined with the soul and spirit which the body had before, at the Last Judgment. Consider the remarkable nature of the lion; if it revives its dead young with its breath on the third day after their birth, it should not seem wonderful to you that God the Father himself raised up his Son on the third day after death. And it is nothing new that God's Son rose from death, for many men rose from the dead before his Resurrection: and if God permitted Elia[29] and Eliseus[30] to raise men from death, then you can see how freely he could raise his own Son from the dead. And Our Lord Jesus Christ, who raised up dead men himself, could easily rise from death, for death could not hold him; death fled from his face, and at his bidding a multitude of dead men rose."

Then the giant said, "I understand what you have said now, but I do not see how he could go back to Heaven."

"That same one," said Rollant, "who could easily come down from Heaven, could easily return up to Heaven. Take example from many earthly matters: a mill-wheel, turning over, climbs up as easily as down; a bird flies in the air as easily up as down;[31] so God's Son ascended easily, after death, to where he had been before. The sun came

[29] Elija.

[30] Elisha; the reference is to *I Kings* 17: 17-24 and *II Kings* 4: 32-37.

[31] Mandach (p. 292) sees the references in this episode to the mill and the lion reviving its cubs (above) as evidence that this was added at Vézelay: "Or on voit, sur la façade de l'abbatiale de Vézelay, une représentation du moulin mystique, du lion mystique, etc." However, J. C. Payen, reviewing de Mandach's book in *Romance Philology*, 17 (1963) points out that there is no mill on the façade: a mill on a capital in the nave symbolizes, he says, the continuity between the Old and New Testaments; nor does he find an example of a lion revivifying its young among the numerous lions at Vézelay (p. 484).

up in the east yesterday, and went down in the west, and the same shall happen today."

(22) Then Ferakut said, "Now I want to fight you, with this stipulation: if I am vanquished, then your faith is better than mine, but if you are vanquished, then our faith is better; and the victory of either of us shall bring glory to his people, while the vanquished shall win eternal disgrace."

Rollant agreed to this. They began to fight together. The giant struck at Rollant with his sword, but he dodged to the left and warded off the blow with his staff. Now, as the staff was cut in two, the giant could get at Rollant easily and got him down on the ground under him. And when Rollant realized that he could not escape from under the giant, he called upon the Son of God himself and the blessed Maria to help him. At once, by the gift of God, he was somewhat revived, and, rolling about under the giant, he had the grace to grasp the giant's sword in his right hand, and struck it into his navel, and left him so.

The giant cried out in a loud voice, saying, "Maumet, Maumet, my god—for I am dying now."[32] At that cry from the giant, the Saracens ran to him quickly, and carried him into the town.

But Rollant returned to his men unharmed. The Christians followed the Saracens who were bearing the giant into the town, attacking violently, and soon won the city and the castle; then all the champions of King Karlamagnus were taken out of the prison.

[32] *a* had apparently omitted a rather essential phrase; cf. PT *Mahumet, Mahumet, Deus meus, succurre mihi, quia iam morior.*

CHAPTER XXV

An Attack and a Defense

A little time later, when the two kings Ebraus and Altomant, who had escaped from the last battle that Karlamagnus waged against Agulandus, had come into the city of Corduba, as was said before, they decided to avenge the disgrace which Agulandus had undergone before Karlamagnus; therefore, they gathered together a great host of heathen peoples and powerful kings. There were so many more of them because[1] they did not trust in fighting against the emperor by themselves; for this reason, to make their will firm, each one made himself as strong as he could, gaining courage to fight with him. Thus these kings sent word to Karlamagnus that they awaited his arrival at the city of Corduba.

As soon as the emperor heard this he turned his army in that direction; and when he came close to the city, the kings came out to meet him with three thousand of their troops. In the front of their host they put foot-soldiers, dressed very wonderfully: they had long black beards and their heads were covered with horns and were hideous in every way, so that they were more like devils or other dreadful monsters than like men. Each of these had in his hands great pipes and hollow drums, with small, shrill tinkling bells.[2] Thus they awaited the emperor.

As soon as he came as near as seemed suitable, he divided his army into three divisions, setting up a first division of the bravest, youngest men, with good horses; the second he made of foot-soldiers, the third of knights. And as the first division of each side came together, these heathens took up their duties, running in front of the French with great outcries, whistling, bellowing, cursing, and all sorts of dreadful

[1] ? Literally, 'that'.

[2] I.e., tambourines.—On the possible significance of the use of words meaning 'tambourine' and the like, cf. Foote, *The Pseudo-Turpin* ..., pp. 42-43.

sounds—striking on their drums, shaking the tinkling bells, blowing on horns and pipes and beating the tambourine. When the horses of the Christians heard such a cursed noise from these monsters and saw their terrifying appearance, they started to gallop away at once and fled as if they were mad and in a frenzy, so that the riders could not by any means turn them back to the battle. The enemies made so great a noise that each and every man mounted on a horse was now impelled to flee: so frightful a din, tumult and uproar was made by these cursed limbs of the enemy that it seemed nothing like it had ever been heard before.

But there is no need to describe this further here; the heathens thus drove the three divisions of Karlamagnus so that no one was so worthy or great that he could make any resistance. Thus the Saracens chased the French like other fugitives up onto a mountain which stands two miles away from the city. The Christians then prepared to defend it, if the heathens wanted to attack them. And when the Saracens saw this, they turned back into the city.

The Christians then set up camp on the mountain and remained until the next day. But God and St. James had so well watched over their men that no one lost his life that day before the heathens. Early in the morning, the emperor called together his wisest counsellors and asked what their advice now was. But they all said that there did not seem to them to be many expedients; however, they all said they would gladly hear what he wished to do. The emperor ordered that all the mounted men in the army have the heads of their horses wrapped in linen cloths so that they could not see the strange, ugly spectacle of the monstrous Saracens; he also ordered "that you stop the ears of your horses with wax or something else, so that they will not hear the noise and terrible uproar of the heathens."

And when this had been done, the Christians rode boldly down from the mountain towards the Saracens, who were delighted at that; they expected to deal with the Frenchmen in the same way as on the day before. But it did not fall out that way for them, for although they had their monsters run out in front, making the worst noise that they possibly could, the horses of the Christians withstood their hubbub well. A great battle now began, for it pleased the Frenchman to strike with their weapons as soon as they could; to repay boldly what seemed to them a fit reward to the heathens, bearing in mind how they had been forced to flee the day before, they had not any intention of sparing either head or trunk of the heathens, if God gave them a chance this second time.

A great many of the Saracens now fell and everyone who could escaped from the dealings of the Frenchmen and thronged about the heathen standard, which was arranged in this way: a very well-appointed wagon stood in the middle of the army, before which there were eight oxen; there rose up from the wagon a red banner with high standard.[3] It was the custom of the Saracens not to flee from battle while they saw the banner standing, and when the emperor learned that he rode before the heathen army, strengthened by the power of God, on the white horse which Balam had sent to him. He cleared an ample way for himself all the way to the standard, and, swinging his good sword at the wagon, cut the standard apart; the standard now fell down, of course, and he then returned to his troops.

But at the moment when the Saracens saw their standard fall down, they became alarmed and fled without any delay. The Christians, however, followed them, with terrible cries, and each of them felled one heathen after another, so that that day they killed eight thousand heathens, as well as the king of Sibil. But Altomant went into the city of Corduba with two thousand, closing all the gates after him.

The morning after, however, he said to his men that they should give themselves into the power of the emperor and become his subjects: and they all agreed to this, because now there was no other hope. Altomant then gave up the city to Karlamagnus, with the understanding that he would then hold the city in fief to the emperor, as long as Altomant lived, and that he would support the emperor in all things he could. And thus it was. Now, we have spoken for a while of how the dealings went between Karlamagnus and Agulandus; we shall hear next a little of what went on in the other part of Hispania at this time.

a (23

A little later, King Karlamagnus was told that Ebraham, king of Sibil, and Altumant, who had flown from the battle at Pampilon[4] as

[3] The description of this wagon has been taken as a crucial clue to the dating of PT; cf., e.g., M-J pp. 72 and 308, Smyser, p. 35, n. 1.

[4] *Pampilun.*

has been said, awaited him at the city of Corduba, wishing to do battle with him; they had gained reinforcements from seven cities: Sibil, Granant,[5] Satin,[6] Dema,[7] Verben,[8] Dabola,[9] Baena.[10] King Karlamagnus turned with all his armies in their direction. And when he came close to the city of Corduba, these kings, with their army, came out to meet him for three miles out of the city, prepared to fight. King Karlamagnus then arranged his army into three divisions, putting his best men in the first division; the second division consisted of foot-soldiers, and the third was led by knights. The Saracens arranged their army in the same way.

And when the first divisions met, there went in front of the Saracens' division many kinds of foot-soldiers strangely dressed in a Saracen way, horned, and like devils, sharply striking tambourines. And when the horses of our men heard the cries and tumult of these monsters and saw their savage appearance, they broke into a gallop and fled as if they were maddened and frenzied so that the riders could not turn them back to the battle. The same defeat befell the two divisions of our men behind. The Saracens became very joyful, and drove our men as fugitives up a high mountain two miles from the city. The Christians then prepared to use the mountain as a stronghold, and made ready to defend it if the heathens should try to come up; but when the Saracens saw this they turned back.

The Christians set up camp there and remained until the next day. That morning King Karlamagnus consulted with all his champions and it was decided that all the riders in the army should have the heads of their horses wrapped with cloth, so that they could not see the ugly strange spectacle of the Saracens. Then they were to stop the ears of their horses so that the horses could not hear the Saracen tambourines.

And when the army was prepared in this way, the Christians fought against the Saracens from the sun's rising until mid-day and felled a

[5] Granada.
[6] PT Sativa; "Játiva, city of Spain," Smyser, p. 123.
[7] PT Denia.
[8] PT Ubeda.
[9] PT Abula; Avila?
[10] PT Baecia; Baeza.

great host of them, since the horses of our men neither heard the noise[11] of the tambourines nor saw the monstrous appearance of the Saracens. Then as the Saracens came together in a host, there was in the midst of their band a wagon, pulled by eight oxen, and there rose up from this a red banner on a tall standard. It was the custom of the Saracens not to flee from battle while this banner stood.

When King Karlamagnus learned this he armed himself with invincible weapons and, strengthened by divine powers, went into the troop of Saracens, pushing them away from him on both sides, until he came to the wagon and chopped the standard apart with his sword. The Saracens then burst into flight and fled hither and thither; a great cry went up in the armies and eight thousand of the Saracens fell. The king of Sibil fell there, but King Altumant went into the city, with two thousand Saracen knights, closing all the gates behind them.

The next day, however, he gave up the city to King Karlamagnus, with the understanding that he would receive baptism and hold the city in fief to King Karlamagnus.

[11] *gnegg*; C-V cites this instance in defining the word as 'neighing', but it clearly applies to the noise made by the tambourines rather than the horses.

CHAPTER XXVI

Jamund Harries the Countryside

Now we shall return to Jamund, the son of Agulandus. A short time after he had parted from his father and gone to dwell in the tower, he had sent the messenger Balam to Agulandus to find out what was happening there, as the saga has told earlier. When Balam returned and told Jamund what he had learned, Jamund had no desire to stay any longer in that same place with the great host that was with him. He therefore divided his troops into three groups, the first of which would go with him; there were twenty thousand in that group. Over the second group he appointed two leaders: Balam and King Triamodes, his kinsman, with many kings, dukes, and earls. They had the greater part of the host with them. Jamund sent them into the further reaches of the realm, while he himself went to the part which was closest to Karlamagnus. He took with him his four chief gods, who have been described before, in whom was all their trust; for this reason Jamund appointed all the least promising men, and those who were young and inexperienced in warfare, to his own troop. The third, and smallest, part of the host he left in charge of the tower.

This flock of evil-doers now travelled widely around Hispania and their passage was a great catastrophe for God's flocks, for they killed Christians and plundered property wherever they could. And because Jamund led this troop, their journey shall be particularly described, since matters are most likely to be eventful in his area.

a:

(24) When Jamund, son of King Agulandus, heard the tidings that Ebraus, King of Sibil, had fallen, and that King Altumant had submitted to King Karlamagnus and accepted Christianity, he was greatly angered, and prayed to his gods Maumet and Terrogant[1] to give him

[1] *Terogant.*

strength to avenge this against his enemies. Jamund now summoned his people to come with as great a host as possible. Seven kings came to his aid, stalwart and mighty warriors; each of them had a huge troop with him. They told Prince Jamund that they would have the lives of King Karlamagnus and his nephew Rollant, "if we meet with them on a battlefield; and you shall take all his realm under your rule."

He thanked them well for these words. When all this host was gathered now, they went to attack King Karlamagnus....

CHAPTER XXVII

Karlamagnus Sends Out Scouts

As soon as Jamund left the tower he started to destroy and dishonor Christians with great zeal. None could withstand him, and he conquered many cities and castles by fire and the sword. He was extremely grim and malicious in his harrying. The most valiant men, who did not wish to renounce their God and bow to cursed heathen idols, he had disgracefully killed, while he ordered the breasts to be cut off women who did not consent to their foul, evil intentions: therefore a great many converted to false belief in idols. At the same time, he gathered so much gold and silver and other treasure that it cannot be reckoned.

Since this persecution waged by Jamund spread widely around the land, Emperor Karlamagnus heard the tidings where he was; but because of the troubles he was already dealing with, which have been described before, he thought he could not go to attack Jamund. Thus he summoned two kings, of whom one was called Salomon and was leader of Bretland while the other was Droim, who governed Gaskunia.[1] To these men the emperor thus spoke: "Since I cannot go as quickly as is necessary to attack Jamund, son of Agulandus, and combat the destruction he is carrying on in the land of my friend James, I appoint you leaders of the troop which shall be sent to scout Jamund's position, so that he may not rush upon us and take us unaware. In case you meet with a small detachment of not too many of their men, you shall have such a troop with you as seems best to you to take along; but send us word as soon as possible when you have need and it seems better to you to remain there."

They accepted this gladly and took to accompany them more than thirty thousand men, then travelled to the area from which they had

[1] *Gaskhunia.*

had word of Jamund's expedition. There they raised their tents near a mountain which is called Aspremont and set ten thousand guards to hold it for a long time. Very well equipped with all armor, they rode up on the ridge below the mountain, and from there down the other side of the slope, stopping at a place where they could see some distance, and looked at Jamund's tower. They divided their troop into battalions, wishing to be prepared in case he should approach them.

a: (24)

... The scouts of King Karlamagnus were soon aware of Jamund's army, and went to tell King Karlamagnus these tidings. The king then held a council with his men and told them he wished to gather his army against Jamund. All his men agreed to this, and now both sides went forth...

CHAPTER XXVIII

Jamund's Misadventures

Just at this time, when the emperor's scouts had gone on their expedition, Jamund was besieging a city held by a king called Kalabre. He conquered it and killed the king, and then he turned back on his way to the tower with his men. They were in a very boastful mood and congratulated themselves on having done well, since they had converted many men to their gods—though they had killed an even greater number—and they had so much plunder that more could scarcely be needed. They now went on their way until they found the French before them, keeping guard on the slope of the mountain, as has been described. Jamund saw that they had drawn up their troop, but that there were far fewer than his own men; so he urged his leaders on to attack them.

But when the Christians saw Jamund coming, they were calm and steadfast and in no way changed their position, intending to grant battle to the heathens if they wished it and to stand fast against them bravely and well. It did not enter Jamund's mind that this band could do them any harm, if it came to proof; he sent bowmen out in front first, bidding them to shoot the French hard and fast, and with them went the younger men, riding with stout spears couched. But the Frenchmen were so well protected that neither spears nor thick flights of arrows were able to penetrate.

When Jamund saw that this was doing no good, he urged on his knights, bidding them to launch a hard attack; but when the Christians saw what Jamund was sending forward now, they drew their swords and couched their spears and gave such stiff resistance that the heathens broke into flight at once, for the Frenchmen's weapons were so strong and rugged that no protection could withstand them. Many in the heathen troop now began to fall, slaughtered, for the French rushed down from the slope with such vigor that whoever stood before them met sudden death if he did not choose to flee. Those who were in the front were the first to turn in flight, while those who stood firm were those who had not yet learned how sorely the French weapons could bite; thus at first flight was very difficult for those who had turned coward: they were being attacked in the front, others stood behind them, and they were in the middle.

God's knights were therefore able to cut the heathen's heads and arms from their bodies. The scouts of Karlamagnus advanced so sharply that they came right into Jamund's division, where they killed his standard-bearer, who was called Estor, and knocked Jamund himself from his horse most disgracefully. But when the Africans saw all that had happened none now waited for the other: each fled as best he could. Some headed away on the mountain, while others tried to get to the tower, but most of them ran into the river which fell into a valley near the battlefield. It is said of Jamund that after he had fallen backwards he rose up quickly and was able to catch a horse which was running about the plain; then he mounted and galloped away from the battle, where there was the greatest of slaughter, ludicrously deserting the gods themselves and all the wealth which he had wrongfully gathered before, turning towards the tower and wishing only to get there. And when a brave knight among the French saw that, he ran after Jamund, threatening the fleet horse on which he was riding with drawn sword, and chased him all the way to the tower. Just as Jamund was galloping into the shelter of the doorway, the knight came upon him from outside and struck at him in such a way that the sword struck the horse behind the saddle-bow. Jamund threw himself from the horse when he heard the sword swinging: that blow was so great that no others would have been needed if it had struck into his head as the knight intended, for the horse was cut right down the middle. The front half went into the enclosure with Jamund while the back fell out onto the field.

Their parting was such that the knight rode back to his men while Jamund stayed behind in shame and distress. The Christians had killed all that they could and put the rest to flight; the battlefield was completely cleared, unobstructed by the heathen host.

a: (24)

... when they met, the divisions clashed and there was hard fighting, until there were so many losses on the heathen side that they turned back in flight. A great part of their host fell...

CHAPTER XXIX

The French Enjoy Victory

After this the Frenchmen went to the ornamented wagons laden with gold and silver and other precious treasures which now stood unguarded; they had many beautiful spoils to share. Now the Christians noticed that one wagon stood out from all the others, for it was roofed over with the most costly fabric and much adorned with red gold. So they went to it, lifted up the covering, and found there four devils, gathered together, each one standing by the others: these were the four gods of the heathen peoples, which Agulandus had had adorned with the greatest pomp before he left for Hispania, as you will have found written.

When Christ's knights found these enemies, they were delighted and took them up disdainfully and threw them out of the wagon onto the ground. They did not find that they suffered any uncanny effect from looking into the eyes of these monsters, although when they returned to him from Arabia Agulandus had boasted that it seemed likely to him that if the Christians saw their wrathful expression all their courage would melt. It now proved quite otherwise, for the Christians raised up four extremely high stakes, tied slip-knots around the feet of the gods, and now pulled them up, now let them drop way down. And they went on in this way so that if any heathens were nearby they would see their disgraceful movements.

Along with this, they spat on them and struck them with tree-trunks and stones, behaving so as to give them all the disgrace they deserved. Now all the French were much gladdened, by God's grace, and they then went back to the kings mentioned before, Droim and Salomon, bringing with them the gods and all the other riches they had gained on this trip. They explained in detail all their dealings, how it had gone between them and Jamund, and showed them the gods, telling them to do whatever they wished with them. They all agreed to let the gods await the arrival of Emperor Karlamagnus so that he might deal with them in any way he saw fit.

Let us leave the emperor's scouting party here for a little while, and tell next of an excellent lord whom almighty God and St. James vouchsafed to send to rescue their land and to help Emperor Karlamagnus.

a: (24)

... and the Christians captured much bounty: including even their gods, Maumet and Terrogant. The Christians took such huge shares of gold and silver that their heirs would never be poor!...

CHAPTER XXX

Girard Sets Out to Help Karlamagnus

At the time when these matters which have just been described were going on in God's Christendom, there reigned over Burgundia[1] a leader who was called Girard, son of King Bonivus.[2] Lord Girard dwelt in the city called Freri;[3] he was a leader of very high rank. In his day there was no better lord in these lands, for he surpassed most kings both in wealth and in wisdom. He was the most valiant of men, very well accomplished, strong, but not tall, polite in his behavior, gracious and loving to good men but grim and extremely harsh against enemies.

Lord Girard was now much stricken in years, as he had lived for a hundred winters, for eighty of which he had served in knightly undertakings: he was the most bold of men at arms and had fought in many battles. God had granted him so much good fortune and so many victories that he had never been on any battlefield without winning a fine victory.[4] He had a wealthy wife and four sons, two of whom were at this time famous knights: the eldest was named Bernard[5] and the younger Reiner.[6] Girard's third son was named Milon,[7] and the fourth Girard;[8] these were young men and had not yet borne armor. Lord

[1] *Borgundia.*

[2] Cf. *A* 50 (ch. LII).

[3] Cf. *A* 29 (ch. XLIII).

[4] *Ibid.*

[5] *Asp.* Ernaut, Ernalt.

[6] *Aemers*; *Asp.* Rainner, Rainier.

[7] Cf. *A* 79 (ch. LXII).

[8] *Asp.* Girardet. — Note that the saga makes no reference to *Asp.* Fouque or Foque (10636), identified in Brandin's glossary as another son of Girart, though the sentence does not necessarily have to be so interpreted; nor does it mention *Asp.* Malré, said in 4236 to be a brother of Ernalt and thus yet another son of Girart. Since the former appears only in a passage after the end of the part of the poem used in the saga, and since reference to the latter is omitted in the A,a version, the B,b redactor would not have known about them. — Cf. Louis, p. 135.

Girard had a sister, who was married to the leader named Milon;[9] they had two sons, Boz[10] and Clares.[11] Lord Girard took these two into his household when they were very young and fostered them well and fittingly, teaching them courtesy and many skills. Then he made them knights, and appointed them leaders over large troops.

Now when Lord Girard heard of the troubles raised by the Africans in Hispania, and that the excellent lord Emperor Karlamagnus had gone there to rescue Christendom with all the might he could muster, it came into his mind that it might be good work on God's behalf to go there to help the emperor with his forces in the last days of his life, fighting for the sake of God against the heathen hosts. And since the excellent lord James the apostle saw his land in need of the duke's coming, he so strengthened Lord Girard's resolve that he called together a fine, great host and prepared for his expedition to Hispania, choosing from his realm fifteen thousand warriors, equipped with the best weapons, clothing, and horses, and all other necessities. With them also went many young men who had not yet taken up arms. In this expedition went the duke's two nephews and his four sons, who were named before, and many other powerful men.

Lord Girard travelled with his host until they came into Hispania. As soon as he arrived there, news came to his ears of how grimly Jamund, son of Agulandus, was trampling down Christian people; at the same time he learned that he was holding the strongest tower in the realm, while Emperor Karlamagnus was in another place at a great distance. And since Lord Girard concluded that he would find the head and source of all the heathen might where Jamund was, he did not wish to try out an attack on any place until he reached the one commanded by the leader, and so he turned his men towards Jamund's tower. It was his great good fortune that on the very next night after the great disgrace which Jamund had experienced at the hands of the emperor's scouts, as has been described, he came so close to the tower that he was no further away than one arrow-shot; they pitched their camp nearby and waited until morning. But on the next day the duke had his host armed, and bade each man to prepare to defend himself if Jamund should come out of the tower; and so they did.

[9] *Milun*; cf. *A* 25.

[10] *Asp.* Beus, Boson.

[11] *Klares*, *Asp.* Claires.

CHAPTER XXXI

Jamund Plans Revenge

Of Jamund, however, it is said that as he sat in the tower he was most displeased over the disgrace he had suffered at the hands of the Christians the first time he had clashed with them; he had lost the gods themselves and the greater part of the troop which accompanied him. And when he was told that Christians had raised their tents right beside his dwelling, this message did not improve his mood: he was filled with great wrath, blamed his men in many ways, and attributed the disgrace he had incurred to their cravenly cowardice. He said that they had so demeaned him that the Frenchmen were boasting over him, and had therefore set up their camp nearby, thinking they had their plans well in hand: it did not enter his mind that anyone might besiege his tower other than those who had put him to flight so scornfully the day before. Therefore he now intended to avenge that ill-fated journey, to ride boldly at the Frenchmen and drive them off with a heavy hand. Thus he ordered all those who were staying in the tower to make themselves ready for attack, and it was so done.

But when Lord Girard saw that Jamund intended to charge at his troop, he said to his men, "Good friends," says he, "follow my advice, and it will serve you well. When they first come out the door at you, do not close with them, but protect yourselves as best you can against their charge. Give them plenty of room to get far away from the tower, for I intend to conquer it today, God willing! We should therefore take care to draw ourselves nearer to the tower as they get further away; and if we can get between them and the tower, then each and every one shall use his weapons as boldly as possible."

All agreed to do as he ordered, saying that they would gladly heed his advice, and would spare neither flesh nor bone of the heathens.

CHAPTER XXXII

Girard Defeats Jamund

When Jamund was ready, he took all the host from the tower and rushed forward at the Christians with great zeal. The heathens shot arrows as hard as steel from Turkish bows, attacked with spears and swung their swords, thinking that in the first rush they would overcome the French. But Lord Girard's men, keeping to the plan which had been laid down, defended themselves well and stood fast, giving way a little so that the heathens advanced boldly forward as they found some giving way before them; and so it went for a while, as the Africans attacked vigorously, but gained nothing at all, as long as Lord Girard could not attack them skilfully from behind: for while they had been exerting themselves in the attack, he had moved towards the tower with a great throng of men, and now he attacked the heathens from the rear after letting out a great war-cry and urged on his men to attack: all that heard this turned quickly, drew their swords, and struck so terribly and so often that no protection could withstand them.

When the heathens became aware of the smarting wounds dealt by the sharp-edged swords, it was not long before their troop burst into flight: each one was glad to escape any way he could, Jamund no less than the others. They headed for the town which is called Hamne. But the Christians pursued the fugitives boldly, killing many of the heathens. Foremost among those driving the fugitives were Lord Girard's two nephews, Boz and Clares, who were named before, who butchered an especially large number of the heathen host. Meanwhile, Lord Girard defended the tower against those who wanted to go there for help.

When Jamund saw his men fall in such great numbers he was sorrowful and wrathful and thought things went ill; he turned the white horse he was riding, thinking to avenge those who had died, and, drawing his strong shield firmly before him and wielding his sturdy spear in both hands, he spurred his horse forward at a good knight and attacked him. But this knight was Clares, nephew of Girard; and when he saw the vigorous charge of Jamund, and judged him to be both huge and strong, he took stock and galloped his horse hard at him, holding his spear firmly couched. When they met, Jamund struck at Clares, and his spear hit the outside of his shield; but Clares veered his horse around and the spear sprang out of the shield, so that he was not wounded. Clares now struck Jamund with such great vigor that he fell disgracefully on his back, soiling the fine helmet which he wore on his head with dirt and mud.

Now, when Jamund leapt up, he did not see any better way to escape than to flee out into the river which fell nearby, and he tried this; he barely made his way across. He parted with them in such a way that Clares took the white horse from which Jamund had fallen.

When all the heathen host had been slain, except those who had scattered, Clares turned back to the tower. Lord Girard had taken control of it and killed all the heathens he found inside. There was no shortage there of food or drink or other choice supplies: there was enough for everyone to choose what he liked. Now there was great rejoicing in Lord Girard's troop, for it seemed to him that their first clash with the Africans had gone very well.

CHAPTER XXXIII

Jamund's Wrath

It is to be said of Jamund, however, that when he crossed the river he fled to the place which he thought would best serve his purpose; there the host that had taken flight quickly crowded around him. Jamund was very angry. Most of his men were distressed, sick at heart and wounded, and many of them said among themselves, "We are miserable and wretched because of the ill fortune which has befallen us; we have lost all our gods, gold and silver, and the greater part of the host which followed Jamund, as well as kings and earls and other most high men of our realm. But what is to be done now?"

They then went to the place where Jamund sat, white-faced, and removed his armor, for he was weary and wet. Then they said to him, "Lord, what is your counsel now?"

He answered wrathfully, "Woe take you!" says he, "What need is there for you to ask me about counsel? Never, as long as I live, shall I be consoled for the grief your faithlessness has caused me. You boasted of your knightly prowess at home in my halls and chambers, where you sat, making merry and drinking my best wine; you said you would take France, and divide among you all the possessions of the Christians, killing them or driving them into exile. Vainly I trusted in you craven boasters, and the wretched persuasion of those who urged me to go to this land with a fine, great host: now they have betrayed me, and done me such great shame that Africa can never produce a remedy."

When Jamund had spoken in this fashion, he summoned the man called Butra[1] and said, "Mount the fastest horse you find in our army and ride quickly until you find our kings Balam and Triamodes; tell them to come to us at once with all the troops that follow them, and

[1] *Butram.*

whomever they can assemble, and tell them in detail everything which has happened to us."

The messenger did as he was told. He mounted his horse and rode day and night over hill and dale until he came to the army of the heathens. There he came first to the tent of the counselor Goram, and told him all the misfortune which Jamund had borne. This tale went around the army quickly. Therefore all the leaders of the host gathered together, and Butra told them in every particular what had happened since they parted, and that Jamund asked them to come to him with as much of a force as they could get.

When Balam heard Butra's message, he considered in his mind the falseness of belief in cursed heathen idols, and the strength of the great faith of Christians; thus the Holy Spirit lodged in his heart, for almighty God intended to have mercy on him because of the generosity he had shown towards Duke Nemes, which has been told of before, when he was in the power of Agulandus and sentenced to death by him. Now he secretly offered a repeated prayer to God, with yearning heart, as you may hear: "Highest father, almighty God, whom Christian men rightly worship and honor, I acknowledge you to be king of all the world and maker of all things; and because I truly believe that the matters of which I have now heard came about through your power against probability when so few men triumphed over such a great multitude, I then pray to your most merciful love that I may not, in my terrible sinfulness, be overwhelmed by your wrath: be patient with me, and do not allow my soul to leave my body before I am baptized and consecrated to you."

Thus he spoke, his eyes wet with tears; and God heard this prayer gladly and let it be fulfilled, as will be revealed later in the saga.

a: (24)

... But when those heathens who survived gathered together helping Jamund to disarm, he was enraged and depressed, sore, and sick at heart. Two of his seven kings had been killed, and all the fiercest and bravest of a hundred thousand men: the better part of the host which followed Jamund had fallen. The miserable, wretched heathens cried out, then, saying to Jamund, "Lord," say they, "what shall we do now?"

He answers, "You are all too downcast. Where now are the fine volunteers and mighty boasters who, in my gold-encrusted halls and rooms in Africa, dallied with fair maidens, giving them sweet kisses and pledges of love, and drinking my best wine? You made yourselves out to be great managers there, talking of getting for yourselves all the honors and wealth of the French chiefs, dividing among you the realm they had inherited; but it is said that men will not cease for either red or white.[2] In vain did I trust in faint-hearted boasters: at their urging, their empty counsel, I undertook this expedition. Curses on you!" says he; "As long as I live, I shall remember this disaster."

Jamund then called his spokesman and messenger, Butra,[3] to him, and said, "Hurry" says he; "tell lord Goram[4] to come to me, and Balam,[5] his father; and also Triamodes,[6] and King Asperan,[7] and Edopt,[8] king of Egypt,[9] and King Jone[10] and Salatiel and King Bordanus:[11] tell them that now a miserable winter of trouble is upon me, and that I have lost Makon and Terrogant and Apollin,[12] and the mighty Jupiter."[13]

The messenger rushed to his horse and made as much haste as he could to carry out his order.

(35) The messenger was now mounted on a swift horse; he went over hill and dale, riding all night, and in the morning when the birds were beginning to sing, he reached the heathen army and dismounted from his horse before the tent of a steward, to whom he related all their mishaps and misfortunes, how many had fallen—one hundred and

[2] This has a proverbial ring to it: relating to wine? It does not appear to correspond to anything in *Asp.*

[3] Here, *Butran*; *Asp.* Butran.

[4] *Asp.* Gorhan.

[5] *Balan* here, and several times in *a.*

[6] *Triamoddis*; *Asp.* Triamodes.

[7] *Asp.* Esparran.

[8] Appears here in place of the 'Cador' of *Asp.* 3697.

[9] *Egipta.*

[10] 'Moysan' in *Asp.* 3697.

[11] *Asp.* Boïdan.

[12] Omitted in *Asp.* here.

[13] *Jubiter*; also omitted here in *Asp.*

seven thousand of the best men—and then their greatest misfortune of all, the loss of their gods.

At that time King Agulandus was at Visa,[14] where he sat in a great hall with his queen beside him; but he knew nothing of this, and no one told him. The messenger told Balam, however, everything that had happened and all of the message he had been given. He had sixty thousand noble warriors with him. When Balam understood the circumstances he called upon almighty God with all his heart and said, "Almighty God, father most high, to you I call with all my heart: you are my maker and creator; you are the highest king and ruler of all, creator of all creatures. And, as I truly believe this, I pray to you and your sacred love not to let my soul be taken from my body before I am christened and signed with the cross." And he wept, with penitent heart...

[14] *Vica.*

CHAPTER XXXIV

Jamund Laments

When the messenger Butra had given the heathens Jamund's message and told them what he wished, they responded well, striking their tents and setting off to meet him with all their troops while sending men where they had the best hope of gaining reinforcements. They gathered together where Jamund was sitting suffering distress and anger, a countless multitude of heathens from various peoples; and when Jamund learned that they had come, he rode out to them with the leaders who were with him, and, raising his voice to speak to them, told all the army to stay on the field. Then he summoned kings and earls, dukes, and all the leaders of the army, and they gathered in the shade of an elm tree that stood nearby, where he dismounted from his horse and sat down on a high seat. He was pale and drained of color, all the former beauty of his countenance had so changed.

Then he said to all who could hear him, "Brave leaders, I have great tidings to tell you, for I have fallen into tremendous misfortune. When we had parted, I went out of the tower which my father gave me to control with my troop, and we took our gods along to lend us strength. For a while we had good luck; we converted a great host to serve the gods and took a great deal of treasure—gold and silver, along with other valuable things. But after a month had passed, we turned back and we met with scouts of Karlamagnus; they attacked us so sharply that we could not make a stand against them. They killed my standard-bearer, Estor, bravest of knights, and many others: but never have I heard my elders tell of so few men driving as many as we were into flight. I had a very narrow escape from there, for they killed the best of my war-horses, which I was riding, knocking me shamefully from its back. And as soon as I got another, I hastened to the tower, forsaking the gods and all the other treasure. But they pursued me until I jumped away from the blow which was intended for me as I reached the tower; but the horse was struck down. I was filled with dread, for never since I have borne weapons have I escaped death so narrowly.

"But because I fled away from Maumet[1] and the gods, they turned their wrath upon me and permitted the Christians to set up their camp right by my tower, to vex me and add to my distress. When I learned of this, we consulted about it and decided to avenge our shame—but we were all the further from lightening our case, for everything went even more grievously for us than before. Many good warriors lost their lives, and we were so driven away from the tower that we can never expect to regain it. Blanched pale with terror, we fled, and I was again knocked off the back of my horse so dishonorably that my bright helmet was soiled right up to the nose-guard. I had no alternative but to throw myself out on the river, which ran nearby, drenching myself completely; nor did I get any help until I crossed it, much wearied by all my exertion.

"I have endured such misfortune as you now hear, good men, deservedly: my father could never chastise me for the disobedience I showed to him. He always wanted me to take counsel with the best of my kin, but I shunned the company of the noblest men and gathered around me the sons of wicked men, giving them honors and blessings, and marrying them to rich wives with great possessions. But they have ill rewarded me for that, for twice I made proof of their service, and both times it proved bad. If I come home to my own realm, I hope to give them the reward they deserve; it was because of their cowardice that I lost my four gods, which causes me great grief and much disquiet in my heart.

"Henceforth I shall not wear a garland on my head, nor listen, in the future, to the sweet song of the birds, nor be entertained by those who are skilled on stringed instruments: I shall not watch a hawk fly nor a hound run nor ask for a woman's joyous grace, when I have lost and mislaid my most mighty lords Maumet and Terrogant. And since I shall never see them again unless you prove your knighthood boldly, I ask you to go after them, and, if that is granted, then I shall make the poorest of you the owner of wealth enough."

[1] *Maumeth.*

The leaders then answered, "Lord Jamund," say they, "bear yourself in a manly fashion. Sorrow makes you speak this way. But know this: all the Christians who have the impudence to meet us in battle shall die shortly, and with your own eyes you shall see us kill them courageously. So do not delay: prepare your army at once."

Jamund thanked them for their fine promises and quickly mounted his war-horse, which belonged to his father Agulandus. He ordered his divisions and appointed leaders of the troops. He put Balam the messenger in charge of the first division, and four kings with him; they had sixty thousand men, very well equipped with weapons, while others had no mailed shirts but only strong leather jerkins. There were many bowmen in the troop who were great and strong, armed with the strongest missiles.

The second division was led by Triamodes, nephew of Agulandus. He had a great multitude of fearless armed men with him. In his division could be seen very sharp swords, good protective jerkins, trusty coats of mail, fair helmets, stout Turkish bows with well-made arrows; every one of them had an axe hanging from his saddle-bow. Although they now bore themselves grandly, and intended to seek out the French scouts, they would never have cause to boast!

Two kings, Rodan and Salatiel, led the third division, with other powerful leaders; they had sixty thousand well-equipped men. There were helmets set with gold and gems, jewelled shields, stout spears with gold-embroidered banners, fine horses with well-made harnesses. The fourth division was led by King Kador and his comrade Amandras, and with them were sixty thousand; they wore gilded helmets, with silvery coats of mail, enamelled saddles and decorated bridle bits. There were many heathens puffed with pride and arrogance, filled with false boasts, swathed in chivalry and worldly finery: but great as they might seem, their insolence would soon be brought down!

At the head of the fifth division were two leaders, King Baldam and Lampas; their troop was both large and well equipped with all armor, weapons, protections, horses, and clothing. The sixth division was in charge of two kings, Magon and Asperant,[2] who were wealthy and of distinguished family. Since Jamund did not wish to tie himself to any

[2] *Alfreant*: apparently in error.

one particular part of the host, he appointed these kings to guard his chief standard, for they seemed best able to defend it well. He appointed, to reinforce them, a hundred thousand men, all well equipped in their manner, for he intended to engage in combat himself wherever he pleased. It is told that he had the sword which was the best of all borne at that time, called Dyrumdali, as well as the shrilling trumpet made of horn called Olifant, both of which Rollant took after his death.

When the leaders of the host had been appointed, Jamund rode forward and divided each division from the next, and the army hurried on until they came into a valley which lies under the mountain Asprement;[3] there was a great plain there where one could see a long way. A very great space was needed for all their army to stand on, for it is said that their host all together was no less than seven times a hundred thousand. Here Jamund had fine tents pitched, of splendid quality: the heathens had such enormous wealth that it was not at all decreased or diminished, although Jamund had twice before been deprived of great treasures, for they had taken all that from the Christians. However, the care with which the tent of Jamund was prepared is described later; now we shall reveal what was happening to the scouts of Karlamagnus, who were spoken of before.

a: (25)

... Triamodes was the nephew of Agulandus, and he had a picked troop of most valiant men, one hundred and sixty thousand strong. There many biting swords could be seen, much good armor, trusty coats of mail and shining helmets, as well as many Turkish bows with well-made arrows; and each of them had an axe hanging from his saddle-bow. Triamodes went out spying after the Frenchmen, but in vain: those wretched, abandoned dogs found that no one, young or old, would be able to escape.[4]

The third division[5] was in charge of Rodan,[6] and Salatiel was a member of this group. They both had sixty thousand well-armed men.

[3] *Asperment.*

[4] This sentence is not in *Asp.*

[5] What seems to be meant here (and in *Asp.*) is that Balam led the first and Triamodes the second.

[6] Boïdant in *Asp.* 3776: 'Rodoans' comes in later.

There were many gold shields there, many helmets studded with jewels, substantial coats of mail and suits of armor, sharp spears and doughty swords, and many gold-embroidered banners made of costly fabric. So much light gleamed from their gilded shields and other shining arms that the land was illuminated on both sides.

Leading the fourth division was King Kador[7] and his comrade Amandras,[8] and sixty thousand men with them; there could be seen many beautiful horses of all colors, with all their war-trappings decorated with gold and precious stones. There were many proud heathens, haughty boasters and vain ranters: but at Aspremunt they were to meet their deaths.

Before the fifth division rode two leaders, King Lampas[9] and Balda:[10] they led sixty thousand of this hateful people. There were so many gilded helmets, shining shields, bright coats of mail, and banners decorated with gold that mountains and valleys shone with their light. — The sixth was led by the two leaders King Asperan and Magon,[11] with sixty thousand of the strongest heathens. These had the best horses in the world: there were none as good in all the host. These swear that they shall seek out Appollin[12] and Makon, and never return until they have arrived where the apostle Peter had built his church.[13]

Then came Jamund, with four kings, and four hundred thousand men with them; these were the most powerful and the most courteous in all the army. With them were ten thousand leaders, all well armed in good coats of mail, strong helmets and thick shields, swords and spears of steel, and there were not three in that division who did not have banners in all this multitude. Now Jamund came galloping out before the ranks, saying that all the army should take its positions; then he called all the leaders in the host to him to tell them his news and plans.

[7] *Asp.* Cador.
[8] *Asp.* Amandras.
[9] *Asp.* Lampal: one of the fourth division in *Asp.*, which gives Rodoans here.
[10] Apparently *Asp.* Butran.
[11] *Asp.* Maargon; elsewhere, Margon, Amalgons.
[12] Omitted in *Asp.*
[13] Not in *Asp.* — The next section does not correspond closely to *Asp.*

Jamund now dismounted from his horse and stood in the shade of a palm tree, gathering around him all the kings and chieftains, earls and dukes and powerful landholders: no mere knights were summoned to the meeting. Lord Jamund sat down on a high seat; he was pale and wan of face, his glory faded. "Gentlemen," says he, "I have come into great difficulty and trouble. My father, King Agulandus, gave me the tower to guard, with a hundred thousand heathen warriors, all well equipped with clothing and weapons; and we had our gods with us, to give luck and safeguard our honor. We converted many Christians to our gods and our faith, and gained so much treasure that I have never seen more in one place. When a month had passed, we turned back, and then we met with ten thousand Frenchmen, scouts of King Karlamagnus. They rode against us so vigorously that we could not resist them, and they killed there Estor,[14] the bravest knight there was in all our army. There was no one who could withstand them, though I have never heard my ancestors tell that so great a crowd as we were could be put to flight before ten thousand men! And I have had so narrow an escape that they slew from under me my best war-horse. When I found another, I hurried into the tower."

And Jamund then disclosed to them how he had escaped the blows which fell on his horse before the gate of the tower as he galloped in. "There is no need to tell you about this at length: such a great peril came upon me that I have never escaped so narrowly from death since I could bear arms. I never again wish to have a garland of leaves or flowers on my head, nor will I, in the future, listen to the song of birds or the entertainment of stringed instrument, nor watch a hawk fly or a dog hunt, or ask for a woman's favor, when I have lost Maumet, my mighty lord."

As Jamund said this, he had no inclination to laugh. "Glorious lords," says he, "anger and sorrow and wrath are in my breast, for we have lost our lord Maumet."

The leaders answered, "Sorrow makes you speak this way: before this evening, all these Christian men shall die, and you shall see this with your own eyes, if you dare be at hand to see us kill them."

[14] *Asp.* Ector, Hector.

Jamund then answered, "We have lost Maumet, and he is very angry with me. He let me be disgraced in his sight when the Frenchmen camped barely an arrow-shot from my tower, and we rode out thinking to avenge our shame and dishonor: there we suffered great loss of life, and I shall never again return to our tower. Now I have not so much as a penny's weight of all my treasure; we have fled down to the castle of Hamne,[15] but the Frenchmen overtook us in flight, slaying many of my men before my eyes. When I turned back to help them, I was thrown off my horse so shamefully that my helmet was buried in earth and mud to the cheekpiece; when I jumped up, I fled away on the river, wet right up to the eyes—nor did I get any help before, wet and tired, I crossed the river.

"My father could never chastise nor advise me; he wanted me to associate with the best of my kinsmen, but I disregarded the best men, and drove worthy men away from me, bringing forward the sons of wicked men and men of low family, giving them blessings and honors, and finding them rich wives with great possessions...44[16]

[15] On the question of the derivation of this name, cf. van Waard, p. 22.

[16] Here, corresponds fairly closely to ls. 212 of *Asp.* — At this point there is a lacuna of two pages, in the course of which the scene evidently shifts to the French camp.

CHAPTER XXXV

Salomon Seeks a Messenger

After the fine victory which, as has been said, the Christians gained when they took Jamund by surprise, they went to meet King Droim and King Salomon and told them about their journey. And since all of them thought it likely that Jamund would gather together an invincible army if he could, they quickly sent scouts up on the mountain of Aspremont so that the heathens could not come upon them without warning. As soon as they had arrived there, they saw the wide plain covered with the heathen army; at the same time, they saw a small detachment of another army, very well equipped, near the mountain. And because they did not know of the coming of Lord Girard, they thought these were heathen spies. They also heard a great commotion in the army.

They therefore rode down the mountain and made for the tent of Salomon, where their leader said to the king, "By my faith," says he, "now we surely have a battle at hand: we saw the heathen army, and it is a great multitude. The plain is covered with them far and wide, and they are very close to us."

When this news came to the Christians, many quickly gave signs of what sort of warriors they were, for those warriors who were hardy and courageous rejoiced in their hearts that they were to meet the heathen troops, while others blanched and were terrified at the prospect. King Droim, hearing of the approach of the heathens, called King Salomon to him and said "Lord, send a messenger to King Karlamagnus to tell him what is going on. It cannot be concealed now that the heathens intend to conquer the land if he does not rush to defend it; since all owe obedience to you, choose whom you please for the journey."

Salomon answered that he would follow that advice, and turned to the knight called Riker,[1] saying, "Brave warrior," says he, "help us in

[1] *Asp.* Richier.

our need and tell Karlamagnus that he should come at once to our aid, for there is no man who is dearer to the emperor than you."

Riker, hearing these words, became somewhat red in the face, and thrust under him the kirtle which lay on the saddle, answering, "May woe be upon me a hundredfold if I do as you say, Salomon,[2] and rush away from this place when I wish to be called a knight: this errand should be borne by someone who cannot offer any help, though it is needed here, and who wishes to save his life and body. If I were to lose my soul for the body's needs I should have little to boast of before God and his saints. Therefore I will not be driven away, but will gain what I can so that my soul may lodge with God's apostles, and especially the apostle James, for whose honor I, and all good men, should stand boldly, for there no coward can trouble me."

Thus answered Riker; so Salomon called to a good knight of their company called Manri,[3] a wise and courteous man born in the city which is called Birra.[4] To him Salomon said, "Most courteous of knights, ride to the emperor and take our message."

He answered, "Hear this, king, which I tell you: in that moment when my chain-mail has burst, my shield shattered, my spear broken, my sword become so blunt that it cannot bite, my body so weak and exhausted that I cannot offer any help, then I shall go on this journey; and if you wish to spare your body, then go yourself where you are directing me."

After that Salomon called Gudifrey[5] the Old, and said to him, "Good fellow," says he, "do as I ask quickly, and ride the swift horse on which you are mounted to the emperor with our message."

He answered with quick words, "By my faith, I will not do that by any means! Do you not see that I have good armor and a fine horse? If it pleases God, I shall boldly defend that which God gave into my keeping and offer to him my soul and body together, if he so ordains; but if you, Salomon, are afraid to die, then go on this errand yourself."

[2] *Salome.*
[3] *Asp.* Amauri.
[4] Berri.
[5] *Asp.* Godefroi.

When Salomon heard such answers, it seemed to him that the message would not go readily; however, he wished to try further, and he thought that it might be undertaken more gladly if treasure was offered as a reward. Thus he spoke to a man called Antilin[6] the Red, who was advanced in age, and spoke to him, saying "Antilin, go and tell our king to come to our aid."

Antilin answered shortly, "What help do you need from him?" says he.

Salomon answered, "You will certainly grant, good friend, that we have no strength in comparison with the overwhelming might of the heathens unless he comes to assist us; but if you will do as I wish and go, I shall give you a castle, and all the district which lies around it, and more than five hundred knights to serve you."

Antilin then said, "You must be an extremely wealthy king, since you are so generous; but you are wrong if you think that I would go back to earn the name of a traitor with your bribe, to hear my companions and peers say that I fled from here out of cowardice. No: by no means shall you manage this. I am not your thrall, and I will not go there at your command or wish; I shall, rather, serve almighty God of my own will, and thus I intend to undertake with my comrades whatever he ordains for us. But if you are afraid to die, then flee as fast as possible while you can save your life of our own accord so that you will not have to bear anything worse than you want to."

When Salomon heard these words from Antilin[7] he was somewhat angry; but, rather than give up, he tried again, a fifth time, saying to Bertram of Mutirborg,[8] "You, chivalrous knight, will surely go and tell Karlamagnus to send twenty thousand armed knights to help us without delay, then to come himself with all his host. If he refuses and will not accept this advice, such harm shall overtake us that he will not soon find a remedy."

Bertram answered, "Lord Salomon," says he, "before you ordered me to go on this errand, you should have considered whether I was

[6] *Asp.* Antelme.
[7] *Antelin.*
[8] Not in *Asp.*

your thrall or not, for you should give such an order to one who is subject to you and would not dare to refuse; but not me, for I shall by no means flee from here before the battle starts, which seems likely to be soon. Can it be, Salomon, as it seems to me, that you are pale and drained of blood, blanched and colorless with terror, so that your feet are shivering and shaking in cowardice? Now if you do not dare to fight, go on this errand as best you can."

At these insulting words, Salomon became visibly angry and grasped his weapons, and so did the knight: a dangerous situation now erupted between them. An archbishop, who was named Samson,[9] saw this; he rode boldly in front of them and said, "Good friends," said he, "do not behave so monstrously; be sensible, and do not fight, for you are brothers, both Christian men. Hear, rather, what I have to say. I will gladly solve the difficulty that stands between you and go on this errand which no one else wishes to do, for I have never taken up chivalrous knightly arms, nor have I ever overcome a man on the battlefield."

They thanked the archbishop for his offer and put their strife aside.[10]

[9] Unnamed at this point in *Asp.*; "the archbishop" usually means Turpin there.

[10] This section, which is missing in the extant A,a mss. because of lacunae, corresponds to *Asp.* lss. 215-219.

CHAPTER XXXVI

Karlamagnus Meets Salomon

When Archbishop Samson was ready he mounted a fine horse and rode away alone, until he came to the place where Emperor Karlamagnus had pitched his tent. Since the strife in that part of the land, of which we spoke before, had now ended, the emperor had determined to send the army after the group of scouts which he had sent against Jamund, and when Samson rode up he was standing in front of his tent, fastening a splendid banner to his spear-shaft. Samson dismounted from his horse, which was terribly exhausted, and walked to Karlamagnus, greeting him and saying, "Good day, lord! King Droim and King Salomon, with all their troop, send you greetings in God's name and their own, and ask you to come to them as quickly as you can."

The emperor looked at his gracious face and said, "God bless you, Archbishop Samson, and all friends of God and of myself! But what news do you have to tell us, that you so goaded your horse with spurs that he is all bloody from it?"

"Lord," says he, "there is much to tell, if there were time; but trust me, for I shall not lie to you. The heathens have drawn very near, and they are so well prepared that soon they will have won the battle and overcome your men."

The emperor then said, "Almighty God, send us there as quickly as possible! And may we still be well advised, through the help of my friend James. Although the heathens wish to plunder the honors and privileges which God granted to him in the regions of earth, it shall not be as they wish, for, while God grants life to me and my men, I shall never, as long as there is need, cease to defend his land and realm from the enemy. Let every man in our host who can bear weapons prepare for the journey."

Soon, now, great blasts oı. the trumpet could be heard. All armed themselves, and mounted their horses, according to the emperor's command; he who was first rode at the front, while the rest crowded one after another, and at the end came the young men and servant boys with tents, food and drink, and the army's other necessities. The emperor went on until he came into the valley which lay on the other side of the mountain of Aspremont; there they rode before Droim and Salomon, who rejoiced greatly at their coming.

The emperor had them stop there, and asked what had happened during their journey, in the time since they had parted. The kings told what had passed between the scouts and Jamund: that the aforementioned number of Frenchmen met the heathens in the midst of the mountain and killed many of Jamund's multitude, driving him into flight in disgrace, and taking a great deal of booty, including the four gods whom the heathens worshipped; they had put Jamund to flight towards the tower, which stood on the other side of this mountain, and had since killed an untold multitude of heathens.

And when the emperor had heard all of this, he gave thanks to almighty God, saying, "Praise and glory be to you, Jesu, son of the maiden Maria, for your deeds of mercy: I acknowledge, in truth, that never could the heathen host have suffered such a defeat from so small a group of your knights if you had not helped them and sent them, to strengthen them, the glorious lord apostle James, who gained that realm by your will and should possess it." Then he said, further, "Good friends," says he, "what disposition have you decided to make of the cursed idols?"

They answered, "Lord, none other than to let them await your arrival."

"I thank you for that," said the emperor. "Bring them forth now, and let us see."

And when the emperor saw how gaudy they were, he said, "Ill spent was the lavish expense with which these fiends were decorated, and too greatly has the enemy blinded the hearts of those who take such for their gods. And so that they should not be so honored as to be broken by the hands of worthy men, give them to whores and harlots, to do with as they wish, rewarding them with all the gold and silver and precious stones they can pry from their decorations."

And it was so done. When the gods had been given to them, the whores were delighted and thought they had been granted a great honor. Then they took their garters and braided them into nooses, and fastened these around the necks of the gods, dragging them around the castle and villages, and later into their dwellings,[1] and when they had done this they took great clubs and smashed them into little pieces, and proceeded to distribute their booty. There were so many engaged in this work that none got more for her share than was worth half a penny.

When this had been done, the emperor called together his army, which had been much scattered, and called the standard-bearer Fagon to him. This Fagon was a wise and valiant man who led a great throng of good knights. He had been the emperor's standard-bearer for thirty-three years and knew well how to serve his lord, so that he was dear to the emperor, who therefore said to him, "Lord Fagon," says Karlamagnus, "look at this fine, large host which I give today into the care of God, and your supervision: now take my golden chief standard, for I shall ride up onto the ridge and look over our enemies, while you stay here with the troops."

The emperor did so; he rode away from the army, taking with him Oddgeir the Dane, Duke Nemes, a Flemish[2] earl, and Baeringur the Breton, with a number of others.

But before Karlamagnus comes over the ridge to see what was going on on the other side of the mountain, it is necessary to tell what was happening at the tower at this time.[3]

[1] Unger's correction: ms. says something like "dragging them behind them roughly, and later taking them into their dwellings."

[2] *Flaemskan*; *Asp.* Flavant.

[3] Based on *Asp.* lss. 220-224.

CHAPTER XXXVII

Girard Rallies His Troops

It has been told how Lord Girard drew near Jamund's tower and drove him into flight, then set about holding the tower; and because he had little reason to trust the heathens, he had a strong watch set over it day and night. One day, when his men were outside amusing themselves, they heard at some distance the horns and trumpets of the heathens, and then they saw a great cloud of dust stirred up by the feet of their horses and a great light shone over the earth from the golden decorations of their armor. When these tidings were told to Lord Girard, he had sixty blasts of the trumpet sounded and assembled his troops outside the tower on a flat, broad plain. All sorts of armor were in evidence: stout and trustworthy coats of mail, fair to see and even better to rely upon; hard shields, with various sorts of gear; gilded helmets adorned with precious stones;[1] sharp swords, fresh[2] to look at, and keenly tempered; stout spears, with fair, broad banners. Fine horses were led out, in the most courtly and becoming harnesses, exceptionally well broken to battle. Each man made ready according to his abilities, then mounted into his gilded saddle.

Lord Girard prepared himself in this way: he took off his underkirtle and put on a thick leather jerkin, throwing over this a coat of mail which reached down to his feet; this was so fine that it never failed him at any time. He set his helmet on his head and girded on his sword, took his spear in his hand, then mounted a strong war-horse. When he had done this, he raised his voice and called out to the host, where there was now much commotion, bidding them to listen to what he

[1] Here *b* begins again.
[2] Literally, 'green.'

wished to say. They quieted at once, for he was so well loved that everyone wished to sit or stand exactly as he wished.

Thus spoke Lord Girard to all his men: "Hear, good warriors," says he, "all honorably dedicated to almighty God! I have now borne shield and sword, like any other knight, for a good eighty years; I have often fought battles for the sake of my honor and for foolish pride. But God, maker of all things, has granted to me that this same banner which my kinsmen and ancestors bore, which we have brought on this expedition, has never come onto the battlefield without my taking the victory. And since in all the years of my life now gone by I stood up for my honor and my realm, now that God has sent me here, I shall do as he wishes so that I may serve him in the last days of my life in repayment for all that he has granted to me, as to many others.

"I also give thanks to you, my good friends, for all the support and goodwill you have granted to me at all times since I came to rule over you; and beyond that, I now ask every one of you to stand forth with all his might, for that life is truly blessed which is spent in the service of God. Accept gladly, then, whatever he ordains for us, be it life or death: those who give their lives for the sake of God shall earn a splendid reward in heaven. But if it should please him to let us return to our realm victorious, I have sufficient riches there, along with fair maidens to give you, so that each man may choose the greatest of honor."

All thanked him for his fine promise. Then Lord Girard arranged his army into three divisions: he put his two nephews Boz and Clares at the head of one, his sons Bernard and Reiner before the second, and led the third himself. Then he had them all join hands and swear that none of them would dare to leave the place which had been assigned to him without the duke's leave. So prepared, they rode away from the tower, down into the valley, until they came to that flat plain which lies beneath the mountain of Aspremont, just at the time which Emperor Karlamagnus went away from the army with Oddgeir the Dane and others to find out about the movement of the heathens, as has been described a little before; and now we shall turn back to them.[3]

[3] Cf. *Asp.* lss. 213 and 224.

CHAPTER XXXVIII

The Men of Girard and Those of Karlamagnus Meet

Now it is said of Emperor Karlamagnus that he rode up on that slope or ridge which was described before, and when he arrived there he saw the heathen host, together with the tower which Girard had been holding: and just then he saw the standard of the duke, who had just gathered his troops around the standard. And since the emperor knew nothing of the duke's arrival he thought this must be a troop of heathens, and he said, "May the Lord guard and protect his troops! Now, indeed, I see heathens, who must have been sent out by them to spy on us, mounted on horseback under the mountainside; they bear themselves most richly. Ride to them, Oddgeir the Dane, and find out what the nature of their journey may be," says the emperor.

"Gladly, lord—as you wish," says Oddgeir, and he spurred his horse. Duke Nemes, the Flemish earl, and Baeringur the Breton went with him, grasping their shields firmly and holding out their stout spears with broad[1] banners.

But when Lord Girard saw these men coming, he called Boz and Clares, along with his two sons Bernard and Reiner,[2] and gave them this message: "My beloved kinsmen,"[3] says he, "now it is time to prepare to serve God. Do you see the four knights riding at us? Surely they are not the least of the heathens! If you can unseat them from their horses, that will be a deed of knightly prowess worthy of note. Ride forward, in God's name!"

They answered, "We will gladly do this, as you ask, even if death were certain; but their situation does not seem to us to be any better than ours. God's will be done, then."

[1] *b*, golden.
[2] *Reinir.*
[3] *b*, friends and kinsmen.

These four knights rode forward at them boldly in a hard charge. It so fell out that Clares met Oddgeir, and the Dane's spear drove down under the handle of the shield so hard that it shattered and pieces fell all over the ground, while Clares struck at Oddgeir's shield above the handle with such strength that the shield burst and there was a cracking sound in the coat of mail; but it did not fail. And although Oddgeir seldom took a fall in a tournament, he fell from his horse at once that time. Then Clares jumped from his horse, and they both drew their swords and started to fight.

But when Boz saw what Clares had begun, he rushed at the Flemish earl and they came together so hard that each of them fell from his horse; they drew their swords, and Boz struck the earl a great blow on the top of his helmet, which glanced off it and struck down on the shoulder; his mail sprang apart and he was greatly wounded, so that he was not able to take part in the next battle after this.

Then Duke Nemes rode at Reiner, while Baeringur went for Bernard; it so fell out between them that Bernard was pushed from his horse, but Baeringur dismounted from his saddle and drew his weapons and they exchanged hard fighting. Nemes and Reiner went at each other—one of them was young, while the other was somewhat advanced in age; each of them behaved in so warlike a fashion that neither spared the other. For a while both were silent: their case would have become very dangerous if it had gone on in the direction towards which it was headed. But God so watched over his men that although each fully desired to overcome the other, no one received any worse injury than has already been told of the earl.

Now, since God regarded them in his mercy, it came into the mind of Oddgeir the Dane to make inquiries of his opponent, and he said, "Who are you, knight?" says he.

The knight answered, "I am called Clares, nephew of the renowned duke Girard of Burgundia,[4] who came here under Asprement a few nights ago to serve almighty God and slay heathens; and who are you?" says Clares.

[4] *Borgunia.*

He answered, "I am called Oddgeir, foster son of the Emperor Karlamagnus."

Clares says, "My good friend," says he, "Welcome!" And he threw his sword away from him and went meekly toward him, while Oddgeir ran to meet him and kissed him joyfully.

In the next place, Duke Nemes asked his opponent who he was. The young knight answered, "I am the son of Lord Girard; men call me Reiner.[5] We arrived under this mountain a few days ago to bear our shields against the heathens."

Nemes then said, "Let us put aside this struggle, good friend, for I am the closest friend of Karlamagnus."

Then they both cast away their swords, and went towards each other, holding up their hands in proof of God's peace.

It went the same way with all these knights. And when the emperor and Girard had seen their conduct, they were much astonished and each one rushed forward from his troop: and when they met and recognized each other there was great rejoicing at their meeting on both sides.[6]

Fragment 2a, Unger pp. 558-9: (*Asp.* 4048-67)

... (not) that Girard had come. Then the king spoke to Oddgeir and Nemes and the Flemish earl[7] and Baeringur the Breton:[8] "I see heathens mounted on their horses, on the slope before us. Ride to them and find out whether they are messengers or whether they have come to spy on our army."

They prepared to charge at them, holding their shields before them and lowering their standard as they couched their stout spears with all their might; but the lord Girard was aware of them at once, and called Boz and Clares, his nephews,[9] and his sons Ernard[10] and Reiner.

[5] *b*, Remer.

[6] Lacuna in A,a continues, but is partially supplied by Fragment 2a, as follows.

[7] *Asp.* "le duc Flavent," 4052.

[8] "le duc Berengier."

[9] Literally, "sons of his sister."

[10] Another sp. for Ernaut; cf. Bernard.

"Lords," said he, "it is now our honor to serve almighty God and avenge him on the heathens. If you can take these four from their mounts, that will show your great skill as horsemen and special fame ..."

CHAPTER XXXIX

Karlamagnus Orders His Troops

As soon as Karlamagnus and Girard met, the emperor asked what the duke had to tell of the heathens. He answered, "Nothing, lord, except that which you know: that they have assembled an overwhelming host. But I would also like to tell you that the tower which you can see, which Jamund occupied for a while, is in my control and I am putting it, together with fifteen thousand good knights, all very well equipped, at your disposal."

The emperor thanked the duke for his splendid offer, asking how he had achieved the tower, and he told him all about it. Then Karlamagnus said, "Praise be to God and to blessed James! It seems to me that there is no one better qualified to direct your troop than you: therefore I shall grant the tower and all the surrounding district to you as long as you stay here."

Girard accepted this. Now Fagon, the standard-bearer, arrived, with all the army, and a great deal of din and hubbub arose when so many men came together in one place. The emperor then rode up on a hill and raised his voice to speak, saying, "God's friends and mine, listen to my words. Truly, almighty God has here brought together a great throng of men from various places for the sake of his most beloved friend the apostle James, to free his land from the evil tyranny of the Africans. I am sure that many have come both for God's sake and for mine, though some only for the grace of God in heaven: yet, many wish to put themselves under my direction and leadership. Therefore we ought to pray that God will let us so perform as to increase his honor and in no way diminish it. And if I return to France victorious, each man shall be greatly rewarded according to his merits."

Lord Girard answered, "Gladly, renowned lord, will we obey your lordship, in the expectation that this will be to our benefit, both in soul and in body."

Next, the emperor arranged the host into divisions. There were four thousand in the first division, the leaders of which were King Salomon, Jofrey[1] and Ankerin,[2] and Earl Hugi of Eleusborg.[3] They had two banners as white as snow and were very well equipped with horses, weapons, and clothing. They all joined hands and swore that they would die rather than flee.

In the second division there were seven thousand; this group was led by Gundabol,[4] king of Frisia.[5] Many banners of various colors could be seen there, shining coats of mail, bright helmets, gleaming swords with golden hilts, and red shields. In the third division were fifteen thousand, and their leaders were Duke Nemes, Lampart, and the brave knight Riker. All of these men were well equipped with good armor bright with purest gold, fresh shields, and stout spears with fluttering banners. In the fourth division he put twenty thousand brave knights whose leader was the good and faithful lord Vernes, with several others; in their division there were steel-hard helmets and bright silver coats of mail, with gold and red banners. There were ten thousand in the fifth division, over which were appointed two kings, a duke, and two earls: it was likely that Jamund would have to labor hard before that troop dispersed!

The sixth division was led by the wise old leader King Droim of Gaskunia, and had forty thousand men; his troop was extremely well equipped with armor and had the swiftest of horses, all strongly armed and well trained. There were seven dukes in this division, all powerful and valiant. The seventh division consisted of many nations: Saxons and Germans, Frenchmen and Flemings, Lotaringi, and with them knights from Pul and Cicilia; here were Fagon the standard-bearer and Oddgeir of Kastram,[6] and there were sixty thousand men in this division. But this troop was to be led by the most famous lord Karolus Magnus, son of Pippin, king of the Franks, and here were placed many

[1] Joifroi l'Angevin.

[2] Ansquetins le Normant.

[3] *b, Oleansborg*; *Asp.* Hüon de Clarvent.

[4] *Gundibol; B, Guldilber.*

[5] *Frisa.*

[6] *b*; "Fagon, the emperor's standard-bearer, and another knight from Kastrum."

great leaders—Duke Rollant, Oddgeir the Dane, and other peers such as these.

Now the army of the Christians has been described; Jamund and his father Agulandus were going to discover that it would have been better for them to stay at home, for, as long as God allowed, these men would oppose them so courageously that all their hopes would be completely overthrown, and so great a defeat would they earn for their greed that they would be led to curse and denounce those who had urged them to this expedition.

a: (24)

... Lord Girard then came to the king, and the king laid his hands on his neck. Girard stood where the king bent over him, and they kissed each other most affectionately. But before the king arose, his headband rolled from his head: Lord Girard then bent down and picked up the diadem, brought it to him, and bowed to him. Now Archbishop Turpin was on the other side; he remembered how Girard had thrown a knife at him[7]—and would have killed him, if he could! He called for ink and vellum, and wrote, translating from French into Latin, of how Girard had dismounted from his horse onto the path, picked up the king's headdress, and brought it to him; and the archbishop added, "He who has been a bad and ill-intentioned neighbor is bound to be bad again tomorrow."

Lord Girard then said to King Karlamagnus, "Have no fear; I have in my train fifteen thousand of the best knights, and they are all well supplied with all arms, so that even the poorest man among them need feel no dread."

"Girard," says King Karlamagnus, "you will be greatly thanked for that."

(27) When Girard had spoken with King Karlamagnus, and given up the tower into his control, the king thanked him, and said, "Hear my words: God has here gathered together a great host of men from Christian lands, and they have not all gathered for my sake, but, rather for the love of almighty God. But you have made me your leader in or-

[7] An episode in *Asp.* which is not given in this saga.

der that God may permit us to bring this business to a good end. When God shall send me back to France, and I return to my ancestral realm, I shall reward you well for your good help."

Girard then answers, "We will give it gladly."
And when he heard that, he thanked him well ...[8]

Fr2.

... Milun,[9] the powerful leader, and Gundabol, king of Frisia.[10] Here could be seen ...[11]

A,a (25)

... banners with various colors, shining coats of mail, bright helmets, the best of golden-hilted swords.—But now King Agulandus and Jamund certainly knew that they would never win France[12] while these men lived to defend it.

In the third division were fifteen thousand, led by Lampart of Freri[13] and Nemes of Bealfer,[14] and third was the valiant Riker. All were well armed in this division.—King Agulandus thought to greatly increase his realm when he sailed away from Africa to conquer all France, but he was never to live long enough to see a penny taken away from there! His weapons would so altogether fail him here that he would curse those who gave him that bad advice.

In the fourth division were twenty thousand brave knights, led by Duke Vernis[15]—and before King Agulandus took France under his power, these men would do him irreparable damage! Thirty thousand

[8] At this point, confusion and lacunae in A,a make any semblance of continuity difficult; however, part of the lacuna can be filled by a bit of Fr2, as follows.

[9] Milon of Poitiers; *Asp.* 4327-8.

[10] *Gundelbof* of *Frisa.*

[11] Ms. *a* resumes here, picking up *Asp.* towards the end of ls. 238.

[12] *a*, power; cf. *Asp.* 4334; Fr. 2, *Valland*, 'France.'

[13] Fr. 2, *Ferre*; not in *Asp.*

[14] Here, "Bealferborg": 'the city of Bavaria.'

[15] *Asp.* Garniers.

were in the fifth division; their leaders were two earls, a duke, and two kings.—Before King Agulandus could win France, these men would do him such damage that he would scarcely be able to remedy it.[16]

(27) ... In the sixth division were sixty thousand. They were the best of knights, armed with good coats of mail and helmets, shields, and all sorts of good armor. At the front of this troop was King Droim, and seven dukes, all strong and gallant men.—If God, in his holy might, wished it, all these would never be overcome by the heathens.

The seventh division was made up of Saxons and men of the south;[17] with them were knights from Cisilia[18] and Rome and from Pul.[19] Frenchmen and Flemings[20] and knights from Loingerus and Loreingus,[21] and Bretons.[22] Lord Fagon rode before them and bore their banner, with another standard-bearer, Oddgeir of Karstram.[23] There were sixty thousand in this group, which was the most mighty one of King Karlamagnus ...

[16] This is the end of ls. 241.
[17] I.e., Germans.
[18] Sicily; not in *Asp.*
[19] Apulia.
[20] *Flaemingjar*; neither of these is in *Asp.* here, but they are mentioned in the next ls.
[21] Two versions of Lorraine?
[22] *Bretar*; not in *Asp.*
[23] Not in *Asp.*; but many of the names in this sequence disagree, so that it is likely the saga source was rather different.

CHAPTER XL

The Arms of Karlamagnus

When Karlamagnus had ordered his troops he dismounted from his horse and went under a tree which had many branches and gave a great deal of shade. He was dressed in a precious kirtle of the finest cloth, which is called esterin;[1] over this he wore a cloak of the fairest cicladi,[2] edged with snow-white fur. He had a hat or cap of sabelin fur on his head, made in the French fashion with wide bands or straps, worked with the greatest of care, and fashioned over this cap were gold knobs, skillfully made. His hose were of the best purple,[3] embroidered with pure gold, and his broad feet were enclosed in courtly shoes, fittingly made.

Karlamagnus now laid aside his cloak and put on the most rugged of coats of mail, made at great expense, for it was shining and bright with the purest silver; parts of it were red, green, or gold, and never had it failed him. Over this, he wore a thick leather jerkin. His helmet was set on his head: so great a treasure that its like would never be found in either the Christian or the heathen army. It was made of the hardest steel the smith could find, fresh in appearance, and there was a ridge around the helmet engraved with flowers and leaves and set with the most precious gems. There were so many stones with special virtues in this helmet that no one needed to fear death while he had it on his head.

After this he was girded with his sword, which was called Jouise:[4] this was an extremely fine sword, large and strong, and engraved with

[1] *b, eximi,* is preferred by Unger and Vilhjalmsson; however, *B*'s *esterin* is obviously the same word as *a*'s *osterin*, a word taken directly from the French, meaning an oriental fabric; none of the three forms is listed in C-V.

[2] *cicladi*, from *a*'s *ciclatun*, representing O.F. *ciclaton* (variously spelled), a silk fabric, sometimes said to be red.

[3] Or, of costly fabric.

[4] *b, Gaudiola* (Joyeuse).

gold lettering from edge to edge. Thus equipped, the emperor mounted the white war-horse which Balam had sent to him, while many great men held his stirrup; then he rode forward in the midst of the army. When he was armed and mounted on his horse, many thousands of men thought that the emperor was a most imposing figure: courtly in appearance, yet warlike; great, and fair to see, with sharp eyes, broad in the shoulders, solid, tall, and strongly built, very powerful; and he could carry his shield especially well.

And when Girard looked at the emperor, he said to those who stood near him, "This lord is no ordinary leader. He may truly be called the emperor of Christian men, for there has never been any man like him, nor is there ever likely to be."

a: (27)

... then he dismounted under a tree which had many branches and spread its shadow afar ...

(26)

Now Lord Girard looked at King Karlamagnus, son of King Pippin. His stockings were of the best purple, stitched with gold thread; he wore a precious gown, of the best osterin[1] and a mantle of ciclatun[2] lined with white fur, with a sable cap on his head. His headband was of pure gold, beautifully made, curving over the hood with gold knobs, rolling richly, made by the craft of the goldsmith: he seemed to King Girard[5] the most royal leader he had ever seen and he repented that he had ever called him the son of a dwarf. Girard's two sons rejoiced greatly ...

(27) ... There he put on his good coat of mail, with a leather vest over it, and closed his gilded helmet over his head, girding himself with the good sword Jouise, engraved all over with golden letters; he then mounted a white war-horse, while they held his stirrups for him. Then they brought his shield to him. The white horse on which the king was mounted had been sent to him by the messenger Balam.

[5] *Gerard.*

The king then rode into the midst of the army, putting the ranks in order. He was magnificent in appearance; broad-shouldered, very tall and strong, he knew how to carry his shield very well indeed. More than three thousand men attended him carefully that day. And when Girard saw the king in his armor, he said to his men, "This man is no ordinary leader: he may truly be called emperor over all Christian kings." ...

CHAPTER XLI

Karlamagnus and the Pope Address the Troops

Now Karlamagnus was mounted on a horse and ready for battle, and his army all about was so well and chivalrously equipped that it was indeed in pomp that this great troop went on its way. There was none of that great number who did not have a war-hat under his helmet. The emperor felt sure that battle was drawing very near, and so he wished to encourage his men with fine words to strengthen them in soul and body and he said, "You all know well that almighty God sent his only begotten son to earth and that he was born of the holy lady and pure virgin Maria into this world to help all mankind, which had been ruined by the sin of the first father, Adam. He dwelt here for thirty-three years and was baptized by John the Baptist, and ordered all who wished to be his servants to do the same, promising to those who follow his commands so great a reward of everlasting bliss that no mortal man may tell or reckon it; but he ordained the dreadful punishment of eternal burning to those who despise them or who plunder his own holy Christendom, which he signed as his own in the shedding of his blood.

"But now it is obvious to all that two heathen leaders, Agulandus and Jamund, have come here near us from Africa to destroy the Christian faith and disgrace the holy places of God, killing us or driving us into exile, intending then to settle in Christ's inheritance: that land which he granted to us, his children. He has therefore sent us here to defend his honors and privileges. Let us bear in mind what we owe to him in service, and how much we shall be rewarded by him. He took upon himself great toil and labor in order to help us, but he was met with scorn and blame and reviling, wounds and torments and crucifixion: he let his hands and feet be pierced with great iron goads, from which ran bright blood. He suffered five wounds on his right side from a sharp spear, from which ran blood and water; but he who pierced him with the spear, who had been blind before, at once gained clear vision when his bloody hand touched his eyes.

"See, good friends, what great deeds our redeemer performed to help us: we should therefore gladly go against his enemies, giving our lives for holy Christianity and meeting death from the heathen weapons, if that is God's will; and if it so befalls you, you shall experience the reward of eternal bliss, where we shall shine in great radiance and rejoice together before almighty God unceasingly."

After this message from the emperor, the pope rode forward, and said, "Hear me, my sons: I am your father, appointed by the good God as physician of your souls; you may therefore trust me, for I shall not lie to you. Our Lord Jesus Christ chose twelve apostles to follow him in this world. The chief of these was the apostle Peter, to whom God granted such power that whatever he bound or loosed should be loosed or bound in heaven and on earth. Know, beyond doubt, that he stands ready to give you strength and to open up the door of heaven's paradise if you go bravely forth under the emperor's standard, especially those who now wish to repent their sins. And in order to dispel all doubt from your hearts, I absolve you of all your sins, with the power which God has granted me on behalf of the blessed apostle Peter, setting you the penance of striking heathens mightily, sparing neither hand nor foot, head nor trunk, receiving for this a true reward from God himself."

All agreed gladly to this condition, and were much fortified by the lord pope's promises; they thanked him and the emperor for their excellent admonitions. The lord pope lifted up his right hand and blessed all the army, and then rode away, with failing voice. Lord Girard then rode to the emperor and spoke to him, saying, "Now, lord, you can clearly see the army of heathens. Lead your first division forward against them while I proceed with my troop, for I would like to come into the midst of the heathen host, if God is willing, to see what my men and I can do."

The emperor answered, "Go in God's name, good friend, and may we meet in good health, God willing!"

The emperor led his troop down into the valley below and waited there for what was to come, earnestly calling on God's mercy and asking for help from his blessed lord James the apostle.

a: (27)

... Such were those on the field at Asperment at the time when King Karlamagnus dismounted from the white horse; a nobleman brought him his shield and sword, and in his gloved hands he took a staff. Now he mounted a huge grey horse brought from Saxony,[1] very swift when bearing weapons,[2] and riding in a princely way, ordering his divisions, he raised his voice and said, "Lords," says he, "a great many of us are now gathered together, as you see. Agulandus and Jamund are on their way to attack us, wishing to take our possessions, unrighteously. But now I ask you, as God sent us here, to defend his honor and glory on this field."

The pope then spoke: "Do not be in such a hurry; I wish to say a few words to you. If you bear yourselves well and righteously under the banner of King Karlamagnus and come to the rescue of holy Christianity, I shall help you, with God's grace, to the most of my ability." Then he lifted up his right hand and blessed them all, and rode away, his voice failing.

... The king now spoke to all the host that was present: "Since Agulandus," says he, "undertook to lay my realm waste and banish my people, if such deeds should be forgiven him he might well mock and scoff at me."

Girard answers, "I tell you truly, lord, if God allows us we shall take vengeance on him and his men." And he said further to the king, "Lord," says he, "I can now see a heathen expedition riding under cover: there are so many of them that they cannot be counted. Now you ride to attack the first division while I go to rally my men: then we shall come and fight with my host. If I can come against them with my troop, I shall take care of the band that comes behind. It is fitting that he who survives this day shall not forget the day as long as he lives." ...

[1] Saxony.

[2] There does not seem to be any precedent for this change of horses in *Asp.*

CHAPTER XLII

The Armies Clash

Now we shall speak of the heathens and how, when they saw the army of Christians approaching, the first division, led by Balam, rode forward and made great din and uproar that could be heard far and wide: blowing shrill trumpets, great horns and stout pipes, beating on tambourines and shields. They let countless banners of various colors stream forth in the wind. Their arms glittered—gilded helmets, bright silver coats of mail, shining shields; the plain was lit up on both sides by their weapons. Right at the front rode Balam, who has often been spoken of before, wearing a doublet of the best purple cloth[1] over his coat of mail so that he could be easily recognized. With him rode forward four kings, who had vowed to find the four chief gods, Maumet, Makon,[2] Terrogant, and Jupiter—or not to return at all. These four were so puffed up with pride that all their trappings were red with gold.

As the divisions clashed together the Christians let out a shrill war-cry and each encouraged the others to go forward. A great terror now struck the heathen host, for many of them thought they were not likely to gain anything at all: their legs trembled, and they were afraid. If they proceed against the Frenchmen in so terrified a state, they shall soon find a suitable resting place!

Earl Hugi, who led the first division of Karlamagnus, and his four companions rode forward boldly from their rank to oppose the four kings who have been described, and such valor was kindled by the Holy Spirit as soon as they rushed strongly into that group that three kings soon lay dead on the field. Balam, meanwhile, struck at Earl Hugi and thrust him from his horse: but since God would not permit

[1] *b* omits "a doublet of."
[2] *Machon.*

it, he did not draw any blood from him. This victory which God and St. James granted their troops in their first attack much heartened the French, who rejoiced and rushed forward with great vigor.

Now the battle began to rage. Much noise was made and wild tumult. There was breaking and bursting in charges, for the French were so determined that none was afraid to advance, and they struck so hard with their keen spears that no armor could withstand them. Many a proud warrior now fell so disgracefully from his horse that he was never able to rise to his feet again; saddles were emptied, while horses ran free when their lords had been slain. Helmets, enclosing split skulls, and hands and feet flew apart from bodies. All went so well for the French that those who had been somewhat afraid before now gained such keen and great courage that no one was braver than they in advancing.

Thus a great crowd of that cursed people fell, until the French came where the heathen bowmen stood: these evil dogs attacked them sharply, shooting hard and often from Turkish bows, so that great danger was at hand. At this time the emperor's beloved kinsman Rollant and Oddgeir the Dane advanced to the front with their peers, and they drove so forcefully against the archers that they pushed them back from their places no less than four arrow-shots; neither stiff bows nor shafts of hard steel availed them, for Rollant gave heavier blows than they! Thus many of the heathens fell, and a few of the Christians as well—but few in comparison.

a: (28)

On the other side, sixty thousand Africans rode forward on the slope. These heathens made a great din and noise as they blew horns and trumpets, pipes and tabors: almost none of them did not have a horn or trumpet, pipe, or tabor. Balam was leading them on a white horse; over his coat of mail he wore a special doublet made of the best purple material, with three lions woven in gold. Four kings also led this division; these four were going in search of their gods, one looking for Maumet, the second for Apollin, the third for Terrogant, and the fourth for great Jove.[3] Each of them was easy to recognize by his arms,

[3] Jupiter in *Asp.* 4424.

which glittered with gold and bright steel. When they saw the divisions of the Frenchmen before them, there was none so strong-hearted in all the host that he was not frightened and shaken in his mind. If they proceed in such terror of the Frenchmen, then what is to be said about them will shortly come to an end!

Four thousand Frenchmen were in the division that was the first to ride forward; of them, four knights went in advance, on good, swift horses. Their coats of mail were made of pure silver, and gold and steel shone on their helmets. These men galloped their horses as eagerly and wrathfully as if they wished to gain God's grace that day by triumphing over all the heathens. Against these four galloped four of the heathen kings, with high pride and arrogance. They, in turn, went toward them as fast as they could, so that they met with such hard exchange of blows that they did away with three of the kings there. But Balam attacked Hugi of Eleandsborg and swept him from his horse, though he could not kill him; and thus the battle began, with a great deal of din. There one could see many kings and knights lying covered with blood, some of them quite dead.

(29) The clash as they met was great and terrible. Spears and golden helmets were shattered, saddles were emptied and horses fled, as the Frenchmen slashed and attacked so wrathfully and mightily that the heathens could not protect themselves from their blows. Many of the Frenchmen who were afflicted with cowardice at first gained courage then, so that later there were no more gallant or better fighters than these. The Christians killed a great many of the heathen people, for in this division there were many who did not have coats of mail.

Bowmen then advanced with Turkish bows and shot so fast and thick that terrible danger was near at hand; but with a French division came a foster son of King Karlamagnus[4] whom God had blessed and sent there, and they charged the heathens and drove them back more than four arrow-shots. ...

[4] Identified as Rollant in B,b, but not so in *Asp.*; cf. 4478-80.

CHAPTER XLIII

Girard Attacks

It is to be said of Lord Girard that when he had prepared his troop he aimed to attack the right division of the Africans and he certainly did not give those before him any chance to rest. Lord Girard spoke these words to his men: "Strike hard as soon as you encounter the army and show whether the swords with which I have equipped you can bite into the thick necks of the heathens. Fear nothing at all, for I am Girard, who shall lead you forward boldly: blessed is he who serves God, both now and in eternity."

They answered, "You shall be able to see whether either we or our weapons prove frail."

Then Lord Clares dashed forward, waving his banner from a stout spear which he held in his right hand; he spurred on the horse he had taken from Jamund and ran at a great king of Africa named Guilimin. He struck at his shield, mail, and body, dashing him dead to the earth, then raised his voice and cried out, "Good comrades, behold! This haughty man has marked our field with his heart's blood: now attack boldly, for the others are not far. Repay today the bread and wine with which God feeds us daily! Slice through flesh and bone, let blood pour out and give a sufficient prey to the raven and wolf, for we shall gain honor and victory."

They did as he urged, drawing their swords and giving the heathens great strokes and strong blows, never stopping to ask whether the man in their way was a king or a thrall. In the nick of time the old Girard turned before a huge knight who had earlier killed many Christians, struck at him with his spear and lifted him out of his saddle, flinging him down to the ground with these words: "By him who made me, you shall never again kill my men!"

Then he rode forward in so manly a fashion that whoever he met fell dead. In this part of the battle there was great loss of life; both men and horses were slain, and some of the duke's troop also fell.—Now we shall turn from this scene, and learn somewhat of how Jamund was faring.

a: (29)

... Lord Girard of Franeborg and his valiant nephews, with fifteen thousand of their most courageous knights on war-horses, armed with the best armor, now rode down from the slope, and aimed at the right wing of the heathen troop, and they were most certainly able to attack bravely. Lord Klares and his brother Basin, with ten thousand of their comrades, led their divisions. Klares rode in front, spreading out his banner on a great spear-shaft; he sat on the white horse which he had taken from Jamund[1] and galloped at Giulion,[2] a powerful African king, striking him in the shield and mail-coat, pushing him from his saddle dead. Then he called to his troop, saying in a clear voice, "Lords," says he, "advance firmly! God must intend honor and victory to be ours, and those who trust in him shall be blessed."

Such good fortune followed Girard that he never came onto the battlefield without winning the victory. Now he spoke bold words to his men: "Fear not at all," says he, "I am Girard: I am not afraid to go before you. He who dies on this battlefield is saved, and happy is he who serves a good lord."[3]

[1] Not so in *Asp.*
[2] *Asp.* 4501: "le roi d'Angalion."
[3] Possibly "the good Lord," but *Asp.* does not seem to indicate this.

CHAPTER XLIV

An Encounter Between Oddgeir the Dane and Jamund

When the battle began in the morning, Jamund began to advance from the chief standard into the middle of the division brandishing the sword Dyrumdali and striking Christians on both sides with such force that neither shield nor coat of mail was any protection: his sword cut through steel and stone as well as through flesh and bone. Thus he did a great deal of damage to the emperor's company, for when he saw his troops slain and giving way he became all the more grim and furious. Oddgeir the Dane could see this, and he said, "Almighty God, it is a great grief to me that this heathen lives so long and slays so many good warriors!"

With this, he turned his horse, grasped his shield before him, and couched his spear for attack, hurrying towards Jamund; he was accompanied by a knight named Arnketill of Normandy. But when Jamund saw this, he said to his uncle[1] Moram, "Here comes a short man towards us, kinsman: what can he expect but to seek his death? He shall find it very soon."

Thus he[2] rode forward, and as soon as the horses met each man struck the other's shield with such force that neither had cause to boast of his lot, for both fell far from their horses. Oddgeir drew his sword, but Jamund drew Dyrumdali: Oddgeir will soon be destroyed, if God does not help him!

Meanwhile, Arnketill rode at a great and powerful leader named Boland and struck down on his helmet so hard that his skull was split to the teeth, and he tumbled to the ground dead. Arnketill then took the horse he had been riding and gave it to Oddgeir, who mounted it quickly and nimbly. Jamund then left them and rode swiftly back to his men.

[1] "Brother of his mother."

[2] *b*, they.

A,a (33)

... Jamund grasped Dyrumdali, the best of swords. Whoever this bit into was dead, for that sword never failed. If he were to live longer, he would certainly win the realm of King Karlamagnus—unless almighty God supported the king.

(32) ... Into the other group of Frenchmen now came galloping Oddgeir, and, with him, Anketill of Normandy.[3] But Jamund, son of King Agulandus, brought about much loss of life in the French division. He struck on both sides and no one was his equal, for his sword never failed. "Almighty God," said Oddgeir, "woe is me that this heathen should live so long!" He put his shield before him, laid his spear down in the correct position, and hurried after Jamund. And when Jamund saw him coming, he said to Bolant,[4] his uncle.[1] "Here comes a man looking for his death," and joyously rode against him..

And when the horses met in swift onrush, each man attacked the other's shield so vigorously that neither could stay on his horse and[5] both tumbled far from their horses. Oddgeir jumped up at once with his sword drawn, holding his shield before him: but Jamund held the great sword Dyrumdali.

At that moment, Anketill rode at Bolant, a powerful man and great leader; and Anketill struck him such a great blow on his helmet[6] that he split his head down to the teeth and threw him dead to the ground; he then took his good horse[7] to Oddgeir, who mounted as quickly as he could: if they had stayed there any longer, they would never have seen Frenchmen again.

[3] Northmandi.—*Asp.* 4717, Ansquetin; however, most of this chapter does not correspond closely to *Asp.*

[4] *A, Morlant,* here and below; *Asp.* Morant, 4872, "cosins fu Agulant"; but Boidant occurs in the passage corresponding most closely in *Asp.*

[5] *a*; "they came together with such hard blows that ..."

[6] "on ... helmet" in *a* only; cf. *Asp.* 4719.

[7] *A*: "the same horse."

CHAPTER XLV

Battle Continues

Now the battle was fierce and savage but there was always the most din to be heard in the part where Rollant rode with his peers, so expert were they in slashing apart flesh with bones. Thus armor was ruined, knights wounded, horses exhausted, and Africans, turning craven, wished to escape, for their host suffered thousands of losses, while the plain became so covered with the bodies of men, horses, and armor that there was no less than half a mile where neither man nor horse could find room to put his foot on bare ground. There is nothing more that need be said of this but that all that day, from the time it started, early in the morning, the battle raged until nightfall. The holy apostle James called many Christian men of the host of Karlamagnus home to a life of eternal bliss that day, rewarding them with an overflowing measure of happiness in eternity for their day's work.

Now, when evening and darkness approached, the fighting ceased and the emperor rode down into a little valley with certain of his men. He was much troubled, for two kings had lost their lives and more than forty earls and dukes, and many other men. He did not grieve over the cause of their death, as if he did not realize that they would be rewarded, but, rather, because there were few left standing to defend the land when so many had gone to God.

A,a (33)

The heathens stayed there as long as they could defend themselves, but those who had come to the battle the first day were of little use on the second. And when the French saw that they were wavering, they killed a great many of them; in that battle also fell twenty thousand one hundred Frenchmen, called to himself by God. When Jamund saw his host pursued, he was filled with dread.

The battlefield was covered with bodies and armor and war-horses, awaiting their lords, for more than half a mile.[1] ...

(30) Beneath Aspermunt, in the valley below, Christians and heathens clashed for two whole days, until the time of evensong had passed on the second day, after starting at daybreak on the day before. So many hard blows and mighty strokes were given there, so many hands[2] and arms and heads cut off, that for more than half a mile the surface of the earth was laid so bare that a horse could not find forage there. On all sides lay shields and helmets and swords, coats of mail and bucklers, armor and dead men. Jamund thought he would win himself a great realm here: but before he could take full possession and have himself crowned by those who had followed him there, there would be few to return home joyfully to his realm.[3] They would leave their lords and leaders, their land and their riches, which would have to be given to those who lay in their cradles, who would have to be fostered for a long time before they could wield a sword.

(35) ... Emperor Karlamagnus, however, was much angered and troubled, for he had lost two kings and more than forty[4] of his dukes and earls, and before they parted in the afternoon he needed them all. As evening fell, he rode into a certain valley, with his troop, to rest ...

[1] Sentence in *a* only; cf. *Asp.* 4750-51.
[2] Up to here, *a* only; *A* resumes here.
[3] *a* adds "and fatherland."
[4] *a*, 60; *Asp.* 4791 "plus de qatorse."

CHAPTER XLVI

Balam Rebukes Jamund

Lord Girard took up night quarters under a ridge; he had lost three thousand of his men. All his best knights stayed on their horses, in their armor, much exhausted by toil and thirst, while other Christians sat on their horses in the midst of the battlefield,[1] over the bodies of the dead. Now there was none so wealthy or high in rank that he did not hold his own horse by the bridle, with his sword in his other hand. None would take such comfort as to loosen his helmet from his head; neither man nor horse ate or drank, nor did sleep come to their eyes, for all thought they had better watch over their horses and weapons themselves when they were separated from the heathens only by a little plain. All endured this night in fear and terror.

Of the heathens, it shall next be said that when the day passed and nightfall darkened many left the field, slinging their shields on their backs and fleeing. But when Jamund saw that he was furious and called out, saying, "Woe upon you, wicked thralls! You have truly betrayed me. Turn back, and do not desert me, for it was your urging that made me so swollen with pride as to attack this land."

But although Jamund was a huge man and called out with raised voice, they did not want to turn back, for they had learned so much about the weapons of the French that day that they never wished to exchange blows with them again, unless they went with overwhelming force. At this time, the messenger Balam came before Jamund and leaned upon the hilt of the sword he was carrying, saying, "You would have accepted my advice, Jamund, if I had persuaded you to believe my words when I came from Karlamagnus when you had sent me to look over the Christian host, rather than suffer the disgrace you have

[1] *b* gives this as the location of the former rather than the latter.

had today. Know, then, that all of the first division which you sent forward this morning has perished together, though a few remain and some have fled. Now it has happened as I said; I told you then to be careful, but you and your men were so far from believing my message that you accused me of taking bribes from the Christians to betray you. Now you have learned who spoke more truly: I, or those proud boasters and arrogant men who said they would take over all the realm. Now you may see how much they are gaining for you."

Jamund answered, "It is true, Balam, that I have trusted them too long; but what is to be done now, good friend?"

Balam answered, "There are now two choices. One is to flee or to surrender to the emperor, and I think that would be the better course; the other is to make a determined stand and suffer death here. For what I said is not false: you will not overcome the French, and no nation is equal to them in valor and chivalry. You can see that they are mounted on their horses, awaiting us."

Jamund answered, "I shall never be caught giving up or fleeing away while we have a much greater host than theirs."

After this they ended their conversation.

A,a (31)

That night the wounded had dismal quarters, where they suffered pain and trouble. King Agulandus had brought this all about by his ambition when he undertook to rob Christian men of their honors and possessions: but before he could win and subdue France and appoint his heirs there, this swordplay would end in such a way that all who survived of his host would become poor and needy—if any were to escape with their lives!

During the night there was a small field between the Christians and the heathens, but neither hill nor valley. No one on either side ate or drank on that day or night, neither meat nor bread nor table-wine, and there was no horse there who tasted corn or hay, as each man held his horse by the bridle and held his drawn sword with his other hand.

Lord Girard, the valiant knight, had felled a knight from his horse, bloodying his spear in his heart's blood: he fell dead to the ground.[2]

[2] An evidently misplaced line.—At this point, the saga skips over several

(35) ... Other Christians stayed on horseback on the battlefield, with dead heathens lying everywhere under their feet. But there was no chieftain there so high or powerful that he did not hold his horse by its reins himself.

All that night Christians kept watch and there was no one in all the army who could take such ease as to loosen his helmet from his head or take his shield from his neck, or who did not suffer some sort of grief or pain; their horses neither ate nor drank.

But Jamund got no honor from this, for his troop was much wounded and more than half had been killed on the battlefield. A great many had fled, disheartened and frightened, nor did they return to the battlefield unless compelled by force. When Jamund saw them fleeing, he spoke, crying after them in a loud voice: "Wicked rascals," says he, "you have grievously betrayed me, for I came here at your urging."

And when he had said this, Balam came up to him and leaned on the hilt of his sword, saying, "It is not surprising," said he, "if you are angry. When you sent me to King Karlamagnus, and I returned, I told you something which I knew to be true; but where now are those boasters who then called me a false traitor, condemning me, and saying I had taken a bribe from his men? They claimed they had seen all their power: but if they had stayed here until day, they certainly would have learned how much they could win."[3]

Jamund then said, "I have made enquiry about them too late, and too long have I followed their advice and urging." Then he added, hard and grim, "Much has now gone amiss for us," says he; "we have lost our four gods, in whom was all our trust, and if we could not drive them off that day, then we shall never be able to win sweet France from their power."

Balam answered, "Lord," said he,[4] "consider now: where are those wicked liars and boasters who condemned my message, saying that it

lss. of *Asp.* and picks up, rather illogically, the action in the midst of the next day's battle.

[3] Latter sentence in *a* only; cf. *Asp.* 4612-13.

[4] *a* adds, "I told you truly, when you sent me to Karlamagnus, and I returned, I then said to you what I knew to be true, which has not been proved by you to be false, that there were never any braver men than Frenchmen." This corresponds roughly with *Asp.* 4625-26.

was false and untrue? Now you may see the Frenchmen before you; they await none but you. We now have two choices before us, either to die here or else to defend ourselves bravely."

The fourth book of this saga now ends here.[5]

[5] I.e., the fourth part of Agulandus (or, the *Asp.* version on which this part is based: cf. Introduction). The saga divides the tale into ten books, but the first three divisions are not indicated in the mss.—A few pages are missing from ms. *A* at this point.

CHAPTER XLVII

Battle Begins Again

Early in the morning when day broke, there was a great deal of frost as the sun rose. Jamund prepared his division, in which there were twenty thousand, for the first attack, and led them himself; against them came four thousand Frenchmen—they were indeed short of men. The battle began with much outcry and shouting. Many of the men were stiff with cold and wounds, for which they did not find much of a cure. Thus the Christians called upon their maker for help, for they were much afflicted by the fall of their comrades.

As soon as the battle began Jamund rode grimly forward into the host of Christians, intending to avenge the harm he thought had been done him the day before. He charged with his stout spear at Anzelin of Varegne, striking against his shield, coat of mail, and body, flinging him down from the horse, and did not care at all who complained of his fall or death. Then Balam rode forth and struck a good warrior against his shield and coat of mail; and just then Oddgeir the Dane came up with a great crowd of knights, and when Balam saw that he drew back his spear and turned back to his men. The man who had been struck was little hurt.

Oddgeir now advanced boldly, striking to either side. He saw that many Christians were now falling, so he did not delay but rode into the midst of the heathen company, and in this attack he captured Butran, who was named before. After this he rode back into his division and asked the interpreter[1] what he could say about the plans of Jamund: he said, "Jamund intends to conquer Karlamagnus with just such a host as he now has, which you can see."

[1] I.e., Butra.

And when Oddgeir heard that, he galloped off to the place where Karlamagnus was with his troop: he had not yet come into the battle, for those who first entered battle were those who had been on the battlefield during the night. As soon as the emperor saw Oddgeir, he greeted him and asked how matters were now going. He answered, "Well, God willing, lord; yet you are still being much damaged, for many good knights are losing their lives. But we comrades who rode forth this morning have captured Jamund's interpreter, and he says that Jamund would rather lose his hands and feet than give up or send word to his father Agulandus. Send, then, to our encampment, and summon hither all the young men. If they come well equipped then I expect that the heathens will grow fewer, for although there are many of them, they have little armor, and prove to be bad warriors as soon as they are boldly attacked. While your men are much wounded and exhausted, they attack so courageously that many heathens fall as against each one of them."

When the emperor heard Oddgeir's words he was troubled in his heart, and said, "Most glorious lord, almighty God, to whose rule and supervision all creation is subject, I am much distressed that the people whom you, my ruler, gave me to govern shall be slain before my eyes by your enemies, who have never loved you and have always hated the holy faith which you ordained to be held and kept. Now they wish to overthrow your honor and seize under their villainous rule the realm which belongs to you and your friends. A great many of your servants now lie on the field, men who were determined to punish them for this disgrace and to cleanse holy Christianity from their tyranny. Therefore I ask for your mercy, that you may strengthen us and cast your wrath over these enemies. I also call upon you, God's holy apostle James, asking you not to take from us your aid, which you have often well granted to us since we came in your service: you know that you are the reason and original cause of my coming hither and if you allow all my men to be killed here, then never shall that be advanced which you promised at the time when you appeared to me, that your honor would be increased in this land by my expedition. Now grant to your knights dauntless courage and cast down the cursed heathens with the power of your great might so that all may praise the mercy of God and your protection, without end."

When the emperor had ended his prayer, he said to Oddgeir the Dane, "Your advice shall be followed, to send after all the host which is staying in our camp; call King Droim and young Andelfreus to me, then."

And as soon as they came before the emperor, he said, "Good friends, go quickly to the camp and tell them I want all the young men and serving boys to prepare themselves for battle and come to join me."

They agreed gladly and rode off to the encampment, where they performed the emperor's errand as it has been described. But now the emperor prepared his division to go forward into the battle; he still had a fine, large host and had his chief standard raised. Rollant and many other leaders were with him.

And when Jamund saw the emperor's golden standard he said to his men, "Now you can see the arrogance of Karlamagnus when he still intends to come to battle with his troop, thinking to defeat us! Let us attack boldly, for the strength of our host is at least four against one and it seems to me that their men have more courage than prudence if they think they can overcome our host."

When Karlamagnus came to battle, he urged his troop to avenge their comrades who lay there dead on the field. The knight Salomon began the first charge of the emperor's troop and charged with his spear against the king called Bordant. This Bordant had around his neck a shrill trumpet called Olifant, and although he was very tall and well equipped his armor was of no help to him. Salomon struck him dead to the ground, grabbing the horn at the same time and taking it. When Jamund saw the king's fall and the horn taken, he was furious, and rushed after Salomon, saying, "It would be better for you, knight, if you had never been born, for now you shall lose your life!" With that, he lifted the sword Dyrumdali high up and struck at his helmet, slashing down into his shoulders:[2] then he took Olifant and tied it around his neck.

[2] The redactor is apparently trying to mend the A,a version confusion here, but making matters worse in the process. Salomon is not, apparently, to be thought of as killed (or even seriously injured) by this blow when he turns up in fighting form in Ch. 52 and later. Unger's summary, however, suggests that he *is* killed here—and confounds the confusion by calling him "Samson," in

Just then the good knight called Ankerin came up, intending to strike Jamund; but he turned quickly and struck Ankerin down through the shoulders, saying, "Woe,[3] Christian!" says he. "You are not going to destroy me!"

When the Frenchmen saw Jamund's great blow, many of them wanted to attack him, and now the battle became very sharp. And when the emperor learned of the fall of Ankerin, he said, "May God slay the heathen who slew you, my good friend; and if God wills I shall gladly avenge you on him, for you were my most beloved foster son, serving me truly from the time of childhood. May God now bless your soul, while we who survive shall press forward as boldly as we are able."

His heart was moved with these words, but he fulfilled them at once, valiantly, and called to his kinsman Rollant, saying, "Let us now trust in God's mercy, and make so hard an attack on the heathens that they are completely pushed back." Then he galloped forward with drawn sword and slashed apart heathens.

At the same time, Rollant attacked on the other side, with his companions, so that many of the heathens fell in the battle here very soon. Now they saw the sharp wands of war[4] piercing their hearts so that blood ran out of their wounds, wounds smarted, coats of mail were torn apart, and men fell dead. While James extends his aid to the Christians in this part of the battle, we shall turn away and tell what was happening in another place.

a: (36)

It was very chilly as day broke, and when the sun came up it wept to see Jamund coming there. Soon the battle was revealed. Jamund made his divisions ready; they consisted of no fewer than twenty thousand

his summaries of both this ch. and ch. 36—the latter being a ch. in which *both* Samson (the archbishop) and Salomon (definitely not confused in the mss.) play parts. Then Unger uses Salomon's proper name in referring to him again in the summary of ch. 69. All this must have misled a number of his readers, including Paris, who duly reports the death of Samson in ch. 47 (*La K-s*, 9-10).

[3] *B*, No.

[4] I.e., swords.

knights, who rode hastily on their way there. But when the Christians saw them, and prepared for their assault, those who dreaded leaving their comrades lamented: they all vowed to God that those who survived would never commit deadly sin as long as they lived! Then three thousand of them rode against that great army, grieving that there were so few against them, and there was a great din as they came together.

Jamund rose in front of his division holding his shield before him and shaking out his banner. He drove a blow at the shield of Anteini of Varigne,[5] whose coat of mail failed him; Jamund stained the shaft of his spear with his blood and hurled him dead from his horse; none refrained from mourning his fall.

Next, the messenger Balam rode forward from his troop and struck the buckler of a strong man, slitting the coat of mail. Lord Girard then came to his aid. The Christians saw much destruction on the battlefield; they let out a cry and attacked, and now so many blows were made, harming bones, that those who were on horseback could be of little help. Horses went with empty saddles all over the field, and it was easy enough to get plenty of good horses there.

King Ganter[6] stood there before King Karlamagnus and the mighty Gernard of Bostdem,[7] Duke Anzelin,[8] Samson, and Eimer,[9] and many another—we cannot name them all. When the king saw them standing before him, he was so moved by grief and anger that tears ran down his beard. He called to God, saying, "Glorious Lord," says he, "almighty God, all creatures live under your guidance; you put in my hands the guidance of these men whom I now see cut down before my eyes by that accursed people who have never known love of you and hate the holy faith which you taught mankind to have and hold. These enemies wish to overcome your friends and establish themselves in your holy realm, where your holy Name is always blessed; but they will never love and honor you. Now I have lost a great part of these, thy men, who are chastising them and cleansing your realm. Now,

[5] Antelme d'Alemagne, *Asp.* 4664.

[6] *Asp.* "le duc Gaifier."

[7] Garnier de Lohierainne.

[8] Antelmes.

[9] Rainnier; Brandin takes this as the Rainer who is a son of Girard, but if so he certainly does not seem to belong in this list.

therefore, I beg for your mercy: strengthen us, and direct your wrath at those your enemies, who wish to overcome us."

And when the king had so spoken, Oddgeir arrived there. His shield had been so cut up as to be useless: there was nothing left of it but the part by which he held it. His helmet was slashed all the way through and his mail was so badly rent on him in many places that the blood gushed from his white flesh. He bore his naked sword in his hand and said to the king, "Lord," says he, "ride as quickly as possible now; we have captured Butran,[10] his spokesman and messenger, who has told us all their counsel. Jamund wishes on no account to send for his father Agulandus: he would rather lose hand and foot first. Now if you wish them to be seized by dread, quickly send men to our camp summoning all to come and join you to help and to avenge their friends."

King Karlamagnus said, "The advice you have given, Oddgeir, is sound and well judged." And he thanked him.

(37) When King Karlamagnus had heard Oddgeir's advice he sent Lord Droim and Andelfraei[11] to his camp, saying, "Tell our army that each and every one of them should come here to me as soon as possible: let him who has no war-horse ride a palfrey." They answered, saying they would gladly do that. Then King Karlamagnus rode out with his division: the poorest knight in this troop was very well supplied with all weapons.

And when Jamund saw the emperor's banner[12] over his standard—there were seven of his most trusted leaders with him, and each had seven thousand knights in his division—[13] Jamund said, "Hear me, lords," says he: "look, you can now see the arrogance of King Karlamagnus, who rides against us with a great host. Although there are many of them, there are yet many more of us, so that we have three against every man of theirs. But I see now that what Balam said is true, and that I was very foolish to doubt his words, although I learned that late."

[10] *Butram.*
[11] Audefroi.
[12] *gullari*: the oriflamme.
[13] The syntax does not indicate which side is being so described, and there is no corresponding passage in *Asp.*

King Karlamagnus now rode forward with his division, past where the slaughtered lay; he left those who were dead lying there. In his division were thirty thousand of the most courageous knights, and two thousand of the king's division were riding in front. Their captains were Anketill and Alemund of Normandy.[14]

Salomon[15] then rode forward and attacked the man called Bordant,[16] who was king of Nubia. His armor could not protect him, for Salomon drove his spear through him and dashed him dead from his horse; then he reached out his hand and took the shrilling trumpet Olivant from around his neck. When Jamund saw that this king had fallen and his horn had been taken from his neck, he cried out loudly, in his language, saying, "Noble knight," says he, "it is a great grief that you were ever born!" He reached out with Dyrumdali and struck down on his back and on the right shoulder in such a way that the sword went straight into the saddle, and with his second blow he struck Ankirim and slashed him down the back; and he took the horn and turned back to his own men, while Ankirim fell dead from his horse.[17]

When the Frenchmen saw that, there was none so brave that he did not shudder with fear at the terrible mortal blow which he had given. If he had had faith in the God of Heaven, no leader in Christendom would have been his equal!

When the king saw that Ankirim[18] had fallen he lamented his fall and said, "Friend," said he, "your fall is a great sorrow, for God fell with you. I brought you up from your childhood, and no man who served me was your equal: if God will ever hear my prayer, I ask mercy for you with all my heart."

[14] This sentence and the following paragraph differ greatly from *Asp.* 4868-4926, and appear to be giving us three different names for the same knight, Ansquetin le Normant. Salomon, Nubia, and Olifant are not mentioned in *Asp.* The saga is clearly confused when Jamund retrieves from Ankirin a horn captured by Salomon.

[15] *Salamon.*

[16] Like the earlier "Bolant" (who is possibly the same character) this appears to be a confusion of Morant and Boidant.

[17] Cf. ns. 2 and 14 above.

[18] *Ankerim.*

And the king raised a great war-cry, and said, "Cut down our enemies!"

They did as the king said, giving hard battle now. They drove their spears, slashed with swords, and if they had held to this long, the others would all have had to yield before them ...

CHAPTER XLVIII

The Next Stage of Battle

Now it is fitting to say something of what the good duke Girard had begun, for it is not to be suggested that he slept or did nothing gainful while there was any such thing to be done. Early in the morning, when there was still only a trace of daylight, he summoned his kinsmen Boz and Clares and other leaders who had stayed the night, as has been said, under the ridge; and he said to them, "My dear kinsmen and friends," says he, "what shall we do now, when we have lost many of our men, and hard battle is at hand—unless it be to confide ourselves to God's providence and be prepared to give our lives, to die for his sake, as when he was so sublime and holy as to suffer death for ours. Let us ride boldly, then, against the unbelieving people of the heathens, and, since the field is so widely covered with bodies that a horse cannot get through, five thousand of our men shall leave their steeds behind here while they go into battle, and help us who are riding to advance."

All agreed to do as he arranged. Then Lord Girard rode into battle, with no greater a host in the first division than two thousand. He moved his troop forward at the right side of the emperor's division, where they fought against twenty thousand heathens who had gathered there; his charge was the hardest, for neither the leader nor those who followed him lacked courage. When the Africans saw the duke coming, they crouched down under their helmets and coats of mail. The Christians rushed forward on good horses, equipped with sturdy armor, and thrust with spears or struck with swords so hard and fast that the heathens could do nothing but try to protect themselves against their charge. Those who stood furthest away shot with stiff missiles, but the duke's men paid no attention to that; they were now so inspired with strength by God that not even the furthest could withstand them. They rushed so furiously that everyone in the heathen host thought that the further off he was from them, the better, and they did not care about holding their places but went off and scattered.

When Lord Girard saw this, he raised his voice and called out, "Glorious knights, guard yourselves well and do not hold back in the midst of the wicked heathens! Stay well together so that each supports the other against their division, seizing that which stands next to us; then let us turn and attack firmly wherever they give way most."

After these words, he spurred his strong war-horse, shook his spear, and thrust it against the shield of a powerful leader who was named Malchabrun, penetrating his jerkin, coat of mail, and body, and shoving him dead to the ground far from the horse. Then he raised his banner, saying, "See, heathens, this comrade of yours, who has bowed down to my old age!" To his men, he added, "Strike hard: God shall strengthen your arms so that the swords can bite sharply; now the case is going so that it truly is shown that our cause is right."

At that time the five thousand whom the duke had told to dismount from their horses came into the battle. They were armed with the best weapons, and gave the heathens strong blows with hard spear-charges, slashed heads from trunks, struck some down through the shoulders and cut off hands and feet. Thus discontent was now voiced among the heathens, for they quickly fell, unarmed, before these newly arrived knights, nor did anyone need to expose the fat of his back more than once to their weapons.

It shall be told here that Lord Girard led an attack to the place where the chief standard of Jamund stood, and, both because the Africans saw the attack become extremely fierce, so that they thought danger was upon them, and because they had found how well and happily the French fought, everyone who could ran off, for the places where any attack or defense could be made were held by them, while the heathens thronged together on top of the dead, who lay thickly over the place.

When the duke had arrived near the division which stood around the standard, they fought back firmly for a while; but as soon as the duke's men arrived in full strength, the division wavered quickly. And when the kings Magon and Asperant, who have been named before, into whose control and guard Jamund had given the chief standard, saw the duke drawing so near, while their men fell one over another, they spoke between them in this way, as you may hear: "Now what Balam said before of the Frenchmen is proved to be true: none is their equal in valor. They are such great warriors that never, while there is life in their breasts, will they give up. But Jamund is now showing his pride and arrogance with unheard-of foolishness when he dares to so carry on the battle without his father Agulandus, and it seems that in the same way that this presumption has arisen in his mind, all of those who follow his counsels shall be overcome by the same folly. Certainly we are great fools if we expect to gain anything in this place when Jamund does not dare to come to help us. What can we expect here but death? Since he neglects his chief standard, it will not help for us to make a stand. It would, thus, be much better to leave these difficulties and go to find Agulandus and acquaint him with what is happening."

The long and short of whatever they said between them was that they agreed to ride away from the standard, without letting Jamund know what they were doing. They got away from the battle with great difficulty, galloped their horses off as fast as they could, and of the rest of their journey nothing is told.

Lord Girard now cleared a broad way, with his nephews Boz and Clares and other very high leaders following him, and after that one of his men after another, all striking on either side, so that the heap of the slain was piled up high on both sides of them as they came forward under the chief standard. When the duke arrived there he said to his men, "Strike boldly! The king of Africa now thinks he has conquered you and taken possession of[1] our land and realm, and that he can drive us into exile or hand us over into terrible torment. Now it shall be seen how well you come forward to defend us. I am old, and it is thus fitting for you to support my old age and attack the better when you are younger."

When he had arrived under the chief standard he attacked with such great valor that no one thought he had ever seen such an attack from so old a man, for with a single blow he struck down dead every one of the heathens which his sword could get near; thus more than ten thousand fell around the chief standard in a little while.

[1] *B*, destroyed.

All who could now fled away, and they never could gather under that chief standard again. It now stood alone, left behind on the field, with the four olive trees which the heathens had put up to hold the platform on which the standard stood, for all of the great crowd of heathens who had been guarding the standard had gone: some had fled, and others were slain. The duke's men were much wounded and exhausted. Lord Girard dismounted from his horse, very weary. Men went to him and took off his armor, taking his helmet from his head and removing his coat of mail, and he sat down, weary after his great labors. Blood ran out of his nose, down onto the helmet, and his men grieved when they saw this. But he said to them, "Do not be grieved for my sake, for nothing distresses me except that there are too many heathens still living. Go forth, then, into the battle and give help bravely to the division of our king. As soon as I have taken down this standard, I shall join you."

We shall now turn away and tell what was happening in another place.

A,a (34)

Now we shall turn to what Girard was doing that morning. He was the shrewdest of men; in his day no better leader could be found, for nothing disturbed him enough to make him grieve or lose heart. With Lord Klares[2] and his brother Basin, he had spent the night in the shelter of a grove. Of their comrades, they had lost three thousand knights.

All of the greatest men were mounted on their horses, clad in coats of mail, with their helmets fastened, their swords girded on, their shields around their necks and tunics folded under them on the saddles, swaying on various sides over the saddlebags.[3] Lord Girard now mourned over the fall of his men, saying, "Lord God," says he, "you suffered for our sake many grievous pains, torture and grim death, and I have come here beneath Aspermunt for the sake of your grace: now I know no other course to follow. As you suffered death for our sake, so do we wish to die for yours."

[2] *Clares.*

[3] *A*: "they had all sorts of weapons." *Asp.* does not seem to detail the scene at all.

And then he said to his men, "Hear me, brave knights: prepare yourselves quickly, and give to God that which we owe to him."

All his men answered that they would gladly do that; they then made ready for battle.[4]

(35) Lord Girard now rode down into the ravine with his troop, sending five hundred knights before him, with ten hundred coming behind as reinforcements ...

a: (38)

Now to speak of Lord Girard; when he came to the battle, he charged into the right wing of the king's[5] division, against twenty thousand men who had gathered there. Lord Girard was never cowardly as he rode in a fierce charge, though he had few followers—two thousand, against their twenty.[6] When the Africans saw the Frenchmen, they began to cower under their helmets and shields, more than twenty thousand of them against the Frenchmen,[7] and they galloped at them, well-armed and on good horses; a great battle arose.

The heathens shot at once from Turkish bows, but the Christian men were not frightened by that and advanced against their division. Many blows were given there as they cut at head and shoulders, breast and back, so that those who had come unprotected in the crowd of armed men could scarcely be distinguished from the others. Thus the Frenchmen made the heathens pay for the horses they had lost through their arrows.

Girard now cried out in a loud voice to his men: "Good comrades," says he, "let us not close ourselves in here among the heathens, but hold together outside their ranks and take whatever we can from them. And let us never take flight: let us, rather, give praise to almighty God, rewarding him for creating us."

[4] *a* adds, "and rode off as quickly as possible."

[5] I.e., Jamund. The whole passage is confusing; the translator would appear to have misunderstood *Asp.* 5003.

[6] I.e., twenty thousand.

[7] Or, more than twenty thousand Frenchmen? In this case the confusion in the passage is massive.

And when he had finished his speech, he spurred his horse Mateplum,[8] shook his spear and spread out his banner and attacked Malkabrium,[9] a powerful chief, hitting him in the shield and armor, knocking him over the back of his horse in the sight of all the heathens. Lifting up his banner, he said to his men, "Knights," says he, "strike hard! Right is on our side."

Before they came into the battle, five thousand of his men dismounted from their horses and proceeded carefully, since they could not ride because of the corpses. Now they came quickly into battle, armed with all the best armor, giving the heathens great blows, slashing heads and shoulders, limbs and bodies, so that those who were alive joined those who were dead. Now when those who were uncovered came into the midst of those who were armed and had experienced their dealings, they did not dare offer themselves again.

Girard cried out to his men and said, "Lords," says he, "strike hard! The king of Africa thinks he has conquered you and wants to destroy our land and banish our people. Now it shall be seen who wishes to defend us and our land. I am, as you know, quite old; nonetheless, if you will follow my advice—if you wish always to have honor as long as you live—then you must not fear for yourselves."

They all answered him then, "We are not afraid for ourselves, lord," say they; "we shall never fail you, as long as we live;"

(39) The Africans were now so hard pressed that the Christians swept all of the field before them and turned towards the Arabians, Turks, and Persians. The field was now completely full of bodies, weapons, and horses, except the part held by the French; no one could help or defend themselves when the French had come so near the chief standard. In their midst, now, spoke Magon and Asperant, who were kings of heathen lands: "As we can now see, the messenger Balam told us the truth about the Frenchmen. They were very mighty men, and shall never lose their courage as long as they live. But Jamund is now showing his pride—as well as foolishness and impudence!—when he

[8] Unger amends to *með sporum* 'with spurs,' but cf. *Asp.* 5026, "Matefelon."

[9] *Asp.* Macabres.

dares to wage this battle without his father Agulandus. Before the sun sets this evening, he will certainly know that this ambition was not suitable for him and many will pay for his foolishness. We shall all be destroyed, both men and captains, if we do not forsake our chief standard."

Now when Girard had come up to the heathens' chief standard, he went after it with the greatest valor, for there never was a braver leader than he. He was then more than a hundred years old,[10] yet there was hardly anyone under the standard that he did not strike; a good thousand of the heathens fell around the standard. Then he spoke to his men: "Lords," says he, "may almighty God strengthen you! Now we can surely know what will be best for us. If I can hold my shield, we shall win over these Africans."

Approaching the standard of the heathens, Lord Girard had the boldest knights with him. He also had a good coat of mail, which never failed, then or later. His two nephews, whom he had brought up from childhood with all kindness and honor, cleared a wide way in the troop of heathens so that every single one fled and forsook the chief standard: they left in such a state of terror and fright that they never again came under that standard.

Then King Asperant[11] said to King Magon,[12] "We can certainly consider ourselves fools, stupid men. Jamund did not dare to come here to help us at all in our great need, but let us look after ourselves. A man can want to follow his leader so long that they are both lost." They then barely managed to get to their horses, and escaped from there as fast as the horses could go.

This long battle took place under Aspermunt. And when King Karlamagnus fought against Jamund, son of Agulandus, and Asperant fled as rapidly as he could with two war-horses, Jamund and the chief standard were deserted. He was fighting in the midst of the army: they sent him no word of their departure, but left the standard alone on the battlefield, where the heathens had brought it on four elephants.[13]

[10] Not in *Asp.* at this point.

[11] *Esperam.*

[12] *Mordans*; more confusion with "Morant"?

[13] Cf. *Asp.* 5126-27.

When Girard had reached the chief standard, he dismounted from his horse. His men removed his helmet from his head and took his shield, and they took him by the hand and led him. His coat of mail fitted closely and he had become very hot from bearing heavy weapons and attacking sharply. They loosened his sword from his side, and sat him down on a ledge there under the standard; blood ran from his nostrils and down into his mouth. All of his men who saw this sobbed in great sorrow. He then said to them, "Do not be grieved for my sake: seek, rather, for that which shall bring you honor later."

Jamund, son of King Agulandus, was now fighting under Aspermunt against King Karlamagnus, who had called to him Oddgeir and Nemes and Desirim,[14] Riker, Fagon and Baerungur,[15] Milon and King Droim[16] and Salomon,[17] for there were not very many leaders there. These were with the king, before his tent. On the other side was Jamund, and with him were Balam and Goram[18] and Triamodis, and King Kador[19] of Africa, and Safagon,[20] Salatiel, and Lampalille.[21] All these spoke among themselves, saying, "King Karlamagnus is a glorious and valiant man, and we shall never be victorious over him."

A,a (48)

... Lord Girard, who had lately captured the heathen chief standard, had taken off his coat of mail and all his armor to rest. Now he sent for his two nephews, Boz[22] and Lord Klares, and they came at once to his bidding. He said to them, "Take four hundred of our host with you now," says he, "and ride as quickly as you can into the battle with the

[14] *Asp.* Desiier?
[15] *Baering.*
[16] *Drois.*
[17] Only Ogier and Naimes are mentioned at this point in *Asp.*; but after the beginning of ls. 278, this depends on another version in any case. In no passage of *Asp.* are all these names associated.
[18] *Goramaron.*
[19] *Kadon.*
[20] Salmaquin? or Sinagon?
[21] *Lamalille*; *Asp.* Lampal; identical with "Lampas," but not necessarily so recognized.
[22] *Booz.*

troops drawn into formation. As soon as I have removed the standard and taken care of the place, I will come to you."

"Gladly, lord," said they ....[23]

[23] Up to here, *a* 48 has no basis in *Asp*.

CHAPTER XLIX

The Fall of Duke Milon

Emperor Karlamagnus advanced very well indeed with his men. He had no idea what Lord Girard was doing, for the battle was huge and widely spread. Neither did Jamund know, as he went stoutly forward, killing many men with his sword, what had happened to his chief standard. And because neither could keep up the same charge continually, men asked for rest and the divisions began to break up, so that something of a gap grew up in the middle; then the battle became somewhat lighter, but the bravest warriors kept on attacking.

Thus King Triamodes, kinsman of Jamund, rushed forward in strong attack, attired in precious trappings and holding a stout spear with a great banner, charging at a French knight. He struck through his shield, body, and coat of mail, and cast him dead to the ground. And when he had drawn out his sharp spear, he did not hold back from the attack but aimed a second time, now striking the good lord Duke Milon,[1] brother of Baeringur the Breton, and drew out his lungs and bowels, hooked on his spear. Then he raised his bloody spear high, thinking the exchange had gone well, and, exulting greatly, turned back to his men, raising his voice and crying out: "Lord Jamund," says he, "be merry and glad: see my fine spear here, how beautifully it flourishes in warm blood, for it pierced right through the chest of two of the leaders of the Christians! Go forward sharply then, for this realm shall soon be completely in your power! These men shall never raise their spears to defend themselves against us again."

When the Christians saw Duke Milon, who had been one of their keenest armed men, dead, they mourned him greatly, but Baeringur the Breton was especially ill pleased. Filled with great wrath, he turned his

[1] Anseis, but not mentioned at this point in *Asp*.

horse with his spurs and galloped after Triamodes, saying, "Stay, heathen, if you dare, for I want to avenge my brother!"

But Triamodes behaved as if he could not hear him and did not intend to pay any attention. When Baeringur came within reach, he drove his spear from the back into the middle of his shoulders so that it came right out through the breast; then he pulled him back manfully and lifted him up from the saddle, and flinging him to the ground angrily, said, "You shall never mount a horse again, though you are big and fat: nor shall you rise to your stiff feet here. You killed my brother and thought all had gone well, but you have now paid so dearly for him that you shall never be his heir."

But when Jamund saw his nephew Triamodes lie dead on the field, he grieved, weeping for his death, and said many words of lamentation in his language. The Africans took the dead body and carried it in their arms into the midst of the army, where they wept and wailed.

A, a (48) As Jamund came into the battle, many great blows were struck...

(32) Triamodes came galloping there, well armed and securely attired, with a stout spear and a magnificent banner; and he drove at the shield and mail-coat of Ansaeis,[1] shoving him out of the saddle in sight of the Frenchmen...

a (46) Triamodes then came galloping up in a fiery charge, spreading out his banner on a stout spear. He attacked Duke Milon, striking at the shield and chain-mail and at his white leather tunic, and drew his bowels out over the saddle-bow. The Christians were much distressed by his fall, for he was a good leader and the most valiant of knights.

Triamodes turned back as quickly as possible, raised his spear with the banner which he had stained with blood from the duke's breast and cried out in a loud voice: "Lord Jamund," says he, "attack this realm diligently,[2] for this man shall never oppose us again."

And as he said this, Baeringur came galloping as fast as his good horse could bear him and shook his spear with great wrath, so that the

[2] A rather odd translation of *Asp.* 5409.

banner sank down — he was so angered that he almost shook the spear to pieces. But Triamodes could not turn back to oppose him, and Baeringur smote him in the middle of the back so that the spear came out through his breast; his armor gave him no help of any more worth than a glove. He bore him dead from the saddle, and when he drew his spear from his body[3] he said, "You shall come down, wicked man," says he, "and never shall you rise up from here, since you killed my brother. But you have now paid so dearly for him that you shall never make use of the possessions that were his."

Triamodes lay there dead on the field. And when Jamund saw that, he mourned his fall, weeping, and spoke many words of distress in his language. The men of Africa lamented his fall with much grief and carried his body in their arms, and many fell swooning in sorrow over his corpse.

[3] *A* resumes here.

CHAPTER L

Jamund in Despair

There next rode forth from the division of Christians the two knights Riker and Margant, one on a well-bred fawn-colored horse and the other on a grey horse with a mane of a different shade. Margant drove his spear at the king who was called Mates;[1] he ruled a realm outside Jerusalem, and was filled with pride and great arrogance, but though he was much swollen with his poisonous haughtiness, it helped him very little, for the sharp spear promptly flew through his body with all its armor.

Meanwhile Riker couched his spear against a close kinsman of Jamund, who had brought from his kingdom the shrilling horn Olifant which Jamund now bore around his neck, and when Riker drove the spear at his breast, Gizarid[2] tried to duck away from the blow, but Riker drew his sword and struck down on his neck, cutting off his head before the eyes of all the heathens.

Both these knights now rode back to their place safely, with God's help. And when Jamund saw these two kinsmen of his, Triamodes and Gizarid, dead, and all the plain covered with the bodies of his men — for God watched over the place of battle, in his great mercy, so that the Christians cut down heathen people like livestock — all of this so oppressed Jamund that his sight grew dim, and he called Balam to him, with heavy sighs, saying, "In truth, I was foolish when I did not believe what you told me truthfully. What is to become of me now? My two kinsmen have fallen. It was they who urged me to come to this land, and I thought I could put my trust in their valor; but now they lie dead. Good friend, give me good counsel now, for I do not know what the end will be to my bad luck."

[1] *B, Mages.*
[2] *b, Gizard.*

Balam answered, "Why does it surprise you that your course goes this way? Things will never turn out well for you or for anyone else who does not care for the realm that is his by right, but desires far more than is reasonable or moderate and wrongfully plunders and seizes the possessions of another. But you were greedy when it would have been suitable for you, as for all those who seemed to be leaders, to make yourself strong and firm, knowing well what was to be expected, not rejoicing overly in your great strength, and to bear any misfortune in a manly fashion. Since I gave the best advice I could to you, and you wished to have none of it, I have nothing to add to it now; everyone can follow the advice he prefers, but you will never overcome the Christians."

Jamund answered, "Whatever others may do, I shall never believe that you are deceiving me."

Then he grasped the horn he had about his neck and blew on it with all his might so that the din resounded widely in all the land around; then he drew his sword Dyrumdali, spurred his horse, and rode into battle against one of the Christians, striking down on his helmet with his sword and slashing into the body,[3] coming down in hard attack.

A,a (46)...Next to ride forward from the king's division were Riker and Marant,[4] one on a pale horse and the other on a grey;[5] the latter attacked a knight called Mates,[6] who was king of the land that lies beyond Jerusalem. He was a very proud man, but all his armor helped him little, for he[7] bore him from his horse on his spear and cast him dead to the earth.

Riker attacked Garisanz,[8] son of Meysanz,[9] a kinsman of Jamund, who had the shrilling horn Olivant, from Africa, around his neck.[10]

[3] *b*, stomach.

[4] *Asp.* Morant.

[5] *a* only; not confirmed by *Asp.*

[6] *a*'s *Morant* is obviously wrong; *Asp.* Macre.

[7] I.e., Marant.

[8] Not in *Asp.*

[9] *Asp.* Moysant; in *Asp.*, however, Richier attacks Moysant himself. Cf. 1. 5428.

[10] Not in *Asp.*

Riker struck at his breast and the spear flew through him. And as his horse bore him away, he drew his sword.

When the pope saw them, he crossed himself, saying, "Holy Apostle Peter," he said, "I entrust these two men to your mercy."

(47) As Jamund saw his two kinsmen fall, and all the field covered with corpses, his countenance grew quite black, and he sobbed in distress and said, "Lord Balam," says he, "what shall become of me? These two kings whom I now see lying here urged me strongly to come here, and I thought they would conquer all this realm for me."

Balam answered, "You speak strangely. He who is not content with the realm which is his by right, and desires wrongfully that which belongs to another, will never come to a good end. It thus befits all who are leaders not to know evil, although misfortune befall them, nor to be too encouraged, though they gain much according to what their friends, who may give them help, seem to say.[11] You sent me to France as your messenger, to summon King Karlamagnus to you, and I told him what you said; he was not at all frightened by the news I brought him, though I threatened him as much as I could, and then he had a hundred of the best horses brought before me so that I might choose whichever I wished of them. I soon found while I was with them that they were the bravest of knights, and that they would never flee.[12] When I returned, it was my intention to tell you all that I had found to be true, and I warned you to watch out for difficulties; but you behaved as if I had betrayed you. Now I do not wish to show you my desire any more, unless it is to let everyone save himself and protect his life, for the Christians will never flee."

Jamund then answered, "It is not fitting for you to blame me." He then took up Olivant,[13] put it to his mouth and blew to encourage his men with its shrilling voice, so that the earth seemed to resound over at least three quarter's[14] length around. He then rode back into the battle, heading for one of the Christians, whom he struck on the helmet in such a way that his sword did not stop until it had reached the middle of his back.

[11] Not much basis in *Asp.* 287.

[12] *a* adds "and they will never be driven out of their realm."

[13] *Olifant.*

[14] I.e., of a mile?

CHAPTER LI

Of Salatiel and Rodan

The battle now began anew. And because almighty God wished to restrain Jamund from harming his flock, he wished to hinder his trollish behavior for a while by letting him hear of the setback Duke Girard had brought about[1] so that thereafter his frame of mind would become worse rather than better. Thus a heathen knight arrived on a fleet horse at the place where Jamund was attacking vigorously, and he led him off from the midst of the crowd, beginning his message in this way: "Oh, oh, Lord Jamund," says he, "much bad luck bears down upon us in all directions: you and all your men have borne great shame and distress today. I am now the only one left of the many who were to guard your chief standard, for this morning a group attacked us that appeared to be of little strength. They were mostly on foot, although better armed than some others: all their coats of mail were double, or better, and as shining as the brightest silver, so tough that they could scarcely be destroyed. There was no helmet on their heads which was not gilded and set with precious stones, and their swords were of steel as green as grass.[2] A short[3] man went before them, with great valor—I am sure he was their leader. And they so dealt with our men that in a short period they killed more than ten thousand."

When he had reached this point, Jamund would not endure it any longer, and interrupted, saying, "Be silent, you wicked[4] man, filthiest of thralls! You do not know what you are talking about. Should I have any faith in a report that the honor of my chief standard is fallen when

[1] "how Duke Girard had staggered"—? This instance is listed in C-V as an example of the verb *svinka*, which is defined as "to stagger."

[2] This appears to be roughly equivalent to "fresh as daisies." It has no equivalent in *Asp*.

[3] *b* adds "and thick-set."

[4] *b*, red; i.e., bloodthirsty?

I gave it into the keeping of two kings in whom I had the greatest trust, and no less than a hundred thousand strong men?"

"Whether you like it or not," said the knight, "you shall hear yet more of it. The two kings have both fled, while most of their troops have been slain; the chief standard has been broken down and is in the possession of the Christians. Believe as you wish: this will be proved true."

And when Jamund thought he could not deny it, such great grief came into his heart that he almost went out of his mind. But after a while he summoned two heathen kings, Salatiel and Rodan, and spoke to them thus, with a grief-stricken look: "Good lords," says he, "we are shamefully beaten in many ways. We have lost our four gods and the greater part of our host has been slain, but, over and above that, we have been robbed of even the chief standard, which my father gave to me as a sign of his great affection. Now since you have taken little, if any, part in the battle, but have a good troop and are well equipped, lend your help bravely now, for much of the host of the Christian king has fallen, while many are wounded and weary and capable of little, so that you can easily overcome them. If this is done, I shall place you highest among all my leaders in this realm."

Salatiel then answered, "Lord Jamund, do not worry a bit, for before evening falls you shall see all the Frenchmen dead."

Jamund said, "It will be good for the eyes that see that, for all the grief, sorrow and distress shall then be cleansed from my breast."

Salatiel now armed himself, took up his weapons, bow, and quiver, then rode away to the battle with his troops drawn up, letting out a great war-cry. God's knights had to give hard war exchange yet again. Many men were slain in both troops, and now a great many Frenchmen fell, for this heathen king Salatiel, who was both hard to deal with and mighty in strength, went around the outside like a huntsman doing various things: he dented armor and broke bones with a great cudgel which he carried in front of his spear, or shot rapidly from his bow, for in all the army there was no archer to equal him. Neither shield nor coat of mail could withstand his shots, for all of the points of his arrows were poisoned; therefore everyone from whom he drew blood was killed.

It happened that Oddgeir the Dane saw Salatiel's course and the way he was distressing many, and, trusting in God's mercy, he rushed eagerly forward to combat him. He made his horse run very swiftly, and when he met him drove his spear into his hard shield. And, since God was watching over him, it flew through the shield, coat of mail, and body, casting him dead to the ground.

Now Duke Nemes rushed forward, splendidly armed and mounted on one of the best of horses, and met King Rodan[5] striking down on his helmet so hard that nothing could protect him: he slashed down into his shoulders, then threw him from his horse.

Oddgeir and Nemes both went back to their divisions then, while Jamund, seeing the fall of these two, said, "We are now few, and less than we were."

A,a (48)... One of the heathens who had escaped was a very agile man who galloped away on a fleet horse which flew as speedily as the fastest swallow or a hawk[6] seeking its prey. And when he arrived where the army was fighting, he rode into the thick of the crowd and asked where Jamund was. When he was told this, he took him by the hand and led him aside, saying,[7] "Lord Jamund," said he, "great trouble and distress has befallen us, and a great disgrace for you. Certain Christians came at us on foot. Never had we seen men armed like this, for they had no mail that was not threefold and whiter than the brightest silver, which never failed to repel weapons. In this troop there was no helmet that was not gilded and set with jewels, and they so attacked our men under the chief standard with their swords that they all seemed as green as the greenest grass; they killed more than a thousand of our men under the chief standard."

As Jamund heard his message, he looked at him with a grim expression and said, "Silence, you foul, sinful man," said he. "You do not know what you are saying. I gave my chief standard to the two kings and ten thousand knights to guard."

[5] *B*, *Alfami.*

[6] The swallow, which seems oddly coupled here, is omitted in *a*; the line is not paralleled in *Asp.*

[7] *A*: "when he arrived before Jamund, he spoke to him in this way:"

The heathen answered,[8] "The Christians have killed them all, driven us away from the chief standard, and captured it."

Then Jamund began to grieve[9] and called to him King Salatiel and the mighty Rodan.[10] "Lords," said he, "we have now been shamefully betrayed. Our four gods were taken away from us, and they hate us for that reason. The Christians have no strength now; some of them have fallen and some are mortally wounded, and their horses rendered useless, so that they cannot come into battle, while your horses are sound and you are well armed. This summer I shall be crowned in Rome; let us now slay the remnant that remains."

King Salatiel bowed to him, and said, "Do not fear the Frenchmen," says he. "This evening you shall see them all dead."

Then he took his shield and bow and quiver with him, and rode with all his troops drawn up into battle.

(49) When these two kings came into battle, they blew their horns and trumpets and beat the tambourine, creating a great din[11] everywhere in the host. The pope then said, "There is nothing else to do now but for all of us to dedicate ourselves to almighty God, who saved our souls by his death. He who now gives strong blows here for the sake of holy Christianity,[12] all his sins both greater and less, I remit today."[13]

Oddgeir then came rushing forward from the French host with a stout spear, covered with a good shield, while Salatiel rode like a huntsman into the battle, dealing wounds among the French with his arrows.[14] No man could stand his shots because all of his shafts were poisoned, so that none could live whom he grazed or pierced. Oddgeir, however, searched for him, and as soon as they met struck him in the shield with so great a blow that all his armor was of no more use to

[8] This phrase is in *A* and Fr2, but not in *a*.
[9] The rest of this chapter does not follow *Asp*.
[10] *a, Roddan*.
[11] *a* adds "and injury."
[12] *a*, on this field.
[13] The rest of this chapter does not follow *Asp*.
[14] *a* adds: "there was no better bowman than he in all the heathen host."

him than a glove, and he struck him dead from the saddle, far off onto the ground.[15]

When Jamund saw King Salatiel fall, he mourned his death, weeping in great distress.

After that, Lord Nemes, the duke of Bealfer, came galloping forward, well and suitably armed, on his best war-horse, Mozel.[16] There was no horse more tireless than this in all this great multitude,[17] and there was no knight more dauntless than Duke Nemes. When he rode at the heathen ranks, he first met with King Alfamen,[18] whom he slashed right down the middle. He left him dead among the corpses.[19] When Jamund saw the fall of this heathen,[20] he said, "Now there are indeed fewer of our men than there were."...

[15] *A*: "he cleft that wicked dog down through the shoulders and cast him dead onto the ground." Fr2 generally supports *a* here.

[16] Morel.

[17] *a*, in his troop; Fr2 agrees with *A*.

[18] *A*, *Fulfinio*.

[19] *a*: "he gave him so great a blow that no protection could help him, and shot him out of the saddle."

[20] *a*: "saw him fall dead from the horse."

CHAPTER LII

Valterus Comes to Karlamagnus

After the fall of Salatiel there was a lull in the battle. Emperor Karlamagnus dismounted from his horse and sat down, calling together the leaders who still survived: Rollant, Oddgeir, Nemes, Salomon, Hugi, Riker; and he said to them, "My good friends, how great a host can now stand under our standards?"

They answered, "We do not know exactly, lord," say they, "but we think it is not less than thirty thousand."

The emperor says, "God knows that is few, in comparison with what is needed; but what would be best to do now?"

Rollant and Oddgeir answered, "This: to attack as best as we can and strike the heathens so strongly that no armor can withstand us; and if almighty God looks after his Christians, as we trust he will, he may give us victory over the heathens."

As they were talking in this way, a knight came there, mounted on a good Gaskunian horse. A piece of a stout spear with a fine banner was fixed in his shield, trailing down so that the straps dragged on the ground. His coat of mail was much broken up, his jerkin slit, his helmet burst open, and blood ran out from under his mail-sleeve, for he had a huge wound in the middle of his shoulders, from which his saddle was filled with blood. The knight greeted the emperor well and courteously, saying, "God bless you and strengthen you, good lord Emperor Karlamagnus!"

Karlamagnus looked at him and answered, "May God help you, whoever you may be: I do not recognize you at all."

"I am called Valterus, from the city of Salastis," said he, "I am one of the men of Lord Girard, who sends me to you: he sends you greetings in the name of God, of himself, and of all his men."

"May almighty God reward the old lord; and where is that good friend?"

"Right under the chief standard of the heathens," said Valterus, "as nimble as a fish, as sharp as a lion, and as merry as a kid: he has struck the standard down, killed some of those who were guarding it, and driven all the rest away in flight."

The emperor praised all-powerful God, and was well pleased, thinking that things might improve now.[1]

Next shall be told what was happening with King Droim and Andelfreus, who were sent to the emperor's encampment, as has been learned before, while Karlamagnus speaks with Valterus and rests.

A,a (49)

... Duke Nemes then turned back to the French host. King Karlamagnus then called to his side Oddgeir and Nemes, Riker and Fagon, King Droim and King Salomon; he asked them, "How many knights do we have around our chief standard?"

"Thirty thousand," they answered.

Karlamagnus then said, "God knows," says he, "that is all too few. Good knights," says he, "what is best for us to do?"

Oddgeir answered, "We shall fight bravely and deal such great blows that no protection shall be adequate to withstand them; and if God loves holy Christendom, he will give us victory over the heathens."

(50) As they said this, **Sir** Valteri came on a good Gaskunian horse; he had on his spear-shaft a great banner, with the strap dragging behind him on the ground. A broken spear had penetrated his shield; his mail had given way, and his armor was slashed. The fastenings of his mail had been slit from his hands, his helmet had been damaged in many places, and blood ran out from under his mail so that his saddlebow was all bloody before him, as were his legs and his feet and spurs. He was sorely wounded in the shoulders and carried his bloody sword in his hand.

When he saw King Karlamagnus, he said "God bless you, King Karlamagnus."

[1] *B*: "... pleased. With the help of James, all might quickly improve."

The king answered, "God give you joy, knight. But I do not recognize you: tell me your name."

He answered, "Men call me Valteri of Salastius. Lord Girard, son of Boy,[2] sends you God's greeting, as do his nephews, the lords Boz and Clares. We have captured the chief standard of the heathens."

"Sir Valteri," says King Karlamagnus, "may that valiant man yet live!"

"God knows," says he, "that he is as hale as a fish and as merry as a kid, so that none of his men strike more strongly than he."

The king then asked, "Where is Lord Girard now?"

Valteri answered, "He is sitting right under the chief standard of the heathens itself, which he captured from them;[3] we have struck down the heathens so mightily that more than ten thousand have died, one after another. Jamund shall die; unless he takes better care, he shall not survive this evening alive."

[2] *A*; Fr2, *Bod*; these are further spellings for Fr. *Bueves*.
[3] Up to here, A,a 50 is not based on *Asp*.

CHAPTER LIII

Karlamagnus Launches a New Attack

As soon as King Droim arrived at the emperor's tents the emperor's message was proclaimed: all of those who could be of any help were to prepare themselves with the best equipment they could get and come to the aid of the emperor and the Christians; lords as well as knights, counselors and their servants, cooks, cupbearers, porters and sentries, and everyone who could use[1] weapons. There was much rejoicing at this, for in this group there were many young men who were very eager to see action and to prove their valor. They now made a great deal of uproar and quick preparations in the tents. He who got there first took the best horse and weapons, while the others mounted stiff old jades. They also cut up fine cloth, velvet and silk or white linen tablecloths, making banners out of them; each prepared himself as well as he could, then mounted on his steed. Many of them were strong and large, foremost among these being the four foster sons of the emperor who served him daily at table or in the bedchamber; they were named Estor, Otun, Engeler, and Grelant.

These were the first to ride down the slope which lay between the camp and the battlefield, and before they came into the valley, Droim and Andelfreus[2] rode on before them and reached the emperor just at the time he was speaking to Valterus, and they lifted up their voices and called out, "God bless you, glorious lord Emperor Karlamagnus, son of King Pippin of France!"

The king smiled, and then asked, "Are our young men coming?"

"Certainly, lord," said they.

"How great a force is it?" asked the emperor.

They answered, "Close to forty thousand."

[1] *b*, get.

[2] *b, Andelfrei.*

When the emperor heard that, he raised his hand, with eyes lifted up to the heavens, and gave thanks to God in such words as these: "Praise be to you, eternal and glorious king, and to your beloved apostle St. James, for now it seems to me that there will soon be a change in our case when all these come against the heathen troops. Then let us cast aside all sorrow and fear, for God may give us his blessed aid!"

After this King Droim prepared to go back to meet the young men to tell them that each of them could take whatever weapons and horses seemed sufficient to him from the battlefield. And so they did: many cast away the equipment they had had before and attired themselves in new armor, also taking fine horses which had been left by their lords. When all were equipped with weapons and armor, King Droim said, "Rush forward manfully, and attack sharply, for there is enough time to avenge our friends before evening falls."

They did so, charging into battle in a great rush. But when the heathens saw the charge of these men they became quite frantic in their hearts, and said "No one spoke more truthfully to us than the messenger Balam: this land will never be conquered, for now there are rushing forth at us people who have not come into the battle before. Their onslaught does not bode well."

And when the young men had come into the battle, there could be heard great din, outcry and shouting, for while these men had never been dubbed knights they still knew how to make the sharp sword bite boldly. The battle soon turned against the heathens, so that each one fell over the next and there was no resistance now: things went for them exactly as they had thought they would. When Jamund saw what was happening—that the Christians were increasing in number while almost all of his own troop had been slain—he despaired in his heart that he would ever win the victory. Thus he looked around for the best way to escape, and when he thought to turn to the right, there was Lord Girard coming, with ten thousand bold knights. Jamund thought he could certainly not go forward that way easily, yet his division was struggling at least three arrow-shots behind him. But when Lord Girard saw that, he turned with a great throng and came down heavily behind him,[3] slaying one after another. Now Jamund saw there was no

[3] "with a heavy cart-load;" cf. C-V p. 269, *hlass*; clearly this idiom is not very appropriate in a Mod. E. translation.

help to be had; he drew back, and found himself before Emperor Karlamagnus with his men.

a (37)... The two messengers which King Karlamagnus had sent to the camp made speed on their journey, and now came to the host and gave them the king's message: that he ordered all to come to him that could be of help. None remained behind, neither lords nor knights, servants, chamber-boys, nor squires, porters nor cooks; those who did not have war-horses mounted on riding horses. Swift preparations could be seen there as they rushed into the tents and swept up the linens, making themselves banners and fastening them on to spears; one took a tablecloth and another a sheet, and tore up the sheet completely. First in the throng were the four foster-sons of the emperor: Estor; Otun; Baeringur;[4] and Rollant,[5] who rode on a hard-ridden jade, better than two arrow-shots ahead of all the others. But more than forty thousand followed them.

A,a (50)... Then Andelfraei came, on a dapple-grey horse. When he saw King Karlamagnus, he greeted the king in the French language and said, "God bless you, King Karlamagnus, son of King Pippin!"

"God give you joy, young Andelfraei," says the king. "Are our boys coming here now?"

"Yes," says Andelfraei. "God knows," says he, "that there are fifty thousand[6] in the first division, and there are none so unprepared in all that throng that he does not have a silken banner; most have gleaming silver helmets and other good armor."

When the king had heard Andelfraei's message, he lifted his hands to heaven and thanked God, weeping. And when that troop came forward,[7] their division stood on two quarters.

[4] Estols de Lengres (who is not mentioned at this point in *Asp.*), Haton, and Berengier: all of whom have, of course, already been active in the saga account.

[5] This is one of the most glaring absurdities resulting from the fusion of sources.

[6] *a*, 50; *Asp.* 40 thousand; note that B,b agrees with *Asp.*

[7] *a*: "...thanked God. When the boys from Albanie came to the field of war..." This may represent a corruption of something like the "a Loon" of *Asp.* 5510.

Now those who wanted to have horses had the chance to take the best that they liked from a hundred thousand, and those who needed armor no longer lacked it, for they could take it from those who lay there dead.[8]

(51) Now when they were all well armed and mounted on good Gaskunian[9] horses, there were no fewer than fourteen thousand, as well as forty[10] thousand in the second division. Duke[11] Droim of Stampes[12] rode out to meet them and said, "You may yet," says he, "avenge our friends in good time."

Now they rode down over the slope. Gold and steel fluttered in the sunshine and a great cloud of dust was kicked up under the feet of their horses.—the heathens said, "No one spoke to us more truly than the messenger Balam: never will that land be gained by us, to our glory. But if Jamund had sent for his father today, Valland[13] would already be under his power; now it will never be won."

Then it was fitting for each one to make good use of his horse. As they came where the battle was, great din and awful uproar could be heard. But when Jamund saw that the battle was turning against his men he urged them to strike and exhorted them, vainly promising treasure and power. When he looked on his right hand he saw Lord Girard coming, with ten thousand knights,[14] and he then drew back his ranks more than three arrow-shots. But the old Girard attacked their backs heavily[3], and quickly felled a great throng of them. When Jamund found he had no support he pulled at his bridle and hurried away as fast as he could.

[8] This is not exactly parallel to *Asp*.
[9] *A* only.
[10] *A*, sixty.
[11] *a*, lord.
[12] *Asp*. Droes d'Estampes.
[13] *a*, all the land; Fr2 agrees with *A*.
[14] *a*: "ten thousand of the strongest men."

CHAPTER LIV

The Flight of Jamund

When the Christians had swept all around Jamund and had slaughtered the heathens so thoroughly that few were left standing, and those who could fled, Jamund found himself in a bad position; but, at whatever cost, he wanted to escape with his life if he could. He looked for the place where there were fewest of the Christians and the battle was slowest, and came through with great difficulty. The two kings Goram and Mordoan[1] were with him: if he could escape then from the hands of the French, he might well be relieved and rightly say that he had never before come through such straits!

Jamund now fled as fast as his good horse could go, riding down along a little crag. He had with him his shrilling horn and his good sword and stout spear, so tough and hard that it could not be broken: it is said that it was made of the wood which is called alder. He rode oppressed with grief, complaining of his troubles, which had taken his men from him, and said, "As mighty and great as I thought I was before, I have now become miserable and wretched. I thought that none could win a victory over me, but it has not turned out so for me today. It would have been better for me to stay home in the realms of Africa and not to have puffed myself up, against the advice of my father. I was certainly making too much of myself when nothing would suit me but to wear a crown while my father was still living. I was a child, and ill-behaved, when I heeded senseless counsel. Because of all this the day of sorrow has come, reducing me to such childlike helplessness that it can never be mended."

Balam clearly heard Jamund maundering and so began to speak: "The sort of utterances you are making, Jamund, would be natural for

[1] *Mordoam*.

a soft woman, who, full of grief, weeps for her husband or the death of her only child. But you have seen too late that pride, with great valor, and, on the other hand, folly, with bad fortune, are not congruous when mixed together; and however you may complain, what has happened remains. If you look behind you you will see something else suitable for great complaint, for eight Frenchmen are chasing you and have no desire to spare your life."

Jamund saw that what Balam said was true, for Karlamagnus had become aware of their escape and fleet horses galloped after them. The first to follow him were Rollant, Oddgeir, Nemes, and four shield-boys. Each of them now rode with all his might, until the horse of King Mordoan became so exhausted that he would not go no matter how he was pricked with spurs or beaten with a heavy spear-shaft. Jamund then said, "What shall we do? I cannot bear to leave behind my master King Mordoan. Let us turn valiantly against those who are following us and thrust them off their horses: then we shall get a mount for our comrade."

"You shall never get away that way," said Balam. "Save your life while you can, and leave those who are doomed to die."

Jamund paid no attention to his words but angrily turned his horse, holding his shield before him and shaking his spear; and since Nemes had the fastest of horses, next to that of Karlamagnus, Jamund met him first, and drove his spear into his shield and the jerkin he wore over his coat of mail. But because, by the grace of God, that did not fail, Nemes fell off his mount before the great blow. As soon as Nemes had fallen down, Oddgeir the Dane came up and struck down on Goram's helmet with so powerful a hand that his head was cleft and the sword did not stop until it reached the stomach; he was thrown dead to the ground.

When Jamund saw Goram fallen, he drew his sharp[2] sword and aimed for the middle of Oddgeir's helmet, but he ducked away and the blow landed further down than Jamund intended. The sword slashed through the horse in front of the saddle, cutting it in two in the middle so that Oddgeir fell over the back part onto the ground. God, however,

[2] *B*, bright.

truly watched over his knight, for if that blow had gone into his head Jamund would have avenged Goram well. Jamund now turned his horse and did not want to linger there any longer; he headed away quickly, for Karlamagnus was then coming.

As he rode off, Balam turned back,[3] galloping his horse swiftly with his spear in both hands, intending to charge at the chivalrous Emperor Karlamagnus; but when he saw this, he pricked his white horse with his spurs and bore down before Balam expected it, striking out at him with his mighty hand so that Balam fell off his horse, whether he wished to or not. The emperor immediately rushed after Jamund while Balam quickly and nimbly jumped up, thinking to catch his horse. But there was no chance of this now, for Duke Nemes had come and so guarded the horse that he could by no means get near him. Both now drew their swords and there began a sharp duel: each struck the other so hard that sparks flew from the armor that protected them. When Oddgeir saw that he rushed up, wishing to help Nemes, his comrade.

But Balam, seeing this, knew he could not prevail now and said to Nemes, "Good knight, do not attack any longer. It will gain you very little to kill me with the help of another, for I swear by him who made me that I will gladly be baptized and signed with the holy faith. If Duke Nemes of Bealfer were close enough so that I might speak with him, I expect that he would come to my aid with valuable assistance."

Nemes then said, "Who are you, knight, and why is Nemes indebted to you?"

He answered, "I am called Balam. Agulandus sent me to Karlamagnus to look over his army, when he had stopped in Baion, and I claim no benefit from him further than he would wish to have done."

Nemes then said, "Thanks be to almighty God, who has so watched over me that I did not do you any shame or harm!"

While they were speaking, Oddgeir came up, shaking his stout spear and intending to drive it at Balam; but Nemes was most displeased and grasped the spear in front of his hand, saying, "For the sake of God and my request, do not do any harm to this man, for no one could help

[3] Balam was Goram's father; see, e.g., *a* 24, at end of Ch. 33.

another more than this man has helped me, if he is the same Balam who came so boldly forward to help me before at the time when I had been captured by the heathens and led before Agulandus, and doomed by him to die. Not only did he offer his wealth to help me but he was prepared to risk his life for my sake if this had been necessary. He also gave the emperor the white horse on which he is now mounted. Thus I certainly ought to give him as much aid as I can and as he will gladly receive."

Balam thanked the duke for his words, reaffirming before them that he wished to give up his former heresy. And as they were coming to an understanding, Rollant rushed towards them and saw Nemes's horse standing on the field before him: he was filled with great fierceness, for he thought that the duke had been killed. He therefore took the horse and mounted it, galloping forward along his way, while the horse that he had been riding before fell dead of exhaustion.

A,a (52)

When Jamund saw that the Christians had surrounded him with more than ten thousand of the best knights, the division of lords Boz and Clares, and when he looked behind him and saw on his right King Karlamagnus coming rapidly, he turned and fled from the press, and if he could escape as he intended he could then truly say that he had never before come through such peril. Jamund now fled, bearing his spear and banner in his hand; it was said that that spear was so tough[4] that it could not be bent or broken. Some men call the wood[5] 'aiol.'[6] Aside from this spear, he had two others of the same wood with him at the battle. He rode such a swift horse that its equal could not be found in all the host. Now he rode down a certain slope and complained of his troubles, saying, "I am wretched and sinful now," says he. "I thought I was so great and mighty that nobody could ever overcome me, but it has not turned out so for me today. I wrongly made charges

[4] *a* adds, and hard.

[5] I.e., of which it was made.

[6] *a, niol*; this translates lines which appear much later in *Asp.*, 8739-41: "Entre ses palmes sa hanste brandissant [Ulien, not Eaumont]/D'un fust d'Alfrique qui n'est mie fragnant;/Fust d'aul l'apelent cele gent mescreant."

against those who[7] are not alive, and I transgressed because I wanted to wear the crown of my father[8] while he was still living. Surely the child who elects to follow childish advice does himself harm and shame."[9]

Balam then answered: "Hear," says he;[10] "you are acting like a woman complaining the death of her only child.[11] Pride and force are comrades who resemble each other closely; he who puts his faith mostly in mischief always lands in difficulties that will be complained of too late. Now since you wanted to do evil, it would be more fitting for others to complain of your going amiss rather than for you yourself to lament like a child or a weak-minded woman."[12]

(53) Now Jamund went on his way, and three kings followed him. He sank back on his saddle-bow in a swoon; then he looked back and saw King Karlamagnus charging after him, with Duke Nemes and Oddgeir, and following them four pages:[13] Estor Delangres;[14] Rollant, on a grey horse;[15] Otun;[16] and Baeringur.

Soon King Magon's horse stopped, as it was exhausted and broken down; neither spurs nor blows would make it move. Jamund then said, "Now I shall not know what to do at all if Magon, my master and foster father, lies behind here. It would be great harm and shame to me to lose him. Let us turn on those who are coming behind us and attack, so that we can take one of their horses."[17]

Balam then answered, "It will not help us much, even if you plunder their riches: they will follow you and kill you, if they can overtake you."

[7] *a* adds, Alas.

[8] *a*, Agulandus.

[9] This sentiment appears to be something of a mistranslation of *Asp.* 5632-34.

[10] *A*: "'See,' says he, 'complaining thus.'"

[11] *a*, your child; *Asp.*, "son amant," 5636.

[12] *a*: "...yourself to misbehave." This paragraph is a considerable expansion of *Asp.* 5636-7.

[13] "Shield-boys."

[14] *a, delagres.*

[15] *a*, a war-horse.

[16] *a, Utun.*

[17] In *Asp.* this passage concerns Sinagon, not Magon.

Jamund paid no attention to what he said but took up his shield and held it firmly before him, lifted his spear and shook it with all his might so that it nearly broke into pieces; then he galloped forward on his horse and directed his spear at Duke Nemes, striking down on the helmet and in all directions, and if his chain mail had not been so safe[18] he would certainly have killed him and shoved him out of his saddle.

Oddgeir the Dane struck at Goram[19] with so strong a hand that he cleft him through the head and shoulders down to the waist, and shoved him dead to the earth.[20] When Jamund saw the fall of his master and counselor, he drew his sword at once, aiming at the midst of Oddgeir's head: the sword flew right down to the saddle-bow, beheading the horse. If the blow had taken off the Dane, then Jamund would have well revenged his counselor! He then pulled at his bridle and fled away. Balam then turned back, clasping his spear as firmly as he could, galloped forward on his good horse, and aimed to attack the courteous King Karlamagnus. But the king defended himself swiftly and attacked him so strongly that he cast him down from his horse, covering his gleaming silver armor with dust.

Balam then jumped up and tried to get at the horse, but when Lord Nemes saw that he drew his sword at once to keep the horse from him; now a hard battle began, with much danger. Each struck at the other with his good sword so strongly that sparks flew widely from their arms. Balam then saw Oddgeir speeding there, holding and shaking his great spear, and with him were Estor Delangres, Otun and Baeringur, and Rollant, on his horse. He saw that he would not be able to defend himself and said to lord Nemes, "Lord knight," says he, "halt, and stop fighting: you will gain little by killing me. I wish to be baptized and consecrated to God and the holy faith; and if I could find Lord Nemes, duke of Bealfer, he would come to my help today."

[18] *a* adds: "that it never failed."

[19] *A, Gorham.*

[20] *a*: "... with so mighty a hand down into the shoulders that he cleft him endlong, and his mail gave way before the blow; he bloodied his sword in the midst of his back, and shot the heathen dog far from his horse: he fell dead on the ground."

Duke Nemes then said, "Who are you?"

"Lord," says Balam, "I am Balam, the messenger[21] who was sent to France by King Agulandus."

Lord Nemes then answered, "Thanks to almighty God!" And he said to Oddgeir, "Do not harm him. No man has ever helped another more than this knight did me in my need." Then Duke Nemes said, "Are you that Balam," says he, "who was of such help to me before King Agulandus, when they sentenced me in my own hearing to slaughter and death? You saved me in their sight, and had borne me such a great treasure of gold and silver, so many bright coats of mail, so many gilded helmets and keen-edged swords, so many good horses, that no man could collect more nor choose or wish for greater treasure. You also gave King Karlamagnus the white horse.[22] Will you now hold to what you have said?"

"Yes, lord," he answered, "that is what I certainly wish and pray for. I give myself to God and into your keeping, for I wish to put my trust in almighty God, to whom the blessed virgin Maria gave birth in Bethlehem."[23]

The Duke Nemes answered, "God knows," says he, "that I will gladly grant you that."

Then Rollant came riding on a tired nag, nearly worn out with toil; he saw Morel[24] standing in the middle of the way. He did not stop to ask questions but jumped onto his back, so grieved that he had never been more so, for he thought that Nemes had fallen.

[21] *A*: "I am the messenger who ..."

[22] *A*: "... 'Do not harm him: no man is more valiant than he. When I was doomed to slaughter and death by the warriors of Agulandus, this man helped me in my need, and saved me in their sight; and he had brought for me such a great treasure of silver and gold that no man could collect more, nor choose or wish for greater treasure. He gave King Karlamagnus the white horse.—hear, good knight,' says he, 'will you ...'"

[23] *Betlemborg*.

[24] *a*, a morel.

CHAPTER LV

The Encounter Between Karlamagnus and Jamund

We shall now return to Karlamagnus and Jamund, who rode far away from other men. Jamund rushed forward; now he had parted with all his honors, for early on the day before he had been followed by no less than seven hundred thousand while now there was not even a shield-boy left to serve him. And because Jamund's horse was extremely swift, the emperor did not catch up with him for some time. Eventually Jamund rode in under the shade of a little elm tree. There he saw a small spring of clear water, which ran up between the roots of an olive tree standing there, and his great weariness and troubles drove him to drink—which was not surprising, for more than three days had passed when he had neither eaten nor drunk, nor had any of the others at the battle; nor had he dared, during that time, to remove his helmet from his head. Therefore he dismounted, took off his helmet and shield, putting them down by the olive tree, and lay down by the water to drink.

But before he got up from the spring Karlamagnus came up on the other side, so suddenly that Jamund could not grasp his weapons, for the emperor watched over them; it seemed to Jamund that he had thus been negligent.[1] Then Karlamagnus said, "Take your weapons and mount your horse, for no mother's son shall taunt me that I killed an unarmed fugitive. But know this: you shall pay dearly for that drink, to which you had no right."

Jamund did so, arming himself and mounting his horse and pulling his shield firmly against his breast, while holding his spear couched. And, since he was a young man, his great exhaustion dropped from his heart as soon as he had had a drink, so that now it seemed to him that

[1] Latter clause in *b* only.

nothing at all could harm him. Thus he spoke in this way: "By Maumet," says he, "you have not found a man running away from you alone! But you have a remarkably swift horse which has carried you so far away from your companions, and you are very well equipped with weapons, for your coat of mail is as fair as the blossom of the apple tree while your helmet is so valuable that whoever wishes to get such a one would willingly set against it three of the richest towns. You must be a man of very high rank, for you have truly shown me that you were never begotten by ordinary people or come from humble kin when you respected me, when you came upon me when I was unarmed, and did me the great courtesy to give me back my arms, which you had in your power before: and I shall reward you well for that. Choose, then, between two alternatives: give me your weapon, and that extraordinarily good helmet, and go back, with my permission, to your men, of your own will; or, if you will renounce your god and become my man, you shall do much better, for all your kinsmen and friends shall be blessed for your sake alone. This choice I offer you will displease none except those who deserve as much of me as you do."

Karlamagnus answered, "You are doing well, Jamund, but I can not agree at all to such conditions between us without trial."

Jamund spoke again, somewhat shortly: "Who are you, who so quickly refuses such an offer from me? Tell me your name."

The emperor answered, "Nothing would make me conceal that from you: I am called Karlamagnus, son of King Pippin of France, emperor of the Christian peoples."

When Jamund heard that, he was silent for a moment, as if he hardly believed his words; then he said, "If what you say is true, then just what I would have wished has happened to me and I do not value all my harm at a penny's worth; for I shall avenge on your body all the griefs which have come into my heart through you and your men. Nonetheless, although I can see that you have great zeal in you, I will still remember the courtesy you showed to me. Give up into my power and rule, as compensation for the harm I have suffered, and to win you freedom and peace, Paris, Rome, Pul, and Sicili,[2] Lotaringia, France, and Burgundia, Brittania and all of Gaskunia."

[2] *Sikeily.*

Karlamagnus answered, "God knows," says he, "you intend to drive a hard bargain; but it would not at all become you to govern so great a realm when you cannot manage it. I expect, however, that God will allot his realms according to his will today, and it is likely that you will have to use a good deal more than words alone."

Jamund now turned his horse with his spurs and ran the length of the field. They came together with such hard impact that neither stirrup nor saddle-girth could hold, so they both fell to the ground. Springing right up, drawing their swords high[3] and nimbly, each attacked the other with the greatest valor, and the combat between them was so hard that there had never been such a battle between two men. It was not, however, an absolutely even match, since the emperor was much advanced in age while Jamund was young, hard, and forcefully strong.

They dealt such strong blows that whole quarters were sheared away from the shields. Now the emperor stepped forward on his right foot and lifted his sword up high, intending to come down on the helmet, but Jamund quickly turned his head away and the blow came down on his right shoulder so hard that his coat of mail burst, and Jamund was severely wounded. When he felt the pain he was very angry, and attacked all the harder.

Karlamagnus noticed that whenever the attack abated a little, Jamund ran his eyes over the helmet he wore on his head; thus he knew that he very much wanted to take it. And that was true, for the more Jamund looked at the helmet the more he wanted to get it. This led him to say, "You are much honored, Christian, that such a helmet suits your head, for in it are stones of such power that I cannot kill you while you are wearing it. But indeed you will have to be clever and skillful in guarding your good helmet if I neither move it nor spoil it, or completely strip it from you: and, by Makon, you will not do that well. It shall by no means be yours any longer, if I am any judge."

The emperor says, "God knows that it shall not become yours, and much disgraced would he be who gave it up to you!"

After these words, Jamund flung his broken shield away and intended to try his strength against the emperor, holding his sword in

[3] *b*, hard.

one hand and grasping at him with the other. But since Karlamagnus knew that he was very weary and that Jamund was stronger, he turned away skilfully and Jamund kept missing him as he tried to grapple with him. And so it went for a while, until Jamund got a hold on the end of his shield and pulled; and when that did not help him, he grasped the band of the helmet and tugged. But the emperor held on to the other side, and they both pulled hard, until the helmet slid off the emperor's head. Now they both tugged at it, while each one held on to the band.

As they were combatting in this way, the emperor knew he would be overcome if they fought it out between them. Grieved at heart he turned his mind to God in heaven, praying him to watch over him so that all of holy Christendom might not be lost and fall under the rule of enemies; he especially put his trust in his beloved friend the apostle James to help him in his great need. And indeed his prayer and invocation were heard, and almighty God would not permit such great harm as now seemed likely, for, just when Jamund had taken the helmet away from him, Rolland came up, carrying a great, stout fragment of a spear-shaft, and he lifted up this cudgel, striking a great blow down on Jamund's helmet.

When Jamund saw Rollant, he did not ward off his blow much, except to speak to them, quite swollen and puffed up with wrath: "I swear by Makon and Terogant and all the power of our gods that your god is far more powerful than all other gods if both get away safely from me!"

He then raised up the sword he was holding, intending to strike down on the emperor's bare head. But as he lifted up his hand Rollant struck him again, bringing his cudgel down on the arm with all his might, so hard that the sword flew down from his hand. Rollant grasped it and struck him at short range, striking into the helmet and splitting it down the middle, and the head with it, so that the sword stopped in his back teeth. Jamund fell face downwards onto the ground, and never stood up on his feet again.

A,a (54)

Now Jamund fled, angry and distressed, for his might had been turned inside out. Early the day before, Jamund had under him seven companies of a hundred thousand; now, there was not left of all his host even the smallest shield-boy. King Karlamagnus was pursuing him. Jamund could not have gone more than, at the most, five quarters when he came to a small grove of elms or olive trees, where a clear spring welled up under the roots of the trees. When he saw this he was greatly drawn to it, since he was very wearied by toil and wakefulness: three days had passed since he had tasted any food or drink, and in the midst of this he had not dared to remove his helmet. Now he dismounted from his horse and shoved his great sword into its sheath, set his shield down against a tree and tethered his horse; then he went to the spring and lay down to drink, drinking his fill.

But before he got up King Karlamagnus came upon him there so suddenly that Jamund could not reach either his weapons or his horse, so that he was much ashamed to have been so negligent. King Karlamagnus then said, "God willing, no man shall be able to accuse me of slaying an unarmed fugitive. Take up your weapons and mount your horse, for I have come to dispute the possession of this spring with you: wrongly you drank from this spring, and you shall pay for that drink dearly."

Jamund quickly took up his weapons and leapt at once onto his horse, holding his strong shield firmly before his breast and couching his stout spear; he said "By Maumet, sir knight," says he, "your sins have led you to do what you have just done. I am not a man you can drive into flight. I see that you have a fine, swift horse, which has carried you thus far away from other men. Your coat of mail is as white as apple blossom; indeed, no weapon has damaged it; and your helmet is as green as grass,[4] all made of the best steel and set with precious gems. Anyone who wished to purchase them might buy with their value three of the greatest towns or castles. But you made it clear to me that you were never begotten by an average man or an obscure family when you refrained from attacking me when I was unarmed, and gave me my horse and weapons. You have treated me so courteously that this treatment shall avail you well. If you will yield your attire up to me here, I will give you leave to go back unharmed. But if you will give up Christianity and deny God, Maumet knows that I will make

[4] Cf. n. 2, Ch. 51.

you so wealthy that all your kinsmen shall be greatly enriched by you."[5]

Karlamagnus answered, "The conditions," says he, "which you have just proposed to me are such that I shall never agree to; it seems to me that you do not wish to get much out of attacking me."

Then Jamund said, "What is your name?"

"God knows,"says Karlamagnus, "I shall never conceal my name from you. I am called Karlamagnus, emperor of Christian leaders; the men of France serve me, and of Germany,[6] Bealver and Loerenge,[7] Mansel[8] and Rome."

It seemed strange, then, to Jamund that he was there alone. He said, "Now it has turned out for me just as I would have wished, for I do not now value my own harm as worth a penny: your body will repay the grief and distress lodging in my breast over the fall of my kinsmen and chieftains." And Jamund then asked again, "Are you that Karlamagnus who has slain some five hundred thousand of the men who fell under my banner? Now I want you to give up Paris to me, as recompense for my distress, as well as Rome, Pul and Sicili, Tutalis[9] and Loereng, Bealfer and Germany,[10] France and Burgunia, Normandy[11] and Brittania and all of Gaskunia,[12] all the way to the borderland of Spain.[13]

Emperor Karlamagnus then answered, "God knows you intend to drive a hard bargain! It is not fitting for you to have more lands when you wish to take them so easily. But I expect that we shall so deal with each other that at our parting one of us shall have little cause to praise his lot."

[5] Last sentence *A* only; translates *Asp.* 5825-27.

[6] *Alimanie, Alemaner.*

[7] Lorraine. Latter two are in *A* only; *a* substitutes *Peito* 'Poitou' and *Bretanie* 'Brittany,' neither of which appear in the corresponding list in *Asp.*, although the others do.

[8] Manseau.

[9] *a, Putalis*; not recognizably in *Asp.*, but neither are most of the others here; this list is much longer than, and has many differences from, that in *Asp.* 5847-49.

[10] *Alimanni.*

[11] *Nordmandi.*

[12] *a, Gaskon.*

[13] *Spani.*

Jamund was a young man, strong and mighty, hardy and daring in his dealings, while the emperor was clever and prudent, trustworthy, and most valiant. They now galloped their horses from one end of the field to the other as far as they could, and each attacked the other so strongly that they both fell from their horses to the earth; no king, no matter how well armed, could have escaped the dust in that fall.

Jamund jumped up quickly and drew Dyrumdali, while the king drew his royal sword Jouise, and they waged such a hard battle between the two of them that never had there been anything like it between two deadly men. They struck such heavy blows that they cut the shields so that pieces flew far around. The king now rose up on his feet and struck down on Jamund's helmet; the sword flew down the right side and slit the coat of mail from the shoulder, wounding him seriously.

When Jamund saw his blood running down, he nearly burst with grief and anger; he saw that the king intended to give him another blow at once and that he would by no means give way before him. Then he saw the golden band around the king's helmet, set with the most precious of gems, and he could no longer conceal what was in his mind; he said, "Christian, you gain a good respite if I cannot cut away that good helmet from you or if I cannot move or spoil it, for I cannot slay you while you have it on your head. Maumet knows that you shall not be able to protect it from me."

Now the king knew that Jamund would take him in his hands unless almighty God and the Holy Spirit helped him. He could not withstand him, so he turned his shoulders when Jamund tried to grasp him with his hands, escaping him thus. Now Jamund saw that the king was guarding himself, and as he looked at the helmet again, and again, he wanted it more than ever the more he saw it. He said, "Christian king," says he, "he who prepared your helmet so splendidly honored you most magnificently. That was the smith of the great king Salomon.[14] I tell you that in your helmet are such stones that he who obtains them shall never find more valuable ones. Maumet knows that it shall not be yours any longer."

[14] The biblical king? Not in *Asp.*

"God knows," says the king, "it shall never be yours: he who yielded it to you would be greatly shamed."

(55) All this took place under an olive tree, where these two chiefs battled in the hardest of encounters.[15] Every time Jamund attacked King Karlamagnus, he retaliated so valiantly that he could not conquer him. Then Jamund grasped the lower part of his shield and tried to cut it away from him. And when he could not do that, he grasped him by the bands and tried to cut the helmet from him: and the king's head was almost bared. But Karlamagnus held the helmet; they both grasped it with their hands.

And when Jamund had nearly taken the helmet from King Karlamagnus, Rolland came riding, and at once dismounted from his horse under the tree; he had a stout piece of a spear in his hand. When Jamund saw him he paid no attention, for he was[16] the most arrogant of men and thought there was no man as deadly as he. The king was then in great distress: if God did not send him help quickly, all of his realm would be lost. But in that moment Rollant rushed up with a great piece of spear-shaft in his hand, and gave Jamund's helmet as great a blow as he could. Jamund then swore by Makon[17] and Terrogant, and all their might and strength, saying, "Far greater in power over all other gods is your god, if both of you leave me as hale as when you came here!"

Jamund was strong, grim, and ill-willed, but King Karlamagnus was no child in his ways. Rollant then clasped his spear-fragment in both hands, intending to give him another blow on the bright helmet. He hit Jamund on the right with such a mighty blow on his arm that the keen sword flew far from his hand. When Jamund knew that he had nothing in his hand except an empty mailed glove, his pride diminished and he blanched, while Rollant grasped the sword at once and struck Jamund's helmet so that blood and brains came out of his mouth and the sword struck into his back teeth: he sank down in such a fall that never again would he stand up on his feet. Jamund had now found that for which he had long sought ...

[15] *a* adds: "each of the two both attacking and defending."
[16] *a*: "swollen with anger and ..."
[17] *A, Machun.*

CHAPTER LVI

Karlamagnus Gives Thanks to God

As soon as Jamund had fallen, Emperor Karlamagnus sat down on the field, overcome with weariness, and said, "I give thanks to you, almighty God, for sending me such a help in my need! You were a very lucky man just now, kinsman Rollant, for Jamund would certainly have overcome me if you had delayed any longer."

Rollant took Jamund's horse,[1] sword, and horn for himself. Then the Frenchmen Oddgeir and Nemes came, with their comrades, and saw Karlamagnus much exhausted, and Jamund dead. When Nemes came up before the emperor, he said, "Good lord, God be praised that I see you safe and alive, for it was most rash to pursue such a champion as Jamund was alone. You must have seen how unlike a fugitive his behavior was when he left us, having felled me to the ground. He had cut the horse of my good comrade Oddgeir in two, so that we both had to go on foot and were unable to help."

The emperor answered, "My good friend, be glad of heart and thank God and his saints, who looked after me better than seemed likely to me for a while: for this heathen fought me so hard over the helmet which I wore that it seemed to me all would have been lost if God had not sent me my kinsman Rollant."

After this they went and fetched some pure water and gave it to the emperor to drink, then washed the blood and sweat from his face, for Jamund had struggled so that the emperor's face was badly scratched where the band of the helmet had gone in. Then they went to where

[1] *B* only, but cf. A,a below. The horse is said to be "Vielantin," the famous *Veillantif* of Roland, in *Asp.* 6078. This tradition is also reported in *Le roman d'Aquin* (ed. F. Joüon des Longrais, Nantes, 1880), l. 1844. Although later parts of the saga mention "Velantif," a connection with Jamund is nowhere mentioned here.

the body of Jamund lay and looked at his broken-off right arm and the skull, split with the helmet down to the teeth. Because of this Nemes spoke to Rollant with great affection: "May God strengthen the hand which gave this dog so strong a blow! Take as your own whatever you want of Jamund's war gear, for we agree that you deserve to enjoy what you won so heroically."

They turned the body of Jamund on its face and carried it up under the olive-tree, throwing his shield over him; then they mounted their horses. But before they rode away, the emperor turned to Oddgeir and Nemes, saying, "If this man had been a Christian, no better man would ever have been born into the world."

A,a (55)

... The emperor then sat down to rest, with little thought of his share of the glory: only that Jamund was dead. For if God had not sent him such help, he would never again have borne the crown. Rollant then took his horse and all his arms;[2] and then the Frenchmen Oddgeir and Nemes came there, dismounted from their horses, and found King Karlamagnus, tired, and bloodstained about the face.

(56) Oddgeir and Nemes dismounted. When Nemes saw King Karlamagnus he became grieved[3] and said, "You acted in a bad and imprudent manner when you followed him alone, when you saw that he had knocked me from my horse and cut down Oddgeir's horse with his sword, putting us both in strange perils as if we were footsoldiers or beggars. He did not act like a fugitive, but like a great viking."[4]

[2] Which, of course, includes the sword *Dyrumdali,* so that this account conflicts with that in ***Kms.*** I (where the sword is given to Karlamagnus after the struggle with Girard of Viana). Such conflicting traditions about the sword are also found elsewhere. It may be of particular interest to note that in *Mainet* (ed. Gaston Paris in *Romania*, 4 [1875], 305-337) Charlemagne (Karles) wins the sword for himself at this early point in his career, but later, we are told (11. 38-40, p. 328).

Puis li fu ele emblee en son tresor plus grant,
Et puis la reconquist Rollandins au cuer franc
Quant it occist Yaumont fil le roi Agulant.

[3] *a*: "They dismounted and met Karlamagnus."—The speech is made by Nemes alone in *Asp.*

[4] *a*: "... like a terrified fugitive when he drove us both from our horses."

The king answered, "Lords," said he, "I shall watch out against such peril in the future; but nothing which has been done was useless. He gave the hardest combat for the sake of my helmet, which he very much wanted, and if God had not sent Rollant to me, to avenge me on him, I should certainly have been doomed to death."

They then took Jamund's body and turned it on its back. Rollant had attacked him so violently that he had cut off his right arm at the elbow. Duke Nemes then kissed Rollant three times[5] and said, "The property which you have now achieved, we agree shall be altogether yours, for you deserve to enjoy that which you have so heroically gained."

Before the king climbed on his horse, they washed the blood and sweat from his face and carried Jamund under an olive tree, where they laid him down. But Rollant had given him such a mighty blow on the back of the head that both his eyes had been knocked out onto his cheeks and brains and blood had come out of his eye-sockets. They turned him on his face[6] and cast his shield over him. Then the king said, "Lord Nemes," says he, "if he had been a Christian, there would have been no man more valiant than he since Christ came into the world."

Nemes answered, "Woe to those who weep for him and to the woman who gave birth to such a son, for he is now given to all the devils."[7]

[5] *a*: "... laid both his hands on Rollant's neck and kissed him three times."

[6] The details are not in *Asp.*, but cf. Roepke, p. 35.

[7] In *W*, it is Naimes who says (twice) what a man he would have been if a Christian, but in other mss. this is said by the king; cf. Roepke, p. 35. The final statement has no parallel.

CHAPTER LVII

The Baptism of Balam

Now the emperor rode back to his men. All of the Christian people were much distressed and troubled, since they had lost the emperor and his companions and[1] did not know where they had gone. The heathen host had then been driven into flight—those who had escaped with their lives. Karlamagnus thus rode to the camp they had occupied, and, dismounting from his horse in front of the large tent which had been Jamund's, went in with his comrades. It was extremely well equipped. There was both plenty of food there and the best of drink which anyone could choose for himself, nor was there any shortage of gold and silver, with precious stones; good table ware, made both after the older fashion and the newer; a large store of the best cloth, both cut and uncut; and there was such a great selection of every kind of battle garment that it is not easy to describe it all.

It seemed good to the Frenchmen to rest here, after long weariness and much toil. Karlamagnus and all his leading men sat down on seats. The lord pope and the learned men sat near the emperor in this tent, praising God for the victory which he had granted to his people. The French relaxed well now, with food and drink which was quite pleasant enough, and there was much happiness among God's people.

This tent which Jamund, son of Agulandus, had brought from the realms of Africa had been made with such skill that the French thought there had never been such a treasure. A thousand knights could sit comfortably in the spacious interior, as well as pages and serving men. The tent itself was made of the most precious brocade, embroidered with gold and silver. In the front of it were set four carbuncles, which cast a light over all the land about so that there was no need to burn candles there at night or during the evening. In it could be heard

[1] *B* only.

beautiful bird-song and the sound of pipes and one could see game pieces that played with each other by themselves. Such great brightness streamed from the carbuncles that the whole valley around was so lit up that no one could come there undetected, and the emperor's men found that they had quite enough light. The emperor and the pope slept in this tent during the night.

In the morning the emperor ordered water consecrated by the clerics, and this was sprinkled on all the hosts, then around the tent, inside and out, and on everything else which the heathens had carried in their hands before. Then the emperor went to the table with all his host and they sat and drank and rejoiced throughout the day.[2] Before the table was removed three men came before the emperor: Duke Nemes and Oddgeir the Dane, leading Balam the messenger between them; and they greeted him well and courteously. The emperor received them graciously, asking who the fine man whom they led might be.

He answered, "I am called Balam. I was sent to you before by Agulandus and Jamund, at the time when you were staying in the town of Baion. I sent you a white horse. And now, very recently, I was so impudent as to attack you, and you knocked me from my horse. And since I clearly understand, because of many of the things that have happened between us, that the religion held by the heathens may better be called a false doctrine than a true faith, I wish to forsake it and take the true faith in baptism, if you will grant this to me. And know, as your God is a witness, that this was in my heart long ago, though up to now I followed my companions."

The king answered, "If you are in earnest about this, as you say, I shall not be reluctant to have you granted holy baptism, if you will accept it."

He answered, "God is my witness that this is my heartfelt wish."

Now the emperor explained the case of the messenger Balam, and the lord pope praised almighty God and said to the emperor, "Do not delay, lord, to fulfill this desire for one who is so good that it pleases God to draw him away from the fiend's maw into his own household."

[2] Latter phrase in *B* only.

The emperor immediately ordered some of the Frenchmen to prepare a deep font, and it was so done. Four bishops went there, with other clergy, and consecrated the font, and at the consecration the emperor asked the lord pope to conduct the baptismal service for this man, which he gladly did. Balam was christened in the name of the Holy Trinity and given the name of Vitaclin, after one of the great lords of Emperor Karlamagnus who had died a short time before. The emperor lifted him from the baptismal font and dressed him himself in the best of clothes, giving him an excellent cloak, which he laid over his shoulders. This man appeared very impressive to all there, for he was handsome in appearance, very tall, strong and powerful, and courteous in his behavior.

There is still more to be told of Vitaclin, but now we shall hear a few words about the excellent lord Girard the Old. After he had conquered the chief standard of Jamund, he went back into the battle again, as was said before. As soon as he knew that Jamund had fled, with Karlamagnus in pursuit of him, he made a very sharp attack, urging his men to advance, and drove the heathens far from where they had been before. And when the afternoon began to grow dark he turned his host toward that tower which he had taken from Jamund, which the emperor had given him to command, while Karlamagnus dwelt in the tents with his men; and they set about letting those who were sound but weary rest, and curing those who were sick and wounded, going about it with such supplies as they could find at hand.

Next, there is something to be said of Agulandus—how well and nobly he received the two kings Magon and Asperant, who had fled from the chief standard of his son Jamund, when they came to his court.

A,a (57)

King Karlamagnus now rode with them to his host, and they found everyone grieving and sick at heart because no one knew what had become of the king. The horses were so exhausted that they were almost useless. If the king had stayed away longer, they would have lost all hope.

When the king arrived, he dismounted from his horse, and they led him to Jamund's tent[3] and took his armor from him; the French then camped there ...

(71) ... That night King Karlamagnus lodged in Jamund's tent, where they had so much food and good drink that they had no need in the world to search for more or better provisions. An enormous amount of gold and silver was assembled there: precious fabrics, a multitude of gold and silver vessels, and all sorts of other goods of pure silver fashioned by the skill of smiths, both ancient and more recent. So many of the slaughtered were represented there by stout spears and sharp swords and all sorts of costly weapons that no mortal eye ever saw so countless a throng, yet these had been dearly purchased, for they had been bought in exchange for flesh and the body's blood. But there were those there who thought that they had avenged themselves against the Africans, and they compensated themselves as well as possible with all sorts of good food and drink, and took a quiet rest.[4]

(72) The emperor, who did not wish any longer delay, sent for an archbishop and had water consecrated and ordered that it be sprinkled over all the host. Then he sat down at table in Jamund's tent with a thousand knights on either side. There was enough room for them all to sit in that tent, with room to spare for pages and cup-bearers to go about their duties.[5]

The ways in which that tent had been skilfully prepared have not yet been detailed: no living man had ever seen the like. Four carbuncle stones were set on poles in the tent, which illumined and made bright all the valley around. Birds sang there continually, while in the evening, during supper, and before and after, those who sat therein were entertained with all sorts of amusements. No one needed to light a candle, and if robbers came by land or sea to destroy cities or castles or to plunder, there was no way they could escape without their attack

[3] *a*, the tent; *Asp.* "tref Aumon."
[4] Last sentence in *a* only; see *Asp.* 7002-05.
[5] *a*: "... pages and serving men."

being seen. The stones gave out such light that night seemed like the brightest day.

(73) Most praiseworthy was that messenger who came to France to give tidings to King Karlamagnus, whom the king felled from his horse.[6] He now came before King Karlamagnus and said, "Lord," says he, "let me be baptized now; then I shall tell you tidings which it is proper that you should know."

"Friend," said the king, "do you wish to hasten this so?"

"Yes," said he. "God is my witness that I have long wished for this."

"God be praised!" says Karlamagnus.

That same day, when the king had eaten, the French prepared a baptismal font and the pope came there to speak with Karlamagnus. "Lord," said the emperor, "see here the messenger of King Agulandus, whom he sent to me in France to carry his message. Oddgeir and Nemes brought him here, and now he wishes to be christened."

The pope answered, "Praised be almighty God!"

Four archbishops then went to consecrate the font, and the pope went to perform the service. Balam removed all his clothing except for his linen breeches, and they submerged him three times; then Karlamagnus came and took him from the water. But anyone who would like to buy the chrism box that was brought forward could not buy it for a thousand marks of silver!

The pope then said to King Karlamagnus, "Lord," says he, "receive and honor this man whom God has given, and cherish him as a friend."[7]

The king answered, "God knows that I shall do that gladly." In the baptism, King Karlamagnus changed his name and gave him a rich cloak. He was a large and powerful man, strong and hardy: in all the Christian army there was no finer knight. He knew well how to sit in a saddle and was the bravest of men. The pope christened him,[8] and he was named Vitaclin[9] after a nobleman who was a friend of the king ...

[6] I.e., Balam.
[7] *a* omits the last clause; either version is an expansion of *Asp.* 7060.
[8] From "he was a large ..." *a* only; cf. *Asp.* 7068-73.
[9] *a*, *Vitaklin.*

(57) ... Girard the Old drove the fleeing heathens away for more than a mile, and none got away from there alive; but the field was covered with bodies and weapons, so that one could not ride over it or come through it. There was so much treasure there that anyone who wanted to could fill his shield[10] and stockings with gold and silver.[11]

Girard the Old dismounted from his horse before the tower: all the good men there were much distressed, for they had been watching and fasting for four days. They all rejoiced when they could rest, and King Karlamagnus[12] sat down to eat.

If King Agulandus had known the news, he would have been much vexed and full of wrath!

[10] *a*, sleeve.

[11] *a* adds: "And when they had taken as much as they liked, there was still so much left that it was sad to see."

[12] Karlamagnus is not there, of course; cf. *Asp.* 6152.

CHAPTER LVIII

Magon and Asperant Return to Agulandus

While the events which have just been described were taking place in Hispania, King Agulandus was staying in the great city of Africa which is called Frisa with his huge host. He heard nothing of what was going on between Emperor Karlamagnus and Jamund. Thus he was now rejoicing in all magnificence, for two powerful kings had come to the city with great fleets. One of them, ruler of a realm which lies far beyond Jerusalem, was called Bordant the Strong, while the other was named Moadas.[1]

One day during their visit, the kings Agulandus and Bordant were playing a game of chess, and when they had been playing for a long time the game began to turn against Agulandus. He took this badly, and said angrily, "Give up the game: for even if I wagered all of Pul,[2] you would certainly never win it."

The king, smiling a bit maliciously, said, "Lord, if I were in your position, I would wager less of the kingdom, for my glove seems worth more than your chances in the game."

While they were talking this way, the kings Magon and Asperant, who have been spoken of earlier, came into the hall, dismounted from their horses, and came before Agulandus as he sat at the game table, greeting him. He recognized them as soon as he looked at them, and asked whether they could tell him of any tidings. They answered, "Lord, there are great tidings."

"What, then?" says Agulandus. "Has my son Jamund conquered Hispania, and killed the Christians, or driven them away?"

"It is not that way at all," say they. "Your son has been fighting with Karlamagnus, and we think that most of the host you sent along

[1] *Modal.*
[2] *B, Ful.*

to follow him have been killed. He gave us his chief standard to guard, with no less a host than a hundred thousand: but on the second day of the battle, a band of people attacked us unexpectedly and amazingly sharply. Their leader was a short, thickset man, and they killed all our host and drove us into flight; Jamund defended neither his banner nor us. Since then we have travelled night and day because of this."

Agulandus then asked Asperant wrathfully, "What can you tell me of Jamund?"

He answered, "By my faith, I cannot tell you any more than I have just related."

When Agulandus had heard the king's words he leapt up, swollen with rage, and shoved the chess board over onto the floor, grasping a large pole which he aimed at the king's head, but he ducked aside. The blow fell on a stone pillar; it was so great that the pillar broke in pieces. Agulandus then said, "You wicked traitors shall be taken prisoner here and hung on the gallows as the worst of thieves, or suffer an even more disgraceful death, for your betrayal of[3] my son and me, your king."

Asperant answered, "Your disgrace will increase the more, deservedly, if you have us killed without a just cause: but neither you nor Jamund need be so conceited as to think you can conquer Karlamagnus."

The kings were now seized, according to the king's order, while he went into a great hall and summoned all the leaders of the heathen host to him and said, "Good leaders, you have all learned what a dastardly deed these two kings have committed against me, betraying my son and fleeing from his chief standard out of cowardice and craven fear. Now in order that no one should dare to act so wickedly toward his leaders, I bid you, for your own lives and for the sake of the overlordship I hold over you, to judge the right sentence quickly, so that their deed may not long go unpunished."

The leaders answered, "No disobedience on our part shall be manifested in this case out of any insincerity towards you."

Twenty kings then went away from the hall into a chamber. Many of them were relatives and friends of the two kings who were now in

[3] *b*, faith to.

bonds. Thus it happened here as often happens when a difficult case is discussed: it did not appear the same way to all. Some spoke for the kings and wanted great mercy to be granted, while others were opposed and wanted to do what would best please Agulandus, and they made various speeches. We shall now tell how disgracefully the case was prosecuted.

A,a (58)

King Agulandus was at that time in the city which is called Frisa; also there were the mighty King Bordant,[4] from the land which lies far outside Jerusalem, and King Modas,[5] with a great host, and they were amusing and entertaining themselves together there, playing chess with King Agulandus from early in the morning until past noon. Now when Agulandus saw that his side of the game was going badly, he became very angry, and said, "You are holding back this game for nothing: I will wager all of Pul against your right glove." Then the other laughed, and said, "Do not give Pul: sword and spear are defending it before us.[6] Yesterday[7] before daybreak Jamund rode forth, and seven thousand knights with him, but I do not know what has happened to them."

Here the sixth book ends, as King Karlamagnus came to rest with his troops after the great struggle and pains of the big battle. The seventh book will now tell of the deeds of Agulandus when to him came Magon and Asperant, who had fled from the chief standard of Jamund.[8]

(59) Magon and King Asperant now came riding in a lather of heat to Frisa, where King Agulandus the Powerful was staying. Their horses were bloodstained from their spurs. They greeted the king nobly as soon as they came before him, where he sat over the chess table. "What are you doing?" said they. "Your son has been fighting with

[4] *Asp.* Boidant.
[5] *Asp.* Moadas.
[6] This speech is credited to Abilans in *Asp.* 6169.
[7] *a* only.
[8] Note that their return, and a large part of the ensuing debate, had already been presented in A,a chs. 40-45.

King Karlamagnus: we, with a hundred thousand men, had charge of the chief standard.[9] Unexpectedly, a band of people came up on our right, and the leader of this troop was a little old man. They killed all our men and put us to flight, and of the twenty thousand there is not one left to bear a shield."

Agulandus then answered, "Asperant," said he, "where is my son?"

"Lord," says he, "by my faith, we do not know at all."

When Agulandus heard that, he nearly went out of his mind, and he grasped a staff which lay beside him and threw it at him. But when he saw the staff flying at him, he ducked away as quickly as he could: the great blow took away half the pillar he had been next to. Then Agulandus said, "You old traitor," said he, "we shall never believe that any man who had been christened might put my son to flight. For your treachery I shall have you both hanged like the worst of thieves!"

Asperant then answered, "I understand your words, lord," says he, "but I expect that you will not regain that which you say I have stolen all winter long."

Agulandus then called to him all the leaders in the host, and they came before him in the great hall which King Jeremias had owned.[10] Agulandus spoke there, saying, "Lords," said he, "hear what wickedness these two kings have declared to me, betraying my son and knavishly turning traitor to him. Now I ask you each to judge what is right in this case."

They answered, "You shall not lack this, lord."

Twenty kings went out of the hall and gathered in a room. These included the greatest leaders, Alamazor and Amustade ...[11]

a; (40) Now we shall speak of the kings who fled away. They rode as fast as they could until they reached King Agulandus and told him all their tidings. Some of those who were present wanted to condemn them, since they had fled from the chief standard, and said that they deserved to die because they had betrayed their lord ...[12]

[9] Part of a page in *a* is missing here.

[10] *Asp.* 6209; Brandin glosses as the prophet.

[11] *Asp.* 6221: "Quatre almacor et uns amustandé," i.e., four governors and an emir.

[12] This summary is not in *Asp.*

CHAPTER LIX

The Council of the Kings

Now when these kings had gathered together in one place the first to stand up was King Amustene, since he was the highest ranking of all and had under his command an army of twenty thousand. He had two fully grown sons and was a close relation of these kings; thus he wished to make a case to clear them of blame. He spoke in eloquent words: "Since wise and knowledgeable men are gathered here, it is proper that each should heed the other's case attentively, hearing what is said with patience. Let us take that which is best and most reasonable from each man's advice, putting aside anger, folly, and impetuosity, choosing, in all calmness, that which is wise. Since Magon and Asperant are my nephews it would not be fitting for me to say much of their quality, but I expect that there is no one who has come to this conference who wishes to make a more severe judgement than is right. Indeed, I fear that if they are not somewhat spared, all this army will be disturbed to no small extent."

After saying this Amustene sat down and King Aquin stood up and spoke harshly: "You are taking on a great deal, Lord Amustene, if you intend to suggest with showy words that these men, although they may be your kinsmen, should not be sentenced to suffer, for it seems to me that their own words doom them to death when they themselves bear witness that Jamund did them the honor of giving them control of his chief standard, with a large troop. But we can all see that they have come here now, though their bodies are not wounded and their shields are not battered—nor are their battle-vests slit, and neither their helmets nor their coats of mail have been broken. It is, therefore, obvious that they have fled in fear and cowardice. We have sent our sons and kinsmen there, and we may be truly terrified about their state. But you, Amustene, expect to be happy and glad in the return of your kinsmen.

It shall turn out quite otherwise for you, for before your eyes I pronounce the sentence that all our griefs should be avenged in their shameful death."

Thus spoke Aquin; he then sat down.[1] Next to stand up was the great leader Galinger the Old, who governed a huge realm and ruled the great city which is called Sebastia. He was a splendid man who wore a cloak of the most precious cloth; his beard was white, and fell down over his chest, and when he began to say something everyone gave him attention, for he was the most eloquent speaker in all the heathen army, calm and deliberate and much honored by all.

Thus he began his message: "Noble lords," says he, "I will tell you how this case seems to me. These kings are noble, doughty, valiant men, and if you wish a rightful judgement to be given in their case, it would seem to me that it would be better to let the case wait until we are absolutely sure how guilty they are. If Jamund comes back safely with his company, let him judge their offense as he likes; but if Makon does not watch over his leaders, and Jamund falls or is mortally wounded, then make your sentence as seems best. If you choose to disregard my advice, I shall have nothing to do with your acts; you know yourselves that I will not judge this case in haste or too great speed without lawful proof, or any other kind, no matter who, great or lowly, may wish it. Nor will I assist in bringing a sentence other than what seems to me to be rightly said. Even if I were offered another realm as large as that I now govern, I would not be worthy to hold my honors if I wrongly judged this case, as it behoves me to say. Let any others who are concerned speak further, but I shall be silent hereafter."

King Mordanturus then stood up and said, "I am amazed that a man who, because of his age, I thought had come to full discernment, now seems to have become little better than out of his senses; you are acting, Galinger, as the sages say: as if your heart were cooled with your conscience as the body withers with age. I am surprised that you seem to put off or delay passing sentence on these kings as not at all guilty of anything against Agulandus or Jamund his son, when, in fact, according to the ancient ordinance of earlier raiders, as it is appointed in

[1] Sentence in *B* only.

the warrior's laws, no worthy man should dare flee further from battle than under the chief standard, there to bear whatever he must in life or death. If these kings had been assigned to the head of a division and they had then fled from battle, so that they did not guard the chief standard out of fear and terror, that might have been regarded with mercy. But that is by no means the case now, when they affirm that they were put in charge of the standard and then forsook it and in this way betrayed their master. Thus I pronounce them self-doomed to the most scurrilous death."

After these words he went to his seat. Next, Gordant of Galizia,[2] which is far out in Garsant, rose up. He was very powerful; his beard and hair were white and he was broad in the shoulders, with stout arms, richly and nobly clad. He raised his voice and said, "Noble lords, you know that I am no child in years or wits, and that thus you may well heed my advice. These kings whom we are now considering are good knights and it would be very harmful to sentence them to death. Do not let this happen, unless it be by the sentence of Agulandus himself: all the more because we do not know how to put this case to the proof. Although Jamund has opposed the will of his father, and of us who are his advisors, in many things, we should honor him anyway since he is the son of our high king, and I beg of everyone to avoid doing anything against him henceforward. Now whatever I say, or would like to happen, it seems probable to me that this case will end in such a way as will tend towards the most trouble, and so I shall not speak any more now."

When Ulien, the kinsman of Agulandus, heard what different arguments the kings made, he did not wish to keep silent any longer and rose up, shaking, and spoke harshly, as he often did: "Hear exactly what I have to say. It is evident that you are not fully agreed on the sentence given to us by our King Agulandus, whose bidding we should fully carry out, for the god himself has made him our overlord. I agree that it was very ill-advised for Agulandus to give Jamund his son a crown and so confirm him in pride and overboldness against himself and all his friends. But although we did not advise this, things are now

[2] *B, Gordiant* of *Galacia.*

the way he arranged it and you can therefore see, good leaders, how disgracefully these kings acted against him when they deserted their lord, abandoned and cast him off, and wickedly left him. They were too much honored before when they received his chief standard to guard, for they fled away wickedly and cravenly and thus betrayed their master. It is, therefore, my judgement that they have forfeited life and limb. Now if there is anyone here so bold as to call my judgement wrong, let him take up his weapon without delay and arm himself against me, and right here I shall cut off his head and show my judgement to be right. And if I do not do just this, may I be cast down into a deep dungeon and left there to starve to death!"

With these words, Ulien silenced the kings and everyone looked at his neighbor. He sat down and turned to the king called Pharaon, saying, "Now I think I have defended the wishes of Agulandus well enough so that no one shall dare to disagree with my case."

When silence had been maintained for a little while, King Pantalas stood up. He looked very wrathful, since his kinsmen were being doomed to death. Thus he spoke in so shrill a voice that everyone there could hear him: "A great deal of impudence has issued from your mouth, Ulien," says he, "as you manifested before all when you doomed to death such brave men as Magon and Asperant. In this way you wish to reward Agulandus for the fine wine with which you stuff yourself every day: by doing what he wants, which will be a great dishonor to both of you. Now whoever may like or dislike it, I must say how this case seems to me. Agulandus should wait until his son Jamund returns, or until he learns truly whether they fled from the battle for good cause or out of cowardice alone, for by Makon, neither Agulandus nor you, Ulien, nor anyone else can judge this case correctly before this. If I ruled so large an army as is now gathered in this city, I should never be so bold as to rush trouble so when nothing has been proved."

Pantalas spoke thus, then sat down. After him King Gundrun the Karueski[3] rose up. He was governor of the realm which belonged to King Temprer, called Birangri,[4] a great land and well settled. A well-

[3] *b, karneski.*
[4] *b, Hiagri.*

spoken man in presenting his case, he was deeply learned in the heathen laws and chief adviser of King Agulandus. Gundrun leaned against a pillar and said, "It does not beseem us to disregard the words and wish of our high king Agulandus when he ordered, in his authority, that we pass a hard and righteous sentence of punishment against these two traitors here who foolishly think that we ought to be pleased with their great betrayal: when these wicked, cowardly thralls fled from their lord Jamund, who, thinking them to be brave champions, gave them command of his chief standard. Since they have proved full of misdeeds and treachery, it is my judgement that they should be hanged like wretched thieves and their bodies then burned on a pyre, for this is the right way to treat wicked traitors. Although their kinsman Pantalas wants to set aside our judgement as soon as it goes against his wishes, I would not give a full penny for his pride and arrogance. If he dares, let him take his sword and fight with me; and if I do not quickly chop his body in two, burn me in flames and cast my ashes to the winds, driving my heirs away from their native land."

When he had said this, he sat down. Then the well-bred leader Acharz[5] of Amflor, a great warrior, stood up and said, "Let us hold to that which was said first and not permit anger or fierceness to intrude in the case. Rather, let us say calmly that which truly seems best to us. But it would have been better for Agulandus to stay home in peace and quiet in his realm of Africa, which is so wide and huge that it is enough for any one king, rather than to seek greedily for the realm of another king, which is of no use to him, destroying men and treasure there. It was also much too hasty a decision when he made his son Jamund leader of so many good men, for it may seem all the more likely, knowing his rashness, that not only these two kings were prompted to leave by great disenchantment, but, rather, all those who followed him in his foolishness. Now because Magon and Asperant, whom you sentence to death, are good leaders and have often proved their faithfulness and brave knighthood, I offer myself and my money as security for them, that they may be allowed to retain life and limb until Jamund returns; but if you will not accept this choice, that is all the advice I have to give in this case."

[5] *b*, *Achaz*.

Acharz thus finished his speech. But King Abilant the Strong answered his argument as you may hear: "Truly, Acharz," says he, "you are not admonishing with wily words, but openly chastising with sharp censure, and if the proper thing were done you should never come before the sight of Jamund or be at all honored by his father Agulandus, when you intend to overcome, with your specious words, our carrying out the behest of our king, and so betray him. Think of this and go away from this place, out of the room, out of our sight, and whisper your counsel in the ears of those who please you; but know that you shall never hear that your advice helped these kings, for it is not meet that their case go any longer unpunished for any man's prayer or wish. Now, right before your eyes, they shall be bound and scourged, and your hand shall not be able to be of the least help to them.

"Rather, fifteen shield-boys shall punish their faithlessness. Each of them shall have in his hand a stiff horse-switch, knitted together with strong leather thongs, and beat them vigorously; but any one of them who does not draw blood from their backs with his blow shall at once get another blow from my right hand. When these traitors have been tormented this way, they shall then be hanged or bound to horses' tails and dragged over hills[6] and stones and thrashed to pieces this way, and afterwards burned in a pyre to cold ashes. That is my judgement, and that of all those who intend to follow me. As for you, Acharz, and the others who wish to follow those who would call that wrong, we shall boldly give you the same sentence, since all of you I count as guilty of agreeing to their treachery.[7] Now speak up loud and clear, if anyone has the courage to speak against my sentence."

King Melkiant then stood up; he was a bold man in argument, and a particular friend of King Amustene. He said, "Certainly, Abilant,[8] you are big and strong, and you think that no one will dare to stir his tongue against you. But so that you may know that you are not that mighty, I shall say what I please without trembling, so that you and your comrades may hear clearly. I have kept silent for a while and

[6] *b*, wood.
[7] *b*, "with these traitors."
[8] *b*, *Adilant*.

listened to what was said here, and I think that those seem to be wisest who are most adverse to the case of the kings; but I think their judgement is made rashly, and with dangerous insincerity to Agulandus, when they call it worthy of death to leave the battle after death was certain. Did they not stay there a long time and fight bravely until all their troop had fallen? Could any two men make much of a bold defense or gain much in the place when before a hundred men could do nothing? They waited, but neither Jamund nor anyone else came to their aid.

"Now say honestly, who of you who now sit here would be so valiant and courageous, at a time when it seemed to him death was certain, that he would not look every way about him for the best way to escape? I can answer myself: none, certainly. All the less would you pay attention to a man who is not related to you, although he were your leader, when even if your father or mother were left behind in the power of enemies you would not consider it if you could better save your own life. You might also consider, if you wish to seek for what is reasonable, how often it happens to those who are engaged in battle that such great fear comes over the hearts of men who before have many times shown their courage that they can think of nothing but escape. But as soon as they are safe from great peril, they themselves wonder why they were so overcome as to flee from the weapons of their enemies, and they would much rather have suffered sudden death than endure such a withering of their former valor. It therefore appears clear, if we consider it correctly, that their flight was impelled not by cowardice but by sudden misfortune. It seems to me these kings have fallen into this misfortune: they fled away when they saw no other hope, nor did they hide themselves in caves or other holes in the ground like terrified fugitives, but came to find the high king himself because they thought that no one was more likely to give Jamund help than his father, when he knew how necessary it was. Now I judge that their deed is far from worthy of death, when I think they have acted properly as good messengers."

So Melkiant[9] finished his case and sat down. Then a great and powerful leader called Sinapis the Clever rose up. He governed a large

[9] *Melkeant.*

realm called Alpre. Sinapis was the closest friend of Agulandus, and had fostered his son Jamund for a long time. He spoke in this way: "Your argument, Melkiant,[10] may seem reasonable if looked at quickly by foolish men. But if it is wisely viewed it will be found of little value because it arises from the great friendship, of which we all know, which you bear for that treacherous king whom I see sitting there near a stone pillar, clad in red cloth—most undeservingly, for he has always led a bad life and even been faithless to his high king, while I have followed King Agulandus with all faithfulness and uprightness. But it is to be wondered at that so wise a man as Agulandus tolerates what he does, for now that man wishes to release these traitors whom he calls his nephews from a right sentence, and not just them but others like them. Thus it is my true wish that Agulandus drive out of his realm first him who is the origin of cunning and wiles, and all his kin, who are now openly disobeying him in this case.

"But then I would sentence Magon and Asperant to suffer the most scurrilous of deaths, the worst we can devise for them. They should not be killed with weapons like good men nor suffer on the gallows like pure thieves; rather, they shall be bound to the tails of wild horses and dragged around through all the streets and then thrown down into a foul pit, so that their guilt[11] shall be evident to all, and so that Jamund shall not hear that we are keeping his traitors peacefully among us. This sentence should be carried out as quickly as possible. Although this sentence of mine may seem wrong to you, Amustene, it shall be so done! I know very well that you are most displeased with my decision, since you have become quite pale and are turning as black as earth: you shall have to swell a great deal more, and become huge with swollen wrath, before you can rescue your kinsman[12] from our judgement, for I shall not recant[13] though you call this judgement wrong. I shall cut off your deceitful head for you, and those of any others who care to speak against this decision."

[10] *Melcheant.*
[11] Or 'penalty'?
[12] *B*, friends.
[13] *B* only.

When the case of Sinapis had reached this point, Madequin the Strong said, "There is no need to discuss this case any further, for I will agree to what Sinapis had decreed."

Then he got up and went to the place where Ulien was sitting and took him by the hand, saying, "Let us go before Agulandus and reveal to him what conclusion has been reached in the kings' case."

They did so, and found the king sitting in his hall on a silk cushion. They greeted him and Ulien then said, "Drive away heavy grief from your breast, for the two traitors have been given such a sentence as you will find agreeable to your wishes."

Agulandus answered, "Are they doomed to death?"

"Certainly, lord," say they. "Therefore do not delay, but bind them between two horses and let their bodies be pulled to pieces. Then let them be pulled by those beasts around all the streets of the town, over stones and mounds. Let them then be broken up into small pieces and thrown into the foulest of pits."

When Agulandus had heard Ulien's words, he became a little more cheerful and prepared to do what has been described to the kings. They were drawn most savagely in the sight of men and women, so that their flesh and blood was spread all over the streets and stones. Many thought this a very harsh punishment, though no one dared say so openly: this affair led to much dissension in the heathen army.

A (59) ... Amustade now spoke first: "Lords," says he, "these two kings are my kinsmen and nephews.[14] I expect that there are none who have come to this council who wish to make a grievous judgement, for they are the bravest of knights; I fear greatly that if they are harmed all of this host shall be disturbed and fall out."

(60) Then King Akvin[15] stood up, speaking wrathfully: "Lord Amustade," says he, "you are taking a great deal upon yourself when you say that no one should harm these men in judgement. Since they have fled from the standard which lord Jamund gave them to guard,

[14] "Sister-sons," Asp. 6228, "... de ma seror."

[15] *Asp.* Antelmes.

when their bodies are not wounded nor their weapons destroyed or proved false, it is apparent to every man that they have doomed themselves. We sent our sons and brothers and close relatives there and are fearful and[16] distressed about their state, but you wish to be gladdened by having your kinsmen freed. But right now, in your sight, they shall be taken captive by these chiefs so that such a judgement may be passed as shall revenge us all!"

a (41) Then old Galinger[17] stood up, a powerful ruler who governed the glorious city of Sebastia;[18] he was dressed in rich and precious furs. He had a white moustache and a white beard hanging to the middle of his breast, with three braids. When he began to speak everyone listened: in all the army there was no man more eloquent than he, "Lords," said he, "if you will listen, I will tell you how things seem to me. These two kings of ours are very noble, strong and gallant men, and though you wish to proceed with the sentence you have judged in their case, it would be better to let the case rest until we have heard the whole truth. If Jamund and his band come back safe to us, then the case should be judged according to what he says about it. But if it is Makon's will that Jamund should fall or be mortally wounded, then judge according to what you can see to be true ..."[19]

... king, and said, "By Makon," said he, "this seems strange to me. Who can tell me that this judgement is wrong? Since Jamund gave them the chief standard to guard, it was fitting for them to do anything but flee back, although they had been put to flight by overwhelming force. It is not fitting for any man to desert the standard, and he ought never to turn from it for any threat of death, so betraying his lord!"

[16] The defective leaf of *a* resumes here.

[17] *Galingrerir; Asp.* Galindres.

[18] *Asp.* Batre.

[19] More than half a page is missing here. The speech next picked up is that of Meadas de Tyr in *Asp.* ; he seems to be indicated in *B*'s 'Mordanturus.' It is probable that the speeches of Floriades and Gorant (*Asp.* lss. 330 and 331) should have preceded this one. (Cf. van Waard, p. 214).

(42) Talamon[20] then spoke in great wrath; he was as grim as a lion whom all animals fear,[21] a powerful man and a mighty leader, king of the land which is called Mememunt.[22] He had red[23] eyes and a laughing, gracious face and was the strongest of armed men on horseback. "Lords," said he, "I know as a truth that it cannot be tolerated if two of our kings have done wrong towards their leader and us all in forsaking their lord, who gave them advancement and honor and put them in charge of many troops. Now you certainly know that I am much grieved by this, for I never expected to see such a thing, whether Jamund deserved well or ill; yet let us wait patiently and let this case stand until we have heard all the truth, then judge according to your will and have them burned on a pyre or otherwise punished. For, by Makon," says he, "my honor hinges on this: if you will not do so, then all our enterprise shall go amiss, for twenty thousand men shall be blood-stained for this cause if the kings are doomed."

King Ulien would not keep silent any longer and said to all the listeners, "Lords," says he, "hear me, and listen: I see clearly that you are all in disagreement about giving a sentence. For what purpose did the king call us all to this meeting? When my lord had assembled his army, before, and brought it here ..."[24]

... "... they have forsaken their natural lord, who gave them the chief standard so that they would guard it and defend its honor, but they fled like wicked, cowardly thralls, abandoning their lord Jamund, who was their ruler. Now give the correct judgement, no matter whom it may displease: that they be hung as the worst of thieves. Then let their bodies be burned on a pyre, for it is fitting to deal so with those who betray their lord. Although their kinsman Pantalas, whom I see sitting

[20] *Asp.* Acesalon.

[21] *Asp.* 6668: "come li on qui ot grant marement," 'like one who suffered great affliction.'

[22] *Asp.* Jubilent.

[23] *Asp.* "vair."

[24] Some twenty lines are missing here. When the ms. picks up again, it is in a speech made by the Saracen identified in *Asp.* as Gondres/Gondrin li Carruier (6439), *Gundrun* in *B*. In *Asp.*, as in *B*, Pantalas speaks before Gondres/Gundrun.

there, wishes to quash our verdict, I would not give so much as a penny for his arrogance and pride. If I have my sword in my hand and he should dare to fight me, if I do not have his head at once, may I be burned in the fire, my ashes cast to the wind, and my heirs driven from my holdings!"

(43)[25] Pliades then cried out wrathfully, as angry as a lion for the sake of his lord: no young man was ever more valiant than he. "I know surely," says he, "that my lord must now be faring wretchedly because of these traitors. Makon will be wrathful at them because they did not help their lord Jamund, wickedly deserting him in battle. These traitors have forfeited life and limb. They should be burned in the fire or suffer an equally hateful death, drawn to death by horses in the sight of all our army. Then let them be cast in a foul pit so that all who hear of it see what becomes of such people. I pronounce the true, right judgment; by Makon, to whom my soul is dedicated, if they have any relative or friend who wishes to dispute the charge with me and says that I am judging the case out of malice and not according to its deserts, let him now stand up, if he is brave enough to defend and speak against this sentence, and take the risk of saying it is wrong! And if I do not take this sword which hangs by my side and immediately strike off his head in the sight of all here, so that you may see him defeated and overcome, then shame on my lord if he does not have me cut down at once."

(44)[25] Next, Gorhant of Florence stood up, a very powerful leader who ruled Kipr and Barbare. Malicious and cunning, he had no equal in treachery and arrogance, so that no knight dared to have dealings with him. He was the brother of Musteni of Karsialand; he was greatly angered that his kinsman was so condemned, and when he began to speak all became silent. "Pliades," says he, "you are very foolish if you wish to deprive these two kings of their lives, for they have done nothing to deserve death. I do not expect you to kill them because Lord Jamund and his troops did not come to their help. They stayed

[25] Not in *Asp.*, but in P_2; cf. van Waard, p. 205.

under the chief standard so long that no one would come to their aid. Of the hundred thousand who were delegated to defend the standard, only two escaped. And since they could not make a stand any longer, they wanted to save their lives, which was not treachery or wickedness or cowardice."

(45) King Malevent[26] then stood up. He was a leader in the eastern part of Africa. Outside of his kingdom no man knew much about it—whether any creature lived in the east or not—except that there was wind there, and heaven above. He had a most wealthy realm: aside from the greatest cities, more than a hundred castles. He was the most gracious of men, handsome and smiling; tall, and fierce when he was enraged, slim of waist and broad in the shoulders, with long, sturdy arms, he had hands as white as snow, with slender fingers, and was clad in an elegant coat of mail. When he was mounted on horseback he appeared to be the most imposing of men. He was princely, clad in rich purple cloth with snow-white furs, and his mantle was embroidered with gold and set with precious stones so that it was worth no less than a hundred marks of silver. He spoke boldly to all the hearers: "By Makon," says he, "lord Amuste,[27] your clan wishes to destroy our race. I am now prepared to prove that neither of these kings deserves to die, and as I say, so I shall prove; and if I do not do so, then may my lord have me hanged."

More than forty hundred heathens now jumped up, all wishing to prove the case with him. He then said, "Come," says he, "prove your words with oaths; if you do not wish to do that, then things shall go badly for us."

Here begins the fifth[28] book, which takes us back to learn what was happening in the battle.

A,a (61)

Then King Akarz[29] of Amflors stood up and spoke with a raised voice: "Lords," says he, "do not be so enraged. We know that Africa is

[26] *Asp.* Maladient.
[27] *Asp.* "sire amustent"; ruler, governor. Cf. n. 11, Ch. 58.
[28] Actually, this should read "sixth."
[29] *Ankaris.*

great and wide, and there are many men of great wealth there who have never desired the realm of another king. It would beseem Agulandus better if he were now at home in Africa, or in another part of his realm, where he could ride with hounds and huntsmen after all sorts of animals, or with the hawks for all kinds of fowls. But Jamund his son and these new-made knights have shamefully taken up arms, and we[30] champions and heroes were gathered here together to find and win honors and powers—if the pride of such boasters as has been mentioned does not maintain that they are braver and more valiant than any other men. But as for King Magon and Asperant the Red,[31] whom you wish to condemn, there are no better knights in all of Africa, nor more mighty to overcome our enemies. It would be a great loss if they were killed or destroyed. But, if the king wishes, let us give security for them until the truth is known as to who won the battle."

(62) Then the bold King Abilant stood up and spoke: "Akarz," says he, "truly, you do not see what is right in this case.[32] Go out of the room and consult with whomever you please, and say what you have heard, but you shall never stand security for these men because it is not fitting that this case should be allowed to run any longer.[33] Now, before your own sight, they shall be bound and scourged and tied both feet and hands;[34] fifteen shield-boys shall follow them, and each of them shall have a horse-whip ready in his hand, with hard knots, in the toughest of straps. Any of them who does not make the blood spring out of the backs of these traitors with every blow shall get a great blow from my right hand. When the traitors have been thus tormented, we shall have them hung and next burned in a pyre. And if this displeases you, our tongues shall just as boldly sentence you to the same doom."

30 *A*, were; *a*'s reading is preferred by Unger, but the sense of the sentence is difficult either way.

31 *Asp.* 6274, Esperrans li ros.

32 *a* has a different reading here, but it is only partially preserved; it is something like "In clear words, you [are not loyal to?] King Agulandus and Jamund;" cf. *Asp.* 2686-88.

33 *a*'s reading here is even less well preserved, but it is probably again closer to *Asp.*, since it contains the phrase "they shall never bear a crown ..."

34 Here another gap in ms. *a* begins.

A (63) Then Amustene of Fame spoke.[35] He was a very clever and powerful man, whose realm lay around Gallia[36] from sea to sea. He spoke in this way: "Gentlemen," says he, "hear what treachery these kings have committed, for which Maumet and all our gods curse them. With great wickedness and baseness, they have forsaken their lord out of cowardice. Jamund made them leaders and gave them great power, honoring them by entrusting his chief standard to them; but they fled, and no one knows what happened to that great host and troop of men. Now it is certainly my judgement that they have forfeited life and limb. But if anyone speaks against this sentence, let him stand up to offer single combat against me. —If I do not have his head before this evening, then I shall surrender all my realm to him."

And there was no one there who took up his challenge.

(64) King Somnel[37] then answered most wrathfully: "Lord Amustade,"[38] says he, "you speak very foolishly; we all know that you were never a friend of our clan. But now I want to tell you why your family has always hated our family: it was because they were never advanced as they wished, since our kinsmen drove your relatives from them and never wished to have dealings with them again. My father brought about what he wished and gave out land magnificently.[39] Asperant is the most excellent of leaders, and so is his comrade Magon. But if you, in your ill-will, hate them, it is not fitting for you to condemn them so shamefully when you do not know who has gained the victory. They have, too, many powerful relatives and friends who will certainly not allow you to condemn them before we know what has happened to our men."

a (40)

... Then King Melkiant[40] stood up and spoke so that all could hear him: "By Maumet," says he, "you are speaking foolishly if you con-

[35] *Asp.* 6316, "l'amustenc de Fenie."

[36] *Asp.* Murgalie.

[37] *Asp.* Manuel.

[38] He is actually addressing "Amustene of Fame" of the previous chapter, not the character designated as "Amustade" in chs. 59-60.

[39] This sentence is difficult; in any case, it appears to mistranslate *Asp.* 6352-53.

[40] Perhaps *Asp.* Maladient, but the speech is that attributed to one Hogiers (*Asp.* 6522-40), after a speech by Maladient.

demn worthy men to death when you still do not know how the battle went or who was victorious. I know this much about Jamund: his youth and boldness, courage, pride, and ambition are such that he would not want to send back word asking for help or comfort in need. And what was so strange in their flight, when they had lost all their troop? If they had stayed there longer, that would have been neither valor nor chivalry, but, rather, great foolishness, since nothing could be expected but slaughter and death, nor would their friends ever be compensated for their loss of life. No matter how they had stood guard, they would have had nothing to show for it. Now, therefore, you act wrongly to judge them in such distress, when their case is clearly proved: if they had stayed there longer all the gold in the world would not have saved them."

Then Kalades,[41] king of Orfanie, stood up. He was a powerful and wealthy man who ruled four kingdoms. "Lords," said he, "bear patiently what has been told you here. Of that which we have heard said, let us take what we find best, rejecting foolishness and choosing wisdom. King Agulandus had all Africa under his rule because he had rightfully inherited it as his patrimony. What necessity drove Agulandus to come here? His kingdom is so great and wide that even if the best mule from Jerusalem we have here were to travel every day as far as he could on the longest day's journey, in seven years he could not travel all around the realm of King Agulandus. Now, he is still hale and able to ride, strong and gallant, and such a knight that I know of none in all your host who can break a stout spear more swiftly than he, or knows better how to cut down with a sword. But in one respect he has done quite wrongly, in that he wanted to crown his son while he was still living, and give him a realm while he was hale and alive: for when Jamund received his father's realm to rule, he divided the kingdom up and gave it to those who have lost all because of their foolishness. After that he had little use for your fellowship.

"Now, scouts have come here from sweet France. You know as a truth that Christian men put their trust in the son of holy Maria, and know well all that has happened among us, and why Jamund disputes possession of this land, and came here over the ocean with a great

[41] *Kalides*; *Asp.* Calides.

fleet. Jamund fell out with his father when he took with him all the youngest men and the best troops, while King Karlamagnus[42] has with him noblemen and all the most honorable and older men. But if the people who now fight with him put him in peril and he loses his life, they shall divide his kingdom among themselves as they like.[43] Now we have forsaken and ruined a great land and kingdom for the sake of this land, though it is no better than the realm of one emperor: this kingdom is quite unlike our realm, which we have left behind us."

A,a (65)

The clever Sinapis[44] then stood up. He was ruler of Alfre[45] and controlled the tower of Antioch; he was a great friend of Agulandus and Jamund, and had been foster-father of Jamund. "Lords," says he, "hear how much these two kinsmen of Noron[46] have transgressed, the nephews of that treacherous king whom I see sitting there by a stone pillar, dressed in red ciclatun.[47] He has been doing ill for a long time, while I have always served the kings. Our king should drive away these men—Akari[48] and Lampalille,[49] Salatiel[50] and King Safagon, Esperigam and King Managon,[51] Estor the Red[52] and King Malgerian,[53] and all their cursed kindred. But as for traitors, we doom them to be

[42] The king in question in *Asp.* appears to be Agulandus rather than Charlemagne.

[43] I.e., Jamund's "friends" may stand to gain by his death.

[44] *Asp.* Synagon.

[45] *Asp.* Halape.

[46] *Asp.* Noiron; Brandin notes (p. 202) "Néron considéré comme un roi ou un dieu sarrassin"; if so, it would seem an unlikely insult.—Up to this point, ms. *A* only.

[47] Cf. n. 2, Ch. 40.

[48] *Asp.* Angart, probably read as Akarz, and possibly correctly, since he supports the "traitors."

[49] *Lampalilla.*

[50] Not mentioned here in *Asp.*, but he is referred to in a later passage, missing in the saga (where it would properly belong in the middle of a lacuna), as if he had indeed supported the appropriate side. But in fact, as things are arranged in both *Asp.* and the saga, he would be already dead.

[51] *Asp.* Garahon, Esoran, Managon.

[52] Epithet in *a* only; cf. *Asp.* Estox li fex.

[53] *Asp.* 6385: "Molt ... mal geredon."

hanged like thieves, then burned in the pyre in the sight of all the host, so that every man may know the cause and how they sinned.[54]

"But if Amustene[55] calls this wrong, then he shall be wrong while we are right.[56] Early yesterday Jamund rode near the Christians, and he placed these traitors under his chief standard.[57] Now we see they have come here safe and unwounded. We do not need to bring charges against such traitors: their guilt is self-evident. Thus it is fitting for us to make haste with this sentence, so that Jamund will not hear that we are harboring his traitors.

"But you, Amustene,[58] whom I see sitting there: you are now losing heart and turning pale. You resemble dust, like a dead man.[59] If you and your kinsmen want this judgement pronounced false, now that you have heard my words, then get your weapons and I shall mount my horse, armed. And if I do not show the judgement to be a true one by taking off your head, then the king may hang[60] me like the worst of thieves condemned to the gallows!"

At these words, all became so quiet that no one offered a single word.

(66) Ulien and King Madekuin[61] then stood up and took each other's hands. They went out of the room into the hall and found King Agulandus,[62] sobbing violently.[63] Ulien then swore by Makon and Apollin and said to Agulandus, "You are all too soft-hearted, lord, over these traitors of the cursed race of Kain,[64] who have indeed committed treachery. Let them now be drawn apart alive and pulled by the tails of horses."

[54] Latter clause in *a* only; cf. *Asp.* 6397.
[55] Now referring to the man previously called "Amustade."
[56] Here we skip to the middle of an oration by Ulien; *Asp.* 6721.
[57] *a* adds: "Making them leaders of his troops." Not in *Asp.*
[58] *a, Samnel; A* agrees with *Asp.* 6733.
[59] An odd rendering of *Asp.* 6735?
[60] *a,* torment; *Asp.* "demener."
[61] *a, Madikun; A, Madekvin.*
[62] *a* adds: "Sitting on a silk pillow."
[63] In *Asp.* he seems to be merely sighing.
[64] *a, Tames*; *Asp.* Cain.

King Agulandus then went out with them into the room where the judges were gathered and spoke in a loud voice: "Have you doomed these traitors?" says he.

"Yes," say they.

"Let them be ut to death as quickly as possible," says he. "Horses shall draw them before the army in the sight of all the host, then all round the town[65] before men and women, young and old. Then all their pieces shall be gathered together and thrown into the foulest pit. Let eighty[66] or a hundred whores be gathered, who sell themselves for silver and will gladly come there; and give each of them a gold coin, and let them urinate and defecate down on them so that everyone can see it. Then let a great fire be lit there to burn them. He who treats traitors any other way deserves to be hung from the gallows himself."

The two kings who had been condemned were now led forth. Agulandus then said, "You wicked traitors," said he, "what have you done with my son? Can you tell me anything of what has become of him?"

"No, lord," say they, "We were not there long enough to know what became of him afterwards. A little old man on a huge grey war-horse was leading a group of men. He was so skilled a warrior that no one could stop him, and he drove us away from the standard and cut down in our sight twenty thousand men. But Jamund was in the other troop, fighting against those who were there, and we know nothing to say of him."[67]

"Makon knows," says Agulandus, "that I would be a fool to question you any further." And he then demanded four horses[68] and had Asperant bound between two and Magon between the other two, and servants ran and lashed the horses, turning them over rocks and crags, so that all the path was made bloody and the stones were covered with their blood and flesh.

After that they were cast into the filthiest of pits, and harlots came there and dropped urine and feces in the sight of all the host; for that

[65] Phrase in *a* only, but cf. *Asp.* 6762.

[66] *A*, ninety; cf. *Asp.* 6764.

[67] From "A little ..." *a* only; cf. *Asp.* 6780-87.

[68] *a* adds an adj., "hard-riding" (or hard-ridden?).

foul work, each one received a gold coin. This performance went on until evening came, and caused much talk[69] in the heathen host. One man said to another, "Jamund has helped these two[70] ill indeed."

[69] *a,* whispering.
[70] *A*, them.

CHAPTER LX

Valdibrun Reports

The day after these events, while Agulandus was sitting at table there came into the city a thousand fugitives from the host of Jamund; there were none in this multitude who were not grievously wounded. Their leader was a knight named Valdibrun. He went forward into the great hall, sorely wounded. He had been thrust through by a halberd in his mail and jerkin so that it had gone into the bone and blood streamed out of this wound, and many others, onto the floor of the hall as he walked there. He greeted Agulandus in a low voice, weakened by fatigue and much loss of blood, and said, "May all your gods strengthen your realm; but consider, in good time, what has happened to Jamund."

"Why are you so tormented, good friend?" says Agulandus. "And what tidings do you have to tell?"

Valdibrun answered, "Much has happened since we parted. When Jamund had taken over your strong tower to guard it seemed to us for a while that everything was promising, and the first time that Jamund went out of the tower with twenty thousand bold young men, taking the gods themselves to lend them strength, they did well both as to treasure and men, converting many Christians to another faith. We burned cities and punished both men and women. And when our affairs had prospered in this way, Jamund turned back to the tower with a great deal of booty. When we met some scouts of Karlamagnus on a mountainside we thought we could deal with them as we had other men, taking their lives and treasure; but it did not go that way at all. They attacked us so sharply that when our encounter ended they had killed a great many men and driven Jamund and all the rest of us into flight, so thoroughly taking the gold and silver that they did not leave us with the smallest penny; and along with the rest, they took the gods themselves. But when Jamund rode out of the tower with his host a second time, to avenge the earlier disgrace and win back the gods, we were so shamefully driven away that the tower was taken from us and we had no refuge to go to from there.

"Then Jamund assembled his huge army and went to confront the emperor himself, and, to tell it quickly, we fought for three days, and although the Christians were few in comparison to our masses, again they pressed us so hard that the last that I know of it is that they drove Jamund into flight, with three kings, and killed every man there. Not one escaped. Such are my tidings," says Valdibrun.

Agulandus, hearing such things, felt little improvement in his heart, and in his great sorrow made as if he had not clearly heard what Valdibrun was saying. He said, "I cannot have understood your words correctly, knight," says he, "for it seems to me that you said that those resplendent gods which I thought would grant us great strength had been captured by the Christians."

Valdibrun answered, "You heard that correctly, lord. They took them from us, and we saw, at a distance, how oddly they dealt with them, for the Christians, with great dishonor and disgrace, threw them down on the ground from the splendid wagon they had been sitting in. Then they went and trod them under foot, spit on their gold-adorned beards and whiskers, and beat them with cudgels and stones. And then they hung them up by their feet as high as possible to annoy us. But I never saw any sign, either great or small, of their power and might there, and I hold that all who believe in such gods are deceived, for it is obvious that they cannot offer much help in another's need when they are not able to save themselves from such dishonor."

Agulandus then answered, with much wrath, "What can you tell me of my son Jamund? Do you know whether he is alive or dead?"

Valdibrun answered, "I do not know that," says he, "but it seems most likely to me that he had fled to the city of Benaris with other fugitives, for I cannot imagine that anyone has been so full of impudence as to kill your son Jamund. Yet, it is not possible to know what the Frenchmen might do, for no bolder warriors than they could ever be found, nor another nation better equipped with weapons."

"This is a great sorrow to my heart," says Agulandus, "that I do not know what has become of Jamund; but what shall we do now?"

Valdibrun answered, "Either turn to rest, and do not risk yourself or your troops under the weapons of the French, or gather together as great an army as you can at once and attack them."

Agulandus answered, "By Maumet, I shall never give up attacking that land and realm which they have wrested from my control; rather, I shall go against them, killing every man, and thus make all their realm subject to me."

And as soon as the table was taken up, Agulandus summoned all the kings and great leaders from the cities and nearby villages, and he said to all those who could hear him, "High kings of Africa, heed my words, and alleviate my grief. Let each man make ready as quickly as possible: do not lose heart, but sound your horns and shrilling trumpets, and summon all your hosts, for we shall ride at the Frenchmen and put down their pride and arrogance, avenging the dishonor they have done to us in many ways, if they dare to await our coming."

Madequin[1] answered the king's words: "By Makon," says he, "if I live for any length of time, the Christians shall soon be dead!"

Valdibrun then answered, "You do not need to be in such a hurry to meet with Karlamagnus, Madequin, for you shall never end a journey less joyfully, though you may have a thousand and they only twenty-one."

Then many trumpets could be heard, sounding all over the city, with much uproar and shouting, as each man equipped himself and his company with the best horses and weapons he could. And when all of the army of Agulandus was gathered, he went out of the city with an untold multitude to the ships and settled in the best cabin with his queen, sailing before a fair wind until he arrived with his ship-army in a fine port of Hispania. There a great river went up and fell down into the valley which was described before, beneath the mountain of Aspremont, in which Karlamagnus and Jamund had fought. And as soon as the time arrived, Agulandus left the ships with all his host and had huge, fine tents pitched. He left his queen to stay on board ship, leaving many well-bred men to guard her. But since he had learned from those who had come from the battle that Karlamagnus might be

[1] *Madeqvin.*

near that place, he divided his host into five divisions and appointed over each division the leaders who have been described.

A,a (67)

When King Agulandus had sat down at table, there dismounted from their horses in the king's enclosure a thousand fugitives, and there was none in their troop who was not wounded. Their horses were much injured, their shields slashed and useless. The most powerful man in the group went first into the hall before the king's table. A halberd had thrust through his armor and his helmet had been struck through to the band so that pieces of it lay on his shoulders.[2] He spoke in a low voice, for he could not speak up:

"Lord," says he, "you have stayed here too long and it is too late. When your son Jamund went to stay in the tower, we rode with three thousand knights and a countless number of bowmen in our troop; and Jamund went before our host to get provisions for us. We had our gods with us, to convert Christian men to our faith. We attacked cities and castles; Jamund had all the leading men who did not wish to renounce their God killed and the breasts of their women cut off. In this expedition we captured a great deal of treasure. When a month had passed[3] we turned back. Then we met scouts from the army of King Karlamagnus as we rode down from a mountain,[4] and we thought to charge against them there; but neither bow-shot nor spear-thrust was of any use. Estor,[5] our standard-bearer, fell there, and there we lost our four gods. So many of our men drowned in the river that one might cross with dry feet on their bodies. There I saw a Frenchman pursue Jamund until he came to the gate[6] of the tower, where he killed the horse under him;[7] and they took from us[8] all that we had gathered: we did not have so much as a penny's worth left."

[2] Details about the helmet in *a* only, but cf. *Asp.* 6822-23.
[3] *A*: "When Jamund had parted with us"; *a* agrees with *Asp.* 6839.
[4] Last phrase in *a* only; cf. *Asp.* 6841.
[5] *Entor.*
[6] *a*, yard, court-yard; but cf. *Asp.* 6850, "porte."
[7] *a* adds, "half of such a blow would have been enough."
[8] *a*'s *him* is obviously not as good.

(68) The king then answered, "Is it true, Valdebrun, that our four gods were captured?"

"Yes," said he. "We have now been fighting against King Karlamagnus for three days. The Frenchmen are few in number, but you could not find any men more valiant. They all have protective caps under mail, and chain-mail down to the feet.[9] They captured our chief standard and drove us into flight—all of our multitudes were of no help to us. But Jamund stayed behind with four kings, Balam and Goram,[10] Mordruin[11] and Sinagern.[12] When they captured our gods, they struck them with spear-shafts and sharp flints, in our sight; and then they were dragged by four elephants[13] on the ground, turned upside-down: and they did not manifest their miraculous powers and might. I think that the belief that such gods can help us is false.

"Lord," said Valdebrun, "understand what I am telling you: we clearly saw their scouts.[14] The captains were twelve dukes and two crowned kings, and their host was sixty thousand knights.[15] The king's own troop was a hundred thousand, but we have killed a quarter of their host. Now, lord, if you wish to attack that land, ride as quickly as possible. Do not be distressed, for they are not sufficiently numerous to withstand you. If they were prepared as a meal for us, they would not serve to half fill us."

The king then answered, "Valdebrun," says he, "you fill me with grief, for you can tell me nothing of Jamund."

"Nothing certain," says he, "except this: if he is still alive, he has gone to the city of Beiuere[16] to rest there."

[9] *a* only, but cf. *Asp.* 6864-65.

[10] *Gorham.*

[11] *a, Mordium.*

[12] *Asp.* 6876-77: "Aumes remest soi quart de compagnon,/Ce fu Huber, Goran et Sinagon."

[13] *a*; a later passage in Part V of the saga identifies this word (alifantum) with the unicorn, but this does not seem material here where either beast is, at least, surprising: no doubt this is why *A* gives *olive trees* instead. See *Asp.* 6882 for what appears to be at the bottom of it.

[14] *A*'s "the French host and their scouts" does not seem justified by *Asp.* 6889.

[15] *A*'s forty thousand does not agree with *Asp.* 6891.

[16] *a, Befueris*; nothing corresponds to this in *Asp.*

(69) King Agulandus then became very angry and said, "Ho!" said he: "Africans, do not be distressed or slow, good knights. Blow the horns and trumpets now and ride to their help as fast as you can, taking twenty thousand knights with you. Madequin and Almazor shall lead them, and Akarz[17] of Amflor and Ulien shall lead a second division, with thirty thousand following them. Following me, guarding my body and honor, shall be Moadas[18] the Red and Galinger[19] the Old, Abilant[20] the Great and Amuste,[21] and with them their two haughty sons. We shall attack the Frenchmen, quelling their pride and arrogance. If we should have my son Jamund with us, we shall soon be quite sure who is most valiant."

Valdebrun then answered, "Lord," says he, "know certainly that you do not need to be so eager to attack the Frenchmen: if there were a thousand of them and you had forty-two thousand, they would be no slower to attack you than you them."[22]

Agulandus stood there weeping, full of grief, and plucking at his beard. But his army all began to blow the horns vigorously and a hundred and forty thousand rode out of the city, leaving behind, however, a large host to watch over the ship and guard the lovely queen, than whom no woman would ever have been more beautiful if she had accepted Christianity and put her faith in God.[23] Twenty thousand knights guarded and served her.

(70) King Madequin then spoke to his men: "Maumet knows that if I am allowed to live for any time all the Christian men who come before me shall be dead."[24]

[17] *Akard.*

[18] *Modes*; the epithet appears to be derived from *Asp.* 6918, "Moadas et Uliens li ros."

[19] *Galingres.*

[20] *Ambilant.*

[21] This now means the original *Amustade,* as do all further references to any form of this word.

[22] *A* omits "the Frenchmen ... slower to attack you," presumably through scribal omission.

[23] Latter clause omitted in *A*; it renders (approximately) *Asp.* 6935-36.

[24] The following abrupt change of subject results from the translator's chapter division; the sequence still corresponds exactly to *Asp.*

In the second division there were thirty thousand. There one could see many coats of mail, bright armor, gilded helmets, good horses, the sharpest swords and the best bows;[25] Akarz[26] of Amflor and Manuel, his cousin,[27] led this division, and Floriades led another. His troops were armed differently: they had neither armor nor coat of mail, but had the best of spears. If these were pursuing fugitives, they intended to press near, but if they were pursued they could move more swiftly than dogs;[28] another leader of this group was the powerful Chalides.[29]

Eliades[30] was in charge of the third division. His men were well armed. They were altogether forty thousand of the proudest and grimmest of men. They would do much harm to the Christians, unless Christ prevented them.[31] In the division of Agulandus himself were Ulien and the great Moadas, Galinger the Old and Abilant. Amustene however, rode along sobbing, suffering great grief for his nephews, who had been drawn to pieces by horses in his own sight. If Amustade had let his mind be known, his intention certainly was to be avenged on the Africans.[32] In this division all were well armed, and there were many Turkish bows, with the best arrows. If God did not help Christians now, few of them would remain alive after the moment when they met these men in battle!

(71) You have heard how Agulandus went to seek out the Christians, until he encountered them; we shall now speak of the proceedings of King Karlamagnus and his men.

[25] *a; A* summarizes "the best war weapons."

[26] *Akart.*

[27] "Son of his mother's sister;" *Asp.* "ses niés."

[28] This odd comparison appears to be a misunderstanding of *Asp. cers* 'harts,' possibly 'hinds.' Another OF word for hind is *biche*, which is obviously similar to Norse *bikkja* 'bitch.'

[29] *Asp.* Galides.

[30] *a, Eleadas.*

[31] Latter clause *a* only; cf. *Asp.* 6962.

[32] Not in *A*; first part of this sentence from Fr2, rest from *a*.

CHAPTER LXI

Vitaclin Alerts Karlamagnus

Karlamagnus was in the tent of Jamund, with the lord pope and other great men, while another host surrounded the tent. The emperor had no knowledge of the expedition of Agulandus and on the same day that the Africans landed not far from the French camp, Lord Vitaclin, who had been called Balam before he was baptized by Emperor Karlamagnus, came and greeted him courteously; then, speaking to him secretly, said, "Noble lord," says he, "I ask you and the lord pope to come aside with me, away from other people."

The emperor did so, taking the lord pope by the hand, and the three went out of the tent together, leaving the others there. Then Vitaclin began to speak: "Since that which I hoped for long before has now come to pass and I have become God's liegeman and accepted the holy faith, so that from henceforth I shall be under the guidance of God and you, Emperor Karlamagnus, it thus behoves me not to conceal from you these matters which I think it necessary to bring to your attention—for if I did, I would certainly be a traitor. I wish to tell you of the singular qualities of this tent, which neither you nor any of your men has observed.

"Look up under the knobs of the poles, and you shall see above, in front, a dragon made of gold; in that dragon you can see a mirror, which is of such a nature that if a man gazes into it steadily he will see whatever is happening on sea or land in nearby places. Now, good lord, look into the mirror, and you shall soon see sailing into the land an enormous fleet: heavy warships, long sailing ships, galiots, with great longships. King Agulandus has come here with an overwhelming army, and they are coming into harbor a short distance from your camp. You can also see, if you will, that he is coming ashore with all his army, having tents pitched, and arranging his army in four divisions while he intends to command a fifth himself, and it is obvious that he does not intend to return to his realm until he has met with you."

The emperor went and saw all these things, just as Vitaclin said; he therefore said, "God be praised that he has appointed such a man to serve him as you are, Vitaclin! Now, send messengers to Duke Girard at once, bidding him come to me."

It was so done; men were sent to the duke's tower. And as soon as lord Girard heard the emperor's message, he made himself ready and summoned his nephews, Boz and Clares, and his two sons, who were named before, to accompany him, and they rode off to the camp. And when the emperor learned that the duke had come he went to meet him most gladly and embraced him, and took his right hand himself, while the other two noblemen went on the left: thus they led him in their midst. Karlamagnus then said, "May God reward you for the great trouble you have recently endured in manfully coming to the aid of his Christianity! But I am amazed that such a leader has not taken the title of king."

Duke Girard answered, "I have no wish to bear the name of king, for such a dignity does not seem suitable to me. Although I am a duke, I can, with God's help, well keep my realm in peace and quietness, defending it from Christians, Vikings, and heathens. But it only rightly fits that one to bear the dignity of a crown whom it pleases God to magnify so that he may serve him the better, to support holy Christendom and strengthen law and justice, suppressing and despising wrong practises and opposition to God, and keeping men of good family about him and gladly accepting good counsel from them, as he knows their faithfulness. It befits a king to govern strongly and give generously; he who does not wish so to do is not fitted to bear the title of king."

The emperor said, "You speak rightly, Duke Girard; but I am sure that you have these qualities."

Then all four of them—Karlamagnus, the lord pope, the duke, and Vitaclin—went together into a special place. The emperor told the duke all that had happened. As soon as he looked into the mirror, the duke saw the army of Agulandus, arranged into five divisions. Then he said to the emperor, "Agulandus is surely coming here, and it is most likely that he intends to avenge his son Jamund. But although their host is a countless multitude, our God is so mighty that, for the sake of the intercession of his holy apostle St. James, he can disperse the heathen curs before the weapons of his flock as he did before. But woe upon those who desert you in this need," said the duke to the emperor. "My men and I, although we are now all too few, shall, rather, offer such hard attack to the heathens that many shall be foully served."

The emperor thanked the duke for his words, then said, "Brother Vitaclin, you were with the Africans for a long time. Tell us clearly about their leaders and equipment, and which commanders Agulandus will have appointed over his divisions."

Vitaclin answered, "Indeed I am acquainted with the foremost leaders of Agulandus, and thus I shall correctly describe to you the equipment of each of them before evening falls, while you take thought about what I can tell you."

The emperor said that it would be so. Vitaclin then began to speak: "You may see, lord, that nearest to us, by a forest, stand many small tents of the whitest linens or the best silk; over the largest of these tents you can see a great banner of red fabric. This is the mighty Madequin. In all of the realm of Africa there is no bigger or stronger man than he, and he leads strong, skilled armed men into battle. On the other side, over against the river, another division of Agulandus is setting up camp with fine tents. Their leaders are, I believe, the powerful lord Acharz of Amflor and his kinsman Manuel; I recognize their equipment easily, for I was often in counsels with Acharz, and I wish to tell you that he sent all the most valiant men of his host to Jamund.

"Up by that large, dark forest, you can see great tents, which are not much ornamented; these are inhabited by a remarkable people: there are none more ill-intentioned or unruly than they. They are hated and shunned by most good men and no one cares for them. They have scant and poor bread to eat, and eat it late,[1] like criminals. They do not value horses or good armor. Birds and game are their principal food; there are no better archers than they, for none can escape their shafts. They do not put their trust in spears, nor do they arm themselves with swords or axes. They are so fleet that no horse can match them; if they

[1] I.e., they eat little? Or slowly?

pursue futigives, they are pleased, but if they flee they howl like dogs and are soon overcome. Their leaders are the mighty king Kalades of Orfanie[2] and Floriades.

"Up on the ridge that rises from the shore on the other side, there are a great many tents with gilded knobs. The people who dwell there are all from one country. They produce better wine and bread than other nations and are very wealthy in gold, silver, and precious stones. They are handsome in appearance and courteous in their manners, well equipped with all sorts of armor and bold in battle. They are led by two leaders, both great champions, named Eliadas[3] and Pantalas.—In the fifth position you may clearly recognize, lord, the chief banner of Agulandus itself rising up: I believe that many kings and great leaders have been appointed to guard it, and I expect that so many of the powerful men of Africa have come here that few remain behind.

"I have told you what I know to be true, and now you should consider what move to make. There seem to me to be only two possibilities: either give up your realm to Agulandus or defend it as valiantly as God gives you strength to do."

Karlamagnus answered, "No, my good friend; as long as God gives me life, I shall not give up my realm to the heathens. But many thanks, Vitaclin, for the faithful service you have shown to us."

A,2 (75)

... Then he took the hand of King Karlamagnus, and the pope went out of the tent with them. Vitaclin said, "Now that I belong to God, and to you, it is not fitting for me to conceal anything."

"God knows," says King Karlamagnus, "you have done well in this, and because of it you shall receive a proper reward from God."

(74) Then Vitaclin said, "If I concealed anything from you, I would be a true traitor.[4] Now look up into the mirror in your tent, up on the poles mounted on dragons. See, now, the mighty fleet that is sailing into the harbor, with a countless host. Now we can see the tower in the

[2] *b*, *Orfama.*
[3] *b*, *Abadas.*
[4] *A*: "I do not wish to conceal anything from you."

city of Risa and all the outworks of the city. Now we can see five battalions: and they shall not turn back before they encounter us. Take counsel, then, as to what we should do: whether we should wait or flee."

"God knows," says Karlamagnus, "that I have not come here to Aspremunt[5] to flee or to give up my realm to heathens."

Karlamagnus then looked into the tent's mirror[6] and he saw galiots and longships and many warships, and a countless number of great ships sailing. And then he saw the tower in Risa, its pillars and battlements, and he sighed, in the distress of his heart. Then he saw that the pope was weeping, so distressed that both his eyes were wet[7] and tears ran down his cheeks. Karlamagnus then said to the pope, "Stop at once: do not behave so, for you may distress all our army this way. Make haste, rather, to Duke Girard, and tell him to come quickly to consult with me."

The pope answered, "I will do that gladly."

With the message that Karlamagnus had given him, the pope went off, and four archbishops accompanied him. When they reached their quarters, they mounted their horses at once; and when they arrived at the tower, Lord Girard was standing there washing his hands, ready for dinner. The pope stepped forward and blessed him, saying, "Emperor Karlamagnus has sent us here. He sends you a message which we shall not conceal,[8] bidding you come to him as quickly as possible, for he wishes your advice."

The duke answered, "That may well be," says he; "but I shall eat with my troop first, since we have tasted no food[9] these three days. But as soon as I have eaten, I shall come: only a traitor would fail in this need."

[5] *Aspramunt.*

[6] *A*'s addition here, "and saw that the pope wept," does not seem right, as Unger indicates in his note: but it must be derived from *Asp.* 7100.

[7] From the beginning of this sentence, *a* only; no apparent basis in *Asp.*, but note that *A* has already introduced the motif. If we follow the *A* reading here, there would, of course, be a new sentence here, and the weeping would be that of Karlamagnus only; but in *Asp.* 7105 it seems to be the pope.

[8] Clause in *a* only; cf. *Asp.* 7122.

[9] *a*; "neither meat nor drink."

When the duke has eaten, their horses were led forth and saddled and Lord Girard mounted his horse, and, with his two nephews and his two sons, rode up the slope. When they arrived in the midst of the army encampment, they saw there great wealth in gold and silver, and an untold number of good war horses: he who had never before had one as good could now help himself to enough there.[10] Lord Girard then dismounted from his horse, while Droim and Andelfraei[11] held his stirrups. Karlamagnus received him at his right hand, with two other noblemen on the other side, and he greeted King Karlamagnus with loyal good faith.

Then King Karlamagnus said to Lord Girard, "Why is it that you are not a king?"

Girard answered, "I do not wish it, lord, for I am not worthy of such great honor, nor have I the means for it; but I hold my realm in peace. Great emperor, do not be displeased with me. It only suits one to bear a crown whom it pleases God to make great, and improve the state of, so that he may serve holy Christianity and destroy wrongful laws, supporting and strengthening all good and keeping near him men of high birth and good conduct, governing the kingdom suitably, promising little but giving generously.[12] He who does not wish to live in this way, it does not suit to bear a crown."

The pope then answered, "It is certainly fitting for one who treasures wit and wisdom to attend to your words. Emperor Karlamagnus sent me after you; he wishes to tell you a strange circumstance: never have I[13] heard of anything like it."

Now these three leaders, with Vitaclin the fourth—no one else was in their confidence—went at least four[14] arrow-shots away from the rest of the host and the pope then spoke: "Look, Lord Girard," says he, "at the mirrors on the posts in the tent; then you can see all the shore where the river falls down into the sea. There are so many

[10] Last clause in *a* only; cf. *Asp.* 7143.

[11] *Amfraei.*

[12] A difficult passage, translated as much according to what it should mean, in light of *Asp.*, as what it actually says. But the omissions and differences from *Asp.* ls. 357 are interesting.

[13] *a*, you; the phrase is not in *Asp.*

[14] *A*, 3; cf. *Asp.* 7185.

galiots, longships, and broad-beamed ships, and warships, that they can scarcely be counted. See the Africans going up into these ships: there are four[15] battalions of them, aside from those under the chief standard. Unless God will now watch over us, it will be too late for others to come to our aid."

Karlamagnus pointed out what was happening in the mirror to him with his finger. Then he spoke softly in his ear: "Do not say anything that will distress our army."

Girard answered, "Lord," says he, "I agree with you, indeed."

King Karlamagnus then said, "Is that not King Agulandus and his chief standard? We shall have to undergo battle.[16] Vitaclin, brother," says he, "give me information, so that I can know their arrangements, and what their preparations mean."

"Indeed, lord," says he, "God knows that I can well do that, since I am now staying with you and have no inclination to go back to them when I have lost my son.[17] There is no need for me to make a long story of it: before evening I shall show you everything so that you will see it with your own eyes."

(75) "See, lord," says he, "in the fir-wood, where the first of the heathens are now setting up camp, with so many tents of the best silk and the whitest linens.[18] And there where you can see the greatest purple banner set, it is that of the powerful Madequin;[19] in all of Africa no one is his equal. The African leaders have all come here together, with not one of powerful family remaining behind. He has with him all the best knights of Africa, intending to avenge those who fell yesterday. He has also sent for his kinsman Jamund."[20]

[15] *A*, 5; cf. *Asp.* 7192.

[16] *a*, five battles; perhaps this sentence represents a misunderstanding, or scribal confusion, of a previous line in *Asp.*, 7198.

[17] *a*, only son.

[18] Latter in *a* only, but cf. *Asp.* 7212.

[19] *Madkuin.*

[20] In, apparently, skipping the passage of *Asp.* 7219-31, the translator seems to have lost the sense; but he seems to be rendering a passage not in this edition, as appears from what follows.

The pope answered him, "By the faith which I owe to St. Martin,[21] it is truly fitting for Emperor Karlamagnus to honor you and cherish you especially!"

Vitaclin then said, "See, now, lord, in the winegrove on the other side, along the river which runs through the valley: another division of heathens are taking shelter there. This is the division of Akarz of Amflor.[22] I was often in counsels with him. He sent every knight of any worth to Jamund; but all of those he sent to his lord Jamund were killed together yesterday on this field.—On the wayside near that great wood, a remarkable people are now setting up camp; they are very ill-natured.[23] Such are their customs, that no one loves them and no one will do good for them. They have little bread and eat late;[1] they set no store in good armor or war-horses and do not give as much as one rotten apple for farm-work: they all live by hunting in the woods. Nowhere in the world are there as good bowmen:[24] nothing escapes their shots. But if they take flight[25] and put aside their bows, they trust in their spears, and no horse is fleeter than they.[26] These are the troops of Kalades[27] of Orfanie.

"Look further, lord, against the crag by the spring:[28] there are many rich tents decorated with gold. These people are from a blessed land where the best bread and wine is found,[29] the most plentiful gold and silver, white and grey furs, and the best war-horses. These are the most courteous of men. Women love them greatly, and they are much given to the company of women. Eliades and King Pantalas are their leaders and lords. Now, lord, have no fear: all of those with them who were the best knights lie here with their comrades, slain on this field."

[21] *a, Marteine; A, Martinus. Asp.* St. Denis, but cf. note 20 above.

[22] Most of what follows here is not in Brandin's text of *Asp.*, which lacks a passage after 7218, here rendered. We rejoin that text in the later passage about the bon vivantism of Eliades and his troop.

[23] *a*: "no one is more ill-natured."

[24] *a*, hunters.

[25] *a* adds, "when nothing will help."

[26] *a* adds, "to catch them."

[27] *Calades*.

[28] Cf. *Asp.* 7219.

[29] *A*, grows, but cf. *Asp.* 7222.

The pope then said, "By the holy faith," says he, "we shall be your friends!"

"Lord," said Vitaclin, "understand my words well. After your men pursued and overtook our men who were with Jamund, and took our four gods, never again did our affairs go right. Now, lord, if you wish to hold your realm in peace, ride as quickly as you can towards them; but if you wish to flee and give your kingdom up to them, they will gladly receive it."

After these words, the emperor laid his hands on his neck and said, "If you are steadfast in this, you shall be dear to me among my advisors."

CHAPTER LXII

Karlamagnus Finds New Recruits

When Emperor Karlamagnus had learned the truth about the army of Agulandus, he said to Lord Girard, "Give your advice, lord Girard, as to how we should proceed now that we know that Agulandus will soon be coming to attack us. There is no time to send back to our land for troops, and although I have only a small army, I do not intend to flee."

The duke answered, "Lord," says he, "God and his holy apostle James shall strengthen your will. And since you have many young men fit for battle who have not yet proved themselves in action, let horns be blown throughout the army and summon to you every young man who can bear arms and dress himself in armor, of greater or lesser rank, and have them all given arms. The emperor should send trusty men into nearby places, summoning both scholars and laymen, rich and poor: let no one remain behind who can offer us any help, whatever his rank, power, or dignity may be."

The emperor thanked him for his advice, then said to the lord pope, "Since there is none in our host to whom I feel warmer affection and who has done more to free holy Christendom than you, holy father, I ask you to gather your honorable fellowship and call to God's battle all the people you can assemble, and prepare for battle as you wish, for all are bound to listen to your orders."

The lord pope gladly agreed to the emperor's request, going on his way with learned clerks. When he had left the emperor called four trumpeters and ordered them to sound horns throughout the army announcing the message which has been described. And as soon as these tidings had flown around the camp, those who had been in the earlier battle quickly came to the emperor's presence, well equipped with weapons. Then each man hurried to be before the others, thinking that he who was swiftest would fight best, so that in a little while there was a great multitude of young men come before the emperor's tent.

Karlamagnus then raised his voice and said, "Praise be to almighty God!" says he: "This throng is great, and fit to be God's defenders against enemies. Since many of your fathers are now dead, and those who still live are much oppressed by age and great toil, we want you to rise up in their places and become knights, taking whatever honors are due to each. If you will willingly agree to this, I shall make you so wealthy that thenceforth your kinsmen shall have every blessing, if God allows us to return safely to our native land."

The young men were delighted by the emperor's promises and agreed to do as he wished. Karlamagnus said, "Then go to where the dead are lying now and let each one of you take armor, as well as horses and other knightly gear."[1]

They did so: riding to where the battle had been, they went among the dead and found there many fine weapons, gilded helmets, bright silver coats of mail, hard shields, and the best of swords. They needed no further choice among such abundance but stripped the dead where they lay there. Then, taking fine horses with enamelled bits and gilded saddles,[2] they rode back to the camp and gave their horses enough grain for the night.

The next morning each one took his equipment and mounted his horse and they all rode to the emperor's tent. Foremost among them were the four shield-boys, Estor, Baeringur, Otun and Engiler,[3] who particularly attended Rolland, the young nephew of Karlamagnus; he therefore dubbed these four knights first, out of affection for his kinsman, then the others, one after another. He raised all of those who had received weapons from servitude, making them free men, and appointed to them all the honors proper to knights, releasing them from all tributes and duties of commoners and the demands of overlords. And they all agreed to give homage to the holy apostle Peter and the emperor and kissed the right hand of the emperor, submitting to him and promising to follow his command and wish and to do all they could to strengthen holy Christendom.

[1] *b*: "and ride back so equipped."

[2] *b*: "enamelled saddles and gilded bits."

[3] *B*'s attempt to eliminate inconsistencies has fallen down badly here.

Then Karlamagnus called Rollant to him, and, taking him by the hand and embracing him with great affection, said, "Truly, I ought to love and honor you more than any other, for, in the sight of God, you gave me my life, through his mercy; and because of this I believe that God has granted you great good fortune. I therefore put all these young knights under your command, that they may grant you all honor as their leader. I expect that in this way they will most strengthen my honor to overcome God's enemies, with such a chief to lead their troop."

Rollant thanked the emperor for his fair words and they all agreed gladly to this. After these events, Lord Girard took his leave to go away and rode to the tower with his kinsmen. All of those who were there came to meet him rejoicing and asked how he found Karlamagnus. The duke answered, "All praise and glory to God: he is well and in good spirits, though he now has much business in hand, for he is making many knights of men of various lineage without inquiring whether they are rich or poor. We should therefore follow his example and dub all the young men in our troop knights."

All answered, "May God support this counsel of yours, and let it be well carried out according to your provision."

Girard then called Ancelin, a powerful leader, and said to him, "Take my sons Milon and Girard with you to Karlamagnus; give him my greetings, and tell him that I ask him to dub my sons knights."

Ancelin did as he was asked, and they mounted on horses and rode to the emperor's camp, went before him, and greeted him suitably. He received them well. Then Ancelin said, "Duke Girard sends you his greetings and asks that you arm these two sons of his whom you see standing here."

Karlamagnus answered, "Gladly, good friend," says he, "shall I do his bidding, for there is no braver man bearing weapons than he."

After these words, the emperor took the hand of young Milon, the elder of the brothers, and spoke to him, saying, "Are you the son of Girard of Burgundia?"

"Certainly, lord," says he.

Karlamagnus then said to Eisant the Breton, "Bring us the sword which bears the holy cross in red gold."

He did so, taking the sword and bringing it to the king. The emperor drew it and gazed at it, speaking thus to young Milon: "Since you are the son of so brave a leader that no better was ever born to the title of duke, it is probable that you will become a good leader yourself, and for his sake I shall honor you. I give you this sword, and with it the wealthy town of Utili, which is now vacant, under our rule, with none but a young maiden governing it; she shall be yours, and I do not think that you will find anyone fairer than she is. You shall always have our friendship and be appointed among my best knights."

When he had spoken these words he girded Milon with the sword and attired him in other clothes, while he bowed humbly to the emperor, thanking him in fair words for such honor.

After this young Girard was led forward. He was a manly youth, nobly brought up, fair to look at, with strong arms. The emperor said, "Sir Eisant, bring me hither the greatest of the swords which belong to me."

Eisant took the sword and laid it on the knee of the king. Then Karlamagnus said, "This sword belonged to the renowned son of a knight, who inherited it from his father; with this sword he conquered the two great cities of Gand and Lelei, and the realm that lies around them. And since you, young Girard, have the proper right of a knight, I gird you with this sword, adding with it the best armor; may God give you with this sword a long and good life, victory, and true desire to serve his Christendom."

With that, a white horse was led forward, equipped for battle with the best armor. The emperor gave this to young Girard with affectionate friendship.

A,a (76)

Duke Girard then began to speak: "Lord king," says he, "let horns be sounded around all the army now, so that all the youngest men shall come to you as soon as possible, those who bear weapons, mail, and helmets and know how to arm themselves, while I go back to my men and comfort them, for I wish to prepare to carry out our plan."

The king answered, "That is well advised." He then called four heralds[4] to sound horns all around the army and bear his message and

[4] C-V lists neither *a*'s *bauaegismenn* nor *A*'s *beaueismenn* (possibly

command. These four rode all around the army, crying out and making known the king's command: "Come to the king, all young armed men, serving men, shield-boys, cooks, porters, chamberboys, stewards' servants and pages, under-cupbearers and link-boys: all shall be armed who can be of any help, and to those who do well in this his need, he has promised to make you rich."

Soon these tidings were known to all around the army, and the first to come were those who had been in the former battles, clad in mail and helmets. The king then said, "If God sends me safely back to France, our native land, I shall make you such great and wealthy men that all your families shall be exalted through you."

They rejoiced at this, and rode more than a mile to the site of the battle, where they found many fine weapons: gilded helmets, gleaming silver coats of mail, hard shields, the best[5] swords; and they took them for themselves, choosing the best horses with gilded saddles. Then they rode to their tents and unsaddled the horses, and they rested during the night, with plenty of grain and fodder.

(77) The emperor's four foster-sons, Rollant and Estor, Baeringur and Otun, heard all that was happening. They consulted together, saying, "What shall we do? The emperor is treating us as prisoners. There is now no serving-boy so miserable that the king has not given him arms, if he wishes. Let us now go and learn if we shall have any armor from him, and if he denies us, let us go away and leave him."

Rollant then answered, "May God bless your advice,"[6] and did as they said. Rollant mounted his horse and his comrades went with him. They found the king sitting with little company, for there were no men by him except his dukes Oddgeir and Nemes and Flovent. The king was sighing, in the grief of his heart, and tears ran down his cheeks. The dukes spoke to him: "Cease, lord, this sorrow: Agulandus is dead if he encounters us."

"Lords," says he, "do not say such things. When we fought on the field before, we had kings and earls and great dukes and mighty

Bavarians; cf. glossary entry for same), but the meaning of *Asp.*'s "baniers" seems needed in the context.

[5] *a*, bright.

[6] *a*, our plan.

leaders: of the most powerful of them, we lost three hundred thirty-seven,[7] and now I shall have the support of those who before were the serving-men of others. For this reason my heart nearly breaks with grief."

And then he did not wish to say any more, since the pope and lord Girard had asked him not to say anything about what they had seen. In that moment Rollant arrived and dismounted from his horse. When he saw Duke Nemes, he took the hem of his mantle with his other hand in Oddgeir's belt clasp and led them both a little aside from where the emperor was. Rollant then said, somewhat angrily, "What does Karlamagnus say? Why is he holding us as prisoners? We came into this army with him like beggars: I rode on such a worn-out cart-horse that my teeth were almost shaken out. He shook me so that I have never known anything like it. Now if Karlamagnus will not give us arms, we shall leave him."

Oddgeir then embraced him and kissed him affectionately, saying, "You shall soon[8] be armed."

(78) Duke Nemes and Oddgeir the Dane knelt before King Karlamagnus. Duke Nemes then said, "Lord king," says he, "your nephew wishes to become a knight."

"God knows," says Karlamagnus, "that may well come about in good time; but our kinsman Rollant is still too young to bear arms."

Young Rollant then answered him, "God may have mercy on me: though I am young, I am no coward, and I have won the best of swords. I have also served you with the cup at table, and Estor Delangres has carved food for you. But if you will not make us four companions knights, then other serving men will have to serve you, while we shall look out for ourselves."[9]

"Rollant," says the king, "I shall not deny you that, when I remember that when I was under an olive-tree I saw you dismount from your horse as swiftly as a greyhound and come to me with a piece of spear-

[7] *A*, 347; cf. *Asp.* 7324.

[8] *A*, perfectly; "soon" is somewhat closer to *Asp.* 7349.

[9] Possibly the idiom here should be translated "go away;" there is no corresponding line in *Asp.* to throw light on the meaning.

shaft made of apple-wood; and when Jamund thought to drive his sword into my heart, you struck him[10] such a great blow that the sword flew out of his hands when he tried to attack me, and his arm was cut off below the elbow so that he never used his hand again.[11] If you now ask me for a favor, there is no need for the intercession of Oddgeir or Nemes. Ask on behalf of twenty or thirty, a hundred or a thousand: all shall take weapons at your bidding who will and can bear them."

And when Rollant heard the emperor say this, he wanted to fall on his knees. But King Karlamagnus took him by the hand and kissed him with great affection, saying, "It is truly fitting for me to honor you, good nephew, above any other mortal man, because your good care gave me my life."

Emperor Karlamagnus then had horns blown before all the tents to summon all to come before him. There one could see all the young men going to their chests to take out their purses, with plenty of gold and silver and costly fabric, deciding on gifts, for every one of them there had received so much treasure that they did not know how they could take care of it.

(80) The emperor was now in the tent of Jamund, where he made many knights of various lineages, without making any inquiries as to whether they were the sons of rich or poor men. He had given the privileges and honor of knighthood to all, releasing all that were so freed from their dues and obligations to the king. When they knew of this release, and that they had been freed for Rollant's sake, they submitted to the king, dedicating themselves to almighty God and St. Peter[12] the apostle, and said to King Karlamagnus, "Lord king," said they, "let us now attack that cursed people as soon as possible. We shall so slaughter them in your sight that they shall never find a remedy for their damage and shame."

The emperor made haste with his business and chose from that crowd three hundred and thirty-seven men: as long as they lived, these

[10] *A*: "... as a lion's whelp, with a little piece of a spear-shaft in your hand, and struck Jamund ..."— *a* is closer to *Asp.*; cf. 7371-75.

[11] Last clause in *a* only; cf. *Asp.* 7377-79.

[12] *Petrus*.

would defend God's faith and the emperor's person[13] and realm, and in his sight they would later be able to strike off the heads of the heathens. When King Karlamagnus surveyed the boys, he thought of their fathers who had fallen; he would have these with him when he hardly expected to come back himself. Considering this grieved him so that he could by no means stand on his feet. He sat down on a piece of cloth, leaned on the pillow, and sighed in deep grief.

King Droim and King Salomon, Duke Nemes and Oddgeir, led young Rollant before Emperor Karlamagnus, and they had three hundred swords brought forward. One was the sword which would not do for a craven youth to bear: Eisant the Breton[14] bore that sword in his hand. King Karlamagnus then drew the sword and said to King Droim, "There is no sword here as good or as fine as this."

Oddgeir said, "Lord," says he, "try out the sword on the stones which stand before your tent."[15]

The king answered, "God knows," says he,[16] "we shall not do that."

Karlamagnus held the keen sword Dyrumdali in his hand. He then put it in the scabbard and girded his kinsman Rollant with it, and he spoke to him, smiling, in gracious words: "I gird you with this sword in the expectation that it will bring you honor in valor and knighthood as long as you live."

When Emperor Karlamagnus had said this, the pope blessed him and all the others thanked God.[17] And when Karlamagnus had girded Rollant with this sword, Duke Nemes knelt down and bound the right spur on his foot while Oddgeir bound the left one. Before Rollant took off his helmet or sword, three hundred and thirty-seven men came quickly and Karlamagnus took the rest of the swords; and with the first he girded Estor Delangres; then, Otun and Baeringur, Hugi[18] and Jofrey[19] and Engiler[20] of Gaskunia, and then all those who followed

[13] *A*, honor.
[14] *Nizant brezki*; *Asp.* Enisent.
[15] *a*: "before the door of the tent;" cf. testing scene in *Kms.* I, ch. 44.
[16] *a* only.
[17] *a* only.
[18] *Asp.* Guon.
[19] *Asp.* Yvoire.
[20] *A, Angler*; *a, Angiler.*

them. All these Karlamagnus made knights. Then he said to his kinsman Rollant, "You have earned much praise," said he; "all of these I put in your control."

And they all submitted to Rollant, pledging perfect allegiance, and to preserve the king's honor and service.[21] Then the king said, "If God sends me safely back to France, and it pleases me to take my rest and go hunting, then you shall go with me to tame unruly men of my realm."

(81) The emperor then gathered together eleven of the knights whom he knew to be most valiant, and he laid both hands on Rollant's neck, saying "Good nephew," says the king, "You twelve shall be peers; these men shall go with you wherever you wish, and do your will. If God sends me safe back to France, you shall follow me and cleanse my land. There is nothing more I wish to tell you now, but to follow my counsels and accept my affection."[22] ...

(79) Now Lord Girard left the king's court, and lords Boz and Clares went with him. They dismounted from their horses before Girard's tent and earls and nobles came to meet them, asking how the emperor was. Girard answered, "God be praised, he is well and hale. Now all the serving men are to become knights, and we shall all follow the same practice."

All of them then answered, "May God bless our plan, and let it be accomplished according to your advice."

Girard now called his nephews and his two sons to him, and said, "Lords," said he, "now all are to bear weapons who are able; and if God sends me back to my realm, I shall well reward you for that."

When Lord Girard had made his arrangements there was a crowd of three thousand of them there. Then he spoke of his sons[23] Milun and Girard,[24] whom he put in charge of Duke Ancelin,[25] saying, "You

[21] The latter is not in *Asp.*

[22] To this point, the chapter is not paralleled in *Asp.*

[23] *a,* men.

[24] At this point in *Asp.,* it is Ernals who is mentioned; see l. 7426.

[25] *Asp.* Antialme.

shall go to King Karlamagnus and give him greetings in the name of God, conveying my friendship. Ask him to give my sons arms; then bring them back to me."

The duke answered, "I shall do that gladly, lord."

Then they leapt onto their horses and went to the headquarters of King Karlamagnus, where they met with powerful leaders and many of their other people, who were having their brothers and sons and serving-men made knights. Karlamagnus said that the earls and dukes should dub their own men themselves. The leaders said among themselves, "King Karlamagnus has certainly put us to this trouble needlessly!" But they did not know what they were talking about, since they did not know what the army had to expect.

(81) ... When Emperor Karlamagnus was in his tent, he took young Milyn and said, "Youth," says he, "it is fitting to speak the truth to you: you are the son of Lord Girard of Burgundia. A better duke never took arms, and his kinsman cannot fail to be a good man. I shall give you power and honor in the city of Mila, which now has no heir but a daughter. If she is as I expect her to be, no one could be found more lovely than she anywhere in the world. I shall give her in marriage to you, with a great dowry. You and Nemes and Oddgeir and Fagon shall follow me and be my counselors in my household."

Then King Karlamagnus called Eisant the Breton to him, and said, "Where is that excellent sword with the gold cross set on it?"

He brought the sword, and, falling on his knees, gave it to him, kneeling courteously. When the king received the sword, he drew it and considered it carefully; then he called Duke Nemes and Oddgeir to him. "You saw," said he, "that yesterday I was girded with this same sword when I loosed the helmet from Jamund's head and laid him under an olive-tree. And now, brother Milun," says he, "it is most fitting to honor you. I give you this sword, along with the maiden; you and Nemes and Oddgeir shall be my chief counselors, and serve me at table always."[26]

(82) That same day, while the emperor was in his tent, he received young Girard, who was fair-haired and very handsome, with big,

[26] "at table" in *a* only; cf. *Asp.* 7552.

strong arms. Karlamagnus said to him, graciously, "You are the son of Girard, bravest of knights." To Eisant he then[27] said, "Eisant, brother, bring me the greatest of my four swords."

He came and laid the sword on the king's knee. Then the king said, "Lords," said he, "this sword belonged to the son of a knight; with it he conquered Gandri and Lalei,[28] the richest of cities, and Gullaran, and all the realm that lies around the city; nowhere could a better sword be found."

The king then girded him with this sword, in the sight of a great multitude. And when he had girded him with the sword, the king said, "All of the realm of Gandri[29] was won with this sword. Christendom was almost overcome and conquered, but God's providence raised up this sword, and it restored peace and strengthened all our Christian brethren. May God give you victory and long life with this sword."

The king's saddle was then set on a white horse, and the king gave it to him, with the gilded saddle and bridle. And when the king had given him the horse, white as a flower, with its rich trappings—a hundred marks would not have bought his equipment! ...

[27] *A* omits address to Girard; cf. *Asp.* 7560-61.

[28] Cf. *Asp.* 7567: "Qui conquist Gandie et la loi en un jor;" the next line is equally distorted.

[29] *Gandre*.

CHAPTER LXIII

More Help for Karlamagnus

Now it is told that the lord pope went, at the emperor's request, around towns and villages, hamlets and castles, calling every man who was able to be of any help, whether young or old, learned or simple, monk or servant, rich or poor. He made as much haste as he could, and returned to the camp when Karlamagnus had finished giving armor to the young men; thus he went to meet the pope, helping him dismount himself with all courtesy, and led him into the tent, where they all sat down together.

And when the emperor learned what the pope had accomplished he raised his voice to say, "Praise be to almighty God for his mercy, for now he has sent many good warriors in place of those who fell in the earlier battle, whom he recalled home to himself from our control. Now, so that no one may wonder what we are doing assembling troops and dubbing new knights, let it be known to all that Agulandus has come to our neighbourhood with an overwhelming army; it is probable that he thinks he has grievance enough against us, when he has lost his son and the greater part of the host that followed him. But God has so provided, in his care, that Agulandus has never had a victory to boast of in our earlier dealings, and I hope that such will continue to be the case. Although we have very few troops in comparison with his, we should not be at all afraid, but put our faith in God and entrust ourselves to his mercy and the intercession of St. Peter—kneeling especially in earnest devotion to his great friend, my apostle James, lord and ruler of this land, that he may manifest protection for his servants so that it may become clear to all that those who wish to stand up manfully in his service have a dauntless advocate.

"And since we must go to battle, in which none may be free of fear as to whether God shall grant him a longer lifetime, it is our prayer and wish that you, apostolic lord, sing Mass in our tent as soon as it is morning, offering up the Body of the Lord to help all the world, especially us who are there present. Then all our men shall take the holy sacrament from your hand, and strengthened by the absolution of sins given by you, they shall be prepared for battle. Now each and every one is preparing himself to be worthy of God's miracles."

The lord pope thanked the emperor and all the others for their words, and gladly agreed to do his will. And as soon as day came, the pope prepared himself and other learned men for Mass, and they sang the divine service in a good and seemly manner up to the gospel. Then all the newly dubbed knights came to the altar, giving a great deal of treasure: gold, and silver, that one could have lived on for a long time if one took care. And when the point came in the service when all the host was to take the Body of the Lord, all the clerks went first to the holy altar, then the emperor, and afterwards everyone else, one after the other. But before the lord pope left the altar, he spoke beautifully before the people of the manifold mercy of God towards mankind, showing clearly what those who truly serve their redeemer receive as a reward; along with this, he revealed the misery and wretchedness which is the lot of those who forsake him and tread down holy Christendom, and he encouraged everyone with fine words, especially the new knights, to stand manfully now under the emperor's banner, promising remission of sins to all of them for this.

After this the lord pope had brought from its chest the holy cross of the Lord, which was described before in this account, which he brought with him from Rome to Hispania. And when it was revealed, everyone fell humbly to the ground, venerating that blessed relic, which is more valuable than any precious stone. The lord pope then spoke with tears in his eyes: "My sons," says he, "look with your eyes on that glorious holy relic, which is splendidly glorified by the pure blood of our Redeemer;[1] on this he suffered a painful death for our sins, and under this sign you shall now advance, in the expectation that just as our invisible enemies are put to flight by its power, so shall also the visible enemies of God and holy Christianity be confounded and all their might brought to nothing if God manifests to them his great holiness."

[1] *b*: "body of our lord Jesu Christ."

After these words, he lifted up his right hand and gave them all his blessing. Each one then went back to his tent and ate and drank as he pleased, while the sons of Lord Girard rode back to the tower and told the duke how generous the emperor had been to them, and what had happened among the Frenchmen afterwards. Lord Girard was delighted with the honor which the emperor had shown to them.

When the emperor had sat at table for as long as seemed proper to him, he ordered the trumpets sounded, that each man should prepare himself and his horse for battle; and when that was done he divided his host into five divisions. He put in command of the first division his kinsman Rollant, with twelve peers, giving him three thousand young men to follow him. Before the second division he set King Salomon and Earl Hugi, who were Bretons; they had the victorious standard which had once been carried by St. Milon when he was in Bretland, and their division was five thousand men. The third division was to be led by the brave leader King Droim of Gaskunia and Duke Nemes, and they had seven thousand. The fourth division was led by the good leader Gundebol, king of Frisia. Segris and Enser were in this division, which was made up of Saxons and Normans. Karlamagnus himself intended to lead the fifth division, with Fagon[2] the standard-bearer, Vitaclin, and many other good men: it is said that he had only sixteen thousand, or a few more, in his chief division.

Then the emperor took a long reed-wand in his hand, mounted his sturdy war-horse, and separated each division from the next as far as seemed good to him. And before he turned his horse back, he called Oddgeir the Dane and said, "Good friend, since I know the zeal and valor of my kinsman Rollant, and that he often does not watch out for himself because of his courage and his eagerness to serve us, I ask you to watch over him closely in this battle and help him in any way you can, for there is no man I love more and it would be a great grief to me if anything were to happen to him; though Rollant is still young, there is no man more courageous than he."

Oddgeir answered, "Gladly, my lord, shall I do your will in this, standing by him: though I cannot see any reason to give him any

[2] *B*, *Magan*.

supervision when he is valiant in all things, although I am older. But may the God of Christian men do with us all according to his mercy."

We shall let this rest here for a while, and turn to what we spoke of before.

A,a (84)

... The pope and his people made haste and prepared the fourth battalion so carefully that there remained behind neither cook nor page, porter nor chamberboy, nor steward, clerk, or priest who could be of help. The emperor had equipped them all now with helmets and coats of mail, sword, and good horses.[3] So well had he prepared them that no one could have objected that a troop might be better equipped than this ...

(82) ... the pope hurried about his offices. And since there was neither church nor minister there, his[4] archbishops consecrated all the field about and established the pope's chaplain in his tent. The pope then prepared for Mass. Never would he sing Mass with a larger group of newly made knights to hear it!

The pope sang the Mass, while Archbishop Bendikt[5] read the epistle. The pope himself read the gospel, and four archbishops led Rollant, the nephew of King Karlamagnus, to the offering,[6] where he and his comrades[7] offered so rich an offering that the strongest mule could not have carried it.

The pope then spoke: "Noblemen," says he, "listen to me. When our Lord delivered us and[8] diminished the power of the enemy, driving him from heaven, God spoke then, and decreed, in order to fill the empty place, the creation of the band of angels. He created all things in six days, and on the seventh day he rested from his labors, and did not work with his hands. Adam, our father, God made of earth, and

[3] Sentence omitted in *a*, which inserts it below.

[4] *a* specifies four: not so in *Asp*.

[5] *a*, *Bencitus*.

[6] *a*, altar.

[7] Latter in *a* only; cf. *Asp*. 7600.

[8] "delivered us" is an addition to *Asp*.—which does not seem very sensible.

fashioned in his own likeness; from his rib he made Eva. And he gave them power over all created things, except for one fruit, which he forbade them to eat. But soon the Adversary betrayed Eva, and Adam stupidly let her urge him.

"When all the world had been created, God came into the world and was baptized by John[9] the Baptist. Then he suffered death for our redemption."[10]

He then called for the piece of the holy cross on which the Lord suffered which he had brought with him.[11] When the pope held up the cross, all fell on their knees and bowed with great devotion, making their prayers in purity of heart; and the pope blessed all the host and gave them leave to go. They then went off with their weapons and armor.

(84) Hear, now, what the courteous emperor Karlamagnus was about. He had arranged five divisions and intended to use them as five battalions. His nephew Rollant was in the first division, while Duke Oddgeir was to be the emperor's standard-bearer that day; there were two thousand knights in Rollant's division, all young and strong men.

In the second division were King Salomon, and with him knights from Normandy[12] and Peitu and leaders from Gaskunia and the leaders Erkibauth and Hugon.[13] In the third division was the hardy leader from Spain,[14] and the lord Duke Nemes, Earl Jerimias,[15] and Rikard[16] the Valiant ...

[9] *Johannis.*

[10] This sermon is drastically condensed from the version in *Asp.*

[11] Last clause in *a* only; cf. *Asp.* 7671.

[12] *Northmandi*: these are not the same groups reported in *Asp.* 7748.

[13] *A*: "Erkibauth and Hugon the Hardy of Hispania were in the third division." *Asp.* Erquenbaut and, presumably, Huon; but cf. Hues, below; these are all in the fourth or fifth groups in *Asp.*, and there may have been conflation of similar names. Brandin's glossary indicates they are both the same man, who would then be in two divisions at once.—Cf. also *A* 106, below at the end of ch. 70, for detail of the Breton banner.

[14] Desiiers de Pavie?

[15] *Asp.* Jeremie.

[16] *Asp.* Ricars.

... In the fifth division were Gundebol[17] and Segis, Enser,[18] and the Normans[19] who came after them, and those who lived in Saxony.[20] Karlamagnus then laid down his shield, and, taking up a long switch in his hand, he rode about, ordering his divisions.[21] Karlamagnus now ordered his divisions to prepare for battle, and separated them from each other, and he did not stop until he had gone from the first to the last.

(85) ... The king was now riding before his troops, exhorting them to defend his land and God's faith, and preparing every division to ride forth suitably. He then called Oddgeir to him, speaking playfully,[22] and said, "Lord Oddgeir," says he, "keep your promise to me and watch over my nephew, for he is a young child and there is no one alive of whom I am as fond."

Oddgeir then answered, "Hear what Rollant says: he swears he will never be my friend as long as he lives unless he can strike the first blow in this battle."

"God knows," says Karlamagnus, "I will grant that gladly. I entrust him to the care of almighty God." And the king gave his blessing and rode away, his voice failing him.[23]

[17] *A, Gundibol; a, Gundulbit.*

[18] *a, Ensis; a* omits *Segis.* Neither appears to be in *Asp.,* unless the two represent drastic misunderstanding of the French here: see *Asp.* 7769-70.

[19] *Normandiar.*

[20] *Saxland.*

[21] Here *a* inserts the sentence omitted above (cf. n. 3).

[22] Or smilingly? *a,* sighing; nothing in *Asp.* suggests either.

[23] The chapter division here follows *A*, which is closer to the order of *Asp.* than the slight rearrangement of *a*, for which see Unger's note, p. 336.

CHAPTER LXIV

Agulandus Sends Messengers

When King Agulandus had raised his camp and arranged his host in divisions, he summoned seven kings, the wisest of all his advisors, and spoke these words to them: "It seems strange to me that my son Jamund has not come back to join me, for it seems likely to me that he would have heard of our coming thither if he is staying in any place nearby. I wish to tell you that I thus suspect that he may not be free to come."

Then Madequin the Mighty said, "Lord, I have something very strange to tell. No night has passed since we sailed to this land when I have not dreamed strange and unheard-of things. I thought I saw Christian men so wonderfully clad that from head to heels they seemed to me to be protected with the hardest steel, so that no amount of labour or waking harmed them; and so strangely did they deal with us that it seemed to me the white and red of brains and blood were mingled together in the heads of our men. Now I cannot understand what this might signify."

The kings thought his remarks amazing, and did not wish to make any answer. King Maladien spoke next: "It is a great marvel, Agulandus, that so wise a man as you are should wait so long to hold battle with the Christians, rather than ride quickly towards them when there are so few of them. It is true that this Karlamagnus has shown much boldness in his arrogance when he dared to await you with his small troop, but it is evident that he cannot know that you have such strength against him. Although our situation has been such that we would seem to have lost a great many good men, there are yet more who will not leave here if we come to battle again. Therefore let us try once more to see whether this Karlamagnus will change his mind and come to his senses: send to him persuasive men who will clearly explain your power, wealth, and multitude of men, firmly presenting your message. If he will subject himself to you and obey you, good; if he refuses your conditions, he and all the Frenchmen will be killed, if they are so proud and arrogant."

Then Ulien answered, "Lord king, do not delay to carry out that advice of King Maladien, for it is good and wisely put. Appoint a second to go with me and we shall carry out that errand well in all respects, as you command."

Agulandus answered their words and sent for Galinger the Old, telling him this plan and bidding him go on this errand with Ulien. He agreed gladly and prepared himself in a fine courtly way, binding on his feet gold-ornamented spurs and covering himself with a most precious cloak. He put a crown set with precious stones on his head and then mounted a strong mule, while many men held his stirrup. And when the old man was mounted, they put an olive branch in his hand as a sign that he came in peace as a messenger. He was a splendid man; his white beard fell in braids down onto his chest, while his hair fell in locks onto his shoulders under his crown.

Ulien leapt onto a fleet horse that had proved better than any two others. He had put over his clothes a silk jerkin with gold-embroidered leaves, and he carried a gold-enamelled shield and a sharp spear with a great and handsome banner. They rode away from Agulandus, one of them prepared to present the king's message calmly and eloquently while the other would threaten with rough words, if this should be necessary. Thus these two messengers of Agulandus rode on until they drew near the first division of the emperor. Ulien let his banner flutter in the wind and both of them rode well in their stirrups, carrying themselves as well as possible, so that they would make a strong impression on those who saw them. They rode impressively past the three first divisions, saying nothing, and paying no heed to anything along the way.

When they came into the midst of the host, a tall and distinguished man on a gray horse rode in front of them, to whom Galinger called out, raising his voice and saying, "You, man, riding there, tell me clearly; where is Karlamagnus, king of the Frenchmen? I cannot recognize him, but we have been sent to him by the mighty King Agulandus."

Now this knight was the noble lord Karlamagnus, who had just been dividing his battalions, as has been told. And he, hearing this man's voice, turned his horse towards him, and said, "Good friend," says he, "here I am, right by you: you need not look any further for me."

Galinger then answered, "I have no greeting to bring you,[1] for our king[2] bears no favor or good will to you, nor do any of his men; but hear the message which I bring from him."

"Gladly, good friend," says he; "deliver your message as frankly as you wish; none of my men shall mistreat you."

"So that you may know," said Galinger, "how patient Agulandus is, he bids you send to him his four chief gods, safe and unharmed, along with tribute of a thousand horses laden with pure gold and silver and other precious treasure, as well as the same number of immaculate beautiful maidens. This much you shall pay him for your life and that of your men. But if you wish to retain your honors and realm, he bids you take your crown from your head, set aside royal garments and array yourself in haircloth, going barefoot and bearing your crown in your own hand; come forward thus, falling on your knees, and humbly put your head in his power. If you will do this, then we, his advisors, will kneel down by your side and ask for mercy for you, and I think that certainly he will gladly[3] give you back your crown and honors if you will submit to him".

Hearing the words of Galinger, Karlamagnus smiled a little into his beard, and calmly replied, "You carry out your leader's errand well and impressively; but God knows that the heathen king assigns me a very difficult duty. I would give my lord a poor reward for the many and great honors he has granted me if I voluntarily gave, out of weakness, Christendom into the power and rule of heathen peoples. Karlamagnus would have lived too long if he bought a heathen king's friendship so dearly as to renounce his God, who is an immortal king, to serve and venerate cursed idols, who are dumb and dead.[4] No!" says he, "God forbid that it be so done. Rather, to tell you the truth, never, while

[1] *b* adds "from King Agulandus."
[2] *a*, he.
[3] *b*, at once.
[4] *B*, deaf and dumb.

there is life in my breast, shall I lay my honors and my crown at the knee of Agulandus.

"Nor is there to be found in our realm as much gold and silver as he wants—and may God never allow us to desire it selfishly, except to strengthen holy Christendom and honor good knights. Such lovely maidens as Agulandus wishes to have sent to him are now far away, locked in strong cities and castles so well that no man may harm them; and it would be most improper for Christians to give brides to lie with heathen men in lechery. The four idols which you called your gods are not at hand now to send to him, for a few days ago they were given to our harlots, who broke them up into little pieces."

When Ulien heard what the king said, he became extremely angry; he frowned, quivered, raised up his banner and shook his spear, and, leaning on his saddle-bow, said, "Whence came such great boldness in your heart that you receive the message of such a king so haughtily? The only reason he made this offer is that it seemed to him degrading to have you and your host slain. But since you will not accept his good will, there is no doubt that Agulandus has come with an invincible host, intending to kill all who follow you and take you yourself prisoner, binding you with strong chains. He will take you with him to your chief city of Rome, and there he will crown his son Jamund and give him all Italy to govern, while he drives you and all Christians into slavery, unless you will gladly obey them."

The emperor answered, smiling, "It is most foolish to intend one government over all the world, and, with God's permission Agulandus shall be slow to crown Jamund in Rome, for he shall not come there easily on his own feet."

Galinger then said, "Lord king, tell me, what is it that you have such faith in? Have you any more troops than those which I now see here? They seem to me very few in comparison with the force of Agulandus, for his first division, which Madequin leads, has twenty thousand big, strong men, and there are many in every other. Thus I can come to no other conclusion but what your people will be scattered like leaves in the wood,[5] and I think you must all be doomed to die."

[5] *b*, driven like leaves before the wind.

The emperor answered, "Perhaps it shall be so; but you cannot see our greatest strength, for that is not in the hands of mortal men or images, but rests in truth with the one God and his saints."

Ulien answered, "Do as Agulandus commands and let tribute be prepared."

Karlamagnus said, "Wait patiently for a short time, while I consult with my men."

Quickly the emperor returned to his camp and sent word to Duke Girard to come to him. As soon as the emperor's message reached the duke, he rode with his kinsmen without delay, and before he came to Karlamagnus he dismounted from his horse, walking to where the emperor sat, where he fell on his knee and kissed his right hand, saying, "May God reward you, good lord, for the honors you have granted to my sons."

The emperor answered, "All that was little, as set against what you deserve."

After that he told him that messengers were there from Agulandus, and described their errand. When the duke had heard all about it, he said, "Good lord, to give a great deal of good advice: send Agulandus the head of Jamund, his son, which will be much better and more suitable to lay upon his knee than your crowned head. I expect that this offering will astound him greatly, and the more displeased he is with it, the better. But do not be at all afraid to fight. Let each of us help the other, while God helps us all; woe upon them who do not drive their twenty thousand boldly to flight with the two thousand who follow me."

The emperor did as the duke advised, sending two knights, Baldvini and Riker, to the olive tree, under which lay the body of Jamund; and when they got there, they cut off the head from the trunk, and the right arm with its ring on a finger. They took these two parts with them, leaving the trunk behind, and rode back, casting their burden down at the feet of the emperor. Then the lord Karlamagnus called to Galinger and Ulien, raising his voice and saying, "Come here, messengers, for now the tribute is ready at hand."

At first, when they heard tribute mentioned, they became extremely glad; but when they saw what it was, they had quite a different surprise than they had expected. Karlamagnus then said to them graciously,

"Now although those things which Agulandus, your king, asked for are not ready at hand, the word of such a leader shall not be ignored at all, especially when he has sent such men to us. Receive, then, four precious things, and take them to your king: that is, the head of Jamund, with his helmet, and his arm, with the ring on a finger. Tell Agulandus that he shall embrace this rather than the gold crown of the Emperor Karlamagnus, and that if God permits, we intend to treat him as we have Jamund."

When Galinger looked at the head of Jamund so prepared, he sobbed loudly, and said, "Oh, Lord Jamund, a terrible day's journey have you had, when this has become of you! But what are you doing, accursed Makon, to let your best friend be so hatefully dealt with?"

The king answered, "It was likely that he could not give any help to others when he could not save himself from disgrace and disaster. But take, Galinger, whatever you wish to carry with you, the head or the arm of Jamund, and take it to Agulandus."

Now, though he did not much want either, he took the hand, while Ulien took the head; and when that was brought to him, he grew fierce over the head, sighed greatly, and said, "By Maumet, Agulandus will take a great revenge on him who dared to kill his only son! Take my glove," he said to the king, "in challenge, and have your best man meet me in single combat. If I defeat him, let all of you accept our faith; but if he conquers me, then I will be converted to yours. But know that if you and Agulandus meet, all of that host is doomed to death. Your fate is upon you and you shall be destroyed."

Karlamagnus answered, "Speak well, and keep your temper: that will be better, for your nostrils are so broad that you do not care what it is proper for you to say. God rules over our fate, not your words. It is more probable that he will see who is right in this case, he who attacks this land or I who defend it. Now take the head to Agulandus with these words: he shall never bear a crown in holy Rome."

With these words they parted, much to Ulien's displeasure.

A,a (83)

We have heard how Rollant and his comrades became knights; now we shall turn to Agulandus. He had sent for six kings, who came to him. He then said, "Lords," said he, "I am greatly puzzled about my son Jamund. He has been fighting against the Frenchmen for three days now, and has sent no message to me."

King Abilant answered, "By Maumet, he is behaving like a witless child:[6] they have lost our four gods."

Then Madequin[7] said to Agulandus, "Lord," said he, "I am much amazed; every night I have had strange and unheard-of dreams. The Christians are strangely[8] armed: they are covered with steel and iron from head to heel and neither work nor sleeplessness harms them. They have mixed together the white flesh and red blood of our men."

King Maladient[9] spoke next: "Lord," says he, "you are acting most ill-advisedly, since King Karlamagnus has only a small troop, when you do not ride against him at once. He is far too presumptuous and has put too much trust in a small muster of troops when he dares to oppose you. Send word to him demanding that he give us back our four gods, renounce his god, and accept our faith. Allow him to live if he renders tribute from this realm of seven hundred mules and camels, all laden with pure gold and silver,[10] and four hundred[11] of the loveliest maidens, to be given to whomever you please. He himself should come to you barefoot, in woolen clothing, before your feet, to give up his crown. If he will not accept these terms, he will be quickly slain."

Ulien then said, "We are letting this plan wait too long. Now let a second one mount his horse and follow me, and we two shall go on this errand."

Agulandus then sent for Galinger[12] the Old, and when he had come he put golden spurs on his feet, clothed him in a rich mantle, and set a rich bejewelled golden crown on his head. Then he mounted the best mule, and they held the old man's stirrups while he mounted. They

[6] *A* leaves out the childishness, but cf. *Asp.* 7693: here it is Agulandus himself speaking.

[7] *A, Baldeqvin; a, Maddikvin,* and so in *Asp.*

[8] *a* adds "suddenly."

[9] *a, Maladin ; Asp.* Maladient.

[10] *a* omits gold; cf. *Asp.* 7715.

[11] *a*, 300.

[12] *Galingri.*

then brought him an olive branch, as a symbol of his mission. He was white of beard and handsome in countenance: no old man could be found to equal him.

Ulien then mounted a dapple-grey horse: in all the heathen host there were not ten horses better than this. He was clad in a silk tunic embroidered with gold leaves, and carried a gold-stained buckler and a keen spear with a great banner. He was mighty and strong.

These were the messengers of King Agulandus.—Here the seventh book ends, and the eighth begins.

(85) Just then the messengers of King Agulandus arrived, with Galinger bearing the olive branch. He had a white beard, and his mantle was so great that it trailed down to his heels.[13] His hair was braided into narrow braids and hung over both shoulders. Ulien rode on a dapple-grey horse, which could not have been bought with the same weight of pure gold. He wore a tunic, and had a bright helmet on his head, a sharp sword, and a keen spear with a shaft of applewood, from which his great banner blew in the wind. He was a mighty man, tall, with strong arms, and if he had been a Christian there would have been no woman so beautiful that she would have been able to refuse him. These had come to bring the message of King Agulandus: one to threaten, and one to fight, if anyone wished to do so ...

(86) Now the messengers came and rode around the nearest division, until they came into the midst of the troops. Galinger was the first to speak: "Brother knight on the grey horse, you who ride before this division, show me Karlamagnus, king of the French, for I cannot recognize him. We are messengers from the mighty king Agulandus."

Karlamagnus then answered, in a loud voice: "Here I am," said he, "you need look for me no longer."

The heathen answered, "I bring you no greeting, for I have no grace or good will for you. Send Agulandus Makon[14] and Terrogant, Apollin and Jupiter the Great, if you wish to keep your life."

[13] *a*: "that it covered all his ornaments."
[14] *a*, *Maumet*.

"Friend," said Karlamagnus, "your lord has a grim and evil heart if he wishes to say such things."

Galinger answered, "We are messengers, and come to give this message: let us take our gods now, and make ready as soon as possible one thousand and seven pack-horses with a full load of pure gold and silver, and the same number of immaculate maidens.[15] And you shall come barefoot, in woolen clothing, and bear your crown in your hands, as one of those who drive horses and earn their living with beasts of burden. When you come to Agulandus, you shall fall on your knees before him; and if you will renounce your god and accept our faith, then you can redeem yourself and your realm. When you have done this, we will ask our lord[16] to have mercy on you and he will then give you your crown."

"Lord God," said Karlamagnus, "these heathens offer me a hard duty, for I have never learned to go barefoot. The gold and silver for which you ask[17] might take some time, but the maidens are so well hidden in strong castles that no man can get at them. And two days ago our men gave your four gods to harlots, who broke them in pieces."

Galinger then began to swear and shook the olive branch so that it almost flew apart in all directions, while Ulien frowned and raged like a madman; he shook his spear so that the iron nearly flew off, raised up his banner and leaned on the spear, saying, "Karlamagnus," said he, "Agulandus, who sent me here, rules all of Africa. When he sent the army to Europe,[18] he sent his scouts ahead with our four gods and Jamund, his son, occupied the city of Sueri[19] for a full month. When they left they took our four gods with them. Agulandus is now coming to search for you until he finds you; he will have you with him at Rome, where he is going to crown his son Jamund and slay all those that believe in Christ."

"By my faith," said Karlamagnus, "he will never do that, God

[15] *Asp.* specifies 1700; see 7835-37.
[16] *a*, king.
[17] *A* only.
[18] *A, Eropa; a, Eyropa.*
[19] *Asp.* 7870: "en fuere."

willing. Neither shall he have gold, silver, or maidens. Know that those who will pay him tribute have not been born."

Galinger then said, "Lord king," says he, "have you any greater host than that which I now see here? In the first division there are few men, and the weapons which they bear belong to our men. King Madequin,[20] kinsman of King Agulandus, has, to oppose these, twenty thousand in his division, apart from other divisions. By Makon, all your men will be taken like fruit from a tree."

"Lord king," said Ulien,[21] "control your wrath. Two hundred and sixty thousand are now riding on their way here. If you were meat slaughtered and chopped up in the kitchen, when there are so many of us, our host could not even be half-filled by you; our king, however, has ordered that you be taken prisoner alive, for he wishes to slay you himself."

Now the emperor sent the pope[22] and Nemes and Oddgeir and Salomon hastily to lord Girard to ask him and his sons to come to the king; when they arrived, he walked out on the field with them. "Lords," said he, "listen to me now. Over there are messengers from King Agulandus. They want their gods and one thousand and seven pack-horses loaded with gold and silver, and the same number of maidens; and they want me to go myself barefoot, in woolen clothing, and bow to him and lay my crown there, renouncing holy Christianity and holding to his faith."

(87) Girard the Old began to answer: "Lord," says he, "it will not do for you to be angry. Eighty winters have now passed since I put a helmet on my head. Send for the body of Jamund, where it lies under the olive tree, and dispatch it to Agulandus as a suitable offering for him, for that will make him angry and enraged. Each of us shall strengthen the other against his vengeance, and God will help us all: woe to those who cannot drive off twenty thousand of their men with two thousand!"

[20] *Mandeqvin.*
[21] *a*, he; but in *Asp.* it is Ulien; see 7898.
[22] *a* only; cf. *Asp.* 7912.

Baldvini[23] and Riker then went after the corpse, while the messengers now came to deal with the king and said, "Let our tribute be made ready."

"Friend," said Karlamagnus, "I have just sent men to fetch it."

The king's men came to the olive tree, where they found Jamund. They cut off his broken arm, taking neither the ring from his finger nor the helmet from his head, and Riker carried the corpse[24] while his comrades bore his shield, hand, and head. When they came to the plain where the king was, they laid down the body of Jamund.

When Galinger saw that, he was filled with alarm, and became as silent now as he had been talkative before. And when Ulien looked at the body, he recognized the helmet and the great finger-ring. Rollant had struck an amazing blow, making both eyes fly out of his head and lie on his cheeks. Ulien spoke: "Makon,"[25] he said, "what are you doing, when you did not make your power known?"

"Friend," said Karlamagnus,[26] "you have certainly lost your god.[27] Early yesterday he was given over to harlots. With strong sledgehammers and keen steel pikes, they have completely broken up his body. I find that you have been threatening me. Now take this tribute: the head, arm, and shield of the man who, in his arrogance, fought against me; you shall never get any other tribute from me. You and Galinger came here to threaten me, telling of the power of your king and the tribute he demanded—your four gods, gold and silver, and maidens (whom it would be shameful to give to heathens as whores!), and my crown, fashioned of the finest gold: these he shall never get in all his life while I wield my sword. As for the four gods he[28] wants, I do not have them, since I had them given to harlots, and they broke them in pieces and dragged them behind them into their tents; each of them got so little of them as would hardly be worth half a penny. I

[23] *Asp.* Bernart.

[24] Thus making little sense of the action of cutting off the arm. In *Asp.* they take only the arm and head, and later here these appear to be the parts assumed.

[25] *Makun (A).*

[26] *A*'s "he" obviously will not do.

[27] *a*, gods.

[28] *A*, you; cf. *Asp.* 8002.

have never had so much treasure as you want, nor has God ever let a king of France want[29] so much, unless it is to be shared with his[30] valiant knights. Now go to Agulandus and take him Jamund's head with its helmet, his arm and ring, and if it pleases God, we shall deal with him as we have with Jamund."

Ulien sat on his horse, and Galinger on his mule; they looked at Jamund's head, and the blood running out of his mouth. Both his eyes lay on his cheeks; brains ran out of his ears. One wept, and the other sobbed. Then Ulien drew the right glove from his hand and went before Karlamagnus, saying, "Take my glove as pledge of single combat against whomever you judge to be best: if I overcome my opponent on the battlefield, you and your men shall trust in our gods, but if he kills me, then all the heathens shall put their faith in the true God."

Karlamagnus then said, "Control your temper, and tell Agulandus that his son has now got what he was looking for. I have his horn, sword, and horse, and I have given them to my kinsman Rollant. Tell Agulandus that I sent him his son's head and his arm, from the elbow, and before this evening has come one of us shall know who is in the right: I, who defend this realm, or he, who attacks it."

Ulien then looked at the shield and the arm and sighed three times, shaking his head. "Ah, lord Jamund," says he, "this was a hard day's journey. Tell me,"[31] says he, "where did all these boys who follow you come from? All that little troop is doomed to death and all your faith is useless."

"Friend," said Karlamagnus, "our fate is in God's hands, not in the power of your words. Take the head to Agulandus on my behalf; tell him that head shall never be crowned in Rome."

[29] *A*, have.
[30] *A*, my.
[31] *a* adds "Karlamagnus."

CHAPTER LXV

Agulandus Learns of the Death of Jamund

The messengers of Agulandus now rode away, less cheerful than they had been before and with less wealth than they had hoped. Karlamagnus did not go barefoot before their horses, nor did fair maidens follow for their delight; rather, all they had to look at was a bloody head. In all respects they had gained little. So they rode slowly, in a dismal mood, until they came near the first division of Agulandus, where they met, first, Madequin; he greeted them and said, "Be quick with your tidings, and tell me at once: how is the sturdy Karlamagnus—has he sent us our gods?"

When Ulien heard what Madequin said, he was angry and did not want to answer. Thus Galinger said, "Why are you behaving so cheerfully? Karlamagnus shall not have either your gods or anything else forced from him. Jamund is dead, the gods broken in pieces."

Madequin answered, "Do not carry on with such nonsense! No man would dare to do such shame and provocation to our king."

Galinger said, "Look on the head of Jamund here, if you do not believe me. But Karlamagnus did this prudently, for neither Agulandus nor any of the rest of us would have been sure that Jamund was dead if he had not added clear signs. You can now recognize the ring which Jamund bore on his finger."

When Madequin could no longer deny it, he answered him, sobbing, "Everything will turn to our harm!" and he tore the hair from his head, and all of his companions who learned of this lamented loudly, wailing terribly in the terror and fear that came over them.

The messengers then rode on to the second division, which was led by Acharz of Amflor; and as soon as he recognized the silk banner of Ulien, he turned to meet them and said, "Welcome to our comrades! Have the Christians and their leaders submitted to our faith?"

Galinger answered, "It would be very foolish of them to do that, for all our faith has come to nothing for us, while they are able to conquer all they wish."

Acharz answered, "Why are you so downcast? It cannot be that anything so dreadful has happened as that Jamund is dead!"

Galinger says, "He is certainly dead, as you can see with your own eyes. Look here on this hand with his ring on his finger, while Ulien has his head and helmet, split completely in two, which Karlamagnus sends to Agulandus."

Acharz and all his men became so downcast at this news that no one knew what to do. The messengers rode forth from there to the third division, which Kalades led; he turned to them, saying, "Makon bless you; it was to be expected, Ulien, that you would want the honors—but Agulandus will do as best pleases him. Did the hardy king gladly submit and yield tribute, or how did it go on your long expedition? Were the horses not ready?"

Ulien was incensed by the mockery that seemed to meet him, and answered with great anger, "Woe upon you, the way you babble! It is likely that you, Kalades, and your followers, will soon know just what sort of tribute the Christians intend to give you; and if you do not counter with the same sort you may be completely vanquished. But know that our god has completely betrayed us and let Jamund be killed, while he himself has been given into the hands of whores, who have dealt with him shamefully and broken him apart into little bits."

Kalades went nearly out of his wits when he heard what Ulien said. He cried, "May you be cursed, Makon, for looking after your leader so little! Who can put any trust from now on in such as you? Woe upon you for your meanness: you have ill rewarded those who serve you!"

Then they rode on to the fourth division. And as soon as Eliades and Pantalas saw them coming, they turned toward them, greeting them, and saying, "Welcome, messengers of our king! Where are the fair maidens Agulandus demanded? It will be good for the young men to have them to embrace."

Galinger answered, "The Frenchmen are not as easy to deal with as you think, and I think they have other ideas of how you shall sport with their treasures. Now, Pantalas, that has been fulfilled which many predicted when Agulandus appointed his son Jamund to lead such good knights: that it would lead to great misfortune for us to follow his impetuosity to this land. The Christian people have so much faith in their god that they think anything is possible when he assists them.—I understand little of it, but I heard much said about him there. They have killed Jamund and all his troop and destroyed the gods themselves, nor do they intend to grant Agulandus any honor when they have done such disgrace and shame to him and all his friends. Such is what we have to say—and a great deal more."

Pantalas was silenced and could say nothing. They came next to the chief standard of Agulandus, where many great leaders came to them, all asking them to give them the tidings at once; but they pressed forward with great seriousness and would say nothing to anyone until they came before Agulandus. When Agulandus saw them coming, he was very glad and greeted them first, asking them where Karlamagnus was and whether he intended to come to meet with him, bidding them to speak up and describe their errand clearly. Galinger answered the king, "Since you so command, it shall be done. Karlamagnus certainly intends to come to meet with you, but not in such subjection as to give up his crown and royal honors to you—rather, to hold battle. And it is true to say that we[1] saw no sort of fear touch his heart, nor did his color change in the slightest when we brought him your message. On the contrary, he was well and in good spirits and had ordered his divisions."

Agulandus then answered, somewhat shortly, "Did he send us the tribute?"

"Yes, lord," says Ulien, "such as you may now see."

He cast the helmet and head before his feet and said, "The tribute Karlamagnus sends you is nothing else but the head of Jamund; and so that you may have no further doubt that your son is dead, he sends along clear signs which Galinger can show you."

Galinger laid down the arm on the floor before the king's knee. When Agulandus saw Jamund's head, his heart withered so that all the strength left his limbs, and he fell forward from his seat over the head, quite unconscious. There he lay until the men standing near picked him up in their arms. And when most of the faintness[2] had left him, he

[1] *b*, I.
[2] *b*, strength.

spoke, with grievous sobs, "Oh, oh, my son, you were born to great misfortune, for your eager and imprudent urging has wounded the heart of your father. Yet it is fitting, for I granted you too much power to oppose me when I set a crown on your head; never thereafter did you follow my advice, but, rather, held to the fellowship of those who desired neither my honor nor your own, so that when Estor wished to betray me you made him your standard-bearer: those who killed him are owed thanks!"

After that, he said to Galinger, "Where are our four gods?"

He answered, "Have no hope for them, lord, for the Christians have dealt with them horribly. Whores took them and dragged them, bound them, and finally broke them apart. I am astonished that they let themselves be dealt with in this way, showing no sign of their power, but it seems to prove that they are much less mighty than we thought. If, indeed, they had any might, they would certainly not have allowed themselves to be so disgraced without any vengeance."

When Agulandus heard that, there seemed to him little way to improve matters, and he spoke with sorrow and great rage: "How can it happen this way? Before we began our expedition to this land, we prayed for the aid of the gods, who have helped us well many times; and we paid such homage to them that we sent them out to Arabia, and had them completely decorated with the purest gold and the most precious jewels, thinking that they would defend us all the more. And now our hopes have been turned to what we can see. What can you say, Galinger, of Karlamagnus?"

Galinger answered, "Karlamagnus seems to me the most remarkable of men, with sharp eyes and great good fortune. I heard much said of his god. They said he had come down from heaven into the womb of a certain holy maiden, whom they call Maria, saying that she carried him in her womb for many months and that she then bore him into the world as a little child; and they add to this something which seems against all probability to me, that she was just as untouched a maiden after she had begotten him and given him birth as she was before. This young boy was, they say, like other men, and was baptized by a man who dwelt in the desert, whom they called John. And after Jesus was baptized, they say that he preached the true faith, but the Jews would not tolerate that and arranged to torment him and nail him on a cross; he died, like other men, and after that he rose alive from the dead and mounted up to heaven, where he sits in his high throne, dwelling there forever. And they say that he helps anyone who has faith in him. And I asked what happened to those who did not believe in him, and they said that they burned in eternal fire. They say that they have so much faith in this god of theirs that they intend to go gladly to battle against you and think they will surely gain the victory. But I could not understand this idea of theirs, because, to tell the truth, lord, their host does not compare to a third of your multitude."

Agulandus answered, "Because of the great sorrow which I suffer over the death of my son, I cannot think about what you are saying."

Then the bloody head was taken from the helmet and brought to the king, and he embraced it, holding it to his bosom. His grief and wrath were thus renewed, and it could rightly be said that all around the divisions of Agulandus the same words could be heard, which each one said to the others: "Jamund is dead." And all were oppressed with sorrow and weeping.

But, God willing, that cause of sorrow would seem little in comparison to that which was about to happen.

A,a (88)

... The messengers rode quickly on, and the first man they met was Madequin. "Welcome, messengers!" said he. "How was Karlamagnus, the mighty emperor, pleased? Has he sent us our four gods and the tribute?"

When Ulien heard this, he was enraged to be mocked. Galinger then answered, "You speak," said he, "like a madman. They gave our gods to their harlots, who broke them in pieces with great sledge-hammers. Jamund is dead."

Madequin answered, "Do not spread such nonsense: there is no man so strong that he would dare to offend my lord."

Galinger[3] answered, "Stop your threats. His body lies under an olive-tree. They cut off his head and arm; you can see his head here in this helmet.[4] They did not wish to take the helmet from his head nor

[3] *A*, Ulien, but cf. *Asp.* 8111.

[4] *a* only, but cf. *Asp.* 8114.

the ring from his finger, for they wanted those who had crowned him before to recognize him now."

Madequin then said, "All is turning to our destruction now." And he was struck with such distress that he tore the hair from his head.

When his troop saw that, they all struck their hands together and wailed so that all the division was struck with dread and fear. The messengers now rode forward through a little wood, where Akarz[5] of Amflor was coming;[6] he recognized the silken banner of Ulien at once, and came towards them, saying, "Welcome, comrades: have the Christians accepted our faith?

Ulien answered, "That would be foolish of them.[7] When Jamund took the city of Kalabre, he converted many Christians to our faith, and he had twenty thousand men with him. Then came the strongest of the French knights at him, with ten thousand: when they dealt with our men, our men fled and lost their four gods. The Christians took charge of them and gave them to their harlots, who broke them in pieces, and each one took a small bit. Jamund is dead, with all his troop."

When Akarz heard that, he turned quite black; then he became pale, and all his men were so saddened that no one knew what to say to the other. But the messengers rode on.

When King Kalades[8] learned of their coming, he rode to meet them at once, saying, "Friends," said he, "may Maumet bless you. Are the Christians converted to our gods?"

Then Ulien said, "Our gods have betrayed us. When Jamund captured the city of Kalabre, he converted many to our faith. He had twenty thousand men with him. When the Frenchmen had put them to flight, they took our four gods and gave them to their harlots, who divided them up between them. Jamund is dead, and we are disgraced."

When they had told their message to Kalades,[9] he went nearly out of

[5] *Ackars.*

[6] *A*, came to meet them.

[7] *A*: "That would be your foolishness." Aside from sense, *a* is confirmed by *Asp.* 8134.

[8] *Kaladis.*

[9] *Kalade.*

his wits, and said, "Lord Maumet: curses on you for allowing Jamund to be slain!"—And all of his divisions broke apart.

The messengers now rode on. But Eliades and his cousin[10] Pantalas ran up to them and said, "Has Karlamagnus sent us the tribute and the maidens?"

Ulien answered, "The Frenchmen are not so easily conquered."

Galinger then said, "Brother Pantalas," says he, "in evil hour was Jamund made our leader, especially when he urged us to conquer this land. The Christians have their faith, trusting in almighty God, son of holy Maria. That is he who was bound to the cross, and forgave Longinus for his death when he pierced his heart with a halberd. Jamund lost our four gods, with gold and silver; the Frenchmen have killed seven companies of a hundred thousand of our heathens and done great shame and disgrace to our friends and kinsmen. Jamund and his four cousins are dead."

The messengers rode on from there, forward through the ranks, and came to the chief standard, where they found King Agulandus and the mighty king Abilant, and with them King Rodan[11] the Strong, and Maladient,[12] King Modas[13] the Young, and Laufer.[14] These saw the messengers coming at a distance.

(89) The messengers rode in quickly, eager to tell their news. When the king saw this he rejoiced at their arrival; and as soon as the messengers dismounted from their horses under the chief standard, King Modas said, "Ulien and Galinger, tell us at once, shall we have the tribute?"

Galinger answered, "You are far too rash. We have ridden more than five miles in one way, where there are more than a hundred thousand bodies lying. Karlamagnus is well and in good condition; he is the most bold of armed men, and has long ago put his battle ranks in order. Indeed he does send you an offering. With this golden shield

[10] "Mother's sister's son."
[11] *Rodant*; *Asp.* Boidant.
[12] *Madien.*
[13] *Modal.*
[14] *a, Lemferr*: possibly derived from "l'amustens, li fel" (*Asp.* 8239).

and jewelled helmet he sends you the head of your son, along with his right arm, and to prove that those who send you this tribute are no liars, the ring on his finger is included."

Agulandus looked at the head of his son; but Rollant had struck him with so great a blow that his eyes lay on his cheeks and his arm was in pieces. When the king recognized the ring, his heart withered, and all his might with it, and he lay down on the shield and embraced these remains. And when he recovered his senses, he said, "What has become of our four gods, that they allowed my son to be slain?"

Galinger answered, "Lord," said he, "when the Christians robbed us of our gods, they gave them to harlots and broke them into pieces. I conclude that all who trust in such gods are deceived, and I shall never be able to believe that they can perform miracles."

When the king heard this, he nearly burst for grief. He gazed again and again at the head of his son Jamund and grew very black, so that he became as dark as soot, where before no man had been fairer. "Son," said he, "great is my grief: for your sake I came here on this expedition. Fair son, I crowned you, but you turned against me most unreasonably: never, after you received the crown, did you follow my advice, but held, rather, to the bad counsel of those who desired neither my honor nor yours. Now if their advice has killed you, they should also be killed.—Galinger, brother," said he, "tell me about the ways of Karlamagnus."

Galinger answered, "There is no man living," says he, "who, if Karlamagnus looked on him with wrathful eyes, would not be afraid of his countenance and dread him greatly, and give a great deal to keep his life. The Christians believe in one God, who came down from heaven to help mankind; he took the form of a man from the body of the holy Maria. This holy maiden conceived him divinely, entirely without carnal knowledge of a man. She gave birth to him in Bethlehem.[15] He was baptized in the river Jordan[16] and ordained holy Christianity afterwards: and whoever has perfect faith in that God shall be helped on Judgment Day."

[15] *A, Bathleem*; *a, Bedlehem*.

[16] *a* adds "by John the Baptist;" *Asp.* refers neither to John nor to the Jordan. The saga version here differs from *Asp.* in several ways.

(90) When the messengers came to Karlamagnus, they thought they would take tribute and make the Christians serve their idols and become their valets and stable-boys, while the greatest of them would be shamefully slain; but they did not receive so much as four counterfeit pennies in tribute. They returned, rather, with the tribute they deserved, and brought Agulandus the head of Jamund. Agulandus, seeing his son's head, behaved like a madman in his wrath. "Son," said he, "great is my sorrow that you came with me on this journey. We prayed our gods with all our hearts to help us. I caused them to be worked in a great deal of fine gold from Arabia and the most precious gems that could be found in the world: with the value of those precious stones I could have bought seven of the richest cities. With these gems, I had arms and legs adorned, neck and shoulders, feet and fingers, back and breast, sides and loins, and all of their bodies from the crown of the head to the sole of the foot. You made Estor your standard-bearer, a man who wanted to drive me from my realm and take my realm of Africa for himself; now he has earned what he deserved, for he fell in the first battle. May it be well for the hands that killed him."

Then Agulandus had the head removed from the helmet. And when this was brought, pale and bloody and colorless, which had been so fair and handsome in life, Agulandus kissed the bloody mouth, from which the brains ran out. He embraced the head and held it to his breast. The Africans could then be seen drooping and weeping in grief and despondency, and even the bravest quaking in dread.

CHAPTER LXVI

Turpin Prepares to Bear the Cross

The next thing to be told is how, when the messenger of Agulandus had ridden away, Karlamagnus said to Duke Girard, "My dearly beloved friend," says he, "you have my most cordial permission to go to your men and prepare them for battle, for we intend to blow the signal for attack here."

The duke answered, "May God's will and yours be done. But take special care that the first attack of your men is as sharp as possible, for if the heathens recognize no sign of fear in you they shall soon give way. And if God in his mercy grants that which he worked on their lot before, then I expect they will not be able to stop it; for it is generally the case that those who give way first have the greatest difficulty. And if the first division advances from its place, send the second after it all the more courageously, and let each aid the other and stand as well as possible so that each does not go his own way. I shall come to the attack with my men, as God guides us. I should be glad if we did not give them such an opportunity to rest as when we first met with them."

The emperor thanked the duke for his counsel and said that he expected his kinsman Rollant and his peers to help him well. Then they parted; the duke rode on his way, while Karlamagnus had his royal trumpets sounded, and when they were heard there was great uproar and commotion in the army, as each of them went to the place and under the banner where he was to stand.

When the army had gathered, the lord pope rode forward with a great train of men, most of them dressed in armor, bearing the cross of the lord. And because it had not yet been decided who should bear that precious relic into battle, the pope turned to a warrior in the troop with whom he was well acquainted, who was called Mauri, and said to him, "Good friend, dress yourself suitably and bear the cross of the Lord before our host today."

"Lord," says he, "you speak strangely. How can I, a layman, bear the holy cross? What would I then conquer with the weapons you brought me the day before? I tell you, lord, that I shall not dress in other clothing until this fails me. You will be able to see yourself that I shall serve God and you so manfully that the heathens shall pay dearly for them. Then let another bear the cross, one to whom its holiness is more suitable."

The lord pope then called to his highest ranking and most learned man, whose name was Ysopes, and said, "My son, we want you to bear the Lord's cross before our host today."

"Holy father," says he, "I have promised always to obey your order, but I ask you to give the holy cross to another man to carry because I think I shall kill all too few of God's enemies and yours with my sword if I take it. I therefore ask you to make me free and unhindered by this, and I shall promise that the heathens will not go on from there freely when they meet with me."

While they were speaking, an imposing man mounted on a handsome red horse rode up; he was very well equipped with weapons, of impressive stature, and he bore himself nobly on horseback, with splendid shoulders and strong arms. This man bowed to the lord pope and said, "May God bless and strengthen you, holy father! I have been hearing that you seem to be encumbered with the holy cross and cannot find anyone who wants to carry it. Now, with your permission, I shall solve this difficulty and prepare to bear the cross which they have refused before as a great burden."

The lord pope looked at him and did not recognize the man at first, since armor hid his face. He asked, "Who are you, and from what realm do you come, good knight who so graciously offers to bear this most holy relic and solve our difficulty?"

He answered, with amusement, "Lord, I was born in the north of Pul, in the realm of the king of France, and for more than ten years I was a monk in the monastery of Umages which stands in the city of Kun; from there I was taken and made bishop of the Christians of Reims.[1] My name, lord, may be known to you, for I am called Turpin."

[1] *b, Renes.*

The lord pope said, "My son, you are certainly known to me; and do you wish to bear this blessed relic today?"

"Gladly," says he, "for it is suitable that we who are your serving-men should stand manfully in the front of God's battle, while you pray for grace for us."

Then the archbishop dismounted from his horse and went humbly to kiss the pope's right foot, and received, with joy and gladness, the cross of the Lord. Then he remounted and rode off in the front of the division. And as soon as Rollant and Oddgeir the Dane and their comrades saw Archbishop Turpin had come with the cross of the Lord, they all sprang from their horses and fell on the ground with great humility and paid honor to that sublime and holy relic, then mounted their horses again.

As we come to this point, it is well to tell next what protection and help almighty God openly sent to holy Christendom from his heavenly throne because of the glorious merit of his beloved apostle, for James saw the devotion of Karlamagnus, and he heard the emperor's prayer; and because he did not quite see now how the warfare of the enemy and his comrade Agulandus could be overcome and brought to an end in his land with human strength, he asked his glorious master the Lord Jesus, son of the Virgin Mary, to send him help from the heavenly host, to fittingly pull down and boldly tear apart the arrogant limbs of the adversary. And that was granted at once, for when the cross of Our Lord Jesus Christ had come before the division of the Christians, all who could see over the throng of men and hills of earth beheld three knights, clad in bright armor, riding on white horses down from the mountain of Aspremont so boldly that they did not restrain their horses from galloping; and they stopped right in the front of Rollant's division, taking their place next to Oddgeir the Dane. And since no one recognized them, Oddgeir spoke to the one who led them, wondering why they had ridden there so eagerly. He said, "Sir knight, sitting on the white horse—the proudest I have ever seen—tell me your name, or of what city you are a native, for I have never seen you before my eyes before. And what is your intention, when you ride so furiously?"

The new-come knight answered him in a gentle voice: "Be calm, good friend," says he, "and speak agreeably." It is likely that there are more men in the world than you can recognize. But if you wish to know my name, call me George. Those two who are with me are called Demetrius[2] and Merkurius.[3] I shall not conceal from you that we were sent by our king to help your host. Do not be surprised if I put myself at the head of the division, for everywhere, when I am in a battle, I always carry out the first charge against the enemy; but this time I wish to give that place to this young man, the emperor's kinsman, who stands here beside us, with the understanding that no word of fear shall come into his heart nor words of cowardice rise to his lips, no matter how he may find himself placed."

As Oddgeir thought he understood clearly that these were God's saints, he humbled himself greatly before them, and said, rejoicing, "Praised be that lord who so mercifully looks after his flock! But I ask you, holy champion of God, to watch over Rollant, the emperor's nephew, as he appointed me to."

George answered, "Ride forward bravely all together, and do not say a word before the others of our nature."

Rollant heard what they said and praised almighty God with all his heart, then came boldly forward in their midst, and they all stood together.

A,a (91)

... Karlamagnus called the pope to him, saying, "Mauri[4] has come here: God's friend and mine."

"Praise be to almighty God," says the pope, "I have a large piece of the cross on which the Lord suffered. Now, Lord Mauri, you shall be specially garbed, and bear this most holy cross."

Mauri answered, "You speak strangely. You brought me armor, mail-coat, helmet, and shield, and I sit here, armed and secure, on this horse. I tell you this: I shall never be garbed in vestments before these fail me. I shall serve God and you bravely, and the heathens shall purchase my weapons dearly."

[2] *B, Demitrius.*

[3] *Mercurius.*

[4] "Erengi" is the man named at this point in *Asp.* (8377), but P_5 gives "Amauri," and is thus closer here. Cf. Josef Mayer, *Weitere Beiträge zur Chanson d'Aspremont* (Griefswald, 1910), p. 40.

The pope then said, "Why have you abandoned me so?"

"I have not abandoned you, lord," said he, "unless it now turns out so for the first time."

Then the pope called Ysopus[5] to him: "You," said he, "are the best of clerks; now you shall take this holy relic with you."

He answered, "Lord," says he, "you are being too rash. Why did I take up these weapons and armor? Bring me the weapons in which I was ordained: then I will, in God's name, do all you ask."

A lord archbishop listened to their words; he was mounted on the best of red war-horses. This archbishop was big and strong, a fine man in appearance. Now he rode forward into the middle of the crowd and said to the pope, "Lord," said he, "I have long listened to your words. We are all prepared to say our prayers if it does not please you that we shall fight. I see you are very anxious about a small fragment. If you give me the precious holy relic which that man refused to take, I will gladly accept it, for I do not expect that it will prove a hindrance to me."[6]

The pope responded, "Friend," says he, "where were you born?"

"Lord," said he, "north of the mountains, in the realm of the king of France. For a long time I was a monk in Normandy, in the city called Kuin,[7] in the monastery called Uniages.[8] I was there more than ten years, and they wanted to choose me as their abbot. From there I was chosen and taken to be made archbishop of the city of Reims. You shall know and fully prove by experience that my services shall please you before this evening."

The pope then said, "God knows," said he, "you speak remarkably well. Do not conceal your name from me."

"Lord," says he, "men call me Turpin."

Then the pope said, "God bless you and give you good fortune. Are you so bold a man that you will bear the standard before our troops?"

"Yes," said he, "and I ask you to do this, if you wish to follow my advice. I have a thousand knights, who serve me at table; if you wish them to follow me, then I will be in the division of Oddgeir and Rollant, and as long as anyone is attacking my lord, while I can help

[5] *Asp.* Ysoré; other mss. agree. Cf. Mayer, p. 42.

[6] From "I will gladly ..." *A* only; cf. *Asp.* 8433.

[7] *A, Kum; Asp.* Roën.

[8] Jumeige; *Asp.* 8438.

with my weapons,[9] I want leave to fight. When I return to my church, then I shall perform all the services for which I was ordained."

The pope answered, "It is useless to speak of this; now you want to be both archbishop and knight."

The archbishop answered, "I do not dare, lord, to quarrel with you. If you do not wish to agree with this, then you must get another standard-bearer."

The pope then said, "You shall have leave; but you shall purchase it dearly."

(92) Then they saw the Africans drawing near; horns and trumpets sounded, pipes and tambourines, and a terrible noise arose from both armies. When the archbishop had been given leave, he kissed the pope's right foot and the pope gave him the cross. The archbishop then bowed to the pope and took the cross with great rejoicing, and seven thousand knights followed him. And when Oddgeir saw the archbishop with the cross[10] he dismounted from his horse, and so did all his men, and they bowed to the cross with great good will and wept with joy.

Then Oddgeir said, "Rollant," says he, "I swear to you faithfully that Agulandus is certainly a dead man if he awaits us."

The brave knight Oddgeir at once mounted his horse, as did all his men, and they rode down the slope. But three knights hastened in front before the division, to the troop, saying nothing: no one spoke a word. And when they came to the front, Oddgeir lifted his voice and called to them, "Man on the white horse, who is hastening so, who are you?"

He answered, "Be calm," says he, "and speak politely. Men call me George, where I am known. Everywhere, I am accustomed to lead the first attack in battle; but now I have given the first attack to this young man, with the understanding that no charge of cowardice shall ever come to him from this."

When Oddgeir realized that this was truly St. George who spoke with him, he said, "Lord," said he, "I give him into God's protection and yours."

[9] *a*, counsels.

[10] *A*: "when the archbishop came to Oddgeir with the cross." Cf. *Asp.* 8496.

CHAPTER LXVII

Rollant Fells Madequin

As soon as these knights of God had joined the French division, they saw where Madequin the Great was coming with his division. A great uproar arose, tumult and din, for both sides whooped in great war-cries, blew horns and sounded trumpets, and there was so much noise when all the men cried out at the same time, and so much sounding of great horns, high whistling of shrilling trumpets, strong sounds of stout pipes, and all sorts of noises of horses and mules, with many whisperings of sweet singing bells, that echoes rang from every hill and mountain and the earth trembled far and wide: every road shook back and forth, and indeed one could not say that those men were cowardly who stood there quite unshaken by the uproar. God gave such incredible strength to the hearts of his men that all this pleased them and made them more bold, as if they were about to go into the most splendid of feasts.

But on the other side, a great fear came into the hearts of many of the heathens as soon as they saw the French divisions. Now the divisions slowly drew together until there was no greater distance between them than one arrow-shot, and before they met, Madequin galloped forward on the field on his great horse, as if to see whether they were so courageous as to dare to try themselves against him. But when George saw Madequin, he spoke to Rollant, pulling in his bridle reins, and said, "See," says he, "how this arrogant boaster looks. Do not fear him, although he is big and strong. See how the exchange goes, for it is fitting for you to carry out the first charge of this battle."

Rollant bowed and said, "if that is God's will and yours, I shall be glad to be the first to redden a sword in the blood of the heathens."

Then he swiftly spurred his horse—which had belonged to Jamund—and grasped his spear in both hands, holding his shield close to him; and he rode rapidly, and drove his spear into Madequin's shield. But because he was extremely heavy, Rollant did not knock him from his horse or budge him at all. Madequin drove his spear at Rollant so hard that it went into his shield, but since God protected him the spear-shaft broke apart into three pieces, while Rollant was not wounded. Rollant was filled with great valor and he drew the good sword Dyrumdali;[1] and because this man was so tall that Rollant could scarcely reach his head, he rose up as high as he could and struck the sword down into the midst of Madequin's helmet, slashing his stout trunk and all its armor right down so that the sword stopped in the horse.

There was a great outcry on the field when he fell to the ground. When the heathens saw their leader fallen, they trembled greatly, and said, "Lord Madequin, in no land was there found a bigger or stronger man than you. Wonderfully great power has been given to that little man who so mightily cut your armor apart! By Makon, we have never seen a little dwarf give such a blow; if the other Frenchmen are as strong, Agulandus shall have a hard fall and soon all Africa shall sit in misery."

After Madequin had fallen, Rollant rode boldly forward at the heathens, slaying every man before him. And when George saw what Rollant was doing, he said, "Ride forward to help this man who has so heroically cleared the battlefield for us."

Then God's three knights, Oddgeir the Dane, and eleven peers rode towards Rollant from both sides, and all their division charged in hard battle. The knights of God drew their swords, which were so bright and sharp that light gleamed from them, and they struck down heathens on both sides. When the battle had begun to rage and Africans were falling, while others were defending themselves well and manfully, the glorious lord Archbishop Turpin came against the heathens bearing the holy cross, which was at this time so radiant with the glorious power of divine grace that it shone so brightly that its path gleamed as if it were lit by the rays of the sun; and it seemed so great and terrible to God's enemies that they did not dare look at it, but fled away from its presence as far as they could, until all of Madequin's division had dispersed.

[1] *b, Durumdali.*

But Rollant and his men killed so many men in a short while that it is not easy to tell how many. For while his peers were fresh, no one could expect to live who came before their weapons. And when they could go no further, Rollant, with the power of the holy cross and the support of God's three dear friends, who always went by his side, was to drive the first division of Agulandus off this way, as God arranged; but now, next we shall be told what the brave duke Girard was doing at this time.

A,a (88)

The emperor's host was all drawn up, and they blew fifty trumpets to ride forward, and rode along the slope. And when they had come down into the valley, they saw that all the land was covered with heathens, so great a multitude that it could not be counted ...

(91) Now we shall tell of King Karlamagnus and his deeds. He had now finished drawing up his divisions, and was himself well prepared, and the first division had come down the slope. And when the Africans[2] saw that, there was none so staunch in all their host that his might and strength did not shrink with fear. The heathens then saw that three knights[3] were riding down the mountain in front of the division wearing gleaming silver coats of mail and the best of armor, and they rushed at the first division of the heathens. Oddgeir was the standard-bearer, and Rollant was the other[4] leader of this division, which now rode down from the mountain ...

(93) Now the Africans rode against them from the other side, and their horns and trumpets sounded; the Christians also had many good horns and shrilling trumpets. Madequin[5] was mounted on a horse so swift that there was no better war-horse in all the African army.[6] He wore good armor, with a silver helmet on his head, and was girded with a long sword. His rich standard fluttered in the wind.

[2] *A*'s "French" is obviously incorrect.
[3] Presumably the three saints, explained later.
[4] Not in *a*, but cf. *Asp.* 8374.
[5] *a, Mandikvin.*
[6] *a*: "in all of Africa."

St. George rode forward with Rollant, holding his bridle and saying, "Do not be afraid, though he is grey-haired and huge."

Rollant answered, "Holy lord," says he, "I shall gladly do as you say."

When Rollant had seen this messenger[7] and heard his words, granted by God to help strengthen his courage and teach him knighthood, and when he had been granted the first attack, so that no one would prevent him from this, he saw Madequin, riding out before his division to see who wished to oppose him first. Rollant couched his spear and held his shield firmly before his breast, and they both turned their horses quickly: Madequin struck Rollant in the upper part of the shield, right into the shield, but his chain mail did not fail and the spear burst into three pieces.

Now Rollant charged at him with all his might, and his armor availed him little: Rollant stained all his sword with blood from his body. Their exchange began, as you may hear, as Rollant first couched his spear. This was a spear-shaft so hard that it did not break; although he was young and unused to knighthood—and so it was to be, although he had never been able to ride on a horse.[8] Next he gripped Dyrumdali and drew it, and hurried to strike him. Rollant was small, while he was as big as a giant; thus he could barely reach the sword to his neck and helmet: yet the sword took off all the front part of his helmet, as well as his scalp and right ear, so that the brains fell out. He had long, strong arms. The sword slit the mail in two places over his loins[9] and went straight through into the horse. Every part of his body that the sword touched was cut apart.[10]

When St. George, St. Demetrius, and St. Merkurius[11] and Oddgeir, their standard-bearer, saw Rollant fight so valiantly, riding at the first division of the heathens and cutting down all in his path as they came

[7] *A*, man, but cf. *Asp.* 8542.

[8] The preceding line is not in *Asp.*, but is in P_2; cf. Carl Haase, *Weitere Studien zur "Chanson d'Aspremont"* (Greifswald, 1917), p. 32, l. 34.

[9] Preceding clause is in *Asp.* but not in P_2.

[10] *a*; *A* summarizes the entire paragraph, after the first sentence: "Rollant threw him dead to the ground." Cf. *Asp.* 8567-85.

[11] The latter two were not identified earlier in *Asp.* either.—The names of the saints do not agree exactly with either *Asp.* or P_2: P_2 gives St. Morise in-

to him, they were so mightily encouraged that they felled all who were before them. But no one knew whether those who were felled by the saints were completely dead, only that they lay so still that they could not move or rise up.[12]

(94) Now those three knights who had ridden down from the mountain on white horses had come into the battle. They were St. George, St. Demetrius, and St. Merkurius. Rollant had struck the first blow, as St. George had granted to him. No one knew that such men had ever given such great blows. Fourteen leaders could be seen there, lying beheaded[13] near Madequin. But Oddgeir felled six men, and the Christians were so nimble that the Africans never got at their mail. The Frenchmen were well armed: they attacked those who were bare and felled a throng of heathens. There were not more than two thousand Christians, with seven hundred knights, while the total number of the heathens was twenty thousand.

God sent the Christians his grace there. The heathens broke their formations so that they could never again oppose the French. When the Africans saw that they had lost their leader, they became much distressed and said, "Lord Madequin," say they, "in no country was there a leader as good as you. This was a little boy who killed you: great power was given to such a little dwarf that he cut down the biggest of armed men! If the others are as strong, then Agulandus shall have a hard fall and all Africa shall suffer distress and affliction."

(95) That day Archbishop Turpin carried the holy cross; in all the army there was no more holy relic. And it seemed to the Africans that it was huge and powerful and brighter than the light of the sun, so that terror fell upon them ...

stead of Mercurie, and both give Domins/Domiste rather than Demetrius.—van Waard, p. 202, states that the saga's list, while disagreeing with P_2, agrees with W and P_3; this is clearly incorrect, as far as W is concerned. I have had no opportunity to check the point in P_3.

12 *A*: "move any of their limbs," but cf. *Asp.* 8596.

13 This section is not in *Asp.*

CHAPTER LXVIII

Girard's Men Meet the Troop of Ulien

When Girard left Emperor Karlamagnus, he rode quickly back to his men and called together all the leaders, telling them to prepare for battle. And when they were all so well equipped with horses and weapons that no troop could need to be better or more beautifully prepared than those whom the Duke had provided for, from the honors which God had given him, he spoke to the young men who had just taken up knightly arms and said, "Young men," says he, "make your hearts firm and bold. If your spears fail or are broken, grip your swords at once. Be just as agile at striking as at driving, whichever is of more use. Do not be at all afraid of the wicked, foul men of Africa; pursue their fugitives boldly and encourage each other to be steadfast, for, if our redeemer wishes, we shall take from them all that they improperly hold: land and wealth, gold and silver. Beyond that, I expect greater and more glorious rewards from almighty God for our pains and labor, for it is very good to lay down one's life for his sake."

All agreed to do as he said. Boz and Clares, his kinsmen, he put in the first row of their division. And as soon as the young knights had mounted their horses, they rode eagerly, competing to see who would be the first to redden his sword in the hard bones of the heathens.

The Duke turned behind the troop of Karlamagnus, intending, if it should so turn out, to come into the vicinity of the chief standard of Agulandus, for it seemed to him best to be engaged where the greatest force was gathered in front. Thus he went forward through a little wood, and did not want to mix with other divisions, taking the path to the right toward the chief standard of Agulandus. But some of the scouts of Agulandus were in the wood, and they became aware of the duke's men. One of them rushed off until he reached Agulandus, eagerly bringing the message; he said, "May Maumet help you, for you will now need that ! A group of Christian men are coming towards you, very well equipped with armor, and if you do not guard against them they shall certainly do harm to you."

When Agulandus heard that he was greatly astounded and his heart was touched with fear; so too were all the leaders who had come there with him. It was by the mercy of God that the hundred thousand men whom Agulandus had appointed under his standard should have been frightened, when those who were drawing near them were a group of about a hundred![1] And when the heathens saw the duke approaching, and heard what was being said, Ulien, who has been spoken of before, said, "Lord, do not be afraid of this matter. This lord has few men, not a sufficient force to damage your honors, for I think little of their might. Give me a train of twenty thousand knights and I shall give them a suitable resting place for the night:[2] if I have not killed them all before the sun sets, may my spurs be set on my feet wrong way around and my horse's forelock be taken off, and I myself turned out of favor."

Agulandus answered, "You are a bold knight and likely to give me good advice and faithful service, kinsman Ulien; thus I expect you will help me with your knightly skill. And if we can conquer that realm, I shall give it to you to govern, as heir of your kinsman Jamund."

Ulien answered, "By Makon, I await no more," and he went and kissed his right hand.

Galinger heard what they were saying and said, "It is amazing, Ulien, that you do not seem to recognize what you can or cannot do. Think of this so that you may have the luck to win the victory from the French: you might remember how little they cared for your pride, for you were forced to go with the bloody head of Jamund and were glad to get away from their sight."

Ulien was much enraged by Galinger's words, and if Agulandus had not been so near they might have immediately put each other's strength to the proof. Then, when Ulien had taken leave of the king, he went on his way with twenty thousand men well drawn up. Most of them had neither coats of mail nor helmets. They were attired in thick leather jerkins, with mailed hats on their heads; they had bows and

[1] *b*, ten thousand.
[2] *b*, winter.

quivers, and axes hung from their saddle-bows. Thus equipped, they went against the duke's men.

When Duke Girard saw them coming he called his men together, for they had been somewhat scattered before. He said, "Let us take care that we do not get separated. Let us crowd together and make our division so thickly packed that shield lines against shield and spear against spear; then when they attack we can receive them boldly, and protect ourselves well. Let no one move from his place until the heathens begin to tire, but then give them a determined charge."

They did as he said and fell into so strong and thick a division that if a glove had been thrown over them it would have been a long time before it came to the ground. And as Ulien came at them, lord Clares, the duke's nephew, galloped forward on the plain which was between the divisions, intending to be the first to begin the battle, if anyone wished to turn towards him. But when Ulien saw that he called out to a knight who was named Jafert, and said, "Jafert," says he, "look at that Christian there, behaving himself so haughtily: he is really frightened to death. Ride behind him and fell him before you; then all that division will fall into our power."

Jafert agreed to do this, and, spurring his horse, rode swiftly across the plain, driving his stout spear into the shield of Clares so hard that it stopped in his coat of mail; but the spear broke apart into two pieces. "See, knight," said Clares, "where you have come now."

And with that, he drove through his iron-bound shield and coat of mail and body, flinging him down to the ground, and he lifted his voice and said, "My old master taught me how to cast down arrogance this way!"

Then he went back to his place. Ulien urged his men to advance and the heathens attacked. But they gained little, for they could not break up the duke's host, and whoever came near was swiftly slain. Thus no one wished to come under their blows more than once, and many of the heathens fell, but none of the duke's men. Girard then called, "Advance boldly and drive these wicked curs before us, for they have no strength left."

They did so, giving the hardest of attacks, striking on both sides with cries and shouting, each one encouraging the other to sheathe his sharp-edged sword as often as possible in the blood-warm hearts of heathens. Soon a change could be seen as the Africans ran while the duke's men charged after them, killing every man they met with. Ulien pressed hard forward, and when he saw many fleeing he cried out, raising his voice and saying, "Shame awaits you, you wicked sons of whores! Turn back; do not betray us all this way, running away like cowards instead of defending yourselves manfully!"

But though Ulien cried out loudly, no one behaved as if he had heard him. Duke Girard now advanced at the heathens, riding with all his divisions: for although he was old now, no one needed to expect to live if he met him. Thus in a little while hundred upon hundred and thousand upon thousand of Ulien's men fell, so that the field was covered far and wide with the bodies of men. And when Ulien saw it turn out this way, yet he could do nothing about it, he said to himself, "I have become wretched: what shall become of me? I thought to win all of Italy under my power today and divide the realm among those who serve me, and now I shall have to flee like a most unfortunate man. No: let it never happen that I became cowardly!"

He turned his horse back and drove his spear at the nearest man, throwing him dead to the ground. Then he rode at the renowned knight Valterus, who had killed many heathens with his sword, and drove his spear into his shield, slitting his coat of mail and casting him to the ground dead. And he said, "Maumet knows that you will not defend the land from us any more!"

Now he rode around the outside, grieving over the fall of his men, grasping his sword with great might and killing many of God's knights, driving some shamefully from their horses and fixing others with his spear. In this attack he struck thirteen men from their mounts, and wounded many mortally. When lord Boz, brother of Clares,[3] saw how much harm Ulien was doing, he was filled with great valor, and wished to see whether he could put an end to the heathen's destructiveness;[4] thus he tried to meet with him, and he raised his voice, crying out to Ulien, "Wait for me," says he; "I want to meet with you alone."

Ulien looked at the duke and saw that there were many knights following him. He therefore did not wish to wait, and fled as fast as he

[3] Latter in *B* only.
[4] "Troll-ship."

could, until he stopped at a sand-hill, where he turned his horse and called back to lord Boz, saying, "You knight who wish to meet with me, come here, and by my faith I shall no longer flee from you."

Boz galloped his horse hard towards him while he came forward against him; each drove at the other so hard that neither could keep his seat and both fell off their horses. Ulien's golden helmet was much stained with dust. They both sprang up quickly and nimbly, each trying to get on his feet before the other, and grasped their weapons; and when Ulien looked about, he saw a great crowd of knights riding up to come to the aid of lord Boz. Thus he did not know what to do but rush quickly to his horse, and sticking his spearshaft down beneath him, vaulted onto the saddle; then he rode back as hard as he could to his men, and thus he parted with Boz that time. Ulien, and all of his men who were able to, fled, while lord Girard followed well and courageously, killing many of their band. We shall leave him thus, overtaking the host of Ulien, and turn to George and his comrades.

A,a (96)

Duke Girard of Satreborg,[5] bravest of leaders, ordered his men in three divisions, to make up three battalions of valiant, well-armed young men. "Young men," says he, "be strong and gallant. When your spear is broken, take up your sword at once. Have no dread of the Africans: they are wicked heretics, and if I do not drive twenty thousand heathens to flight with ten thousand men, never listen to my words again."

Girard had now ordered his troops. He spoke before them, urging and encouraging them, and said, "Good warriors," says he, "the Africans are a group of wicked men, useless and cowardly. I shall conquer what they possess from them and enrich our land and realm with their treasure. Now we shall bravely serve God, who has all things in his power, so that we may rejoice in eternal rewards."

They answered him affectionately, and all agreed that they would do his will.[6] Boz and Clares were their leaders and standard-bearers, and

[5] *a, Sakrisborg.*

[6] *a* adds: "in all things."

there were one thousand five hundred of the most powerful knights;[7] each of them vied with the others to show his valor.

Now a heathen spy went stealing away and rode quickly into a little wood, making for the chief standard of Agulandus at once. When he saw the king, he raised his voice and cried out, "Lord Agulandus," said he, "Makon bless you! There are now coming," says he, "on your right, a band of knights; in all the army there are no more handsome or better armed knights. These are believers in the son of St. Maria."

When the Africans heard this news they were all terrified; and when they saw the banner of the duke and all the armed troop, they were struck with great fear. And when Agulandus himself saw them coming, he had no impulse to laugh or be merry. Duke Girard now rode at them with mighty strength. His attack was not that of a slacker: he intended to give the heathens so hard a fight that they had never before experienced anything like it. It was evident how gallant he was, when he dared to combat the king who had fifty realms under his rule. In that division there were a hundred thousand of the best troops of the heathens who followed him. But he was certainly a wise and brave leader, like King Karlamagnus, who dared to attack him with sixteen thousand: before Agulandus could conquer France, he would certainly be grieved and angered!

(97) Duke Girard, a knightly,[8] strong, and grim enemy, rode strongly at them with three divisions, led by the lords Boz and Clares. In the first division were one thousand five hundred knights, and they rode so close together that one could not have seen a sparrow-hawk flying in the midst of their spears. The Africans saw the Christians draw near, with their weapons gleaming in the sunshine, and they rode quickly to tell Agulandus. When he heard this, it seemed strange to him. Ulien then said to the king, "Lord," said he, "do not be afraid: they do not have enough force to do you any harm. Half of our troop eats more meat at one meal than all of them. All their power is not worth a penny.[9] If you will give me twenty thousand knights, I shall so

[7] *a* boldest men.

[8] ? *haeferskr* presumably renders P_2 *chevauche*.

[9] *A*, glove; P_2, I denier.

deal with those who are now coming here that they shall all lie dead before you go to sleep. If I do not do so, then let the spurs be cut from my feet[10] and the forelock be clipped from my horse; that is the proper way to treat a cowardly knight."

Agulandus then answered, "You are a valiant knight, worthy of much praise, and my nephew.[11] I want you to help me now with your advice and knighthood; if we can conquer that realm, I will give it to you, free of tributes and duties."

Ulien then answered, "I shall not wait for anything more," says he. And he went at once to kiss his hand.

But the old Galinger did not by any means wish to agree to that, and he said, "Lord," says he, "now I am very angry. You sent me to King Karlamagnus, and I went as your messenger to demand your rights and make threats on your behalf, and find out their strength. But King Karlamagnus is a great hero, and so are all those who follow him. They will all let themselves be cut in pieces alive before they will renounce their God;[12] they are no cowards, and before you drive them out of this land they will offer you stiff resistance. Do not believe anything that the boaster Ulien says."

Ulien became very angry:[13] he shook and seemed to burn as if he had been set on fire, with his eyes blazing like coals, when he heard what Galinger said. He might have let his anger blaze out through the host and they might have then quarreled badly, if King Agulandus had not been standing by at the time.

(98) When Ulien left the king, he lifted his voice and said, "Follow me," says he, "Makon knows that I shall welcome them as best I can."

He took with him as great a host as he wished, which was more than twenty thousand knights. Agulandus stayed behind under the chief standard, and with him remained Abilant[14] and King Meliades, and Modas[15] the Great, and Amuste, with his two sons. When Ulien had

[10] ? The mss. seem to say "from my hand."
[11] "Sister-son."
[12] *a* adds "and their faith"; there is no equivalent in P_2.
[13] *A*: "Ulien did not say anything."
[14] P_2, Boidanz.
[15] *Moadas*.

drawn up his troops, he made Jafert[16] leader of the first division: this man had followed the king out over the sea. But they were not so well-prepared as they had been before, for they had neither coats of mail nor helmets,[17] only bows, and quivers on their backs, and mailed caps on their heads, with axes bound to their saddle-bows. In all this division there was no other weapon.

Now a division of the French army came towards them. No man has ever seen as many men so well armed as that division, which lord Girard had provided for with all the good things which God had given him. Their leader led such a closely packed division that if an apple had been thrown in their midst a long part of the morning would have passed before it fell to the ground. Clares rode alone out before the division, a good crossbow-shot in front of the others, and raised up his standard.

Then Ulien said to his comrade Jafert, "This division is a gift to us: all Africa shall gain by their[18] arms."

Jafert asked to be granted the first attack and Ulien agreed to this. They rode at once, galloping their horses as fast as they could go, and Jafert rammed into the shield of Clares so that the shield failed; but his coat of mail was not torn, and the spear broke into pieces. Clares now struck at his iron-bound shield, which did him no good at all: the spear plunged deep into his breast.

The Africans rode at the Christians, but they were well-armed with the best of armor and war-horses and drove them off boldly, while the Africans had no coats-of-mail, except for leather vests.[19] The Christians did irreparable harm to the Africans, slashing heads and shoulders, limbs and bodies so that all of them wanted to flee. Ulien cried out to his men four[20] times, saying, "You wicked sons of whores," said he, "you are betraying us when you fail in such great need!"

[16] P_2 Jafer.

[17] The *Asp.* text is picked up again in this sentence; the detail about the helmets is found there, but not in P_2.

[18] *a*, our; *A* is closer to *Asp.*

[19] A detail which is in P_2 but not *Asp.*

[20] *A*, three; cf. P_2: *Asp.* does not specify.

So many lay slain and fallen from their horses that all the field was covered with them. The French were well armed, but the Africans were poor in weapons and bare. As soon as lord Girard came with this troop, they cut down the crowd of heathens at once. The Africans could not withstand them longer when they saw their men so cut in pieces that the plain was covered with their bodies.

Ulien then said, "Wretch that I am," says he, "what shall become of me? I thought to subject all Europe[21] to my rule and divide the realm among my men—to lay Christianity waste and disgrace it, and give honor and strength to our faith; now our enemies are overpowering us, while we, in our misfortune, flee like cowards."[22]

Then he turned back on his good horse, one so good it would be hard to find his equal. Whoever met with him got a hard battle. When he saw Valteri[23] doing a great deal of harm to the heathens, he made for him and rammed his shield and coat of mail; the spear went into his heart[24] and pushed him dead from his horse. When Clares saw that he sobbed with all his heart, while the Africans felled Christians.

There could be seen many good horses, abandoned by their lords, going around the field with broken bridles. Ulien was mounted on a red horse so good that a better could not be found. He rode through the throng grieving over the distress of his men and using his spear with all his might. His spear-shaft was from Africa: it was made of the wood which the Africans call dand,[25] a wood which can hardly be bent or broken. His spear was very sharp. He rode, and found none so proud as to praise or boast of his lot if he met with Ulien: if he struck or attacked, neither stirrup nor saddle-girth was of much help. In these attacks he felled fourteen men from their horses. If he had been a Christian, neither Rollant nor Oliver would have been a better knight than he!

(99) Duke Basin,[26] who had been looking for him all day,[27] now

[21] So P_2; *Asp.*, France.
[22] *a*: "; now I am become like an unfortunate coward, put to flight."
[23] *Valter*.
[24] So *Asp.*; P_2, chest.
[25] *a, dant; Asp.* fust d'aul—cf. n. 6 to ch. 54.
[26] *a, Bosin.*
[27] In P_2 but not *Asp.*

came galloping up and, raising his voice, cried out behind him, "If you turn in flight, you shall fall!"

When Ulien saw the duke, who had looked for him all day, coming holding his spear couched with a thousand five hundred knights riding after him, there was nothing he could do. He turned quickly from the throng and did not stop until he came to a slope, where he took his shield and held it firmly to protect himself, his feet jammed into the stirrups with all his might. Then he raised his voice and cried out to Lord Basin, saying, "By Makon,[28] I consider myself dead[29] if I catch you without companions!"

The duke then advanced on a horse from Gaskunie, with a mane of a different color from its body, given to him by King Droim. When they met on their swift horses each attacked the other with hard thrusts,[30] so that neither could hold his seat in the saddle and both fell in such a way that their shoulders lay in the sand. Anyone who was under the crag near the olive-tree and saw how these two rode the horses could also see that they jumped straight up and took up their shields and spears.

Now Ulien saw the Christians draw near him, and he knew he was likely to meet his death there. He hurried to his horse and, leaning on his spear, mounted: woe to the stirrups which received him! Four thousand Africans now came and surrounded Ulien, to protect him, and Clares could not approach him then.

Messengers now ran to the chief standard of Agulandus and raised their voices crying, "Lord Agulandus," said they, "everything is going badly for us today. The Christians are so clothed in iron and steel that no one can wound them: you shall not see four of your men come back."

When the king had heard their message he was furious and had eighty thousand men under his command prepare themselves.

[28] *A*, my faith; cf. *Asp.* 8769.
[29] Probably this should read "consider *your*self dead." Cf. *Asp.* 8769.
[30] *a* adds "and blows."

CHAPTER LXIX

A Setback for the Heathens

When Rollant had dispersed all of Madequin's division, killing many and driving the others to flight, he next came to the second division of Agulandus, which was led by Acharz of Amflor. A few of the Christian troop had fallen and both men and horses were very tired. When Acharz saw them coming, he was amazed at how quickly they had driven through the first division: but because his host was a formidable one, and well supplied with weapons, they joined battle fiercely, so that there would now be very great peril if reinforcements did not arrive to help Rollant; where human power came from shall be told.

Emperor Karlamagnus had appointed as leaders of his second division King Salomon and Earl Hugi, and when the battle began they had waited to see how it went, as has been said, instead of joining the battle quietly. Soon they could hear blows and great crashes, so that Earl Hugi said, "Lord Salomon, guard the chief standard with most of our troop while I go into the battle with a thousand of the best knights and see whether I can give any help to our comrades. I expect that Rollant and Oddgeir have enough trouble: God grant that they may not come to grief!"

They did this, then, and Earl Hugi rode with a thousand knights. Nor were they equipped like vagabonds, for they had rugged coats of mail and strong helmets and were mounted on fine fresh horses. Hugi asked King Salomon to follow boldly and give them help, and he agreed to do so. Earl Hugi was a powerful man, very tall, and strong in all valor and prowess. He shouted a great war-cry and encouraged his men, saying, "Good friends," says he, "let us ride bravely to our comrades, giving such great blows that no armor can withstand them: let it be seen that there are no better warriors than Frenchmen!"

They did so, striking with their swords on both sides and driving spears hard, again and again; and so they made their way until they came to the front, where Oddgeir the Dane was. And when Oddgeir saw Earl Hugi, he said, "Praise be to God! We comrades are much in need of your arrival."

The earl answered, "God grant that it will be of help: now I have come to the place where I most wished to be."

Now the battle became most furious, for each side performed with all its might. So many of the heathen knights fell that soon the field was covered far and wide with their bodies, for Rollant truly proved that Dyrumdali could bite, while God's holy champions George and his comrades advanced boldly, making many heathens bow before their weapons. Earl Hugi asked Oddgeir the Dane who these three knights were who advanced so nobly; he answered, "My good friend, they are God's saints, George, Demetrius, and Merkurius, whom he has sent to lend strength to his Christians."

The earl was most gladdened by this explanation, and lifted his voice to say, "Let us accomplish as much as we can, stretch out our arms as far as we can: for God's help is now fully granted to us!"

When the battle was raging hardest, Archbishop Turpin came forth with the Lord's cross before the heathen division, and immediately a change took place, as it had before. The troops of Acharz, who had been fighting with great valor up until then, were struck with fear as soon as they beheld the cross of the Lord, while the Christians were much strengthened by its arrival and pushed on in such hard attack that the heathens burst into flight. Thus many a shield could now be seen broken apart, and thousands of heathens dislodged from their mounts; others became pale as coats of mail were slit and helmets slashed open together with skulls.

And while Acharz saw his men fleeing or cut down dead, one after another, he also saw King Salomon coming with his troop, and, in the third place, he saw the holy cross advancing in shining brightness. All of these together weighed most heavily on him, and he said to those who stood next to him, "A great wonder is revealed here today, for there is nothing at all we can do against them with good men; this will be another disastrous encounter for us. Who ever saw such a marvel as that a tree, which I believe the Christians call a cross, should strike such terror into good fighting men that they cannot do anything at all? When it appeared to our division it seemed as though we lost our minds, for we saw nothing with the sight of our eyes, and by no means could we look upon its brightness or come near its power. Our wits were turned, and we behaved like madmen, driven frantic: the more often we looked at it, the more our fear grew. If the lord of the Christians was tormented on this tree it is indeed proper for them to honor it, for never have our gods revealed such might at any time—and, by Maumet, I am not going to stay here any longer!"

He turned his horse, then, and fled rapidly, and so did all his men, until none remained behind. But the Frenchmen pursued the fugitives so sharply that they killed every one they could and two thousand fell among the fleeing host. The French host now scattered a great deal, for each was slaying whichever fugitive was nearer; they chased the heathens a long way through fields and woods, but most fled to the third division and stopped there. Rollant was foremost among the pursuers, with the eleven peers, Oddgeir the Dane, Earl Hugi, and many others of the bravest men, while God's three knights went further behind, in a circuit, with Archbishop Turpin and the holy cross.

The French next came to the third division of the heathens, which was commanded by King Kalades of Orphanie; there was a great multitude of men with him, for Acharz of Amflor and many of those who had escaped with him had now joined him. Rollant then spoke to those who followed him: "Let us move boldly at these wicked[1] curs who stand before us here, for they can scarcely withstand us like good men. They do not value gilded helmets or bright silver coats of mail, for they prefer a rotten sour apple to a fine war-horse with its trapping. Let them find out that Christians know how to make a sword bite!"

Then they all shouted a great war-cry and attacked eagerly. But although those who were before them were not richly dressed with precious armor, they nonetheless came sharply into battle, for they were so skilled with the bow that it almost seemed as if two or three bolts flew from their strings at once, and they were shot so hard that there was scarcely any armor that they did not pierce through. Thus they did a great deal of harm to Rollant's troop, most of all because

[1] *b*, dead.

many good warriors were now losing their mounts before their poisoned arrows. This would have led to terrible peril, unless God in his mercy looked after his men. And it so happened that right at this time King Salomon came, with four thousand of the most valiant knights, and they gave the heathens a hard blow, driving many of them disgracefully from their mounts, so that the Christians who had been on foot were able to get good horses.

Now a stiff battle began again with neither group holding back among those who were able. All the Frenchmen fought valiantly, often staining their bright weapons in streams of red blood. But the most wonderful thing of all was how bold Rollant proved in this battle; he had a heart as bold as a lion, grimmest of animals. He rode from crowd to crowd, biting so with his sword that the hard battle-wand deftly broke many a man's chest apart; and he laid so many heathens on the field that it might be said to be beyond all probability. He reddened his sword so vigorously that he struck strong men in full armor right down the middle, so that the two parts fell down on either side of the horse. All his peers also made a great havoc. Oddgeir the Dane, King Salomon, and Earl Hugi spared neither flesh nor bone of the heathens. When Oddgeir saw how Rollant was attacking, he said, "May God strengthen your arm: he who stands nearest you is better off than he who stands further away!"

King Kalades had raised up his standard in the midst of his division, and Rollant, who could see this, called to his four young knights, Grelant, Estor, Baeringur and Otun,[2] who were named before, saying to them, "Good comrades, what is the best plan? I see where the standard of the wicked Kalades is standing, and I would very much like to break it down. If we can make our way there, this division might quickly be broken up."

Grelant answered, "Attack it courageously and we shall surely be able to break it down, for those who are guarding it have no fit armor."

Rollant said, "May God reward you for your valor! If he allows us to return to our possessions alive, you shall be granted great honor."

Then these four[3] champions galloped away from their men, forward into the midst of the heathen's division, in so great a charge that each

[2] *Othun.*
[3] *B*, three.

and every one fell back well out of their way, so terrified and frightened that no one saw any cause for rejoicing. It went as Grelent thought: many were ill prepared for their blows and strokes, and they broke down the standard and killed all those who were supposed to guard it. And when Kalades saw that, he raged in his heart and aimed at Grelent, thinking to drive his spear through him. But Grelent ducked away from the stroke and drove his spear through Kalades; and just as he tried to push him out of his saddle, the spear-shaft broke, but Grelent drew his sword and cut off his head, saying, "Woe upon you, wicked heathen! You are so heavy that you have broken my good spear-shaft; but all the same, you now have a wound that no physician from Africa will be able to heal."

Rollant galloped his horse swiftly and met Acharz of Amflor. Letting his banner sink down, he drove his spear through his shield and coat of mail right into his heart, and said, "Knight, you thought you did well when you fled away from your division, but now I want to tell you that you shall not go from here on your feet."

Then Rollant drew his sword and struck on both sides. They made so good an attack that in a little while they killed sixty heathens, and two kings over and above that, without losing a single drop of blood.

When Oddgeir missed Rollant, he was much worried, and feared that he might have been driven from his horse or slain; he called to Earl Hugi, saying, "My good companion, let us seek at once for our best of comrades, for Rollant has gone off and I do not know what has become of him."

"Gladly," said the earl. They now pressed into the battle where they heard much shouting and crashing, and Oddgeir called, "Praise be to God! I can certainly see the white helmet of Rollant in front of us: let us fly there and help him."

They did so, riding on the way until they came where Rollant and his comrades were attacking vigorously. Rollant said, "Welcome, good comrades! Let us all make a stand here together."

Oddgeir answered, "My heart would never have rejoiced again if I had lost you."

At that moment Archbishop Turpin came with the holy cross, with God's three knights and beloved friends following him. A great disturbance then arose in the division of Kalades; all the heathens drew back together and lay face down on their shields as soon as they saw that blessed relic, then they drew back and took to flight, with outcry and disorder. But the Frenchmen charged after them and made a proper attack from the rear, striking them down like cattle. In this drive they killed more than a thousand and drove them over valley and ridge. Some fled to shelter in the division of Eliades, and some went up on the mountain like mountain sheep.

But who can tell others what joy almighty God granted to his servants through that great marvel he manifested at that time? For although great, strong heathens stood with all their might and natural knighthood against the Christians for a while, all their valor crumbled and turned to nothing as soon as God manifested before their eyes the power of his holy cross, granting also that his friends should see, with their mortal eyes, his saints, whom he vouchsafed to send them: for the Christians were then as strengthened by their approach and the sight of the holy cross as the Africans were weakened. In that attack many of the Christians had fallen, but very few in comparison to what would have happened in normal human circumstances.

A,a (95)

... Now our knights approached the division of Akarz[4] of Amflor. There were twenty thousand in the first division of Africans; these had had Madequin, whom Rollant slew before their eyes, as standard-bearer. The four following him[5] felled so many that no one could count them.

The holy cross was so bright that all the day was illuminated by its rays and light. But to Akarz of Amflor it seemed strange and amazing how perilously and rapidly they reached his side and rushed upon his men. But Rollant, brandishing Dyrumdali, struck strong blows on both sides; he never shrank with dread after St. George strengthened him, and it is, in fact, said of him that never again did he bring about such destruction of life as in this battle.

[4] *a, Akadz.*

[5] I.e., Rollant.

(100) Now we shall tell of the deeds of Karlamagnus[6] and St. George, who came to the battle every day with three men.[7]

... wonderfully sturdy and proud, powerful, gallant, and courageous. He said to his men, "Lords," says he, "what are you doing, and why are you afraid? Why are you not seeking for these men's inheritance and wealth, which they and their forefathers have possessed? We shall become rich at their expense, taking their blessings and honors; we shall divide their realm and wealth among us. We are at least a hundred against every two of their men. Know, certainly, if you let even one of them escape, I shall never be happy as long as I live."

Then battle broke out, so hard that no one got much protection from helmet or coat of mail. The Christians were much vexed. Their horses were exhausted, and could not run; many could not go as much as a mile.[8] If God did not send them help quickly, Karlamagnus would be afflicted with sorrow and a thousand children in his realm would be fatherless and impoverished.[9]

Now King Salomon came, and with him the men of Angio[10] and Mansel[11] and the Bretons. They rode quietly, making no noise, until they came so close to the battle they were no more than an arrow-shot away. Then Earl Hugi spoke: "Lord Salomon," says he, "stay here with our dragon-standard and I will go to see how our Christian men are faring. Rollant is a child, though Oddgeir is a doughty man: I greatly fear that we may lose Rollant. If we are in need, come to our help."

The king said, "Go, with God's blessing."

The earl then rode away, with a thousand brave knights. These men were not armed like servant boys but had secure coats of mail that would never fail before weapons, and they were mounted on such good

[6] So in P_2; *Asp.* Roland.

[7] An odd rendering of *Asp.* 8815?—The translator, or his source or his copyist, has jumped over something here and left the text in some confusion. As van Waard remarks the fault is probably that of an earlier copyist, since ***B*** 69 has a résumé of the missing action.

[8] *a*, half a mile.

[9] At this point, the sequence no longer conforms to either P_2 or *Asp.*

[10] *a, Angikarmenn*; *Asp.* Angevin.

[11] *A, Oransel.*

horses that there were no better in the world. The earl gave the victory-cry of Emperor Karlamagnus. He had the heart of a lion; this earl was the most handsome and brave of men.[12] He said to his men, "Good knights," says he, "let us ride on our way and aim at the chief standard of the heathens. I bid you strike hard, so that no protection withstands our blows, to the honor and glory of Frenchmen."

The earl could not accomplish so much that he became the equal of Oddgeir the Dane,[13] yet he and Samson and Riker gave strong blows. Oddgeir then said, "Lord Hugi, do you see the knight who is mounted on a white horse, who keeps killing heathens? That is St. George, and the two knights with him are Demetrius and Merkurius, whom God has sent here from heaven to strengthen our Christendom."

(101) Akarz of Amflor now found his men losing heart as the Frenchmen quickly felled them; and he saw the division of King Salomon attacking, and Christians killing heathens, with the holy cross shining and gleaming. He then said to his men. "Our four gods were not worth a bad penny: they gave us into the power of the Christians,[14] and now they have been crushed into pieces. It is fitting that the Christians honor and praise their God. See, here, the cross on which he suffered; we cannot look towards it, and by no means can we approach its power, for it turns our wits and we go mad and frantic. The more often we see that cross, the more we are in trouble. Maumet knows that I do not wish to stay here any longer."

And he[15] fled as quickly as possible.

Akarz of Amflor now fled as fast as he could with his troop, his sword drawn, pale and colorless,[16] while the French cried after them and struck them with spears and swords, conquering so many of them that more than ten thousand heathens lay there dead. The French followed them through a little wood, killing them with all speed; then

[12] Brandin's punctuation of *Asp.* indicates that all these words of praise seem to apply to Charlemagne rather than Huon, and to be part of his address to his men.

[13] An apparent misunderstanding of *Asp.* 9388-89.

[14] *A*, our enemies; cf. *Asp.* 9405.

[15] *a*, they.

[16] *A*, craven.

they came to the division of Kalades[17] of Orphanie.[18] Earl Hugi raised up his voice and cried, "Now it is fitting for us to show our valor! Hit these accursed people hard, these who have no regard for helmet or coat of mail and do not value the best horse more than a sour apple."

They now fought bravely against our men. If God does not watch over them now, and send Salomon and his men, then we shall lose both Oddgeir and the earl!

(102) Now the divisions of Christians and a third division of heathens came up, and the French struck with all their might; then King Salomon came, boldly helping them, with five thousand of the best troops, protected by secure coats of mail and good helmets. These men attacked the heathens so valiantly that they struck through heads and shoulders, limbs and bodies—the Frenchmen gave hard combat there.

One group was bare, the other armed. The bravest[19] became terrified; the rest, frantic. They drew back and howled like wolves, shooting from their horn-bows, so that they killed three hundred of the Frenchmen's war-horses. Because of this many had to go on foot.

(103) The battle became very fierce. Everyone did what he could. Many were disgracefully ridden down by horses, for at this battle everyone was breaking spears with sword blows. Rolland could be seen there, riding through a throng, always giving the heaviest blows. Earl Hugi and Riker conquered greatly, and Oddgeir said, "Rollant," said he, "God knows you are much to be praised. I would not have believed it yesterday if such things had been told me of you!"

"Yes," said Rollant; "If God gives me strength, I shall reward you for this work and faithful service."

Hugi and Riker won a great victory there, as did Duke Oddgeir and Samson, the powerful knight.[20] Rollant then[21] called to his four

[17] *Calides.*

[18] *a, Arfanie.*

[19] I.e., of the heathens.

[20] *A* only. Although Unger's punctuation and note do not suggest it, it is necessary to conflate *A* and *a* here; cf. *Asp.* 9478-80.

[21] *a* only.

comrades, Estor, Baeringur, and Otun, and the young man who was named Grelent, who had been born in Bretland[22] and was related to King Salomon.[23] He entertained King Karlamagnus in his hall and was a foster-son of the emperor from childhood; he even slept in the king's bedchamber. There was no better singer than he, nor anyone who understood more of the craft of poetry, and it was he who wrote the first song in the Breton tongue. But in this need, Rollant armed him. Among the young knights, none was his equal except Rollant.[24]

Rollant now said to his men, "What is our best plan now? Look at the banner standing there which belongs to the wicked Galinger.[25] If we could drive apart the throng in their division, they would certainly perish and be lost."[26]

Grelent answered, "Let us attack them quickly, for they have no good weapons and will never be able to withstand us."

"Yes," said Rollant, "You are certainly the son of a brave hero."— And none was a better knight than he.[27]

Now when young Grelent had agreed with Rollant, they directed their armed men at those who were bare. None of these wished to be in their path, and thus they cut apart the division of Kalades,[28] all of whom were so terrified that they did not know what to do. Now Grelent ran at Kalades and struck his shield and him, and as he pushed him out of his saddle the spear broke and he drew his sword at once and gave him so great a wound that no one could have been found who could heal it.

Then Rollant rushed up as quickly as his horse could bear him[29] and lowered the strong spear with its banner, charging at Akarz of Amflor with such great power that all his armor did him no good; he shoved him dead from the horse at once. Rollant then drew his sword, as did

[22] Britanny.

[23] *A*, Samson; cf. *Asp.* 9483.

[24] *A* adds "and Otun," but cf. *Asp.* 9493.

[25] *Asp.* Calides, who clearly should be named here.

[26] *A*: "we would certainly be victorious;" cf. *Asp.* 9498.

[27] This may be part of Rollant's remarks about Grelent's father; Brandin so punctuates the corresponding line in *Asp.* (9506).

[28] *Calidis*.

[29] *a*, as he could; cf. *Asp.* 9531.

his five comrades, and they[30] felled there more than sixty heathens. In addition, they killed two kings in the sight of their men, without losing so much as a drop of their own blood. They accomplished so much that ever afterwards they were honored as long as they lived. But Floriades and Manuel fled as fast as they could, suffering both grief and sickness of heart.

(104) When Oddgeir missed Rollant, and did not know where he had gone, he was afraid that he might not see him again. And it was not strange that he feared for his state, since he had been put in his care. He said, then, to Earl Hugi, "Lord," says he, "matters have taken a bad turn: I do not know where the king's nephew has gone. But in the troop that is there in front of us, I hear a great uproar, and surely I see Rollant there, under a bright helmet. Now I ask you to join me to help them as quickly as possible."

The earl answered, "We shall do that gladly."

Now Oddgeir arrived where Rollant was and said, "You have not held to our agreement. If God had not given me the comfort of finding you safe, I swear to God that I would not longer bear shield or armor."

Now the Africans had deserted three of their leaders. The holy cross had so terrified them and put them to flight that they all were cast down by cowardice. Almighty God cherished King Karlamagnus and his deeds and the good people whom he steered, for he did not wish them to be lost; rather, he defended them, and sent them his three knights to help them, his friends, in favor with him: so openly that all saw them and recognized them and heard their voices, especially St. George, who led the other two. The Christians were greatly heartened by this while the Africans fell back together and took to flight, with the Frenchmen in pursuit killing them like wolves after sheep ...

[30] *a*, he.

CHAPTER LXX

Rollant's Progress

Three divisions of the army of Agulandus had now been completely overcome by the Christians. Rollant came next to the fourth division, which was led by Eliades and Pantalas. They were great warriors and had never been accustomed to flee from battle, and their troops were better equipped with weapons and clothing, as well as valor and strength, than any other in the army of Agulandus. When they heard a great deal of uproar and loud crashing, and saw attack and pursuit in all directions near them, there were much astonished, and said to each other, "What can be going on here? It cannot be so bad that there are Frenchmen coming right at us, coming so quickly right through three divisions of our men! But if this is indeed the case, then things look very bad for our cause. But whatever has happened to the others, so evil a spirit shall never come upon us as to turn craven and cowardly before the Christians. Those in the first three divisions were probably not as well supplied with courage and weapons as our troop is."

When Rollant had pursued the fugitives until he came close to the fourth division, it appeared that he was short of men, since many of his comrades had fallen and most of those who survived were exhausted by wounds and labor. He therefore called a knight to him, and said, "Go to Emperor Karlamagnus, bringing him my greetings, and ask him to come quickly to help us. Tell him exactly what has happened; especially, how much help almighty God granted him today, through his holy cross and glorious knights."

He went on his way, while Rollant drew his men, who had scattered somewhat in the rush of battle, into a firm battalion. King Salomon had not yet arrived, so Rollant's division amounted to little against so great a multitude, while Eliades had more than fifteen thousand to begin with before they were joined by some of the fugitives. Rollant and his peers, Oddgeir and Earl Hugi, stood foremost of the

Christians, letting out a great war-cry. Bitter battle now broke out for the fourth time. These heathens closed with them so violently that the Frenchmen thought they had not been so hard pressed before that day—these men were agile and daring in battle, and had extremely good weapons.

Rollant encouraged his men, especially the new knights. One of them, of the lowest rank, had fallen in the first charge, but those who survived stood valiantly. Grelant did not hold back from giving the heathens strong blows: he was a very strong, powerful man, When the battle was at its hardest, the knights said among themselves, "Praise be to almighty God," say they, "and to the good lord Emperor Karlamagnus, who took us from servitude and bondage! We have been lucky. Let us attack valiantly while God lends us life and strength, for a quick, courageous death is much better than allowing our leader to suffer shame and disgrace." Then they all cried out together, raising their voices and saying, "Let him never be counted a worthy man who now holds back as much as is worth a counterfeit penny!"—and with this they struck so hard that no helmet or coat of mail could withstand them.

At this moment, Salomon came with his host, and gave a sharp charge. One might see many men overthrown here, including a number of Christians, but by God's will, the heathens fell most often. Rollant, and those near him, began to tire from the great attack.[1] Many good swords were broken in this battle, spears sprang so hard and so often that it was like a shower of arrows. Many bold warriors were driven shamefully from their horses, shields were slashed so suddenly that many lost their lives when the place where the blow fell was before them; coats of mail were slit, helmets riven, and men became pale, their arms weary.

When things had gone on this way for a while, King Droim came into the battle, with seven thousand men, all well equipped with weapons. He joined in the attack as soon as he arrived there. But since they had an overwhelming force to deal with, and they were too few to be a match for the division of Eliades, and because almighty God wanted it to be clear to the French that they were mortal men, so that

[1] *B*: "began to attack strongly those who were there."

they would realize what they owed to him and that their host was increased by a heavenly band, those who had come to the battle first that morning became much exhausted, some because of wounds, but most of them because of heat and the great perspiration caused by all their labor, and the horses were also exhausted, so that many were forsaken then. And as their situation reached this point, the excellent lord Archbishop Turpin appeared with his holy relic, and God's three knights following him. Although the host of Eliades seemed mighty, the same change came over them at the cross's coming as with the others before, so that they said to each other, "Woe upon that standard-bearer who has come here! His standard is so high that it touches the heavens, and so bright and terrible that no one may look at it. Little is our state improved by its coming! Although we had trouble fighting the French before, that was still tolerable for brave men; but now there is nothing we can do. Thus we will do better not to stay here any longer, for everyone who does not flee is certainly dead."

So they did, casting their shields on their backs and taking flight, breaking up the division. But as soon as the Christians saw that, they pursued boldly and felled them one after another. And when Eliades saw his men running, while the French pressed them with all their might, he said, "Never, in the long time that I have been able to stand among brave men, has such a time of misery come over me. It is the truth that those who trust in the pure Christ[2] have tremendous power, for they may conquer all they wish. I thought it could never happen that I should flee from battle, but now it has so come about that while that is bad, everything else is worse. But it is well for those who first leave some of the strong champions of Karlamagnus on the field."

Then he turned his horse in the direction of the twelve peers, who kept on killing Africans again and again, and he drove his stout spear against the first one he met so hard that it slit his coat of mail and punctured his heart. He threw him dead to the earth, then raised his voice and cried, "By Makon and all the gods, there is no point in staying here any longer! I believe I have avenged many of my men in this one who has now been made to bow."—And he spurred his horse and galloped away swiftly in flight.

[2] Literally, "white Christ;" cf. C-V sub *hvítr*, p. 302.

Rollant could see what Eliades had done, and he was much grieved by the fall of his peer; he said, "God, who made me, knows that you would not escape, you worst of heathens, if my horse were not so exhausted: yet you shall have a slight remembrance." He grasped a spear and turned toward him, hitting him behind the saddle-bow. Eliades was slightly wounded. A knight who followed him then said, "You were given a message there, Eliades."

He answered, "It was harmful for me, as he who sent it wished, for if it had struck before as it just did behind, I would certainly be dead. Let us ride swiftly and not wait for another."

The Frenchmen pursued the fugitives so valiantly that they did not realize it when their horses were about to fall down dead;[3] then they proceeded on foot, continuing to stretch their hands forward, never ceasing to slay heathens and pursue them. There is no need to say much more of this, beyond that when Rollant and many others of his comrades were mounted on horses, they attacked a detachment of the heathens which were at some distance from the others, and it is said that they drove them into a circle and surrounded them. They were then so overcome by fatigue that they did not have the strength to attack them; but the heathens did not by any means dare to attack them, so things remained that way on both sides for a while.

We shall leave them there, and say something of the knight Rollant sent to the Emperor. He rode swiftly, as was said before, until he found Karlamagnus, whom he greeted, saying, "May God help you, glorious lord! Your kinsman Rollant sends you greetings and asks you to come to help him and his men at once."

The emperor received him well and said, "Your horse is very tired, knight; but what tidings do you have to tell us?"

"Many, lord," said he. "First, that three divisions of the heathens have been dispersed; the greater part of the host has been slain and the rest put to flight. And it is to be said of your kinsman Rollant that he showed so much valor today that it is beyond all probability. From the time he started in the morning, he has continued with the same vigor all day, until, when we parted, he had come to the fourth division, and was standing there before overwhelming force. There is also this to be

[3] *b* adds, under them.

said, which is most sublime: almighty God granted you unheard-of help today, for his holy cross was revealed as a great wonder. Before it fell more of the heathens than could be counted. Beyond this, there came, early in the morning, three knights, who advanced fearlessly, slaying one heathen after another. I do not know who they are, since I have not spoken with them, but I have heard others say that they were saints, sent by God to help you."

When the emperor had heard the knight's message he was much more joyous than can be told and fell on his knees before God, saying, with hands uplifted, "Much more praise and manifold thanks do I owe to you, almighty God, than I can express. Truly your grace surpasses all things. Blessed be you, good lord James: for all the might God shows us in this land, he grants for your sublime prayer and deserts."

Then he took five thousand of the bravest knights with him, leaving Fagon in charge of the troop that was left behind with the king's chief standard and telling him to follow later. The emperor and his troop now rode swiftly over the field where the dead lay; everyone was astonished at how many men had fallen there in one day. The emperor did not stop until he arrived where Rollant stood on guard, as has been said before, for wherever Karlamagnus met his men, he asked where Rollant was, but they said they did not really know.

When Rollant saw the emperor approach, he turned to meet him with his men. But the heathens at once took to their feet and fled, and because it was very late in the day they were not pursued. When the emperor saw Rollant much overcome by exhaustion he spoke to him playfully, saying, "How is it, kinsman, that your arms have become so heavy that they cannot strike with a sword? Or are your weapons so blunt that they are unable to bite?"

Rollant answered, "I think, lord, that it is some of each."

Karlamagnus then said, "Many a man's strength is worn out by less than you have achieved today, for which God be praised! But now the fighting shall stop for a while during the night, though the rest shall not be long or easy. But you shall rest in the morning, while my men and I attack the heathens."

They answered with one voice, "May such shame never overtake us as to cower in the tents while you fight! It seems better to us to stand or fall by your side, God willing."

A,a (107)

... Now there were of those still living five kings, all fugitives, while three[4] of their leaders lay behind, beheaded; and the Christians killed one thousand one hundred of them fleeing by the crag or valley. But Eliades[5] and his nephew[6] Pantalas were not accustomed to flee, for they were among the greatest of warriors. They heard the din and great blows of the French as the Frenchmen came upon their division. Eliades then said to his counselors, "The Christians are proud, fierce men. If they now find us staggering and losing heart, and if Agulandus hears the truth about this, we shall never be his friends or dear to him.[7] But I do not hold all the pride of the French[8] to be worth one bad penny."

The Christians[9] now came, drawn up in battle order; there were no fewer of them than two thousand seven hundred. The first to ride in the front of the French host were those who were best. In this group were Rollant and Oddgeir, Grelant and Riker and Earl Hugon and the twelve peers. All these rode in such closely knit formation that the wind could hardly get between their weapons.[10] But first in the division were the three saints: if Eliades waited for them, it would be a wonder if he did not repent it! He was a most gallant man, and did not want to flee on any account. But the Frenchmen raised the emperor's victory-cry and made a tremendous din, and they joined in hard battle. Many good men fell there whom God called from this life.

In this battle the Germans[11] and Saxons especially distinguished themselves, and the Bavarians[12] and knights of Ardeneus.[13] The Africans were chivalrous and well prepared. They were mounted on good, fresh horses and killed one hundred of our men, and three of

[4] *a*, 4; cf. *Asp.* 9592.
[5] *a, Kliadas.*
[6] "Sister-son," which does not agree with A,a 88 (see n. 10 to ch. 65).
[7] *a* only from "and if Agulandus ..." cf. *Asp.* 9605-6.
[8] *A*, Christians; *Asp.* 9607.
[9] *A*, French; *Asp.* 9608.
[10] *A*, them; cf. *Asp.* 9624.
[11] "Men of the south;" *Asp.* Aleman (9640).
[12] *A, Bealvei*; *a, Bauaeis. Asp.* Bavier.
[13] *a Ardenaeis*; *Asp.* Ardenois.

those who were chosen as the twelve peers, who were two dukes and a king.

(105) This battle began with great din and hard fighting. There were fifty thousand heathens, while the Christians had two thousand seven hundred. Grelant did not spare the heathens heavy service, helping our men, who attacked so firmly that none could withstand their blows and onslaught; one said to another, "Good fortune," they say, "has come to us: we were valets and serving boys, cooks and shoe-boys, and it is certainly fitting for us to love the noble Emperor Karlamagnus and serve our lord with affection, for he took us from low service and freed us, and made us all knights. We would all rather lose our lives than allow any disgrace to come upon him, or that he be driven from his realm."[14]

When Oddgeir heard what they were saying he raised up his voice and said, "That is well spoken! If God allows me to live until I return to France, I will get into your hands[15] the honors and wealth he has promised you so that there shall be no one who needs anything from the emperor, and I shall present the case of any whom he shall not hear gladly and give support to my request and his need. But I shall be your standard-bearer: now draw around the standard."

They all answered and said, "We will do that gladly."

When these knights remembered how poor they had been when they came to Karlamagnus, and that they had now been made knights, they thanked him in loving words and fair speeches and said that they would rather lose their lives than have the king defeated by Africans. Now they rode at the heathens and closed with them, and struck many strong blows to limbs and bodies. There were fifty thousand of God's enemies, while the Christians had two thousand seven hundred. Now if God does not show his power among Christians, King Karlamagnus will lose his foster-son!

(106) A terrible noise went up and many heavy blows to the neck were struck. The damage to our side might not have been remedied if Salomon had not come, with five thousand knights with raised spears

[14] Last sentence in *a* only; cf. *Asp.* 9662-63.
[15] *a* adds, from the emperor.

and fluttering banners, and the best of shields before their breasts. This leader was a very powerful man. The Bretons cried out and lifted up the victory-standard of St. Milon,[16] who stayed in their land, and they went into battle with strong boldness. Cowardly boasters could not be hidden there—those who let themselves be killed out of despair: for the young men[17] who had just been dubbed knights were so powerful, strong, and swift in giving great blows that they felled a great host of heathens.

In the division led by Rollant, nephew of King Karlamagnus, there were two thousand seven hundred, and in the division of King Salomon five thousand, and a few of them fell in this battle. Just then came Droim, the powerful duke, and with him men of Peitu and Gascons, with sturdy armor and mounted on the best horses—there were none in the troop as good as they were.

The Africans saw that their troops fell, and they saw a third battalion riding at them, with more than seven thousand men, each of whom had good chainmail and a good horse.

A (107)

Now three leaders came forward, sent by God to help King Karlamagnus. Each of them was in the likeness of a knight, and with them was Turpin, the glorious archbishop, who carried the holy cross in his hand. Then the Africans began to whisper among themselves, "May woe take the standard-bearer whose standard is so high that it leans in the clouds, so bright that the rays of the sun are not lighter: it overturns our courage so that we shall gain nothing from them here, except our death."

When Eliades saw that his division was breaking up and he did not see any way to stand firm, he saw no reason why he should not flee; and he fled, reluctantly, at the last possible moment, contending with his gods and saying that all their power was useless. He rode wielding his stout spear. But Rollant and Oddgeir and Salomon mustered their troops: if they drive off the heathens well, they will avenge their own.

[16] St. Mallo, *Asp.* 9709.

[17] Here a page is missing in *a*.

The horses were quite exhausted, and a messenger rode to tell the emperor, saying, "Ride,[18] lord, and help your men. There is no better knight than your kinsman Rollant."

The king answered, "Almighty God," says he, "I give thanks to you."

The king rejoiced greatly, and drew up his division.

A,a (112)

... Oddgeir and Rollant, Grelant and Estor and Riker and Marant, were victorious in four battles that day, so that none who survived dared to stand against them. Our men were wounded, but so many of the heathens were killed and wounded that no living man could count them. Oddgeir and Rollant and their comrades drove the heathens together into a circle, but when they wanted to fight they were so tired that they could scarcely do anything; so they turned back to the division of Karlamagnus ...

[18] Perhaps the translator misread *Asp.* "rices rois," 9781.

CHAPTER LXXI

The Forces of Agulandus Dwindle

We shall next speak of Ulien, who, after he was knocked from his horse by Lord Boz, had ridden away as soon as he could take a horse, with those of his men who had escaped from Duke Girard.

Ulien dismounted from his horse under the chief standard and went up to Agulandus. The duke's men had brought it about that his pride and arrogance were somewhat abated. Thus he now knelt and asked for mercy from Agulandus, saying, "Things have gone badly and unfortunately for me today, for most of the troop that you gave me has been killed; the Christians are so valiant that they do not give way before any man."

When Agulandus heard Ulien's words, he said, "Kinsman Ulien," says he, "why is it that so small a bird now sings over your ship?[1] Has it not turned out as you vowed to us this morning, that the Christians you went out against today would all be dead before the sun set? It now comes into my mind that your flattering and showy words may have been guiding me in this case all too long, and that the principal reason I came to this land was that I had great faith in your knighthood and in those others who said they would conquer everywhere: but that has now proved otherwise. And I shall tell you, Ulien, what seems to me to have happened to us. The man who puts his faith in effeminate, womanish words has no right to rule a great realm, for a woman is always trying to impose on a man, and if she finds him bending somewhat to her will she tries all the more, never leaving him in peace, until she is able to betray him and ensnare him. This is the sort of thing which has happened to us. You have loved me with a woman's frame of mind: you have drunk my wine and eaten my bread, emptied my bags of money, and taken from me good men and

[1] Presumably an idiom.

true; with my goods, you have attracted wicked men to serve you. And I have borne all this patiently, for the sake of the close kinship between us and because I thought that you were such as you often boasted you were. But tell me this, kinsman Ulien, as I shall ask it: why is your bright helmet as dirty as if you had been standing on your head?"

Ulien answered, "There are more necessary things for you to do than to disgrace me with words, for although I have not done well, your other champions could gain little more of a victory. If the Christians meet with you then it shall be seen who is the strongest, for of the twenty thousand who went with me, only three thousand[2] have escaped."

While they were thus speaking, Eliades[3] came before Agulandus, followed by three thousand men. Eliades had not taken the spear which Rollant threw at him, as has been told, from his wound, and he had bled so much that the saddle under him was full of blood, which ran down the side of the horse. He greeted Agulandus, but the king did not recognize him at first and asked him what his name was. Eliades answered, "Lord, it may be that I am unknown to you, but you have seen me before: it is Eliades, son of King Nabor, your kinsman."

Agulandus then answered wrathfully, not believing what he was told, "How could you be Eliades, whom I appointed leader of the fourth division, which is next to us?"

Eliades answered again, "You may believe it when I can tell you yet more: the other four have been completely dispersed and so entirely scattered apart that no one remains behind. Most have been killed and all the rest have fled. Three thousand rode here with me, and I believe that few others survive of the fifteen thousand which you gave me to lead—and there are none of these that are not wounded. Never before have I been in a place that was so hard to hold."

Agulandus was silenced by these words. After a while had passed, he said, "Kinsman, you bring heavy tidings to our ears. But what can you tell me of Madequin?"

Eliades answered, "He is dead, in truth; I was told that he was the first of our men to fall."

[2] *B*, three.

[3] *Eliadas*.

"What is to be done now?" asked Agulandus. "Will Karlamagnus try to attack us here?"

"Certainly, " says Eliades, "we must expect that. He has few troops, for he lost many today, but they have such bold hearts that they will die before they flee or lose courage. Thus, one plan would be to set spies on the four ways leading to the chief standard, so that they may not come upon us unaware in the night, and be ready for battle in the morning: unless you wish to flee to the ships and sail away, as things stand."

Agulandus answered wrathfully, "Do not say so dreadful a thing as that I might run from Karlamagnus and give up to him that realm which is rightly mine when I still have half again as many troops as he has. The choice elected shall be a guard on all the ways which lead to us."

It is said that Agulandus then had no small army: no fewer than a hundred thousand all told. There were many crowned kings there, among whom was Amustene, who was named before. He remained more out of cunning and fear of Agulandus than out of any good will, as he soon proved, for he had not forgotten what a hateful death his two kinsmen, the aforementioned Magon and Asperant, had suffered. Thus he watched for an opportunity to repay Agulandus—and those who had played the greatest part in it—for that, if the opportunity should arise.

Therefore he went to his friends and kinsmen, and said to them, "All of us now know what has happened today, that the greater part of our might has been struck down; but Agulandus has revealed that he does not intend to flee from this battle. Thus we expect that neither he nor any of those who follow him will return to their possessions. I also wish to declare to you, my kinsmen and friends, that the shame and disgrace which Agulandus did to all of us in the hateful death of Magon and Asperant, our kinsmen, displeases me greatly, and if he does not know whether we are pleased or displeased, we are a disgrace to our family, worse than any fugitives. Now I wish to say that for my part, I do not wish to let the matter stand so any longer. My proposal is that at this point we should leave Agulandus and sail home to Africa, dividing the realm among ourselves and your kinsmen. This shall be done in such a way that he has no supicion of the plan; and if you agree, I shall make such quiet arrangements as I wish, and you will follow when I want to go."

They all agreed to this, hailing it as a splendid way to avoid falling into the hands of the Christians while avenging their disgrace. Amustene[4] went to Agulandus at once, up on the hill where the standard stood, and said, "Lord, I have heard the advice of Eliades, and it seems to me that it should be followed. But since it would be a misfortune which would do us great harm if the Christians should come between us and the ships and gain control of them, I ask leave to go with my men in the direction where they lie. I do not think any others could better repulse the French if they came forward there. If, however, there should be a greater need for troops somewhere else at the time when the battle starts, either I or my sons will go that way to help you."

Agulandus received this well, and said, "You have a good troop, Amustene, and thus you can lend us great strength; do as you say."

Amustene bowed to the king and went away. Seven leaders followed him down from the chief standard; all of them were his adherents, and three of them were crowned kings. He had horns blown to summon all his troop together, and it is said of Amustene that as soon as the battle began in the morning he went to the ships with his men and sailed away from Hispania to Africa while he set fire to, or had broken up, those ships which he could not take with him, for he wanted to make sure that Agulandus would get no help from them if he should have need.

Thus Amustene and the leaders with him left; the queen and many other women fled with them.[5] No true and valiant man would ever have parted with his commander so! But it is indeed the truth that this was in some part arranged by God and St. James, for they would have killed many Christian knights, since Agulandus had no band of men left as valiant or well equipped with arms.

Amustene is now out of this saga. But as soon as he had left, Agulandus appointed King Gundrun, his chief advisor, to guard a second way to his chief standard, providing him with more than twenty thousand men. In the third direction, he put the leaders Moadas, son

[4] *Amusten.*

[5] Note that in *Asp.* (and *A*) the queen does no such thing.

of King Aufira, and Abilant, giving them thirty thousand; and in the fourth direction, he put Ulien, with twenty thousand. Agulandus remained under his chief standard, with guards set about it in two or three rows. It may indeed seem that it would not be easy for a few men to touch this, above all places, when the way was strongly guarded. Thus they remained there during the night. There was more dread, fear, and terror in their breasts than any kind of joy or gladness.

Next we shall say something about Emperor Karlamagnus.

A (108)

Now we shall hear what Duke Girard was doing, there by the crag when lord Boz fell from his horse before the proud Ulien, who rode with twenty thousand from the army of Agulandus that day. He thought that he would make all his kinsmen leaders before he grew any older, but the Christians destroyed his plan, for they intended that he should never mount his horse again. Woe to those who gave him a troop! Of the twenty thousand he had with him, seven thousand lay behind there, while those who fled with him would never again wish to take part in such an exchange.

Ulien returned quickly to the army of Agulandus and climbed at once from his horse before the chief standard. Then he came before the king and asked for his mercy, saying, "Lord," says he, "you gave me all of Europe, but now I shall never govern this land."

(109) When Agulandus heard his words, he said, "Kinsman Ulien," says he, "I have listened to your words. Your bright helmet is covered with dirt, your shield is slashed; and I was truly foolish when I trusted you. Because of you I left my land and realm, for you and Madequin[6] robbed me of my son. At home in Africa you claimed to be the best of knights, but now you are useless and craven. Woe is me if I lay my trust in you any longer! Kinsman Ulien," said Agulandus, "I wish to teach you the truth: he who trusts in the advice of women or cowardly men is not fitted to rule a large realm. You have long served with a woman's temper; you have long drunk my wine and drained my treasury."

[6] *Mandequin.*

Ulien then answered, "Lord," says he, "stop quarrelling now and let your troop be drawn up around you to guard and defend your life. You shall then find how much you have gained. We met the Frenchmen on a slope and I suffered a fall there, such that my helmet was up to the nose-guard in the dirt, and I got no help from anyone except my horse—when later I managed to catch him. But after I overtook him, and turned him with my spurs, my helper appeared to have gone mad. We could not stand against the Frenchmen; of our twenty thousand no more than four thousand have escaped, for they will never flee. Yesterday I saw them riding in such close formation that no sparrow-hawk could fly between their weapons. If they come here over the crag and close with our men, then I say to those who hear my words: you will pay dearly for their coming."

Now a knight came in great haste. A spear-shaft was struck through his saddle-bow, with the point in him, and his saddle was full of blood. Three thousand men followed him, and there was none so strong that his horse or his body was not wounded. The leader spoke in a low voice, since he was greatly weakened: "Lord," said he, "it seems strange to me: yesterday you gave me fifty thousand men, and half of them were struck down."

Agulandus answered, "Friend," he said, "what is your name?"

He answered, "I am Eliades, son of King Sobror."[7]

Agulandus answered, "You are my close kin; your father and I were cousins. Can you tell me anything of Madequin?"

Eliades answered, "Yes, lord," says he. "He is certainly dead."

Agulandus became much distressed for the sake of Eliades, who had been so badly dealt with, and Madequin. Eliades answered him, "Lord," says he, "do not be fearful.[8] It was your bad luck to have such boasters and arrogant men. When they were drinking your wine and kissing your lovely maidens, then they were brave knights; but the Frenchmen hold their realm by lawful inheritance from their fathers, and we shall never conquer them with seven times a hundred thousand, even if we had a hundred knights against every two of theirs. There is no doubt, if they should come to fight against you; the Frenchmen are

[7] *Asp.* Fanis (9035).

[8] A rather inappropriate translation of "Ne sciés si iror," *Asp.* 9044.

neither craven nor cowardly, and King Karlamagnus is the most gallant and courageous of leaders. Now three leaders have fallen in these three battles, and those who are still alive are not much more unhindered."

Many of the heathens then made a great din and were dismayed, as the emperor came, with five divisions, and they blew sixty trumpets in one blast. Gold and steel gleamed and glittered, so light and brilliant that the daylight was brightened, and it was no further to the midst of the French division than one crossbow shot. No one so stalwart or proud could be found in either host that he did not waver in his mind and feel dread. Agulandus was then under his chief standard, and five kings were with him who were all bound to him with oaths; none of them had not borne a crown, and their host was drawn up all around in such a great multitude that they could not be counted. But the emperor rode at them with five divisions. Agulandus showed his men the army of Christians, and said, "That host," says he, "is not so much meat as would suffice us for our midday meal: if they were prepared as food for us, we should be wretchedly served. King Karlamagnus does not seem to me to be a wise leader when he fights with me without a great host. He shall therefore get great trouble here; he shall bear iron chains around his neck and hands. If he does not renounce his god and Christianity, he shall be beheaded."

The old Galinger looked long at the king, and said to him, smiling, "You are too hasty in this small matter. Send for Ulien now. The Frenchmen met him today, and never before has he seen such reversal and misfortune."

Agulandus answered, "You are talking too much. Even if they were made of the hardest steel, they could never withstand me."

(110) When Amustene saw Agulandus, he called his sons and said, "Wretched serving boys, worthless fugitives! Magon and King Asperant were my nephews, they who were killed by your army: little did it enter your mind that you are wretched, useless cowards. You had my kinsmen disgraced before my eyes.[9] Now take up my trumpet and standard at once, as quickly as you can, and blow it four times: my

[9] This whole speech is vastly confused by changes from the *Asp.* version. There (9166 ff.) the emir accuses his sons of forgetting the dishonor the king

trumpet is far shriller than Olifant. We shall head for the ships and sail to Africa at once. Then if Karlamagnus fights against Agulandus, he will certainly conquer him and avenge his sorrows. I am no longer young, but you are young men; we shall have all of Africa, and our heirs everlastingly."

They answered, "This is the best and most suitable plan to follow."

Now the ninth book ends and the tenth begins.

A,a (111)

The Africans now charged at the Christians. There were thirty-four thousand Christians,[10] and never were men[11] better armed than they. But the Africans were quite differently armed: they had doublets of leather[12] and were girded with great swords and they carried bows and axes and quivers of arrows. When the Christians met with them they gave many strong blows, slashed heads and shoulders, limbs and bodies, and felled so many that all the field was covered with bodies; there was no room to ride or walk over all the bodies of the dead.

The Africans boasted that they would drive the Frenchmen from their realm, but when they met with the French those who were most wise found that their counsel was foolishness. When Amustene was sure that the host had gathered, he said to Agulandus, "Lord," said he, "hear my words. Three divisions of your host have been defeated and overcome and put in flight by the Christians. I have two sons, who have newly been made knights, and now I want them to go into battle, and I myself with them, with my troops."

Agulandus answered, "That is what I indeed want."

"Certainly, lord," said Amustene. "It is better than you expect." Ten men then followed him away from the chief standard; three of them were crowned kings. But when they parted with Agulandus, it would have been better for him to have had them killed rather than to allow them to depart. They headed away from the host at once, taking

has done to the clan, while here he appears to be addressing the army generally, or Agulandus himself.

[10] Cf. *Asp.* 9146, "trent cinq mile."

[11] *a* resumes here.

[12] *a* adds "and linen."

twenty thousand men with them, and thus left Agulandus. Amustene would not have left him so if he had been a trustworthy man. They might have caused the French to lose much, for they had better than twenty thousand of the best troops.

They went to the ships and boarded them with all their booty,[13] but they broke the other ships into pieces and burned them. Now if Agulandus does not take care, he shall never again set eyes on Africa!

[13] *a* specifies "horses, weapons, and booty."

CHAPTER LXXII

Karlamagnus Advances

Emperor Karlamagnus and his men stayed on their horses all night, right where they were. As soon as the first light appeared, they gathered together in one place, where the lord pope came with his host and Fagon, the standard-bearer. The emperor mustered his troops; there were not more than thirty thousand. Three of the twelve peers had fallen the day before, and many of the men were wounded.

Karlamagnus prepared himself for battle, with four thousand of the best men. He intended to go into battle first that day himself, and told Rollant, his kinsman, to rest first; but he answered, "No; I tell you truly, by God's grace, I am no less fit to manage my sword than I was yesterday."

When the emperor's troop was ready, Archbishop Turpin went to the lord pope and said, "I ask you, apostolic lord, to take the holy cross of our Lord now, for I wish to go forth with my men today and wield my sword sharply. I have heard Karlamagnus and all his men say that today one of two things shall happen, by the will of God: either they will all be slain or this land shall be freed from the rule of heathens."

The lord pope answered, "Gladly, my son," says he, "will I take the Lord's cross and bear it myself, while you and all your men go, in God's keeping, and do your best."

After this the emperor went forth with all his host, except that he left Fagon behind to guard his standard. Many trumpets could be heard sounding, right at the time when the sun first began to rise, red in the sky. And as soon as the heathens heard the shrilling sound of the trumpets and saw the division of the French coming forward, with the glittering of gold-adorned weapons, shields, and helmets, where the morning sun shone on them, their hearts were struck with incredible terror and they said to each other particularly, "This is astonishing:

yesterday many of the emperor's men fell, but now his host seems no smaller than it then was!"

Karlamagnus galloped before his host and the four divisions which were described before in so great an onslaught that the division of King Gundrun gave way as soon as they came up to it. The emperor then drew his royal sword while his men drew theirs; they struck hard and often, so that everyone before them had to fall dead, or flee. This battle began with great uproar, loud crashing, and great outcry. Nor is it to be forgotten that as soon as the battle began there came before the divisions God's three knights, George, Demetrius, and Merkurius, attacking boldly. Rollant and his comrades—Oddgeir the Dane, Samson and Salomon, Earl Hugi, King Droim, Gundebol, Duke Nemes—all gave hard battle, and the heathen host soon lost many men.

The emperor rode forward with great courage, sparing no one, galloping away from his men into the midst of the heathen division, where he met Gundrun and struck down on his helmet. The sword bit sharply, slashing right through his armor down into the stomach. But when the Africans recognized the emperor they attacked with all their might and killed the horse under him; now, on his feet, Karlamagnus was faced with great peril, unless God's mercy granted him strong support. Yet he defended himself so valiantly, continually turning around like a top, that no one dared to assault him.

When the French realized that the emperor was missing they were much distressed, as might be expected. One of them, Baeringur the Breton, could see the plight that he was in. He rushed forward swiftly, saying, "Almighty God, watch over us in your mercy!"

At the same time, he drove his spear right through a great leader, throwing him down on the ground at once, and took the horse. Then he went to where the emperor was defending himself so mightily that the heathens were being flung away from him, leapt from his horse, and said, "God save you, my mighty lord! Please mount the horse by your side at once."

The emperor did as he said and, putting one hand forward on the saddle-bow, while stabbing his spear down in the ground, he vaulted so splendidly into the saddle that no knight could have done it better. Baeringur held his stirrup for him, then mounted the horse that had belonged to the heathen and they rode back to their men, who were more delighted than can be told to see their lord safe and alive. Now he rested a little there.

A huge heathen king soon advanced and urged on the Africans, saying, "This shame which is upon us will be known in every land, that so few men should entangle so great a multitude of our men! Do not let this happen. Attack bravely! Do you not see that the Christians are clearing the battlefield before you because they think you[1] are overcome?"

The Africans did as he urged, choosing from their division those who were strongest and best equipped with weapons. These men galloped forward at the Christians with drawn swords and made so hard an attack that many of God's knights now had to fall: they seemed about to give way. And when Karlamagnus saw that, he said, "My Lord, what do you now intend, and what is to happen? How can Christendom win freedom today if its defenders are to be struck down like sheep this way? Strengthen us, my Lord, so that we can put down the arrogant insolence of your enemies!"

When he had spoken these words, the lord pope came, with the cross of the Lord, and turned before the emperor saying, "Good lord, do not be distressed about Divine Providence, for although some things may not go the way you would choose, it is for no other reason than that God wishes to try your patience, so that you may attribute the victory entirely to him. It will be the more glorious when he grants it miraculously. See, lord, what great blossoms shine on this sublime cross, from which we are all strengthened, by God's mercy."

As soon as the cross of the Lord came into the heathen's sight, it revealed the same power—or more—as on the day before. Thus the Africans who were closest to it began to turn away, while as soon as the French realized this they were emboldened and pursued them daringly. Karlamagnus led his men forward, raising his voice and crying out, "Fight manfully, and avenge our kinsmen and friends!"

Rollant pursued the fleeing host, and in this drive more heathens were killed and severely dealt with than seemed probable. There is no need to speak of this at greater length, except to say that all of this heathen division was completely routed. Some fled up under the chief

[1] They?

standard of Agulandus while others joined the troops of Moadas and Abilant. Now many sounds of distress could be heard among the Africans, cries and bellowing, for many had suffered severe wounds.

Emperor Karlamagnus came at the division of Moadas next; but first we shall turn away from here for a while.

A,a (112)

... Karlamagnus then said, "Lord, God,[2] do not let your holy Christendom be laid low! Give me strength so that I may avenge your friends[3] on these heathen dogs." When he had said this, the king rode forward, and with him went four thousand knights; and they rode into a crowd of heathens against Gundrun the charioteer, a counselor of the heathens. Karlamagnus struck down through his head and all his armor.[4] Before he got away, they wounded the horse under him with fifteen halberds, but by the time Karlamagnus took the horse from which he had killed his enemy, they had killed ten thousand Africans,[5] and all the host[6] recoiled in terror.

As our men went back to their division the Africans grew bolder and gave hard combat, striking many terrible blows, so that a great many men fell. Karlamagnus grieved over the fall of his men, and, raising his voice, he cried out and bade his knights to avenge themselves in God's name.

Now the Bavarians,[7] Saxons, and Bretons fought well; Rollant and Oddgeir and their comrades[8] did especially well. The emperor was foremost in the front and had Jouise[9] in his hand; no one lived who got a blow from this. There the French[10] were so much harmed that no

[2] *A*, only; cf. *Asp.* 9273.

[3] *a*, enemies.

[4] *A*: "... the charioteer, and Karlamagnus struck down into his shoulders as if he were a rotten log." The *a* version is similar to that of P_2.

[5] *a*, "more than ten thousand heathens, so that all the Africans lost heart."

[6] *a*, two (of them).

[7] *A*, *Bealvaei*; *a*, *Bealfij*; this list corresponds to P_2 as printed on p. 184 of Brandin's edition.

[8] *a*: "Oddgeir and Grelent, Rollant and Estor, Riker and Marant." This is closer to the text of P_2, but not identical.

[9] *a*: "his sword Jouis."

[10] *a*, Christians.

one could tell of it; heads and shoulders, limbs and bodies were struck. Then Oddgeir and Nemes came to Karlamagnus and said, "Lord," said they, "much of our troop is fallen. We have no greater a host than fifteen thousand men now, and nine of the twelve peers."

"Lords," said Karlamagnus, "I have heard your words, but so help me God, I would much rather die than flee."

(113) King Karlamagnus and Duke Nemes and Oddgeir saw that their men were losing heart. Then the pope said, "Lords," said he, "do not be afraid: God is now testing you. He saw himself doomed to die, but he bore it resolutely; now do for his sake that which he did for yours.[11] We have never asked for life before, but God has given us victory over the heathens."

"Lord," says Karlamagnus, "you have now spoken my desire. No man should need any other advice."

Archbishop Turpin gave the holy cross to the pope, saying, "Now you shall see if I can be of any help."

The pope agreed to this at once. The archbishop then blew a shrill trumpet to encourage his men, and Agulandus heard the trumpet and said to his men, "Now everything is just as I wish it to be:[12] the Christians[13] are completely overcome and now they want to give up the battlefield to us. Attack the chief standard now!"

They did so, thinking that the Christians would give way. The African army took heart and raised hard combat. Spears flew[14] like showers of arrows, but the Frenchmen withstood them, striking heads and shoulders with sharp swords. Then Ulien raised his voice and cried out to his men four times:[15] "Africans," says he, "have no fear! Avenge your kinsmen, fathers, and brothers, who have been killed by

[11] *a* is closer to the printed texts of *Asp.* in omitting the "moral" drawn here, but *A* may be simply summarizing a good deal more which is omitted in the saga version.

[12] This phrase occurs above at the beginning of Turpin's speech in *a*, according to Unger; there it is clearly mistaken, while here it corresponds to the P_2 ms.

[13] *A*, Frenchmen; cf. P_2, p. 186.

[14] *a* adds "in small pieces."

[15] *a* only; cf. P_2.

the Frenchmen, and Jamund, who fostered you; seek now for land and riches from them so that you may be wealthy and happy."

When they had heard his message they rode more strongly at the Christians.

Girard and his sons and nephews and foster-sons[16] drove them off with the hardest blows they could strike. But if God does not have mercy on the Christians now, disheartened men will have to pay dearly for the valor of the gallant!

When the emperor rode into the heathen ranks, they blew on their horns and trumpets and made a terrible din, and great damage was done to both sides. Oddgeir and Nemes, Riker and Hugi; and Salomon, who bore the emperor's standard, and the Bretons who followed him; young Rollant, who carried Dyrumdali, stained with blood,[17] and those who followed him: all guarded his life and body as best they could.[18] But all would have given up then if Emperor Karlamagnus had not lifted his voice and called out gracious words to them: "Stand fast all, both great and less![19] Defend boldly," said he, "my person and your honor."

King Karlamagnus fought so bravely that all who saw his blows stood in great terror then. He had no easy life that day. His excellent horse was killed under him, but this most strong man jumped up at once and drew Jouise,[20] which he had received when he was crowned; whoever drew near to him was sure to die. Now when the king was standing on his feet, he defended himself so bravely that no one dared to approach him, and many greater and lesser men turned back to surround him. Baeringur of Markun[21] was the first to realize that the emperor was on foot, and he headed toward him at once, striking a great heathen and slashing down into his teeth;[22] he then grasped his

[16] *a* only; cf. *Asp.* 8895.

[17] *a* adds "of heathens."

[18] *A*: "and all his comrades: all fought very well." *a* is somewhat closer to *Asp.* 8909-10, but not an exact translation.

[19] *A*: "Karlamagnus called out and said to them;" cf. *Asp.* 8912-14.

[20] *Jovisse.*

[21] Cf. *Asp.* 8926: "li marcis Berengiers." P_2 lacks this.

[22] *a* elaborates on this, but is not particularly closer to *Asp.* 8929-30: "... a great heathen down on the helmet, slashing down into his teeth, and then struck him from his horse with a second blow."

horse by the gold-laced reins and went at once to the emperor. He dismounted from his horse and gave it to the king, holding his stirrup while he mounted; then he mounted the horse from which he had killed the heathen, and they both went into the battle and felled a great many heathens. When the Frenchmen saw the king return, they had never been more joyful since they came into the world.[23]

[23] *A*: "they rejoiced greatly over his coming." Cf. *Asp.* 8940 and P_2.—Two pages are now missing in *a*.

CHAPTER LXXIII

Duke Girard Launches an Attack

Now we shall speak of the mighty lord Duke Girard, who had spent this night in the little valley which lay to the right a short distance from the chief standard of Agulandus. In the morning he called his leaders to confer with him and said, "Now it is likely, good knights, that, God willing, our enterprise will be brought to some ending today; thus we should by no means take thought for the safety of our persons. I know that we are quite near the hill where the chief standard of the heathens is standing, and because that will be difficult to attack you should pay heed to my counsel. Four hundred of our strongest and best armed men should dismount, and gather together, as close as possible to each other, holding their shields thickly up over their heads, being girded with swords and wearing coats of mail down to the feet and raising their spears before them. You shall go that way up under the ridge, while those who are mounted on horses shall surround the outside, with all their strength. And if God grants that we can come up under the chief standard in a group so drawn up, there shall be enough to conquer. And, I forbid any of my men to ride forward at all, whatever may come against us, without sheltering us as well as possible, so that we throng forward on the way into their midst; I suspect that they will not be able to do much."

They all said they would be glad to do just as he arranged. When what has just been said had been done, and all the men on foot had gathered together first, and then the knights on horses had gathered thickly around them, they made their way up onto the slope which was between them and the heathens. Ulien could see them coming and he went to Agulandus and said, "Trouble is now advancing towards us from all directions. Now the group which I met with yesterday is coming upon us here, and those who meet with them are certainly dead men."

Agulandus answered, "That must be our comrade Amustene with his train."

"No," says Ulien; "I clearly perceive that after what had happened to them, they will not come here to you."

Agulandus said, "Go, Ulien, against this troop."

Ulien was forced to do so, with twenty thousand men, galloping forward with great outcry and uproar. And when the duke saw that, he said to his men, "Pay no attention to their cries and shouts. Let us stay calm and cautious, letting them make whatever fuss they like; let us stand fast and make our way as quickly as we can get there. But look at that man who is rushing furiously forward, under a golden shield; he rushed at us boldly yesterday. God be praised that we managed to give him what was due for the debts that we owed him! I suspect that he will gain little better tribute today than he got yesterday. Now I ask you all to take up your weapons, as I shall, and kill every one that dares to come close enough; but do not get out of your places at all. Go for the one that is close enough at hand."

They agreed to do so. Ulien urged on the advance, thinking that now they would avenge the disgrace he suffered the day before. The Africans shouted a great war-cry, shot arrows and drove with spears, struck with swords and threw stones. But although they went on this way they gained very little from it, for Girard's men did not break from their places the least bit but killed a great many heathens: no one was left to report the news who was in the way of their weapons!

And when Ulien saw it was no use, while Africans lost heart and avoided getting near them, it seemed to him it would be easier to encounter them in another place and he turned off in another direction, going forward into the division of Moadas, where he took a place. But Duke Girard accomplished exactly what he had intended, for the heathens were continually driven back as his men attacked, until the duke had come right up under the ridge on which the standard stood.

Now some heathens had come up to the standard and said to Agulandus, "If these men, who are coming up at you, are not vanquished, all your men will soon be dead."

When the duke had drawn this close, he said, "Praise be to God! He has looked after us well, in his mercy, for we have not lost a single man, but we have cast down many of the heathens. Now let us mount our horses and make a determined attack on the heathens. On the other side of the ridge, I hear great shouting and loud crashing; the emperor must have arrived there. Now every man do his best: may God and the holy cross grant that we take the victory at last."

They charged up at the heathens now, silently, in close formation, holding their shields before them and brandishing keen halberds, while the Africans came to meet them. Hard battle was again joined. The duke advanced slowly, for it was hard for his men to attack as they moved upwards, and thus many of his men fell—but far more of the heathens. The battle was then at its fiercest. Those who were nearest were struck hard and often with their swords, so that precious stones sprang far and wide, cut away from gilded helmets, while coats of mail burst, the steel gave way, and warriors went pale from grievous wounds which each side dealt out to the other. But before something happens of great significance in the duke's attack, we shall turn back to the emperor, and say what he was doing with his men.

A,a (112) While Agulandus was waiting for those who went away from him, Girard made haste and came secretly riding into a valley. His troop was a thousand and seven hundred,[1] and they were gathered around him in such close ranks that the wind could not come between their weapons.[2] It will be strange if he does not repent.[3]

When Ulien saw this he nearly burst for grief, and said to Agulandus, "Lord," says he, "now there are coming at us here people with whom I met today. They killed seven thousand men before me."

Agulandus replied, "Is it not the troop that Amustene led away from here?"

"Certainly not, lord," said he. "Know certainly," says Ulien, "that whoever does not defend himself as best he can is a dead man."

After that preamble, fear and terror came upon Agulandus, and he told Ulien to be ready to do his will. He left there, wrathful and frantic, and mounted on his horse, having twenty thousand men with him under the chief standard, and met lord Girard there.—But Amustene had

[1] *a*, 1107; cf. *Asp*. 9204.
[2] *A*: "... could scarcely come between them," but cf. *Asp*. 9206.
[3] So *Asp*. 9207; presumably "he" refers to Agulandus.

gone on board ship and destroyed all those that he did not want to have with him. Now if Agulandus does not take care, he has lost his share of Africa!

The seven hundred men whom Girard turned over to Boz and Clares were well armed. And when the ill-natured Ulien saw that, he rushed on them at once in so hard an attack that there was no one of their troop who did not fear death. Lord Boz and Clares closed with them so well that they killed a great number[4] right at the beginning: but whether they wished to or not, they had to give way, and returned to Girard's division.

When he saw his nephew, he was furious and gave way to his wrath, calling him the son of a whore: "Never," said he, "were you the son of Duke Milon, when you are so terrified by heathens!"

A (114) Listen, good friends, to this fine saga about the good emperor Karlamagnus. Hear of the valor and courtesy of the Christians, the love and devotion of valiant men, the courage of the king's troop, and about the hardy Duke Girard. He was the son of the powerful King Bovin;[5] a better duke never held high rank. When Lord Girard saw the standard of Ulien, he called to him Boz and Clares, Ernard and Riker[6] and Milon: "Good knights," says he, "let us not hold back. See him who sits there under the golden shield, who rode at us boldly today: God be praised that we can give him a good reckoning for the debt we owe him! Now I bid you not to make any attack with your spears until we have gathered together as closely as possible, with everyone holding his shield firmly before his breast. Thus prepared, we shall ride at them, if they dare to stand before us."

Now Girard rode, with this troop drawn up. He had with him one thousand five hundred knights, and Boz and Clares were their standard-bearers. Ulien now came with four thousand men, who had stiff bows and good armor; they cast arrows and shafts at them. However, they found no shrinking cowards before them, but resolute knights, such that no duke ever had better, and they did not dare to rush at the duke. Ulien found that the Frenchmen would not give way before

[4] In *Asp.* it is clearly their own men who are slaughtered here.
[5] Another form of Fr. Beuvon.
[6] Cf. *Asp.* 9872: "Ernalt son fils et Renier..."

shouts or threats or arrows; they headed toward the chief standard of Agulandus. But before he had fastened his standard he saw heathens fleeing on his right side. Ulien could not stop them from breaking their ranks and splitting up, and Girard and his troop had come so near the chief standard that they were within two arrow-shots. Girard then told his troops to stop. He called to his sons and nephews and all his chief friends: "Lords," says he, "surely God has been watching over us, since we have not lost a man. Christians have rushed on the Africans; I can hear them now urging the men on. Now I ask you to join me in helping them boldly."

They answered, "That, we will gladly do. We are well armed, and those dogs are badly equipped, or worse than weaponless. May God and the holy cross will that we do battle with the heathens and that we render them leaderless!"

Now four hundred of them dismounted from their horses—those whom the duke chose as the best and boldest—while the others took their horses; and they proceeded in close formation, covered with their shields, bearing sharp pikes,[7] girded with good swords. When the Africans saw them, Agulandus said, "These are not our men. If we do not defeat those who are advancing on us, those who are now behind us will kill us."

Agulandus was now under the chief standard. With him were twelve heathen kings, and around them so great a host that no one could count it, but they were all alarmed about Amustene and thought that he was staying away for a long time. In that moment Girard came, with four thousand men in long mail who rushed at the heathens, striking out at them; and they so cleared the way before them that there was not so much as one arrow-shot between them and the chief standard.

Yet Karlamagnus would have little to exult about there (nor Nemes, Oddgeir, or Rollant), if God almighty, who rules all things, had not sent him his three knights.[8]

Lord Girard, and his sons and nephews, now came at the heathens, armed in steel and iron so that none could conquer them. They struck

[7] C-V defines the word used here as 'pot-hook;' it must correspond to *Asp.* 9939 "piqois agus," javelins, or something of the sort.

[8] Cf. *Asp.* 9934, apparently referring to Girard.

heads and shoulders, breasts and trunks, and threw down one after another dead. When they saw they were being destroyed, they fled, with others following, until they came under the chief standard. The Africans then said to Agulandus, "If these men catch up with us, the standard will not be able to help us much."

When Agulandus saw that he almost went out of his mind, for his men fled to him, each one observing the others.[9]

[9] This is not a very clear construction; *Asp.* offers no clue.

CHAPTER LXXIV

Ulien's Fall

When the Africans saw that the Christians had slain and ripped apart all the division of King Gundrun, advisor of Agulandus, some thirty thousand rode forward in great wrath. Their leaders were Moadas and Abilant, who were so proud and puffed up that they considered no man to be their equal. Thus they blasted on huge trumpets and made enormous uproar and tumult, with outcries and clashing of weapons, thinking that they would thus shake the courage of the French. They bent stiff bows, shooting so hard that the strings cried out. But the Christians were not as frightened as they had thought, for when Rollant heard their noise he took up his shrilling horn Olifant, set it to his mouth, and blew so loudly that it could be heard under the chief standard of Agulandus and all around the army. All the Christians did the same, with everyone who had a trumpet sounding it. Their war-cry seemed much more alarming to the heathens than might be thought, for many of them were filled with terror and fear.

This battle began with loud noise and hard meetings between brave men. Emperor Karlamagnus attacked with great valor, while they defended themselves manfully. God's three knights did a great deal of harm to the heathens and many men, both Christians and heathens, were now knocked from their horses, one falling over another so thickly that the mounds of the dead were piled high. Oddgeir the Dane, Duke Nemes, Salomon, and Baeringur the Breton charged before the flock of heathens hard, and it happened that they were all felled from their horses; when Karlamagnus saw that he did not like it at all, and called up to heaven saying, "What are you doing now, my noble lord James, apostle of God? Are these[1] my champions to be killed before my very eyes? This would be a great grief, and I tell you truly, ex-

[1] *B*, three of.

cellent champion of God, that I should never have a happy day afterwards!"

Then he rushed forward in great wrath, striking to both sides, until he met with Abilant, on whose helmet he struck down with his keen sword so that it did not stop until it reached the middle of his stomach; and he cast him dead to the ground. Then Rollant came to the place where Oddgeir the Dane and his comrades were defending themselves on foot well and manfully, and with Rollant were Grelant, Otun, and several of the peers, with five hundred knights. And when he saw how things stood for his companions, he said, "Oh, oh, my good friends, God knows that you have now come to a difficult point! It will be well for the man who can dispel your distress."

They threw the heathens back from them in two directions, but they were surrounded on all sides. Grelant spoke: "My master Rollant, these heathens are mounted on very good horses. Let us get them and give them to our men who are in need of them."

Rollant answered, "Let us do as you say."

Then he rushed at a huge heathen, driving his spear through his shield, coat of mail, and body, lifted him from the saddle, and said, "You heathen dog, go to your home!" He threw him down dead to the earth, but grasped the horse, and took it to Oddgeir with these words: "You have often shown me many courtesies, and thus I ought to repay you for these good things. Take here, good friend, this fine horse which God has given me and mount it quickly."

Oddgeir did so. Grelant rode another way at another heathen, striking down on his neck with his sword so hard that he cut right through the coat of mail and his neck, so that his head fell off and rolled far away; he took the horse and led it to Duke Nemes. And it was not long before Salomon and Baeringur had horses. Then they all charged forward together, clearing the way roundabout, cutting heathens down through the shoulders so that the heads of some of them flew off and the hands and feet of others, loading one on top of another; they paid no attention at all to whether they lay on their backs or face down.

It had now come about that the Africans did not need to learn what strong blows the French could give, for they chopped them right up for the cauldrons prepared for them in hell, from which the roasting heat wells up, never waning or coming to an end. Thus Rollant and his troop pressed forward until they rode forth on either side of the emperor. And when he saw Oddgeir and Nemes, he rejoiced and said, "Praise and glory to you, sublime lord James! You have now truly gladdened my heart. Now, kinsman Rollant, let us attack well and manfully; almighty God will soon grant us the victory."

Then he took up his royal trumpet and sounded it, high and shrill, so that Fagon the standard-bearer could hear it clearly where he was with his band. Therefore he said to his men, "God knows that Karlamagnus now seems to need our help, for I have clearly heard the sound of his royal trumpet. Let us then prepare ourselves and ride as quickly as possible to help the emperor with all our might; let us meet the heathens with such strong blows that all their courage deserts them."

They answered, "Lord Fagon, let us go as you say. As soon as the wicked Africans find out what we are doing, they will flee like drakes from a goshawk, and they shall take their leave and lie on their backs with gaping mouth, under the feet of the horses."

Lord Fagon rode with a thousand knights, all well equipped with weapons and clothes, and before they began to fight Fagon said to his kinsman Remund, "Take the emperor's standard and guard it zealously, while I see whether my good sword is able to bite."

Fagon was mounted on a good Gaskunian horse. He had an excellent helmet on his head, set with precious stones. He came to the battle where Moadas was at the front and shouted a great war-cry to encourage his men, and they started with so hard a charge that those who were nearest to them fell back from them, all entangled together. But Fagon met with Moadas and drove his spear into his shield so hard that it broke and gave way; then it pierced the coat mail and penetrated the heart. He lifted him from the saddle, saying, "There you go, big man: you will not be going any further."

Then he threw him away from him, turned his horse well and nimbly, drew his sword and struck down on the helmet of King Matusalem, striking right down through his shoulders. Lifting his voice, he cried out to his men, "Do your best: do not spare sword or spear against the heathens. Let them see whether we know how to do something more than eat and drink!"

They did as he asked and lay three thousand heathens on the ground. Now the Africans in that part of the battle began to take flight. Ulien, who had come into the division of Moadas, as has been said, came forward rapidly and saw the Africans losing all courage and fleeing after the fall of their leaders. Thus he then called out to them, saying, "Ill do you reward Agulandus for the great honors he has given you when you run away from him! Do not act in so flagrantly shameful a fashion as to flee any further than under his chief standard, which you can see still stands."

But though he said such things, they paid no attention to him; rather, each one headed where he thought he would be most likely to find help. Ulien spurred his horse and rushed at a good knight named Edvard, cutting through his helm and head right through to the teeth. After this he met with the brave knight Riker, driving his spear into his shield. But when Riker saw this, he turned his shield around with such great strength that Ulien's spear was shattered from above the socket, while he struck his sword down on his helmet;[2] and when it broke Riker said, "Guard yourself, knight!" He followed this with a blow so powerful that he struck down through Ulien's shoulders, felling him to the ground.

At this time the lord pope came with his holy cross to the front of the division; God's three knights were with him. There was no need for any action, for such great fear and terror came over all of the heathen host that everyone forsook his place. Some fled into the mountains or woods, and some under the chief standard, to Agulandus, whom they urged to flee. There was a great crowd there now, for the emperor had arrived under the ridge with his host and they were all charging up towards the chief standard, while Duke Girard attacked on the other side, no further away from the place where the standard was placed than scarcely two arrow-shots.

A (115) The Africans deserted their place under the standard all together; then they took a stand and defended themselves, and many great, heavy blows were struck. But Karlamagnus was the most courteous of emperors, and Rollant was his nephew, and Nemes the most

[2] This seems to mean that Ulien struck Riker.

polite knight in all the king's court.[3] The Frenchmen rushed at the heathens as they came down into the valley, and they waged a hard battle there. The bold men from Orfanie shot spears and shafts and caused much loss of life.—Unless almighty God looks after the Christians now, they have never met such grievous blows as this.

Eliadas and Pantalas, his comrade from Orphanie, took a stand and defended themselves under the mountain. Great uproar arose, cries and exhortation, with so much loss of life that no man ever saw more. When those from Africa saw that great multitude fall, father and kinsmen, sons and brothers, they said, "Now our trouble grows, and if we do not avenge them we shall be traitors. Out on those who do not now strike into their shields!"

And they did this, slashing their shields. When the French drove them off with great blows, dread seized the men of Orfanie, so that all their power and courage deserted them, and, fearful and terrified, they escaped as best they could.

(116) When Emperor Karlamagnus saw the Africans shrink back, and those from Orphanie running and deserting, he cried out at once to his men: "Follow them now," said he, "and strike hard!"—and the Frenchmen rushed after them. They charged them and struck them and broke off spears in them, and their cry could be clearly heard under the chief standard, and each of them fell on the backs of the others. They made their three hundred steel and iron spears and swords be known there so that never after could they find a cure to heal themselves, and they fled, so completely that no one remained behind on the battlefield.

(117) After these had been overcome, they then met thirty thousand of the strongest people. The leaders of this host were Moadas, son of King Aufira,[4] and Abilant, son of King Monspira,[5] and they drove

[3] The translator must have lost the sense of *Asp.* here; he seems to be rendering 9990 ff., but to have been somewhat led astray by the contemplation of courtly qualities. Perhaps what is meant might more accurately be described as "chivalry."

[4] Here in *Asp.* (10039) "fils le roi de Tyr," but in 10175 "fil de roi Pharaon."

[5] *Asp.* "le roi de Mont Espir."

them back under the standard, whether they wished or not.[6] But Fagon called out then, for he did not want to flee. He said to his men, "Now we shall have a good chance to avenge our friends and serve God."

When the Africans saw his men vanquished, they all came down from the mountain with bent bows: thirty thousand of them, bearing sharp spears and newly sharpened swords, axes, and steel pikes. Their leaders, Moadas and Abilant, were so strong and proud that they did not hold any man worth a straw. When they met with the Frenchmen, they charged at them; but they resisted them so bravely that those from Persia were much enraged, and many strong blows were struck there, and the heathens fell down, one over the other, falling so thickly that no one could recognize his father or son. Oddgeir and Nemes were both struck from their horses, and so were Salomon and Riker and Baeringur. When Karlamagnus saw that he was most displeased, and he lifted his voice and cried out, "Lord God," says he, "What are you doing? If you take these men from me, I shall never have strength nor power, and never again shall I bear a shield into battle."

He held the royal sword Jouise in his hand, striking on both sides, and did not stop until he reached the midst of the heathen troop. Then he struck Abilant on the helmet, so that the sword went right into his teeth, and lifted up a victory-cry, which the Frenchmen heard: more than seven thousand came to him at once. Rollant, his nephew, and Hugi and Grelant came on good horses, and they cut through the throng and fought by the king's side.

When Karlamagnus was aware of their arrival, he said, "Make sure that the battlefield is well controlled by our side."

And they cried out at once with such a shrill war-cry that all who were under the emperor's banner heard it. As soon as Fagon heard that, he said to his men, "May God strengthen us," said he: "Now Karlamagnus is in need of troops, and God shall do as he sees fit."

(118) When Fagon found that the king was in need of troops, he said, "Good warriors," says he, "let us ride as quickly as possible and help the emperor."

[6] *Asp.* makes it clear that it was the French, not the heathens, who were driven back this time; see 10041.

They said they would gladly do as he wished. When the king knew that Lord Fagon had arrived, he said to his men, "Lords," said he, "what are we doing? If they take our men now and put them in irons then I shall never again return to my land."

And he cried out his battle signal, and said, "Let us ride boldly and cut down this standard which is the greatest of all!"

They did so, riding in formation for better than a bolt shot, and the Persians[7] gave way whether they wished to or not. Lord Fagon bore the king's golden standard. He had been the emperor's standard-bearer for thirty-three years. He gathered the thousand knights of his troop so closely that they would ride a long way before an apple thrown into their midst would fall to the ground. He then spoke graciously to his men: "Good warriors," said he, "I have nourished you all, and exalted you, and have brought you here to a strange place. See here before us a hated people. Now earn my goodwill from me well: encounter the heathens with such strong blows that all their courage deserts them, bearing however much noise and outcry they make."

They answered him stoutly, "We shall so ride, lord," they said. "The Africans shall now meet their fate so suddenly that three thousand of their men shall lie with their mouths gaping open, while we shall safeguard your honor so well that God shall know of it for ever and ever."

(119) Now lord Fagon[8] rides into the battle. He was a counselor of King Karlamagnus and had long borne his standard; never had he fled from battle. A thousand knights followed him now and he intended to make a terrible attack on the heathens, though he had few men to meet with such a great multitude as the troop of the Almacians.[9]

Fagon then called to him Remund,[10] leader over Ozakarent,[11] a brave and gallant knight; he was Fagon's nephew,[12] and he had great

[7] *Persar.*
[8] *Fagun.*
[9] *Almacii*; *Asp.* 10148, "la gent l'almaçor."
[10] *Asp.* Raimon.
[11] *Asp.* 10149: de Moncontor.
[12] "Sister-son," as in *Asp.* 10152, "fils de sa seror."

faith in him. He gave him the chief standard and said to his men, "Strike the heathens, and do not be afraid!"

And they did so, riding forward, striking, and stabbing with all their might. No Persian was so well armed that he did not shrink for terror. And they came first to the troop of Moadas, and both young men and old fled to the chief standard of King Agulandus. Now Fagon, the king's counselor and kinsman, rode in front of the troops, the bravest of knights. He was a good arrow-shot in front of all the others, well armed and on a good horse, nobly clad in a good steel helmet, a thick coat of mail and a strong shield painted with a picture of a lion, bearing the best of spears. He rode into the thick of the rank ahead of him and attacked Moadas, son of King Aufira, who was a nephew of King Agulandus and son of the lovely Angelien,[13] queen of the city of Balatim.[14] Fagon attacked him and cut through his life and all his bowels, for the spear went right into the back of the saddle-bow and he knocked him dead to the earth.

And when he turned, he drew his sword and struck at the helmet of King Matusalem,[15] and threw him from his horse dead; then he raised his voice and cried out the king's victory signal. When his men heard him, they came rushing, with so much uproar that in their first charge they struck three thousand heathens to the ground, all calling on Makun for help.

(120) When the Africans saw the Frenchmen coming, and Moadas and Abilant fallen, and found that they could no longer stand firm, they escaped as quickly as they could to the mountain and woods. And when King Karlamagnus saw that he thanked God suitably for the victory. Then he said to his men, "Bold knights," says he, "let us make haste and strike the heathen dogs!"

And they struck so valiantly that twenty thousand fled quickly away from the battlefield. Spears could be heard breaking there, and coats of mail giving way; three thousand Persians[16] fell there as the flight began, while many fled to their chief standard for help.

[13] *Asp.* 10177: "De sa seror la bele Engelisson."
[14] Not in *Asp.*
[15] *Asp.* Matefelon.
[16] *Persiemenn.*

(121) When Ulien saw his men struck down he almost burst with sorrow that he could not come to their aid nor stem their flight, for the men in front were advancing. He struck Edvard[17] and slashed down through his teeth, throwing him down dead to the earth. Ulien was a most bold knight, and when he saw he could not hold back the Africans he said, "You wicked evildoers and sons of whores, where now are the boasts you made when you were contending in the hall of Agulandus, where you drank his wine and counted the Frenchmen and all their strength not worth a bad penny? But they are valiant men, as you can see. You will never get so much as a pennyworth of this realm if you do not make a stand under the chief standard."

But they went on their way, without a glance at the standard,[18] riding so vehemently that the father did not await his son nor the son his father. When Ulien saw the Frenchmen kill more than a hundred Africans, he took his spear, with its stout shaft of apple-wood, and rushed as quickly as possible to attack the shield of Riker, who was the son of Antoine and nephew[19] of Duke Nemes and grandchild[20] of Baeringur.[21] When Ulien met with him, he cleft his shield at once. But Riker was an excellent knight; his coat of mail was strong and did not give way. Ulien's spear-shaft broke off at the socket, and Riker struck him with so great a blow that he struck right down through him: the sword did not stop until it reached the saddle-bow, and he cast him dead to the earth.

When the Africans saw that, they fled away over mountain and valley; none remained to look after the chief standard. When Agulandus saw that, he almost jumped out of his mind, and said to his men, "Where now," says he, "are my counselors, who advised me to challenge this realm? They should be helping me now in my need." And there was no one so bold that he did not advise him to flee. There was now a great uproar by the chief standard, and the Christians piled the Africans one on top of another. Everyone who could hurried to protect his life, fleeing as fast as they could...

[17] Neither the character nor the incident appears in *Asp.*

[18] Or, pretending not to see it.

[19] "Sister-son."

[20] "Daughter-son."

[21] *Asp.*: "Neveu Antelme, fils fu au duc Renier, / Né de la fille au baron Berengier," 10251-52; no doubt another Berengier.

CHAPTER LXXV

The Fall of Agulandus

Agulandus sat under his chief standard. It seemed to him that things had taken a serious turn for the worse, for the Christians had now conquered all around. Thus he now advanced from the hill, drew his sword, and struck on both sides so mightily that he did not fall short. But when Agulandus had gone, Lord Girard attacked boldly and soon reached the chief standard and struck it down, urging on his men vigorously. More than a thousand knights fell in this attack before the standard was cut down.

When the Frenchmen saw that the standard had been cut down, their courage and daring grew. They piled the heathens one on top of another, and a great din rose up all around as they all came in to one place together. And when Agulandus saw the standard fall, he nearly went out of his mind. He did not wait long for anyone to hold his stirrup, but sprang onto a strong horse and headed away through the crowd, so frantic and furious that he hardly knew where he was going.

Agulandus took the road that goes to the city of Risa, but there was a big ditch before him, so deep and wide that there was no way he could get over it. He was forced, by necessity, to turn aside from it. But when Duke Girard became aware that Agulandus had gotten away, he lifted his voice and cried out, so that both his men and the emperor's could hear him: "Follow Agulandus, for he has fled away! Let us never suffer such great shame as to let him escape; there will never be a better time to give him his reward than now."

He turned his horse with his spurs and rode with a great throng to the place where Agulandus was, for when he could not pass the ditch, he had turned back to the battlefield and joined his men. There the Africans had crowded around him and were defending him with all their might, and the duke charged, followed closely by Boz and Clares[1]

[1] *Klaris.*

and many of the French. A hard battle began there, a bitter meeting; the heathens kept falling one after another, but those who could get away fled. Now much running and chasing could be seen all over the field as the Africans ran away with the French in pursuit.

Emperor Karlamagnus came with a great number of his men to help the duke. But before the emperor arrived, a good knight named Antonen,[2] an advisor of the duke, rushed forward and killed the horse under Agulandus, then turned back to his men. Agulandus was now on foot and his men were falling around him in all directions, while some of them fled, when he saw Karlamagnus and the French coming at him. He thought of the danger which was overtaking him from behind on the other side, and he said, "Wretched have I become, when I thought I would have all of France. Now I know I have no hope of victory or escape. Let those who can save their lives, but there is nothing left for me to do but defend myself while I have the strength. It is more suitable for me to fall near my friends than to flee away defeated from the battlefield."

Then he threw his shield away from him and took the haft of his sword in both hands, striking so that everyone who stood before him was killed, until the sword could not do any more without breaking off under the hilt. Then he was given another sword by his men, and went on in the same way, and more, and performed such terrifying feats that after a while it could not endure and broke in pieces. Finally the Africans gave him an extremely big axe which none but the strongest of men could manage. It is said that the shaft of this axe was made of horn, strengthened by bands of iron. No iron-bound shield or two-fold coat of mail could withstand it.

Emperor Karlamagnus had now come up with his host, killing heathens so thoroughly that Agulandus now stood completely alone, defending himself so superbly and killing so many knights that the emperor forbade his men to attack him. He stood there alone, holding the axe. The emperor invited Agulandus to accept Christianity and acknowledge the true God. But he answered this message quickly: "There is nothing to be gained now," says he, "in making me such an offer, for I will by no means accept a new faith and renounce my gods

[2] *b*, *Anton*.

out of fear. Attack boldly, like brave knights, but my axe shall take the first to attack."

At that moment, Clares[3] rushed at him. Agulandus struck at him, and struck him down through his shield so that the two pieces fell on either side of him; but before he could use the axe again, Clares drove his spear at him so hard that his coat of mail gave way, and it plunged into his body. But Agulandus grasped the shaft and broke it in pieces from above the socket. Then Duke Girard struck down on his helmet, and the blow came around the outside, sprang down on his shoulder and cut into the breast; Agulandus looked down at the blow. It was not long then before Rollant turned and struck at his neck with his good sword Dyrumdali so mightily that the head and neck flew away from the trunk. Agulandus fell dead to the ground, though he did not wish to.

The Christians shouted in a great victory cry and proclaimed the death of Agulandus so loudly that it was heard throughout the army. Great gladness and rejoicing came to the hearts of the Christians, and they gave many thanks to Almighty God.

A (121)

... The battle lasted longest under the chief standard, and the troop of lord Girard diminished greatly there, for a thousand of his knights fell. But Agulandus was put to shame so thoroughly that ten of his kings were felled, and his dragon-standard broken down. When our men saw that the chief standard of Agulandus had fallen, their courage and daring grew. Karlamagnus fought so much that necessity drove him from his horse, and he struck many great blows there.

When Agulandus learned that his men had been overcome, he became terrified and did not wait there any longer; he turned away in fear and desperation and headed for Risa.[4] A victory-cry was raised behind his back: if he wants to ask for tribute now, he will get what he deserves!

(122) Karlamagnus now stopped on the battlefield. He did not have enough might to follow the fugitives, for so many of his troops had

[3] *Claris*.
[4] *Riso*.

fallen that there was not a quarter left. Agulandus had headed for the chief standard, but the Christians had driven him off and had felled ten hundred thousand before him. Boz and Clares felled many proud men to the ground. Lord Girard, however, rode to Risa; but before he arrived there, it happened that the fugitives led him into a ditch, which had been dug from the mountain in the woods, and he was forced to turn back. Then Boz and Clares came to him and made a vigorous attack. As the heathens came poorly armed, while the Christians were well equipped, so many of that hateful people fell there that no living man could count them.

(123) Then Agulandus took a stand on the battlefield, and his men turned back around him and defended themselves. But the Frenchmen killed so many that they could scarcely be counted. The old Antoiene, a splendid man, killed the horse under Agulandus so that he could not escape in any way. But Karlamagnus rested in his tent then, and called to him Oddgeir and Nemes, Fagon and Riker, Hugon and Droim and Salomon; and he said, "Now place the tent near the standard."

And they did this. Then Karlamagnus called to him Rollant and Estor and Grelent, and with them a thousand of the best knights, and said, "Ride," says he, "and come to the help of Girard, boldest of men."

"Gladly," said they; "never shall we fail him."

King Karlamagnus then called to Nemes, and Oddgeir, Droim and Salomon, Fagon and Riker, saying, "Lords," said he, "prepare to ride over the slope and help lord Girard as fast as possible."

Fagon was their standard-bearer. They rode quickly over the slope. When the Africans saw that, they decided to flee, since it would not help them to close with them. There were four thousand Frenchmen who had come to help, all well armed, and they rode in such close formation that if a glove had been thrown in their midst they would have gone further than a crossbow shot before the glove fell to the ground. When the Africans saw them coming, they found that whoever stayed there would gain a quick death, and they all fled together; father did not wait for his son, nor son for father.

(124) When Agulandus saw his men cut down, and the French riding at him, he said, "Wretched am I, and sinful. I intended to own

all France and divide this realm among my noblemen, but now they have been cut down, and I expect neither to live nor to get away myself. Let those who can save their lives, but for me, who can do nothing else but defend myself as best I can, it is more fitting to die by my friends than to flee this battlefield defeated."

He had a good sword in his hand and struck a fatal blow to everyone he could come near. Agulandus was now both wrathful and sorrowful, for his horse had been killed under him and his men so struck down that none remained except twelve kings who had followed him from Africa. But one could not find a stronger man than he, nor one slower to know fear, though his men could not even be of as much help to him as to re-mount him on a horse, and no matter how many weapons they gave him, he broke them all. They prepared for him an axe made of elephant-horn[5] all bound with iron clasps; this was the best of axes, for no steel helmet nor two-fold mail could withstand it. And when he had taken the axe none was so bold that he dared to approach him, and he stood there alone for a long time.

Karlamagnus then said that none should attack him with weapons and sent a monk to him with this message:[6] if he will renounce Makon and accept Christianity, acknowledging the true God, he might have many good things in his days. But he said he would not accept a new faith and renounce his god out of cowardice, and it was no use to attempt this with him.

The Frenchmen then struck around him and killed all of his closest troops who were there to protect him. And he defended himself very bravely and killed many men in front of them. And then Clares came riding at him and struck his shield in front of him into pieces; but before he could strike him any blow, he buried his standard in the heart of Agulandus. But Agulandus broke the spear. Then Clares struck down on his helmet and slashed down into his breast, and he

[5] Or unicorn horn? Cf. n. 13 to ch. 60. *Asp.* 10443, "pumier:" applewood?

[6] In *Asp.*, it is Girard who makes this offer to Agolant. The whole scene is Girard's final triumph: Karlamagnus and his men do not arrive in time to share the glory.

fell on his knee. Now Rollant came up[7] and cut off his head, while all the others who had come with him fled: no one knew what to do with himself for sorrow and terror. But, to tell the truth, not ten knights of them escaped, they were so altogether cut down. A truce was given to all the women and maidens, however, and Christian knights took them[8] later when they abandoned their false doctrine.

[7] In *Asp.* the end of Agolant is accomplished by Claires unaided.—From this point, the saga writer gives a hasty summary of *Asp.* for the rest of the chapter.

[8] I.e., in marriage.

CHAPTER LXXVI

Karlamagnus Praises God and St. James

After the fall of Agulandus, Emperor Karlamagnus sat down on the field, for he was greatly exhausted, as well as all the others. But it is not easy to say with how many words of thanks he praised the Lord Jesus and his glorious apostle James for the manifest help of the wonders so gloriously revealed over the relic of the holy cross, as well as for the visible advancing of God's three beloved friends. It was now beyond doubt that almighty God had sent them from his heavenly host, since as soon as the battle had ended they vanished from the sight of men's eyes and were nowhere to be seen. What occurred elsewhere can be read in the sagas of the saints, which tell how heavenly power has been revealed through the aid and service of God's excellent beloved friends.

Karlamagnus then went to his tent, bidding everyone to take rest and quiet after their labor. And when the time came, he had them go about the dead and search for where his men had fallen, nor did he go any further until all the Christians who had fallen in this battle and the one before were given the most honorable funeral service. And when that was done he went all around the region of Hispania and restored Christendom, where this was needed, raising up monasteries and churches where Agulandus and his son Jamund had earlier broken them down.

A (125) After this victory was won by Karlamagnus, he travelled over all Hispania and Galicia, and all the surrounding territory, and christened all the people, killing those who would not acknowledge the true God; and he had churches consecrated and restored all that that wretched people had defiled and destroyed. Then he appointed governors to rule that land, both from his own men and from those who had accepted his rule. But after that great battle, all the heretics in that land were so destroyed that no resistance was offered to him afterwards in Hispania.

King Karlamagnus then went, in peace and quietness, and rested his troops, and had all of those who had fallen carried to holy places where they would be prayed for by the clergy. And when that was done, it is said, King Karlamagnus went home to France, and stayed there in peace for several years afterwards. His homecoming was much needed, for many there had been creating considerable disturbance.[1]

[1] The last chapter returns to PT as a source, and is based on chs. 18, 19, and 27-29 of PT.

GLOSSARY OF PROPER NAMES

Karlamagnús Saga, IV

References in this glossary are to the chapter in which the name appears; cross-references to I, II, and III refer to the first volume of the saga. Most ms. variant spellings are cross-indexed; listings include people, places, nations, horses, swords, pagan gods, and saints, but not references to God or Jesus Christ.

ABIA *see* Arabia

ABILANT THE STRONG (also spelled Abilan, Adilant, Ambilant), PT Boidanze, *Asp.* Abilans, Abilant; a Saracen lord, 59, 60, 64, 65, 68, 71, 72, 74

ABRAHAM (Biblical), 24

ACENNOA (also sp. Atennoa), PT Acentina, Aceintina; city in Spain, modern Guadix, 2

ACHARZ OF AMFLOR (also sp. Achars, Achaz, Ackars, Akard, Akari (?), 59, 60, 61, 65, 69, Akart, Akarz, Ankari), *Asp.* Acars de Flors; a Saracen king

ACHIS (also sp. Akis, Aguisgranum, Aquisgranum), PT Aquisgranum; Aachen, Aix-la-Chapelle. Cf. I, *Eiss*, 1, 4, 9, 10

ADAM (Biblical), 24, 41, 63

AEMERS *see* Reiner, son of Girard

AFRICA, AFRICANS (sp. Afrika, Affrica, Affrika, etc.), *passim*

AGABIA, AGAPIA PT Agabia; an island off Tunis, 8, 21

AGENNA, town of Agen in Gascony, 20, 21

AGULANDUS, PT Aigolandus, *Asp.* Agolant; King of Africa, *passim*

AKARI, a Saracen lord; probably another sp. for Acharz, q.v., though appearing in *Asp.* as Angart, 59

ALEMUND OF NORMANDY, *Asp.* Ansquetins li Normand? a French knight; *see* n. 14, ch. 47

AKARZ *see* Acharz

AKIS *see* Achis

AKVIN *see* Aquin

ALANDALUF, PT Alandaluf; Andalusia (region of Spain), 2

ALBANIE, a place; *see* n. 7, ch. 53

ALBASPANIA, ALBASPINA, Aubespin, in France; *see* Reinald of Albaspina

ALEXANDRIA, city, 8

ALFAMEN, ALFAMI (also sp. Fulfinio), a heathen king, identified by the B-revisor with Rodan, q.v., 51

ALFING (also sp. Alfuskor), PT Aphinorgius et al.; king of Majorca, 8

ALFRE *see* Alpre

ALFREANT *see* Asperant

ALFRIG OF BUGUNIA, Auberi le Bourgoing; PT Alberious Burgundinus—cf. I, *Anherri of Burgunia*, 11

ALMACIANS (sp. Almacii), *Asp.* la gent d'almacor; a heathen people, 74

ALMAZOR, *Asp.* almacor; a Saracen lord, 58, 60

ALPRE (also sp. Alfre), *Asp.* Halape; land ruled by Sinapis, q.v., 59

ALTOMANT, ALTUMANT, ALTUMAIOR (also sp. Astumairo, Estimaior), PT Altumaior; King of Corduba, 8, 23, 25, 26

AMANDRA, AMANDRAS *Asp.* Amandras; a Saracen, comrade of Kador, 34

AMFLOR, AMFLORS *see* Acharz of Amflor

AMMIRAL, PT Admirandus (i.e., emir); King of Babilonia; cf. III, 24

AMUSTADE, *Asp.* amustande; a Saracen lord (emir); cf. Amuste et al., 58, 59, 60

AMUSTE, *Asp.* amustent; name or title of one of the Saracens, properly a title meaning ruler or governor, it is used apparently referring to Gorhant of Florence (q.v.) but elsewhere as a name for other characters: *see* Amustene, Amustade, 59, 60, 68

AMUSTEN, AMUSTENE, *Asp.* amustande, amustenc 'emir;' a Saracen lord, confused in A,a with one generally called Amustade, 59, 60, 71, 73

ANCELIN, *Asp.* Antialme, Antelme; a French duke, probably the same as Anzelin, q.v., 62

ANDELFRAEI, ANDELFREUS (also sp. Amfraei, Andelfrei), *Asp.* Andefroi; a French knight, 47, 52, 53, 61

ANGELIEN, *Asp.* Engelisson; mother of Moadas, sister of Agulandus, 74

ANGLER (also sp. Angeler, Angleriz, Anglier), *see* Milon of Angler

ANGIA, England (so understood by the A,a translator); PT Anglia (cf. also England), 1

ANGIO, Anjou, 69

ANKARIS OF AMFLOR *see* Acharz

ANKERIM, ANKERIN (also sp. Ankirim, Anketill, Arnketill); *Asp.* Ansquetins li Normant, 39, 44, 47

ANKETILL *see* Ankerim

ANKIRIM *see* Ankerim

ANSAEIS, *Asp.* Anseis; French knight, 49

ANTEINI OF VARIGNE *see* Anzelin of Varegne

ANTILIN THE RED (also sp. Antelin), *Asp.* Antelme de Tors; French knight, 35

ANTIOCH (sp. Antiocha), the city; cf. III, 59

ANTOIENE, (1) *Asp.* Antelme, but see note; father of Riker, q.v.

ANTOIENE, (2) a knight who may or may not be intended to be the same in A; see Antonen, 74, 75

ANTONEN (also sp. Anton, Antoiene [2]), French knight, advisor of Duke Girard (B), 75

ANZELIN OF VAREGNE (also sp. Anteini), *Asp.* Anseis; French knight, 47

ANZELIN, *Asp.* Antelme, Antelmes; a French duke, not the same as Anzelin of Varegne since he appears just after the latter is killed, in A,a only, 47

APOLLIN, heathen god, understood as part of a sort of Moslem trinity, 33, 34, 42, 59, 64

AQIN (also sp. Akvin, Aqvin), *Asp.* Antelmes; a Saracen lord, 59

AQUISGRANUM *see* Achis

AQUITANIA, AQUITAINE (also sp. Akvitania, Aqvitania), district in France; see also Engiler, duke of Aquitaine, 1, 11

AQUITANIA (also sp. Akvitania), mythical city, 11

AQVIN *see* Aquin

ARABIA (also sp. Abia), 2, 6, 7, 8, 65

ARABIANS (sp. Arabiamenn), 17, 48

ARASTAGNUS, ARASTANG (also sp. Arakstan, Aragstanus), PT Arastagnus; king of Brittany, 11, 22

ARDENEUS, *Asp.* Ardenois; the Ardenne; 'men of the Ardenne' are also sp. Ardenaeis, 70

ARGUA, PT Arga; Spanish river, 23

ARMENIANS (sp. Armeniar), 24

ARNALD OF BERNALD, Hernaut de Beaulande; PT Arnaldus de Berland/Bellanda, 11, 22, 23

ARNKETILL *see* Ankerim

ASPERAN, ASPERANT, *Asp.* Esperrans li ros; the Red (also sp. Asperam, Espiram, Alfreant—see ch. 34, n. 2) a Saracen king, 33; 34, 48, 57, 58, 59, 71

ASPERMENT, ASPERMUNT *see* Aspremont

ASPIN (also sp. Ospin), PT Ospinus; king of Agapia, 8

ASPREMENT (also sp. Asperment, Aspermunt, Aspramunt), a mountain, said in the saga to be in Spain, 27, 34, 35, 36, 38, 45, 60, 61, 66

AUFIRA, *Asp.* Pharaon? a Saracen king, father of Moadas (q.v.), 71, 74

AUGUSTUS, (Roman) emperor, 11

AVIT (also sp. Avid), PT Hivitum (et al.); King of Bugie, 8

AZA, PT Axa; town of Dax, Aix-en-Gascogne, 4

BABILONIA, Babylon, 24

BACALES (also sp. Bakales), PT Burrahellus; king of Alexandra, 8

BAEJARALAND *see* Bealfer

BAENA, PT Baecia; Baeza, Spanish town, 25

BAERING, BAERINGUR THE BRETON (also sp. Baeringr), PT Berengarius, *Asp.* Berengier one of the twelve peers (cf. I), 11, 36, 38, 48, 49, 53, 54, 62, 69, 72, 74

BAERINGUR (not the same as above), grandfather of Riker, q.v., 74

BAION (also sp. Benona), Bayonne, 11, 12, 13, 14, 16, 19, 54, 57

BAKALES *see* Bacales

BALAM (also sp. Balan), *Asp.* Balan; a Saracen king, messenger of Agulandus, 13, 14, 15, 16, 19, 25, 26, 33, 40, 42, 46, 47, 48, 50, 53, 54, 57, 60, 61

BALATINE, city, presumably in Africa (not in *Asp.*), 74

BALDA (also sp. Basda), PT Bascla; the Basque territory, 1

BALDAM, a Saracen leader; copying error for Butran? 34

BALDVINI, PT Balduinus; Bauduin, half-brother of Rollant; (cf. I), 11

BALDVINI, a French knight, possibly the same as above, but appears here in place of *Asp.* Bernart, 64

BARBARE, Barbary? Heathen city or land, 59

BASDA *see* Balda

BASIN *see* Boz

BAVARIANS (sp. Bauaeis, Bealfij, Bealvaei, Bealvei); *Asp.* Bevier, 70, 72

BEALFER, BEALVER (also sp. Baejaraland, Bealfuer, Beiare, Berare), Bavaria; see also Nemes, Duke of Bealfer (cf. I), 1, 11, 55

BEGON, PT Bego; Begon de Belin, brother of Garin le Loherant, 11

BEIARE *see* Bealfer

BEIUERE, BENARIS (also sp. Befueris), a city; not mentioned here in *Asp.*, 60

BENDICT (also sp. Bencitus), an archbishop; not in *Asp.*, 63

BENONA *see* Baion

BERID, BERNALD (also sp. Berit, Bernind), *see* Arnald of Bernald

BERNARD OF NOBILIS, PT Berardus de Nublis; French knight, 11

BERNARD, *Asp.* Ernaut, Ernalt; son of Girard of Burgundia, 30, 37, 38, 73

BERTA, sister of Karlamagnus, mother of Rollant; also called Gilim (cf. I, Gilem), 11

BERTRAM OF MUTIRBORG, a French knight, 35

BETHLEHEM (sp. Betlemborg, Bathleem, Bedlehem), 54, 65

BIRANGRI (also sp. Hiagri), *Asp.* Brugier; land ruled by Gundrun, q.v., 59

BIRRA, *Asp.* Berri; city; cf. Biturica, below, 35

BITURICA, BITURIKA, Bourges;

see also Lanbert of Biturica, 11
BOLAND, BOLANT (also sp. Morlant), *Asp.* Boidan, Boident, et al.; a Saracen king; cf. Mora, Bordant, 44
BONIVUS (also sp. Bod, Bovin, Boy), *Asp.* Beuson, Beuves, Beuvon; father of Girard of Burgundia, 30, 52, 73
BOOZ *see* Boz
BORDANT, Saracen king of Nubia (in A-version), apparently *Asp.* Boident; possibly blended with *Asp.* Morant (cf. Mora and Boland) and probably the same as Bordanus, q.v., 47, 58
BORDANUS, *Asp.* Boidan; a Saracen king, 33
BORDDAL (also sp. Bordel), Bordeaux; see also Jofrey of Bordel, 22
BOSTDEM *see* Gernard of Bostdem
BOVIN, BOY *see* Bonivus
BOZ (Also sp. Basin, Bosin, Boson, Booz), *Asp.* Beus, Bos, Bozon; a nephew of Girart of Burgundia, brother of Clares, 30, 32, 37, 38, 43, 48, 54, 61, 62, 71, 73, 75
BRETLAND (see also Brittania), Brittany (cf. I), 27, 63, 69
BRETON, BRETONS (sp. Brezki, Bretar), see also Baeringur the Breton, Eisant the Breton; cf. III, 39, 63, 69, 72
BRITTANIA (also sp. Bretanie, and cf. Bretland), Brittany; see also Arastagnus, king of Brittania, 11, 22, 55
BUGIA, BUGIE, a city near Tunis, 8, 21
BURGUN, BURGUNIA, BURGUNDIA (also sp. Borgundia, Borgunia), Burgundy; see also Girard, duke of Burgundia; cf. I, Burgonia, 11, 30, 55
BUTRA, BUTRAN (also sp. Butram), *Asp.* Butran; a messenger of Jamund, 32, 34, 47

CADIS, Cadiz, city of Spain, 2
CAPARIA *see* Kaparia
CAROLUS MAGNUS *see* Karlamagnus
CENOMAN *see* Ornonianens
CHALIDES, *Asp.* Galides; a Saracen king, possibly *Asp.* Calides and thus the same as Kalides, Kalades; so understood by the B-redactor; 60
CICILIA, CISILIA *see* Sicilia
CLARES (also sp. Claris, Klares, Klaris), *Asp.* Claires etc.; nephew of Girart of Burgundia, 30, 32, 37, 38, 43, 48, 54, 61, 62, 68, 73, 75
CLAVE (also sp. Slave), PT Blavium; Blaye (French city), 11
COMPOSTELLA, Spanish city of Santiago de Compostela, said to have been formerly called Librarum Domini, Pro., 1, 2
CONSTANTIN, CONSTANTINUS,

Prefect (or duke) of Rome, 11, 22, 24

CORDUBA (also sp. Korduba), Cordova; see also Altomant, king of Corduba, 8, 23, 25

DABOLA, PT Abula; Avila, city in Spain, 25

DEL (also sp. Eleon, Elon), PT Hoellus; earl of Narras; Hoël de Nantes, 11, 24

DEMA, PT Denia; Denia, Spanish town, 25

DEMETRIUS, DEMITRIUS, St.; *Asp.* St. Domin, 66, 67, 69, 72

DESIRIM, *Asp.* Desiier? a French knight, 48

DIONISIUS, St.; St. Denis (q.v. in III), 3, 4

DROIM OF GASKUNIA (also sp. Drois), *Asp.* Droon/Driu le Poitevin; a French king, 27, 29, 34, 36, 39, 47, 48, 52, 53, 61, 62

DROIM OF STAMPES, *Asp.* Droes d'Estampes; a French lord, apparently not the same as Droim of Gaskunia, 53

DYRUMDALI (also sp. Durumdali), Durendal, Rollant's sword; cf. I, 34, 44, 47, 50, 55, 62, 67, 69, 72, 75

EBRAHUM, EBRAUID, EBRAUS, EBRAVIT, PT Ebraum, Ebrahim; King of Sibil (Seville), 8, 23, 25, 26

EDOPT, (Saracen) king of Egypt; not in *Asp.*, 33

EDVARD, a French knight (?), 74

EGYPT (also sp. Egipti), cf. III, 33

EIMER, *Asp.* Rainnier; a French knight, 47

EISANT THE BRETON (also sp. Nizant), *Asp.* Enissent, Enisent; a French knight, 62

ELEON *see* Del

ELEANDSBORG, ELEUSBORG (also sp. Oleansborg), *see* Hugi of Eleusborg

ELIA, Elias, Elijah, the prophet, 24

ELIADAS, ELIADES (also sp. Abadas, Eleadas, Kliadas), *Asp.* Eliades; a Saracen lord, son of King Sobror or Nabor; cf. also Meliades, 60, 61, 65, 69, 70, 71, 74

ELISEUS, Elisha, the prophet, 24

ENGELER, ENGILER (also sp. Angiler, Angler), PT Engelerus; Duke of Aquitania or of Gaskunia; Engelier/Angelier; I: *see* Engeler, 22, 53, 62

ENGLAND, (sic: cf. Anglia), 1

ENSER (also sp. Ensis), a French knight, not in *Asp.*? 63

ERKIBAUTH, *Asp.* Erquenbaut; a French knight, 63

ERNARD *see* Bernard

ESPERIGAM, *Asp.* Esoran; a Saracen knight, 59

ESTOR (also sp. Entor), *Asp.* Ector, Hector; standard-bearer of Jamund, 28, 34, 53, 60, 65

ESTOR THE RED, *Asp.* Estox li fex; a Saracen knight, 59

ESTOR DELANGRES, *Asp.* Estols

de Lengres; a French knight; cf. Eystult below, 53, 54, 62, 69, 70, 75

ESTURMID (also sp. Esotrant), PT Esturmitus; a French leader, 11

ETHIOPIANS (sp. Ethiopes), 5

EUROPE (sp. Eyropa, Eropa), 64, 68

EVA, Eve (Biblical), 63

EYSTULT (also sp. Eistul, Gistubert), PT Estultus comes lingonensis; Earl of Lingun; identical with Estor Delangres, as listed above, but apparently not recognized as such by the translators, 11, 22

FACUNDUS, St. (also sp. Fakunus), 16

FAGON (also sp. Fagan, Magan), *Asp.* Fagon; a French knight and standard-bearer, 36, 39, 48, 52, 62, 63, 70, 72, 74, 75

FAKUNUS *see* Facundus

FAME, *Asp.* Fenie; a heathen land; see also Amustene of Fame, 59

FANTIM (also sp. Famni, Partin), PT Fatimus, but see note; king of Marab, 8

FERAKUT (also sp. Ferakuth, Ferakurtt), PT Ferracutus; a giant, 24

FLEMINGS (sp. Flaemingjar), 39

FLEMISH EARL a (sp. Flaemskan); *Asp.* Flavant, 36, 38

FLORENCE, city or land ruled by Gorhant, q.v., 59

FLORIADES, *Asp.* Floriades; a Saracen lord, 60, 61, 69

FLOVENT, *Asp.* Floevent; a French duke, 62

FRANEBORG *see* Freri

FRANCE, FRANKS, FRENCH, FRENCHMEN (variously spelled), *passim*

FRERI (Freiborg, Franeborg), town (Berri?) said to be seat of Girard of Burgundia; see also Lampart of Freri, 30, 39, 43

FRISA, city, said to be in Africa, where Agulandus takes temporary residence; cf. Visa, Risa, 39, 58

FRISIA (also sp. Frisa), see also Gundabol of Frisia; I, Frisland, 11

FRISIAN SEA, 1

FRISIANS, 22

FURRA, king of Nafaria (Navarre); Forré, PT Furra; I Ful, 24

GALICIA, province of Spain, Pro., 1, 2, 24, 76

GALIZIA (also sp. Galacia), *Asp.* Garilant; Saracen realm; cf. Gordant of Galizia, 59

GALILEE (sp. Galilea), 1

GALINGER THE OLD (also sp. Galingres, Galingri, Galingrerir), *Asp.* Galindre/Galindras; Saracen king of Sebastia, 59, 60, 64, 65, 68, 69, 71

GALLIA (1) *see* Gaul

GALLIA (2) *Asp.* Murgalie; a Saracen realm, 59

GAND (also sp. Gandre, Gandri), *Asp.* Gandie; city, 62

GANDEBELD, GANDEBOL *see* Gundabol

GANDRI *see* Gand

GANTER, *Asp.* Gaifier; a French king, 47

GARA, PT Garinus; duke of Lotoringia (Lorraine); Garin le Loherant, 11

GARISANZ *see* Gizarid

GARSANT, Saracen realm, possibly a second derivative of *Asp.* Garilant; see Galizia, Gordant of Galizia, 59

GARZDIN, GARZIN (also sp. Garthin), PT Garzin; mountain, Montjardin; I: *see* Mondangim, 24

GASCONS, 24

GASKUNIA, GASKUNIE (also sp. Gaschunia, Gaskon, Gaskonia), Gascony; cf. I, Vaskunia, Gaskun, 1, 4, 17, 27, 39, 55, 63, 68

GAUDIOLA (also sp. Gandiola cf. also Jouise), PT Gaudiosa; Joyeuse, the sword of Charlemagne; I: *see* Giovise, 19

GAUL (sp. Gallia), France, 1

GAUTER OF TERMES, PT Gaulterus; Gautier de Termes; I: *see* Guazer of Terus, Valter of Terins, 11

GEBENES (also sp. Gibbon, Gilin), PT Gebennes; Geneva, 11

GEORGE, St. (sp. Georgius), 66, 67, 68, 69, 72

GERIN (also sp. Gescir), PT Gerinus; one of the Twelve Peers; —see also I, 11

GERMANS (sp. Suthrmenn; literally, "men of the south"), *Asp.* Aleman, 39, 70

GERMANY (sp. Aleman, Alemanie, Alimanni, Theothonia, Thyverskan, Thydversktland), 1, 4, 55

GERNARD OF BOSTDEM, *Asp.* Garnier de Lohierainne; a French knight; (cf. Vernis), 47

GIBBON *see* Gebenens

GILIM *see* Berta

GIRARD (also sp. Geirard), *Asp.* Girart d'Eufrait or de Fraite; Duke of Burgundia, *passim* from ch. 30

GIRARD, *Asp.* Girardet; son of Duke Girard, 30, 49, 62

GIZARID (also sp. Garisanz, Gizard), a Saracen; not in *Asp.*, 50

GIULION *see* Guilimin

GOLIAS, PT Gelerus/Galerus; Gerer, 11

GOLIATH, the Biblical giant, 24

GORAM, GORAMARON (also sp. Gorham), *Asp.* Goran, Gorhans; son of Balam, q.v., 33, 48, 54, 60

GORDANT OF GALIZIA (also sp. Gordiant of Galacia), *Asp.* Gorant of Garilant; a Saracen king, 59

GORHANT, Saracen king of Florence (same as above?), 59

GRANANT, Granada, city of Spain, 25

GRELENT, *Asp.* Graalens, Graelent; a young French knight, 53, 69, 70, 74, 75

GUDIFREY THE OLD, Godefroi de Bologne, 35

GUILIMIN (also sp. Giulion), *Asp.* "le roi d'Angalion"; an African king, 43

GUINARD, PT Guinardus; a French

leader, 11

GUINELUN (also sp. Guilulun), PT Ganalonus; Ganelon; cf. I, Guenelun, 11

GULLARAN, *Asp.* le dognon; a city, 62

GUNDABOL, GUNDEBOL (also sp. Gandebeld, Gandebol, Gundelbof, Guldiber, Gundilber, Gundibol, Gundilbol, Gundulbit), PT Gandeboldus, Gandelbadus; king of Frisia; Gondebeuf le Frison, 11, 22, 39, 63, 72

GUNDRUN, *Asp.* Godrin/Gondres/Gondru le Carruier; called "the Charioteer," a Saracen king, 59, 71, 72, 74

HAMNE, a town (with a castle), 32, 34

HARO, PT Ato/Hato; Oton, one of the Twelve Peers, 11

HEROD AGRIPPA (sp. Herodes), Pro., 1

HISPANIA, Spain, but usually means the whole Iberian peninsula, including modern Portugal and parts of France, *passim*

HUGI, *Asp.* Guon, Guielin; a comrade of Rollant, 62

HUGI OF ELEUSBORG, Hüon de Clarvent; there are two French knights of this name in *Asp.* who are distinct (see ll. 7750 and 7754), but easily confused, as; e.g., in Brandin's index, 39, 42, 63, 69, 70, 72, 74

HUGON, *Asp.* Huon (and Hues?); called "the Hardy" in A only; probably the same as Hugi of Eleusborg, q.v., 63, 70, 75

ITALY (sp. Italia), 1, 6, 11, 22, 64

JACOBUS *see* James

JAFERT (also sp. Jafer), *Asp.* Jafert; a Saracen, 68

JAMES, St., the Apostle, son of Zebedee (sp. Jacobus, Jocobus), *passim*

JAMUND, *Asp.* Eaumon/Eaumont, etc.; prince, son of Agulandus, *passim*

JERIMIAS, (1) the prophet Jeremiah understood as an Eastern king? see note, 58

JERIMIAS, (2) *asp.* Jeremie; a French earl, 63

JERUSALEM (sp. Assolum, Jorsala, Jorsalaland, Jorsolum), cf. I, II, III, Pro., 1, 5, 50, 58, 59

JEWS (sp. Gydingar), Pro., 1

JOFREY, Joifroi l'Angevin, 39

JOFREY, comrade of Rollant; in place of *Asp.* Yvoire (error?), 62

JOFREY OF BORDEL, PT Gaiferus; Gaifier de Bordele/Gaufroi de Bordiaus, 11

JOHN, St., the Apostle, brother of James (sp. Jon, Johannes, Johannus), Pro., 1, 4

JOHN THE BAPTIST (sp. Johannes, Johannis), 41, 63, 65

JONE, a Saracen king, not in *Asp.*, 33

JON *see* John, brother of James

JOUISE (also sp. Jouis, Jovisse), Joyeuse, the sword of Charlemagne; see also Gaudiola; I, Giovise, 40, 55, 72, 74

JORDAN, the river, 65

JOVE, heathen god (Jupiter, q.v.), 42

JUOR, PT Yvorius; Ivorie, one of the Twelve Peers; I, Ivori, 11

JUPITER (also sp. Jubiter), pagan god, understood as part of a Moslem trinity; same as Jove, q.v., 6, 33, 42, 64

KADOR (also sp. Kadon), *Asp.* Cador; a Saracen king, 34, 48

KAIN (also sp. Tames), Cain, 59

KALABRE (1) king of a city conquered by Jamund; cf. Kalabre (2), 28

KALABRE (2) *Asp.* Calabre; Calabria; said to be a city conquered by Jamund, 65

KALADES (also sp. Calades, Calides, Calidis, Kalde, Kaladis, Kalides), *Asp.* Calide, Calides; Saracen king of Orfanie; see also Chalides, 59, 61, 65, 68, 69

Kaparia (also sp. Capara, Caparia), PT Caparra; city of Spain, 2

KARANT, PT Charanta; the river Charente, 21

KARL, KAROLUS, KARLAMAGNUS, Charlemagne, *passim*

KARSIA, KARSIALAND, a country; *see* Musteri of Karsia

KASTRAM (also sp. Kastrum, Karstram), *see* Oddgeir of Kastram

KIPR, a Saracen city or land, 59

KLARES *see* Clares

KORDUBA *see* Corduba

KUERNA, place? not in PT: see note, 24

KUIN, KUN (also sp. Kum), *Asp.* Roën: city in Normandy, 66

LALEI *see* Lelei

LAMALILLIE *see* Lampalille

LAMBERT *see* Lanbert

LAMPALILLE (sp. Lamalille, Lampalilla), *Asp.* Lampal; Saracen knight; cf. also Lampas, 48, 59

LAMPART, said in *a* to be "of Freri," in Fr. 2 "Ferre"; French knight; Lambert de Berri? Not in *Asp.*, 39

LAMPAS, *Asp.* Lampal; a Saracen king, 34

LANBERT OF BITURICA (also sp. Lambert, Lanbertus), PT Lambertus; Lambert de Berri; I: Lambert of Berfer, 11

LATORIGIA *see* Lotaringia

LAUFER (also sp. Lemferr), a Saracen; possibly from a misunderstanding of *Asp.* 8239, "et l'amustens, le fel ...", 65

LELEI (also sp. Lalei), a city; cf. *Asp.* 7567, "la loi," 62

LEOFRANDUS, PT Leoprandus; deacon of Achis (q.v.), 1

LIBRARUM DOMINI *see* Compostella

LINGUN, LINGUNIA, PT Lingonens; Langres, city in France; see also Eystult, earl of Lingun, 11

LOERENG, LOERENGE, Lorraine, but it is not clear that the trans. knew this since he uses quite different spellings: cf. Lotaringia, 55

LOINGERUS *see* Lotaringia

LONGINUS (Biblical), 65

LOREINGUS *see* Lotaringia

LOTARINGI, men of Lorraine, 39

LOTARINGIA, LOTORINGIA (also sp. Latoringia, Loingerus, Loreingus, Loringia), Lorraine; see also Loereng, Gara of Lotoringia, 1, 39

LUCRINA, LUCTENA, LUCTUOSA (also sp. Luktena), PT Lucerna ventosa; town in Spain, 2

MADEKUIN, MADEQUIN, *Asp.* Mandaquin; (the Strong, the Mighty, the Great) (also sp. Blandeqvin, Maddekvin, Maddikvin, Madekun, Madekvin, Madikun, Madkuin, Mandequin, Mandeqvin, Mandikuin, Mandikvin), a Saracen leader, 13, 59, 60, 61, 64, 65, 67, 69, 71

MAGON (also sp. Mordans), *Asp.* Margon et al.; a Saracen king, 34, 48, 54, 57, 58, 59, 71

MAIORK *see* Mariork

MAKON, MAKUN (also sp. Machon, Machun, Mahoun), Mahomet, Mohammed, understood as a Saracen god; same as Maumet, q.v., but here taken as a separate deity, 6, 9, 33, 34, 42, 55, 59, 60, 64, 65, 67, 68, 70, 74, 75

MALADIEN, MALADIENT (also sp. Madien, Maladin), *Asp.* Maladient; a Saracen king; see also Malavent, Melkiant, 63, 65

MALAVENT, *Asp.* Maladient: cf. Maladien, Melkiant; a Saracen king, 59

MALCHABRUN (also sp. Malkabrium), *Asp.* Macabres; a Saracen, 48

MALGERNIN, a Saracen king; derived from *Asp.* 6385: see note, 59

MALKABRIUM *see* Malchabrun

MAMONON *see* Manio

MANIO (also sp. Mamonon), PT Maimo et al.; Saracen king of Mecque (Mecca), 8

MANRI, *Asp.* Amauri; a French knight, 35

MANSEL (also sp. Oransel), *Asp.* Mansel; Manseau, in France, 55, 69

MANUEL, *Asp.* Manuel; a Saracen lord, cousin of Acharz; see also Samnel, 60, 61, 69

MARAB, MARAK, Morocco, 8

MARANT, MARGANT, *Asp.* Morant; a French knight, 50, 70

MARIA, MARIE, St. the Blessed Virgin Mary; see also I, II, 1, 4, 24, 36, 40, 54, 59, 65, 66, 68

MARIORK (also sp. Maiork), PT Maiorice; Majorca, 8

MARKUN, place? apparent misunderstanding of "Li marcis"—see note, 72

MARTIN, St. (sp. Marteine, Martinus), 6

MARY *see* Maria

MATEPLUM, *Asp.* Matefelon; horse of Girard of Burgundia, 48

MATES (also sp. Mages), *Asp.* Macre; a Saracen king, 50

MATUSALEM, *Asp.* Matefelon; a Saracen king, 74

MAUMET (also sp. Maumeth), PT Mahummet; Mahomet, Mohammed, generally understood as a Saracen god; see also Makon; in III also, 2, 6, 17, 24, 26, 29, 34, 42, 55, 59, 60, 64, 65, 68, 69

MAURI, *Asp.* Erengi, P_5 Amauri; a French knight (or cleric?), 66

MAURI, Moors, 5, 17

MECQUE, MEKUA (also sp. Meana), PT Meque; Mecca, 8

MELIADES, a Saracen king; possibly Eliades, q.v., 68

MELKIANT (also sp. Melkeant, Melchant), a Saracen king; name seems derived from *Asp.* Maladient, but character conflated with one 'Hogiers,' Maladient's opponent in the argument of *Asp.* ls. 327, 59

MEMEMUNT *see* Talamon

MERKURIUS, St. (also sp. Mercurius), 66, 67, 69, 72

MEYSANZE, *Asp.* Moysan, Moysant; a Saracen, kinsman of Jamund, 50

MILA, *Asp.* Mile; a city (offered by Karlamagnus to Girard's son Milon), 62

MILON (1) Duke (of Poitiers), brother-in-law of Girard of Burgundia, father of Boz and Clares, 30, 73

MILON (2) (also sp. Milun), a French knight; identified with Milon of Poitiers by Brandin, but appears to be a brother of Baeringur (Berengier); see *Asp.* 5420.

MILON OF ANGLER (3) (also sp. Milon, Milu, Justo), Milon d'Aiglent; cf. I. 11, 13, 16, 19, 73

MILON (4) *Asp.* Mile, Milon; son of Girard (also sp. Milun), 30, 39, 48, 62, 73

MILON (5) St., *Asp.* St. Malo; (also sp. Milun), 63, 70

MILUN *see* Milon

MISTURIOS (also sp. Misterios), PT Mauros; Moors? May correspond to PT Mauros, 5

MOABITES, Morabites, Almoravides, Pro., 1, 5

MOADAS, MODAL, MODAS, *Asp.* Moadas li ros; called the Red, the Great (also sp. Moda, Modes, possibly Mordanturus, q.v.), a Saracen king, 58, 60, 65, 68, 71, 72, 73, 74

MONSPIRA, *Asp.* Le roi de Mont Espir; Saracen king, father of Abilant (q.v.), 74

MORAM (also sp. Bolant, Morlant), *Asp.* Morant, apparently conflated with Boidant in *a*; maternal uncle of Jamund, 44

MORDANTURUS, *Asp.* Meadas, or Moadas (q.v.)? A saracen king, 59

MORDOAN (also sp. Mordoam, Mordoans), a Saracen king; name appears in B in place of Magon (q.v.); see also Mordruin, 54

MORDRUIN (also sp. Mordium, Mordoan [q.v.]?), *Asp.* Moridant or Morant? a Saracen king (in relevant passage, Huber), 60

MOREL, MOZEL, *Asp.* More, Morel; the horse of Nemes, 54

MUSTERI OF KARSIA, a Saracen, brother of Gorhant of Florence, 59

MUTIRBORG *see* Bertram of Mutirborg

NABOR, Father (in B) of Eliades, q.v., 71

NAFAR, NAFARA, NAFARIA, Navarre, 1, 24

NAGER, PT Nagaras; Najera, town in Spain, 24

NARDI, a Saracen people; see also Pardos, for which this may be a misspelling, 5

NARRAS, Nantes, city of France; see also Del of Narras, 11

NAUNAN *see* Nemes

NEMES (also sp. Naunan, Naunal), Duke of Bealfer; Naime, PT Naaman; see I, Namlun; III, Nemes, *passim*

NOBILIS, PT Nublis; the city of Nobles or Noples taken by Rollant and Oliver; cf. I, 11

NORMANS (sp. Normandiar), 63

NORMANDY (sp. Nordmandi, Northmandi), cf. I, III, 44, 47, 55, 63, 66

NORON, *Asp.* Noiron; Nero? (see note), 59

ODA, city in Spain, 2

ODDGEIR THE DANE, Ogier le Danois; see also I, III, *passim*

ODDGEIR OF KASTRAM, a French knight, possibly the same as Oddgeir the Dane; both are described as standard-bearers, 39

OLIFANT (also sp. Olivant), a horn, captured by Salomon (?) from Bordant (*a*) and by Rollant from Jamund (B,b), 34, 47, 50, 71, 74

OLIFER *see* Oliver

OLIVANT *see* Olifant

OLIVER (also sp. Olifer), Olivier; see I, 11, 68

ORFANIE (also sp. Orfama, Arfanie), *Asp.* Orcanie, Orfanie; a Saracen country, 59, 61, 69, 74

ORNONIANENS, PT Cenomannicus; le Mans, 11

ORPHANIE *see* Orfanie

OSPIN *see* Aspin

OTUN, PT Odonis, Odon de Lengres; (1) father of Eystult, 11

OTUN (also sp. Thun, Utun), *Asp.* Haton. One of the Twelve Peers? 53, 69, 74

OZAKARENT, *Asp.* Moncontor; region ruled by Remund, q.v., 74

PAMPHILONIA, PAMPILON, PAMPILUN, PT Pampilona; Pamplona, city in Spain, 2, 21, 22, 23, 25

PANTALAS, *Asp.* Pantalis; a Saracen king, 59, 61, 65, 70, 74

PARDOS, a Saracen people; see also Nardi, 5

PARIS, see also I, III, 3, 4, 55

PARTIN *see* Fantim

PEITO, PEITU, Poitou? 63, 70

PEROCIUM MARE (also sp. Perxotium), PT Petronum; sea, El Padron, 2

PERSIA, PERSIANS (sp. Perse, Persar, etc.), 5, 48, 74

PETER, St., the Apostle (generally sp. Petrus), 34, 41, 50, 62, 63

PHARAON, *Asp.* Pharaon; a Saracen king, 59

PIPPIN, Pepin, father of Karlamagnus; cf. I, III, 1, 39, 40, 53, 55

PLIADES, a Saracen, 59

POPE, the (presumably the Pope Milon of I, etc.?), 22, 23, 41, 50, 51, 57, 61, 62, 63, 64, 66, 72

PORTUS CEPHEROS, PORTOS CISEREOS, PT portus Cisereos; (also sp. Cisterios, sephereos), Port de Cize, a pass through the Pyranees, 21, 22

PRIMITIBUS, PRIMITIVUS, St., 16

PUL (also sp. Ful), Apulia; cf. III, 39, 55, 58, 66

RAMERUS (also sp. Reiner) PT Rainerus/Reinerus; Renier de Genvres, father of Oliver; I, *see* Reinald, 11

REIMS *see* Rens

REINALD OF ALBASPINA (also sp. Arinald, Reinbald, Romald, Romblad), PT Reinaldus de Albo Spino; Renaut d'Aubespin, 11, 22, 24

REINER (also sp. Aemers, Reinir, Remer), *Asp.* Rainner, Rainier; son of Girard of Burgundia; see also Ramerus, Riker, 11, 30, 37, 38

REINS *see* Rens

REMUND, *Asp.* Raimon; a French knight, nephew of Fagon, q.v., 74

RENS (also sp. Reims, Reins, Renes, Rensborg), Rheims; see also Turpin, archbishop of Reins, Pro., 1, 11, 66

RIKARD THE VALIANT, *Asp.* Ricars li preus; a French knight; Ricart de Jovent, according to Brandin, 63

RIKER, *Asp.* Richier; a French knight, 35, 39, 48, 50, 52, 64, 69, 70, 72, 74, 75

RIKER, a son of Girard? Appears in place of *Asp.* Renier (9872), 73

RISA (also sp. Riso), *Asp.* Rise; city, presumably in Africa; actually represents Reggio, in Calabria, where Agolant's headquarters are said in *Asp.* to be, 61, 75

RODAN (also sp. Rodant, Roddan, Roduan), *Asp.* Rodoans, Rodoant, a Saracen king; cf. also Alfamen, 34, 51, 65

ROLLANT, Roland, *passim*

ROMALD *see* Reinald

ROMAN EMPIRE, 1

ROMARIK, ROMATICUS, PT Romaricus, Romaticus; a French knight, 12

ROME (sp. Rom, Roma), 6, 11, 19, 22, 24, 51, 55, 63, 64

SAFAGON, *Asp.* Salmaquin? Sinagon? Garahon (6382?) a Saracen; he appears to be an enemy of Sinagon, but this list badly confused; *see Asp.* 682-683, and cf. *Kms.* a 65; see also entry for Sinapis, 48, 59

SALASTIS, SALASTIUS *see* Valterus of Salastis

SALATIEL, *Asp.* Salatiel; a Saracen king, 33, 34, 48, 51, 52, 59

SALEMCADIS (also sp. Salemkades), PT Salamcadis; heathen idol: the colossus of Cadiz, 2

SALOMON (1) Solomon, the Biblical king (?) 55

SALOMON (2) companion of Eystult; probably the same as Salomon of Bretland, q.v., 11

SALOMON (3) *Asp.* Salemon; king of Bretland (also sp. Salome, Salamon), 27, 29, 35, 36, 39, 47, 48, 52, 62, 63, 64, 69, 70, 72, 74, 75

SAMNEL, *Asp.* Manuel; a Saracen king; cf. Manuel, 59

SAMSON, *Asp.* Sanson; Duke of Burgundia, one of the Twelve Peers; see also I, III, 11, 47, 69, 72

SAMSON, Archbishop, 36

SANTUN, SANTUNES (also sp. Samtun), PT Sanctonas; Saintes, city in France, 21, 22

SARACENS (sp. Saracenar, Saraceni), *passim*

SATIN, PT Sativa; Játiva, a Spanish town, 25

SATRE (also sp. Sakris, Sakris borg, Satreborg), a city associated with Duke Girard; not in *Asp.*, 68

SAXLAND, Saxony, cf. I, 41, 63

SAXONS (sp. Saxar), see also I, 39, 63, 70, 72

SEBASTIA, *Asp.* Batre, a Saracen realm ruled by Galinger, 59

SEGIA (also sp. Seggia, Seggja), PT Ceia; river Céa, in Spain, 13, 14

SEGIS, SEGRIS, a French knight; not in *Asp.*, 63

SENDENE, SENDINE, the city of St. Denis, Pro., 1

SICILI, SICILIA (also sp. Cicilia, Cisilia, Sikeily), Sicily, 39, 55

SINAGERN, *Asp.* Sinagon; a Saracen king, 60

SINAPIS THE CLEVER, *Asp.* Synagon, king of Halape; Saracen king of Alpre; but see immediately following report, *Kms.* ch. 68, *Asp.* 6876, 59

SIRIA, Syria, 24

SOBROR (also sp. Nabor), *Asp.* Fanis; father of Eliades, q.v., 71

SONA, SONORA, city in Spain, 2

SORDUE, PT sanctum Iohannem Sordue; town of St.-Jean de Sorde, 4

SPAIN (sp. Spani), see also Hispania, 55

SUERI, *Asp.* "en fuere demora"? city, said to be occupied by Jamund, 64

TALABURG, PT Talaburghus; Taillebourg, castle near Saintes, 21

TALAMON, *Asp.* Acesalon of Jubilent; Saracen king of Mememunt, 59

TEMPRER, *Asp.* Tempier; a Saracen king, 59

TERHPIN *see* Texbin

TERMIS *see* Gauter of Termis

TEROGANT, TERROGANT (also sp. Terogant), *Asp.* Terragant; "Termagant," heathen deity, 6, 26, 29, 33, 34, 42, 55, 64

TEXBIN, TEXPHIN (also sp. Gezbin, Texphin, Terhpin), PT Texephinus, Terenphinus; Saracen king of Arabia, 8

THIDREK, PT Teodericus (Thierri l'Angevin, according to Smyser); a French knight, 11

THOLOSA, Toulouse; I: *see* Tolosa, 4

TORKVATUS, St. (also sp. Torqilatus), St. Torquatus, a disciple of St. James of Compostella, 2

TRIAMODES (also sp. Triamoddis, Triamodem, Triamodis), *Asp.* Triamodes; a Saracen king, nephew of Agulandus, 26, 33, 34, 48, 49, 50

TURKS (sp. Tyrkir), see also I, III, 24, 48

TURPIN, Archbishop of Rens (Rheims), 39, 66, 67, 69, 70, 72

TUTALIS (also sp. Putalis), district of Italy? 55

ULIEN, a Saracen king, nephew of Agulandus, 6, 13, 59, 60, 64, 68, 71, 72, 73, 74

UMAGES, UNIAGES, *Asp.* Jumeige; a monastery, 66

UTILI (also sp. Mila, q.v.), town given to Milon, son of Girard, by Karlamagnus, 62

VALDEBRUN, VALDIBRUN, *Asp.* Valdebrun; a Saracen, 60

VALLAND, France, 53

VALLE VERIDE, PT Vallis Viridis; region of Spain, trans. as "green valley" in A,a, 2

VALTERI, VALTERUS (also sp. Valter), of Salastis, a French knight, 52, 53, 68

VAREGNE, VARIGNE *see* Anzelin of Varegne

VEHENNA, VENNA, Vienne; I: see Viana, Pro., 1

VENOSA, VENOZA, a city in Spain, 2

VERBEN, PT Ubeda; a Spanish town, 25

VERNES, VERNIS, *Asp.* Garniers; a French duke; cf. Gernard of Bostdem, 39

VIA JACOBITA, "The Way of St. James," said to be a street near the church between Dax and St.-Jean de Sorde (cf. Sordue, Aza), 4

VISA (also sp. Vica), city said to be in Africa; no doubt the same as *Asp.* Rise: cf. Risa, 23, 33

VITACLIN (also sp. Vitaklin), *Asp.* Guitekins; baptismal name assumed by Balam, q.v., 57, 61, 63

VILHJALM, PT Guielmus, Willelmus; brother of Gauter of Termis, q.v., 11

YSIDORE, YSODORE, St. (sp. Ysidorus, Ysodorus); St. Isidore of Seville, 2

YSOPES, YSOPUS, *Asp.* Ysore; a cleric (or knight?), 66

ZEBEDEUS, Zebedee, father of Sts. James and John, the Apostles, Pro., 1